Inside Defense

Also by Derek S. Reveron:

Flashpoints in the War on Terrorism

America's Viceroys: The Military and U.S. Foreign Policy

Promoting Democracy in the Post-Soviet Region

Also by Judith Hicks Stiehm:

Nonviolent Power: Active and Passive Resistance in America

The Frontiers of Knowledge

Bring Me Men and Women: Mandated Change at the U.S. Air Force Academy

Women's Views of the Political World of Men

Arms and the Enlisted Woman

It's Our Military Too! Women and the U.S. Military

The U.S. Army War College: Military Education in a Democracy

Champions for Peace: Women Winners of the Nobel Prize for Peace

Inside Defense

Understanding the U.S. Military in the 21st Century

Edited by

Derek S. Reveron and Judith Hicks Stiehm

INSIDE DEFENSE

First published in hardcover in 2008 by PALGRAVE MACMILLAN® in the United States—a division of St. Martin's Press LLC, 175 Fifth Avenue, New York, NY 10010.

Where this book is distributed in the UK, Europe and the rest of the world, this is by Palgrave Macmillan, a division of Macmillan Publishers Limited, registered in England, company number 785998, of Houndmills, Basingstoke, Hampshire RG21 6XS.

Palgrave Macmillan is the global academic imprint of the above companies and has companies and representatives throughout the world.

Palgrave® and Macmillan® are registered trademarks in the United States, the United Kingdom, Europe and other countries.

ISBN: 978–1–137–34300–0

Library of Congress Cataloging-in-Publication Data

Inside defense: understanding the U.S. military in the 21st century/edited by Derek S. Reveron and Judith Hicks Stiehm.
    p. cm.
    Includes bibliographical references and index.
    ISBN 0–230–60260–6
    1. United States—Armed Forces—Handbooks, manuals, etc. 2. Civil-military relations—United States. 3. United States—Military policy. I. Title: Understanding the U.S. military in the 21st century. II. Reveron, Derek S. III. Stiehm, Judith Hicks.

UA23.I49 2008
355'.033073—dc22   2007052845

A catalogue record of the book is available from the British Library.

Design by Macmillan India Ltd.

First PALGRAVE MACMILLAN paperback edition: July 2013

10 9 8 7 6 5 4 3 2 1

Transferred to Digital Printing in 2013

Contents

List of Figures and Tables

Acknowledgments

This is by far the most ambitious project I have ever tackled, and it required many people to produce. First and foremost, Joan Johnson-Freese and Tom Fedyszyn in the National Security Decision Making Department at the U.S. Naval War College continue to create an atmosphere where good teaching and scholarly research can occur without compromising either. The Naval War College is a very dynamic college with supportive colleagues and very bright students. I believe very much in the notion that "one learns most while teaching others," and it is a privilege to teach the people I do and where I do it. Many of the contributors to this volume also provided valuable input on both the scope of the project and my chapter. In particular, I am grateful to Kathleen Mahoney-Norris, Steve Wrage, David Burbach, Leah Hutton Blumenfeld, and, of course, Judith Stiehm. Finally, a project like this could not be completed without the editorial guidance of Toby Wahl, who believed in the importance of exploring these questions about the U.S. military. And as always, I greatly benefited from Kirie Reveron, who tirelessly reads all of my work and is the best sounding board any scholar can have. She sets the conditions for me to think, research, and write.

Derek S. Reveron
Jamestown, Rhode Island

Introduction

Political scientists regularly tell their students that the defining element of government is its monopoly over the legitimate use of force. They rarely mention force again. This is true even though our powerful and lethal military consumes an enormous share of our tax dollars, is an important tool in international politics, plays a role in domestic politics, and is an essential constituent of our society even if it is set somewhat apart from it.

Nevertheless, the 9/11 terrorist attacks of 2001, the Southeast Asian tsunami of 2004, and the earthquake in Pakistan and Hurricane Katrina along the U.S. Gulf Coast in 2005—coupled with ongoing military operations in Iraq and Afghanistan—have catapulted the U.S. military onto the front pages and TV screens everywhere and every day.

Because the military has been so active in so many places and with such a variety of missions, we believe it is important that students, policymakers, and, indeed, every citizen consider the new roles the military plays in international and domestic politics. *Inside Defense* brings together scholars, policy experts, and practitioners in an effort to provide a comprehensive view of the U.S. military as it is today.

Section 1 of this volume focuses on the military's role in international politics. While the military's unique mission is to defend freedom by "fighting and winning the nation's wars," it has increasingly been charged with non-warfighting and foreign policy responsibilities. While the missions mentioned above may have captured most of the headlines, the military has also been involved in less publicized activities—for example, training militaries around the globe, delivering medical care in cooperation with other countries and nongovernmental organizations (NGOs) in the Caribbean and Latin America, and supporting the National Oceanic and Atmospheric Administration (NOAA) and the World Wildlife Fund in Africa. Many of its activities are undertaken because federal civilian personnel and resources are simply not available. The military's aircraft, mobile medical facilities, water purification units, trained personnel, and other capabilities make it a crucial player on the international scene quite apart from any participation in military conflict. While Dana Priest's *The Mission* and Derek Reveron's *America's Viceroys* describe an increasingly militarized foreign policy, the implications of that militarization need to be explored. State building and stability operations were considered doubtful during the Clinton administration. During the G. W. Bush administration, they have expanded and are now considered essential to national security.

Our authors specifically address the need to develop a coherent strategy in which strategy, operations, and tactics work toward the same goal. They also examine the competition between the Department of Defense (DoD) and the Department of State and the military's role in diplomacy. How the military—and, in particular, the chairman of the Joint Chiefs of Staff (JCS)—advise the president, and the degree to which international law is honored, invoked, or revoked are also considered.

Section 2 looks at the military's interaction with U.S. governmental institutions and with political actors. The Constitution defines the respective responsibilities of Congress and the president, but it is important to know how things "work" and what authority the judicial branch exercises as well. The fundamental premise is that the military is flat-out apolitical. While it was always the norm that officers were apolitical, the norm was once that they didn't even vote! The authors in this section discuss partisanship within the military and what some might describe as politicians politicizing the military by using military credentials in their election campaigns and associating themselves with the military in public appearances. Civilian officials may authorize or direct actions for political reasons, which the military finds unethical and/or unwise. Recently, torture has been the subject of debate. What many may forget is that the first to argue against new rules which expanded interrogation techniques were active duty military lawyers. The budget, of course, is central to any discussion of the military, and it continues to increase.

Samuel P. Huntington's half-century-old *The Soldier and the State* continues to shape any discussion of civil-military relations. Recent work by Peter Feaver, Eliot Cohen, Richard Kohn, and Michael Desch has made the discussion current and vibrant. Some had thought that the tensions between the military and the executive during the 1990s were particular to the Clinton administration. However, strains have increased during the current (Bush) administration. Secretary of Defense Donald Rumsfeld found it hard to "transform" the force into a "light," agile, and information-age military capable of defeating any future adversary anywhere. The planning and conduct of operations in Afghanistan and Iraq have further exacerbated relations.

In Section 3, theory and current practice are reviewed and the role of retired senior officers is discussed. In addition to new elements, such as the contracting of security services, the participation of women in combat and near combat, and the role of NGOs is described. Finally, the practice and philosophy of the citizen-soldier is brought up to date. Civil-military relations are not just a matter between officers and elected officials. More fundamental is the relationship between individual citizens and the organization that defends them.

Introduction to the Paperback Edition

An Update

Five years after publication of *Inside Defense*, the US military continues to play a major role in international affairs. While the United States concluded military operations in Iraq in December 2011, it continues to have a significant diplomatic and commercial presence there. At the same time, the United States surged combat operations in Afghanistan and launched a concerted effort to train Afghans to assume responsibility for their own security. Now the US-led coalition of 50 countries plans to redeploy all combat forces by the end of 2014. The original goals of representative government (including ethnic diversity and gender rights and quotas), and of economic development in addition to peace and stability have proven difficult to realize. Indeed, the United States' current objectives for concluding the two Bush-era wars have changed to merely giving indigenous forces the capacity to provide for their own security and stability, and to ensure that there is no threat to the United States from either country.

Though Iraq and Afghanistan have occupied much of the attention of the public and of the national security community since 2009, President Barack Obama has initiated a rather robust security agenda. Missile defense has continued to mature as a program. Thus, President Obama has ordered the deployment of US Navy ships to Spain to protect Europe from Middle Eastern missiles, although he changed course from Bush administration plans by canceling missile defense sites in eastern Europe. In addition, the United States supported Libya's "Arab Awakening" with air combat operations enabling anti-Qaddafi forces to seize control of the country. Further, the administration maintained decades-old pressure on Iran's nuclear program with cyber attacks and by reinforcing Persian Gulf countries' capacity through weapons sales, enhanced security partnerships, and the development of missile defense sites. Finally, President Bush's Africa Command has brought increased attention to security partnerships in Africa and a focus on transnational threats such as piracy, terrorism, organized crime, and illicit trafficking. President Obama has also continued to use the military for humanitarian operations, notably deploying the military to post-tsunami Japan in 2011, but also regularly to the Caribbean, Africa, and Southeast Asia.

President Obama has also expanded the size and use of Special Forces and drones. Dramatically, the Special Forces accomplished the 2011 raid deep inside Pakistan that killed Osama bin Laden. Drone strikes are regularly made inside Afghanistan, Pakistan, and Yemen. In fact, remotely piloted vehicles fill such an important role in President Obama's counterterrorism strategy that more new Air Force Academy graduates are being trained to pilot drones than traditional jet aircraft. This approach to countering terrorism with Special Forces and drones reduces the footprint required for US military operations and are near casualty free for US forces. These operations tend to favor assassination over capture and inevitably involve "collateral damage." This means unintended civilian casualties and economic damage, which can result in "blowback" and anti-Americanism in general. For example, in the Iraq war collateral damage has been estimated to include as many as 100,000 Iraqi lives and costing trillions of dollars. (It is difficult to quantify true costs and the estimates vary widely, but costs like these need greater attention and discussion prior to military operations.) Further, after the US military withdrew from Iraq, civilians continued to be victimized by insurgents who continue their fight against the new government in Baghdad.

Although some call for a reduction in US global commitments or at least for a more restrained use of force, President Obama's 2012 defense strategy document reaffirms a global posture centered in the Asia-Pacific region and the Middle East. The official strategy suggests that the United States will maintain an ability to go anywhere (sub-surface to outer space) and to act in any situation (major combat to humanitarian assistance). This ambition is untempered by the reality that US policy has not been especially successful in meeting goals, which have included a representative, stable government based on a solid economy. This is true even in a nearby, benign environment like Haiti. This seems to suggest that a commitment to military primacy may not be the best way to achieve some US foreign policy goals. In fact, the emphasis on military primacy appears to have had a negative impact on other nation's opinions of the United States. According to a Pew Research Center poll of global opinion, support for President Obama's international policies fell in Europe from 78 percent in 2009 to 63 percent in 2012 and in predominately Muslim countries from 34 percent in 2009 to 15 percent in 2012.[1] Still, the same poll revealed that President Obama remains the most popular leader in the world.

For the first time in many years the military budget (which has been increasing each year even when all spending for the two major wars are omitted) has become a matter for both public and Congressional discussion. If the goal of reducing discretionary spending by $1.2 trillion over a decade is to be reached, there will have to be major budget cuts, but the military's share of those cuts is still uncertain. Still, Congress has begun to reduce the size of the Army and Marine Corps by about 15 percent, which will return them to roughly 2005 levels. This will alleviate some fiscal strain since much of the defense budget involves health care and salaries.

The military's stance on social issues continues to evolve. The decades-old ban that prevented homosexuals from serving openly has ended. The military even celebrated a gay pride event at the Pentagon and the promotion of a lesbian general in 2012. The military also has been wrestling with respect for and treatment of mental health problems and is developing new responses to an increased number of reported sexual assaults. It is also working to further the integration of women into certain combat positions. The Navy has opened the submarine force to a limited number of officer women and there are discussions with Congress about removing restrictions on women's participation in ground combat. This is in recognition of the role women have already played when attached to ground units and in recognition of the fact that there is no longer a "battle front" with "lines" between combat and support.

While these are substantial changes, our basic thesis has not changed. In spite of more than a decade of combat operations, looming budget reductions, and a variety of social changes, the military remains a powerful tool for American presidents and they have not been loathe to use it even without a Constitutionally-specified declaration of war by Congress. The military's size, technology, equipment, and remarkable capabilities allow presidents to defend America and also to support friends, allies, and partners, to supply humanitarian assistance, and to provide "presence" through Navy ships, Army training, and Air Force exercises even in distant regions. While some continue to argue for reducing the military's role in foreign policy, for reducing its budget, and to call for an assessment of what is actually accomplished versus goals articulated, politicians of both parties continue to support a massive, well-equipped, and future-oriented defense establishment. However, questions remain about what is actually required for US security, and also about the most economic way to fulfill those requirements. With this in mind, we reaffirm what we wrote five years ago, "Because the military has been so active in so many places and with such a variety of missions, we believe it is important that students, policymakers, and, indeed, every citizen consider the new roles the military does and should play in international and domestic politics."

Impact of the Wars

Since November 2001, the United States has had a substantial number of forces deployed in combat zones—2.4 million in Iraq and Afghanistan. Unlike in previous wars, US casualties have been low. In Iraq, 4,400 were killed and 30,000 were wounded. In Afghanistan, about 2,000 have been killed and 15,000 have been wounded. While physical wounds have been low relative to other wars, the psychological impact of the wars will resonate for years to come. Post-traumatic stress disorder (PTSD) is at epidemic proportions and suicide deaths compete with combat casualties. To address these important issues, the military is now making a concerted effort to de-stigmatize psychological disorders and to instill in its leaders an obligation to help service members recover.

The impact of recent wars significantly affects the military's thinking about and planning for its future. Today's junior officers are principally experienced and think about counterinsurgency and counterterrorism. It is unclear if these leaders will continue to embrace these missions or reject them as the Vietnam generation of officers rejected the tactics of their generation. Indeed, some senior leaders are questioning the population-centric orientation of the military with its emphasis on "winning hearts and minds" and US force protection. They worry that the military and the US public will not be ready for a conflict with a peer military.

Thus, much of the institutional military is again stressing the potential for a major conflict that could take place on the high seas (or under them), in space, or cyberspace. In fact, President Obama's Secretary of Defense wrote in the 2012 defense strategic guidance:

> This country is at a strategic turning point after a decade of war and, therefore, we are shaping a Joint Force for the future that will be smaller and leaner, but will

be agile, flexible, ready, and technologically advanced. It will have cutting edge capabilities, exploiting our technological, joint, and networked advantage...It will have global presence emphasizing the Asia-Pacific and the Middle East while still ensuring our ability to maintain our defense commitments to Europe, and strengthening alliances and partnerships across all regions.

Refocusing the military on a potential competitor like China or regional challengers like Iran and North Korea is welcomed in the halls of the Pentagon, but forces in the field and at combatant commands continue to concentrate on counterinsurgency, building partners' capacity, and responding to natural disasters. Thus, the Pentagon boasts about the most expensive air battle fighter ever built, the F-22, but not a single F-22 aircraft has flown a combat mission in Iraq, Afghanistan, or Libya. Though a single program, the F-22 is an important symbol of an unresolved tension within the national security community between those that see a future dominated by tensions among great powers and those that see the past as prologue. For the former, the lesson of the last 12 years seems to be that the military should focus its efforts on preparing for large-scale, war fighting against a peer since counterinsurgency is a losing proposition. The novelist Mark Helprin captured this position in an op-ed:

> leaving divided, violence-plagued, tinder-box nations hostile to American interests, friendly to its enemies, and largely unchanged despite our mission of transformation is not victory.[2]

On the other hand, there is a group that says the future will continue to be characterized by the United States leading coalitions to combat subnational and transnational forces such as insurgents, terrorists, pirates, and criminal enterprises. This group uses stability operations in the Balkans and counterinsurgency operations in Iraq and Afghanistan for its examples and rejects "never-again" pronouncements about nation-building. Marine General Charles Krulak's 1999 characterization of a future "three-block war" attempts to formulate the possibilities.

> At one point in time, one block, they've got a child in their hands, they're wrapping that child in swaddling clothes, they're feeding it, and it's called humanitarian assistance. The next moment, they're keeping two factions apart—that's called peacekeeping. And what you're seeing is the third block, every once in a while coming into the second, and the third block in the three-block war is what we call mid-intensity, highly lethal conflict.[3]

Krulak attempted to drive strategic thinking and planning toward the types of conflicts he believed United States was most likely to wage. In the three-block scenario, the military would be fighting, peacekeeping, and delivering humanitarian assistance at the same time. The era of large-scale maneuver warfare reminiscent of World War II and Cold War scenarios was not a part of his vision. However, the institutional military did not adopt his three-block view. For Krulak and others like him, this was a mistake. Arguing against a fixation on conventional and large-scale warfare alone, he said, "We're not going to see the son of Desert Storm anymore. You're going to see the stepchild of Chechnya."[4] The Pentagon ignored his vision and, instead, under Bush's leadership, stormed into Iraq and Afghanistan.

While major combat was a success, what happened after the first several months demonstrated an inability to anticipate and prepare for what comes after regime change. In Iraq and Afghanistan, it took several years before the United States attempted to build the institutions it destroyed and rediscovered the need for counterinsurgency. With no clear successes in Iraq or Afghanistan, it appears that a tendency to eschew state-building activities and to focus on a major conflict may be reemerging. The Pentagon seems to be saying we will never do operations like Iraq or Afghanistan again. Restraint in post-Qadaffi Libya and apprehensions for civil war Syria suggest the United States is heeding former secretary of Defense Robert Gates' advice that "any future defense secretary who advises the president to again send a big American land army into Asia or into the Middle East or Africa should have his head examined."[5] Nevertheless, many at the Pentagon are talking about a potential great power like China. Consequently, calls to pivot to the maritime theater of the Pacific are welcomed by many in the national security establishment. While future presidents are likely to receive a range of advice, it is the (lack of) budget that may alter options and impact the military's role in international affairs.

Looming Budget Cuts

There is a direct connection between national security and the economy—a strong economy generates revenue that can be allocated for defense and an innovative economy creates new technologies that can be employed by the military. Importantly, the defense industry also provides a large number of well-paying jobs. The Pentagon now explicitly recognizes the importance of the economy to what it can do. In 2011, then Chairman of the Joint Chiefs of Staff Admiral Mike Mullen declared that the national debt is the single, biggest national security threat.[6] He noted that the interest on the national debt is nearly the size of the defense budget and that an increasing debt would negatively affect future military spending. Thus, the US military would be unprepared for future military operations.

Currently the United States' expenditures on its military is almost half that of all the world's military expenditures. It overshadows all potential competitors combined. Only the United States is able to place over 100,000 troops 8,000 miles from home and sustain them indefinitely under combat conditions. This capacity, not nuclear weapons alone, is what makes the United States a superpower. However, this capacity is costly—$655 billion in 2012. Over the last decade, the military budget grew by several hundred billion dollars. Some of the increase is explained by the cost of the wars, but there were also significant new outlays in scientific research and personnel costs. In fact, the US military spends more on health care than India or Germany spends on its entire defense budget. In fact, the US budget for personnel (salaries and benefits) is larger than China's entire defense budget.

There is a current effort by the military to rein in personnel and health care costs. However, Congress is often reluctant to cut personnel benefits, thus weapons may eventually become the focus of the cuts. This generates concern at the Pentagon, which believes the United States may lose its edge if weapons programs are cancelled to pay for health care and retirees. As Arnold Punaro, a consultant on the Defense Business Board noted "we're going to turn the Department of Defense into a benefits company that occasionally kills a terrorist."[7] To avoid this scenario, some advocate reducing personnel size and emphasizing technology. For example, an Arleigh Burke destroyer (DDG) has a crew of about 350, while the new class of Littoral Combat Ship (LCS), which fulfills many of the same functions, only needs a crew of about 50. While LCS and DDG are not equivalent, technology and doctrinal change are said to offset individual platform differences.

The Limits of Military Power

Obviously, the budget will affect the future focus of the military, but so do the lessons learned from recent wars. After Vietnam, a number of changes were made that dramatically changed the US military. First, the Abrams doctrine shifted key specialties from the active component to the reserve component. This slowed the nation's ability to wage war (it took six months to call up reservists and National Guardsmen and to build the force needed for the 1991 invasion of Iraq). Second, the all-volunteer force was enshrined in part to have a constant pool of professional forces, but also to avoid conscripting unwilling personnel and, importantly, to tamp down opposition to military action since only volunteers would be involved. Third, the Weinberger Doctrine advised strict criteria for military intervention, which was intended to prevent gradual escalations leading to full-scale combat. Finally, the Powell Doctrine advised overwhelming force if a commitment was made.

During the George W. Bush presidency these lessons were set aside (save the all-volunteer force). Today, the military is very usable, and presidents have been using it without benefit of a Congressional declaration of war since World War II. Congress can reduce funding as a means of control, but has chosen not to do so. Too often major conflicts have resulted from a series of small steps rather than from serious debate and national commitment. The military, however, has learned one important lesson, that it cannot achieve national objectives alone. Thus, it regularly calls for interagency reform and for more development and diplomatic experts in the field. However, civilian departments lack both the personnel and budgets needed for participation in large-scale operations.[8]

Secretary of State Hillary Clinton is attempting to change diplomats' focus on national capitals and to move more personnel to austere environments, but she has not been able to change the Department of State's orientation to match the Defense Department's expeditionary mindset. Further, Congress is unlikely to fund what would be needed for civilians to do nation building even if there is reluctance to do it in the military. Similarly, the Defense Department's expeditionary orientation is difficult to apply to both combat and noncombat settings. Journalist Rajiv Chandrasekaran has documented some of the unreality of the US "whole-of-government" efforts in Iraq and Afghanistan. Writing about Afghanistan, Chandrasekaran wrote,

> For all the lofty pronouncements made about waging a new kind of war, our nation was unable to adapt. Too few generals recognized that surging forces could be counterproductive...Too few soldiers were ordered to leave their air conditioned bases—with the siren's call of Baskin Robbin's ice cream in the chow halls and big screen televisions in the recreation rooms—and live among the people in fly-infested villages
>
> Too few diplomats invested the effort to understand the languages and cultures of the places in which they were stationed. Too few development experts were interested in anything other than making a buck.
>
> Too few officials in Washington were willing to assume the risks necessary to forge a lasting peace. And nobody, it seemed, wanted to work together.[9]

The military may recognize its limits better than do civilians, yet it is civilians with grand development and diplomatic goals that direct the military. Still the challenges to development and to diplomatic goals in a country like Afghanistan now seem obvious. The military may be able to check insurgents and may successfully develop a professional Afghan Army, Air Force, and national Police. However, it is unclear what kind of civilian government will finally emerge, whether Afghan elites will stay after 2014 to rebuild the country, and it is unclear how or even if the economy will develop.

Success in Afghanistan can be claimed only if Afghan President Hamid Karzai can reinforce Afghan local, regional, and national leaders, can build functioning institutions, and can provide for security against Pakistan, the Taliban, and other insurgent groups. The Afghan economy must also develop to sustain the population and a professional military and police. Again, 11 years of unresolved conflict suggest that external actors can have only a temporary and/or marginal effect on a country's circumstances. Only nationals can establish a nation's sovereignty and effectively provide for their security, government, and prosperity. This is a lesson that seems both to be learned and not learned by military and civilians within US national security circles.

As we reflect on other efforts to build states or reinforce failing states, the results seem grim. Proponents of nation building point to successful cases in Japan, Germany, and South Korea, however, there are few contemporary examples where external actors such as the United States have achieved announced objectives of creating security, representative government, and a developing economy.[10] The United States has supported Colombia since 2000; this has been called a success, yet the government there cannot bring resolution to a 50-year-old civil war. In the Balkan countries of Bosnia-Hercegovina and Kosovo, economic and political development have progressed little since the late 1990s. All these cases are instructive, but the case of Haiti continues to be the most revealing. With no war as a shadow hanging over development efforts, with extensive US involvement, and with proximity to US shores, little stability or prosperity can be claimed after a half century of US effort.

Future Directions for the US Military

Ten years after the 9/11 attacks and the invasion of Afghanistan, one thing is clear—the United States is still committed to being able to use its military globally. Beyond counterterrorism efforts like those to combat al-Qaeda, US strategy attempts to support sovereign governments like Egypt, Saudi Arabia, Philippines, South Korea, and Colombia in order to ensure regional stability, support counterinsurgencies, and to thwart international terrorism. While much has been made of linking US national security to international security, too few realize that intervening in other countries' insurgencies carries its own risks.

US military strategy is now to "partner" with nearly every military in the world. Over the last decade, the American security assistance program has expanded from about 50 to 150 countries.[11] Funded through the Department of State, security assistance is implemented by the Department of Defense. Military-to-military relations have thus become as important as diplomat-to-diplomat relations in some countries. This type of assistance ranges from bringing foreign officers to the United States to teach them how to pilot helicopters and to attend our War Colleges, to helping countries control their maritime space by providing ships, intelligence, and training. Regime type is not a discriminator; the United States works closely with democratic regimes like Japan and non-democratic regimes, even kingdoms, like Saudi Arabia and Bahrain.

The organizing principle for military strategy was in contrast to the Cold War, when, countering a "peer competitor" such as the Soviet Union, the concern was US "vital interests"; "weak states" and mere "interests" (of others as well as those of the United States) preoccupy strategic thinkers today. The 2011 National Military Strategy of the United States underscores this noting: "In this interdependent world, the enduring interests of the United States are increasingly tied to those of other state and non-state actors."

The rationale for providing security assistance globally is based on the assumption that instability breeds chaos, and chaos could threaten the United States. Therefore, the United States should support other countries through military-to-military contacts, equipment transfers, and combined training activities. Since the United States has such a dominant military, countries increasingly choose to partner with the United States to take advantage of US assets. The United States welcomes military partnerships because they broaden our influence, give us access to strategic locations, and promote international security.

Admittedly, security assistance does not always translate into influence or even stability.[12] Even countries such as Israel, Pakistan, and Egypt, which receive enormous support from the United States are (and have to be) responsive to domestic politics. Still, the new model of security assistance is a far cry from what the US military practiced through much of the twentieth century. Then, military assistance meant installing US-friendly governments through the power of the bayonet (Panama), promoting insurgency to overthrow unfriendly governments (Nicaragua, Iran, Afghanistan), and arming friendly regimes regardless of human rights records (Saudi Arabia). The United States now aspires to create partners that can manage their own threats to security and stability. While beginning to understand that there are clear limits to what the United States in general, and the military in particular can do, it appears that both Democrats and Republicans see a continuing, major role for the US military in supporting global stability. As the United States moves beyond Bush-era military commitments, future research needs to address three key questions. Is such an ambitious program the best way to achieve national security? Is this approach in the best interests of ordinary US citizens? Is an internationalist United States what US citizens want?

Derek S. Reveron and Judith Hicks Stiehm
November 2012

Notes

1. Global Opinion of Obama Slips, Drone Strikes Widely Opposed, June 13, 2012. http://pewresearch.org/pubs/2284/obama-usimage-image-abroad-global-economic-power-drone-strikes-policy-military-terrorism-china-economy

2. Mark Helprin, "A Primer for American Military Intervention," *Wall Street Journal*, July 5, 2012, p. A11.

3. "An Interview with Charles Krulak," *Newshour with Jim Lehrer*, June 25, 1999. http://www.pbs.org/newshour/bb/military/jan-june99/krulak_6–25.html

4. Ibid.

5. Robert M. Gates, quoted in Thom Shanker, "Warning Against Wars Like Iraq and Afghanistan," *New York Times*, February 25, 2011.

6. Michael J. Carden, "National Debt Poses Security Threat, Mullen Says," *American Forces Press Service*, August 27, 2010.

7. Quoted in Elisabeth Bumiller and Thom Shanker, "Panetta to Offer Strategy for Cutting Military Budget," *New York Times*, January 2, 2012.

8. For alternative approaches, see Nikolas Gvosdev and Derek S. Reveron, "Waging War, Building States," *Policy Review*, October 2010. http://www.hoover.org/publications/policy-review/article/49846

9. Rajiv Chandraskaran, *Little America: The War Within the War for Afghanistan* (New York: Simon and Schuster, 2012), p. 331.

10. For detailed analysis of nation building efforts, see James Dobbins, *America's Role in Nation-Building: From Germany to Iraq* (Washington, DC: Rand, 2003).

11. Derek S. Reveron, *Exporting Security: International Engagement, Security Cooperation, and the Changing Face of the U.S. Military* (Washington, DC: Georgetown University Press, 2010).

12. While a student at the US Army War College in 2005, the chief of staff of Egypt's armed forces argued in a paper that the American military presence in the Middle East and its "one sided" support of Israel were fueling hatred toward the United States and miring it in an unwinnable global war with Islamist militants. See David D. Kirkpatrick and Kareem Fahim, "In Paper, Chief of Egypt's Army Criticized U.S.," *New York Times*, August 16, 2012.

Part I

The Military and the International Setting

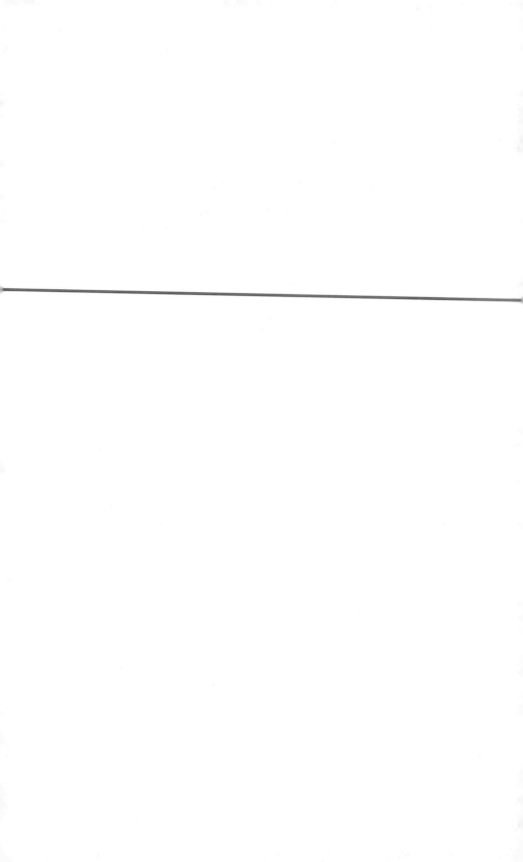

1

Strategy in War

Stephen Biddle

The conduct of war is among the most important acts of the state. In the past century alone, failure in this undertaking has toppled governments and imposed hostile occupation for hundreds of millions from Paris to Warsaw and from Tokyo to Jakarta. Military failure in World War I destroyed the Ottoman, Austro-Hungarian, German, and Russian empires and created a host of new states in Eastern Europe and the Balkans. Allied military victory in World War II made global superpowers of the United States and the Soviet Union, and split Germany into two countries. The success of Soviet arms ended Latvian, Lithuanian, and Estonian independence, and resulted in a generation of subjugation under Soviet satellite rule for the peoples of Eastern Europe. Pyrrhic victory in two world wars exhausted Britain and brought an end to its global economic hegemony. Failure in internal war has toppled governments from Afghanistan to Vietnam; variations in the conduct of such wars can mean the difference between decades of misery in grinding stalemates, as in Lebanon, or in a rapid, decisive conclusion, as in the Sinai in 1967.

But, although its effects on international politics are profound, the conduct of war is often neglected by political scientists, who focus chiefly on war's causes rather than on its conduct. This overlooks a rich—if undertheorized—literature by historians, soldiers, and strategists. A more systematic engagement with this literature would enable a more sophisticated treatment of both research and teaching about war and international relations.

A comprehensive review of this enormous literature is beyond my scope here.[1] Instead, I will provide an introduction to the subject by presenting some key distinctions and organizing principles, and by sketching a few of the more important debates about the subtopic of major interstate war. While this excludes much, it is at least a point of departure for the study of strategy, and it may serve to illustrate the richness of the subject matter. The later chapters in this book explore these ideas in concrete terms as strategy relates to the U.S. military, its relationship with the State Department, and its use as a foreign policy tool. This theoretical chapter lays the foundation for that discussion using as a framework the distinction between the *levels of war*. Much as international relations observes a distinction between levels of analysis (system, unit, individual), so strategic studies distinguishes the *grand strategic, military strategic, operational,* and *tactical* levels of war. Each involves a different set of issues, a different range of variation in state practice, and different considerations for success. Proficiency at one does not necessarily imply proficiency at another, and no one dominates the others as a determinant of success or failure in war.

Grand Strategy

Grand strategy is the level of war most familiar to most political scientists. It defines the state's ultimate objectives and prescribes means for pursuing them, including the military, economic, diplomatic, social, and political instruments of national policy. American grand strategy in the Cold War, for example, defined U.S. objectives as fundamentally defensive (the containment of what was seen as an expansionist Soviet opponent). To this end, the United States employed, inter alia, a combination of alliances and a large peacetime military establishment to balance Soviet power; the use of free trade and economic expansion at home to ensure an economic base sufficient to sustain a large ongoing military program; the economic and diplomatic isolation of the Soviet bloc; and a political effort to maintain domestic support for international engagement by emphasizing the perceived threat from the Soviet Union.[2] By contrast, German grand strategy in 1939 was fundamentally offensive; it sought territorial expansion. To achieve this, Germany emphasized unilateral military means, with only limited efforts to secure allies, and with an expectation that the economic resources of conquered territories would enable continued expansion.[3]

Grand strategic choices are frequently controversial. In the United States, for example, the Cold War saw a debate between advocates of the containment doctrine sketched above and supporters of rollback, who sought to shrink the Soviet sphere of influence in Eastern Europe rather than merely to prevent its expansion.[4] With the end of the Cold War, debate shifted to the comparative merits of an American pursuit of global primacy as opposed to an emphasis on cooperative security, selective engagement, or even isolationism.[5]

Today, the U.S. grand strategic debate is over the role of democratization, unilateralism, and preemptive warfare. Since 2001, neoconservatives have advocated a non–status quo policy of transformational democratic change in hostile regimes, to be pursued multilaterally and peacefully if possible but unilaterally and militarily if necessary.[6] Realists, by contrast, have increasingly sought international stability even at the cost of tolerating illiberal regimes, and they have argued for avoiding unilateral military action and for restricting the use of force to defensive action with support from broad alliances for the purpose of preserving local balances of power.[7] Official U.S. grand strategy has not been clearly articulated in the post-2001 era. Basic questions, such as those concerning the identity of the enemy or the nation's aims in the war, have been left unanswered; although official statements had been drifting toward the neoconservative view by 2004, events in

Iraq had so undermined this approach as to leave the grand strategic direction of the war largely adrift by January 2007.[8] A new approach is needed, but none has yet emerged.

Military Strategy

Military strategy prescribes how military instruments are employed to achieve the goals set by grand strategy in a given theater of war. The United States in the Cold War, for example, employed a number of complementary military strategies to achieve the goal of balancing Soviet power in Europe and Asia. *Nuclear deterrence* aimed to dissuade the Soviets from aggression by threatening overwhelming retaliation. A *continental strategy* of defending key European and Asian allies with conventional ground and supporting air forces aimed to defeat aggression if it occurred, or, failing that, to provide time for *nuclear compellence* to restore the territorial status quo. At times these were complemented with a *maritime strategy* of using U.S. naval action to threaten horizontal escalation against the Soviet periphery and to pressure Soviet client states overseas.[9]

As with grand strategy, military strategy is often controversial. Among the more prominent debates at this level have been the recurring disagreements between advocates of *strategic bombing* (which entails coercive attacks against enemy centers of industry, population, and political control to secure national aims) and more conventional continental strategists who advocated air support of ground troops.[10] Cold War nuclear strategy saw a sustained debate over the requirements of deterrence and the employment of nuclear weapons, yielding a series of American nuclear doctrines, including *massive retaliation* (in which any Soviet aggression was to be deterred by a threat of overwhelming nuclear attack against the Soviet homeland); *flexible response* (in which limited aggression was to be met initially with a limited response, escalating only as necessary to compel a return to the *status quo ante bellum*); and the *countervailing strategy* (in which deterrence was focused on a threat to destroy Soviet leadership and military targets, rather than Soviet society at large).[11] Maritime strategists debate the merits of Mahanian approaches focusing on the coercive control of sea lanes and oceangoing commerce, as opposed to Corbettian approaches in which naval power is used to project force ashore via amphibious assault and air or missile strikes against land targets.[12]

Unlike grand strategy in the Cold War, where the United States made a reasonably clear, consistent choice of one among several competing alternatives, U.S. military strategy for major war has usually been service-specific; hence, at any given time, multiple military strategies have been officially sanctioned. Typically, the army favors continental strategies. The air force normally favors strategic bombing (as opposed to "tactical" bombing in support of a land war). The navy had long preferred Mahanian approaches, but has now shifted toward a Corbettian emphasis, which has been the Marine Corps' traditional preference. This strategic pluralism probably conduces to better policy because of the vigorous competition of ideas. However, it also promotes interservice conflict as advocates of different means of securing military ends compete for peacetime budgets and wartime missions.

Operational Art

Operational art prescribes how military forces are to achieve theater strategic ends by interconnecting a series of battles or engagements or airstrikes (sometimes called a "campaign"). During the Cold War, for example, the theater strategy of continental defense in Europe was implemented via a number of successive operational-level doctrines. The doctrine inherited from World War II conceived U.S. offensive campaigns as a sequence of battles and actions: (1) *concentration* of a disproportionate fraction of U.S. forces on a narrow front; (2) one or more *breakthrough* battles, in which this concentrated force fought its way through the enemy's prepared defenses on that front; and an ensuing (3) *exploitation* and *pursuit*, in which the attacker's forces, now free of the need to overcome prepared defenses, accelerated and fanned out to overrun less-protected supporting infrastructure many miles behind the front, causing systemic collapse of the defense as a whole.

U.S. defensive campaigns, by contrast, were designed to thwart an enemy's use of an approach like that described above. This would be accomplished via the use of deep dispositions that would forestall breakthrough in a series of delaying actions at the threatened point, while withheld reserves were counterconcentrated to that point from elsewhere in the theater. These reserves could then be used to set up a climactic counterattack, or to reinforce local defenses at the threatened point.[13]

This approach was replaced in 1956 by what is now called the Pentomic doctrine, which relied on tactical nuclear weapons to destroy the enemy without the series of maneuver battles called for in orthodox doctrine. Concentration was judged too dangerous in the face of nuclear firepower, which in friendly hands was deemed sufficient to breach enemy lines or destroy enemy assaults without conventional breakthrough battles. Instead, dispersed ground forces were to direct nuclear fires and exploit their effects via widely distributed small-unit actions at many points across the theater.[14]

The Pentomic doctrine was found to be impractical, however, and was abandoned by 1962 in favor of a return to orthodoxy in the Reorganized Armored Division (ROAD) system, which closely resembled previous doctrine. The ROAD doctrine was in turn displaced by the "Active Defense" of 1976, in which a new firepower source—early-generation guided antitank missiles—was judged to render traditional breakthrough battles impossibly costly, and defensive depth superfluous. Instead, defensive campaigns were to be waged by concentrating antitank weapons near the initial point of contact for an early decisive battle before the attacker could penetrate in depth. The withholding of reserves was discouraged in order to maximize forward combat strength, and counterattack was all but forbidden in the face of the defensive firepower expected from the enemy's guided weaponry. Maneuver was limited to lateral displacement of forward defenders to match the attacker's local concentration at the point of attack, and theater campaigns as a whole were designed to avoid the need to retake lost ground or to penetrate into enemy territory.[15]

Like the Pentomic doctrine before it, Active Defense was soon found to be too static and too dependent on firepower, yielding another return to orthodoxy in the form of the "AirLand Battle" doctrine of 1982. AirLand Battle restored the traditional emphasis on orchestrating a series of sequential battles fought in depth, with heavier reliance on counterattack to regain lost ground, and larger reserves. It added to this an increased reliance on deep airstrikes against military targets on enemy territory in order to facilitate breakthrough and exploitation when on the offense, and to disrupt the enemy when on the defense.[16]

AirLand Battle, though revised several times after 1982, remained the heart of U.S. Army doctrine through the 1991 Gulf War. Since then, however, it has been subject to challenge from advocates of a related series of ideas often termed "network centric warfare" (NCW) or "rapid decisive operations" (RDO). Advocates of NCW/RDO see the potential of long-range precision strikes based on new networked information technologies as obviating the need for both traditional massed ground battles and sequenced campaigns of concentration, breakthrough, and exploitation phases. Instead, they believe that standoff precision firepower delivered simultaneously throughout the depth of the theater by air and missile forces can destroy an opponent's ability to resist. Ground forces, then, are reduced to a secondary, supporting role.[17]

Though commonly described as novel, today's NCW and RDO doctrines bear a striking resemblance to the two earlier postwar responses to apparent increases in firepower in their rejection of both concentration for breakthrough and sequential campaign design. Whether NCW and RDO will go the way of the Pentomic Division and the Active Defense remains to be seen, but a renewed doctrinal debate is certain.

Operational doctrine for interstate continental warfare, however, is far from the only subject of debate at this level of war. The proper conduct of counterinsurgency and counterterrorism campaigns has attracted increasing attention.[18] And, of course, other military strategies, such as strategic bombing, have generated their own debates at the operational level over the best way to integrate individual engagements into campaigns that can provide theater success. For strategic bombing, for example, target selection and time phasing of strikes have been ongoing controversies.[19] For Mahanian navalists, the relative merits of different means of controlling seaborne commerce have been hotly debated; the orthodox approach of destroying hostile capital ships in a battle at sea in order to blockade key ports has been regularly challenged by advocates of widely distributed commerce raiding by submarines or light surface ships.[20] Corbettian navalists now disagree over the need for amphibious invasion—as opposed to deep strikes by aircraft or missiles—as the best means of projecting naval power ashore.[21] At any given time, each service will have an officially sanctioned operational doctrine, but those doctrines, which are not always mutually compatible, are continuously debated and frequently changed.

Tactics

Tactics prescribe how the individual battles or airstrikes that make up a campaign are to be conducted, and they ordinarily dictate how small units are employed (e.g., platoons, companies, battalions, ships, or squadrons). By contrast, operational art concerns the activities of large formations (e.g., army divisions or corps, naval task forces, or wings of aircraft), and theater strategy concerns the direction of the largest formations, such as armies and army groups, fleets, and "numbered air forces" (i.e., multiple wings of aircraft).

Among the more important issues in the history of tactics have been the balance of arms and the use of terrain. Prior to World War I, European armies saw infantry as the decisive arm, with artillery, cavalry, and other branches serving only to prepare for or support the critical clash of opposing foot soldiers. Terrain was understood to be important, but the emphasis was on large-scale features (e.g., commanding high ground) and on enabling or disabling the maneuver of massed formations that tended to close with the enemy in the open. These tactics yielded slaughter in the opening battles of August 1914.[22]

With traditional infantry-centered tactics having clearly failed, European armies abandoned them wholesale by as early as March 1915. In their place came a new system of artillery-centered tactics in which the very lethal firepower of modern artillery was harnessed in an effort to destroy defenses before exposing friendly infantry to enemy fire. As the French put it, "*l'artillerie conquiert, l'infantrie occupiert*": the artillery conquers, the infantry occupies. This was a dramatic reversal—in a matter of months, ostensibly conservative military institutions demoted the dominant arm of the previous century to the role of mere support for an artillery branch that had been considered a minor technical arm before 1915. This stood a lifetime of military experience on its head and constituted, arguably, the most sweeping revolution in the history of modern strategy. Yet it, too, failed, yielding the great trench stalemate of 1915–17.[23]

By 1918 a new system had taken shape, in which the infantry-centered tactics of 1914 and the artillery-centered tactics of 1915–17 were both replaced with a new combined arms approach in which infantry and artillery cooperated as coequals. In the new approach, artillery was used not to destroy defenses outright but merely to suppress them, restricting their freedom to fire on advancing infantry. That infantry now dispersed into small, independently maneuvering formations that could use minor local terrain features for cover and concealment, dashing from one small patch of cover to the next while the artillery kept the defenders' heads down. This tight integration of mutually supporting arms and careful use of microterrain by small subunits made it possible to sustain an advance in the face of enemy fire, and restored movement to the battlefield by the spring of 1918.[24]

The resulting "modern system" of tactics proved both effective in enabling ground forces to win battles in the face of enemy fire and remarkably robust over nearly a century of technological change. Since 1918 it has become something approaching a transnational norm for sound tactics. But while it is militarily effective when fully implemented, it has the disadvantages of extreme complexity and political unattractiveness, yielding significant variance in the actual conduct of battlefield tactics.[25]

Moreover, technological change has periodically tempted tacticians to abandon the modern canon in favor of heterodox approaches designed to exploit increasingly lethal firepower or, most recently, improvements in information availability. The operational-level doctrines associated with the Pentomic Division and the Active Defense, for example, were accompanied by tactical-level innovations emphasizing passive, static dispositions in prepared defensive positions, with a minimum of forward movement in the face of the apparently too-lethal nuclear and precision-guided conventional firepower. As at the operational level, however, it was found that static tactical defenses could be overcome by combined arms attackers. In both cases, the conduct of battles returned to the modern system norm when the Pentomic Division and Active Defense were abandoned.[26]

Today, proponents of standoff precision strike and networked information technology advocate new tactics that strive to avoid giving battle at short range on the ground by destroying the enemy at great distances via remotely delivered firepower. The ground forces that remain are to disperse into small, widely distributed elements and to act chiefly as scouts to acquire targets for long-range air and missile attack.[27] For major combat, today's tactical debate turns centrally on the ability of such methods to succeed against opponents who employ the modern system to reduce their exposure.

In both operational art and tactics, the last century of warfare has thus seen a repeated pattern in which new technologies have tempted militaries to design new approaches around the apparent increase in firepower provided in turn by the new artillery of 1914, the battlefield nuclear weapons of the 1950s, the first-generation precision-guided antitank weapons of the 1970s, and now the stand-off precision weaponry and networked information of the 1990s and the early twenty-first century. Heretofore, such heterodoxy has proven impractical, and orthodox doctrines and tactics have always returned. Whether this will happen again remains to be seen.

But, this is not the only debate among students of tactics. As with operational art, tactics for counterinsurgency have attracted increasing attention, especially as the war in Iraq has unfolded.[28] And just as strategic bombing theorists and Mahanian or Corbettian navalists have debated differing approaches to operational art, so they have disagreed over the best tactics for warfare as well.[29]

All of these debates are important. And all of the levels of war are important. No one trumps the others. Brilliant tactics and operational art can be undone by errors at the strategic or grand strategic level, as was the case for Germany in World War II, and as may yet prove to be the case for the United States' 2003 campaign to topple Saddam Hussein.[30] Conversely, unsolved problems at the tactical and operational levels can preclude success at the strategic or grand strategic level, as in the great trench stalemate on the Western Front from 1915 to 1917 or in Saddam Hussein's conduct of the Gulf wars in 1991 and 2003.[31]

Success in the conduct of war often requires competence across the levels of war. Similarly, teaching and research in political science and international relations can profit from a familiarity not just with the politics of war at the grand strategic level, but also with at least some of the basic issues in the conduct of war at the military strategic, operational, and tactical levels as well.

Notes

1. For partial but useful overviews, see, for example, Peter Paret, ed., *Makers of Modern Strategy* (Princeton, NJ: Princeton University Press, 1986); John Baylis, James Wirtz, Eliot Cohen and Colin Gray, eds., *Strategy in the Contemporary World: An Introduction to Strategic Studies* (New York: Oxford University Press, 2002); Colin McInnes and G. D. Sheffield, eds., *Warfare in the Twentieth Century: Theory and Practice* (London: Unwin Hyman, 1988); John Collins, *Military Strategy: Principles, Practices, and Historical Perspectives* (Washington, D.C.: Potomac, 2001).
2. See, for example, John Lewis Gaddis, *Strategies of Containment: A Critical Appraisal of Postwar American National Security Policy* (New York: Oxford University Press, 1982).
3. See, for example, Norman Rich, *Hitler's War Aims* (New York. W. W. Norton, 1992).
4. See, for example, Gaddis, *Strategies of Containment*, pp. 128–9, 155–6.
5. Christopher Layne, "Offshore Balancing Revisited," *The Washington Quarterly* 25:2 (Spring 2002), pp. 233–48; Barry Posen and Andrew Ross, "Competing Visions for U.S. Grand Strategy," *International Security* 21:3 (Winter 1996/97), pp. 5–53.
6. See, for example, Robert Lieber, *The American Era: Power and Strategy for the 21st Century* (New York: Cambridge University Press, 2005); David Frum and Richard Perle, *An End to Evil: How to Win the War on Terror* (New York: Random House, 2003); Charles Krauthammer, "The Unipolar Moment Revisited," *National Interest*, Winter 2002/03, pp. 5–17.
7. See, for example, Francis Fukuyama, *America at the Crossroads: Democracy, Power, and the Neoconservative Legacy* (New Haven, CT: Yale University Press, 2006); Anatol Lieven and John Hulsman, *Ethical Realism: A Vision for America's Role in the World* (New York, Pantheon, 2006); Zbigniew Brzezinski, *The Choice: Global Domination or Global Leadership* (New York: Basic Books, 2004).
8. For official articulations, see *The National Security Strategy of the United States of America* (Washington, D.C.: The White House, September 2002); *National Strategy for Countering Terrorism* (Washington, D.C.: The White House, September 2006). For a critique of U.S. grand strategy as underspecified, see Stephen Biddle, *American Grand Strategy after 9/11: An Assessment* (Carlisle, PA: U.S. Army War College Strategic Studies Institute, April 2005).
9. On American use of continental and maritime strategies in the Cold War, see Robert Komer, "Maritime Strategy vs. Coalition Defense," *Foreign Affairs*, Summer 1982, pp. 124–31; John J. Mearsheimer, "A Strategic Misstep: The Maritime Strategy and Deterrence in Europe," *International Security* 11:2 (Fall 1986), pp. 3–57; Joshua Epstein, "Horizontal Escalation: Sour Notes of a Recurrent Theme," in Robert Art and Kenneth Waltz, eds., *The Use of Force*, 2nd ed. (Lanham, MD: University Press of America, 1983), pp. 649–60. On nuclear strategy and European defense, see David Schwartz, *NATO's Nuclear Dilemmas* (Washington, D.C.: Brookings, 1983); J. Michael Legge, *Theater Nuclear Weapons and the NATO Strategy of Flexible Response* (Santa Monica, CA: RAND, 1983), RAND R-2964-FF.
10. Cf., for example, Robert A. Pape, *Bombing to Win* (Ithaca, NY: Cornell University Press, 1996); Barry D. Watts, "Ignoring Reality: Problems of Theory and Evidence in Security Studies," *Security Studies* 7:2 (Winter 1997/98), pp. 133–49; Richard Overy, *Why the Allies Won* (London: Pimlico, 2006).

11. On the history of Cold War U.S. nuclear doctrine, see, for example, Lawrence Freedman, *The Evolution of Nuclear Strategy* (New York: Palgrave Macmillan, 2003); Tami Davis Biddle, "Shield and Sword: American Strategic Forces, 1945 to the Present," in Andrew Bacevich, ed., *The Long War: American National Security Policy, 1945 to the Present* (New York: Columbia University Press, 2007).

12. See, for example, Philip A. Crowl, "Alfred Thayer Mahan," in Peter Paret, ed., *Makers of Modern Strategy* (Princeton, NJ: Princeton University Press, 1986), pp. 444–77; Alfred Thayer Mahan, "Commerce Destroying and Blockade," in Allan Westcott, ed., *Mahan on Naval Warfare* (Boston, MA: Little, Brown, 1942), pp. 91–9; Julian Corbett, *Some Principles of Maritime Strategy* (Annapolis, MD: U.S. Naval Institute Press, 1988 ed. of 1911 orig.); Michael Howard, "The British Way in Warfare: A Reappraisal," in Howard, *The Causes of Wars* (Cambridge, MA: Harvard University Press, 1984), pp. 169–87; Geoffrey Till, *Seapower: A Guide for the Twenty-first Century* (London: Cass, 2004); Norman Friedman, *Seapower as Strategy: Navies and National Interests* (Annapolis, MD: U.S. Naval Institute Press, 2001); Andrew Lambert, *Foundations of Naval History* (London: Greenhill, 2006).

13. Robert Doughty, *The Evolution of US Army Tactical Doctrine, 1946–76* (Ft. Leavenworth, KS: U.S. Army Combat Studies Institute, 1979), pp. 2–12; *Field Manual FM 100-5, Field Service Regulations, Operations* (Washington, D.C.: Department of the Army, 1949), ch. 8. Army field manuals represent an important resource for official descriptions of operational art and tactics, yet one that is typically overlooked in political science scholarship. They can now be obtained online from a variety of sources. Many historical manuals have been digitized by the U.S. Army Combined Arms Research Library at Ft. Leavenworth and posted at: http://cgsc.leavenworth.army.mil/carl/contentdm/home.htm (under "Obsolete Military Manuals"). Current manuals are sometimes made available to the public online by the army and sometimes not; the site is open as of this writing (January 2007), and can be found at: http://www.army.mil/references/ by following the links for "Army doctrinal and training publications." Nonofficial sources include http://www.globalsecurity.org/military/library/policy/army/fm/index.html; and www.enlisted.info. Nonofficial sources are not necessarily as current, but are more consistently available.

14. Andrew Bacevich, *The Pentomic Era* (Washington, D.C.: National Defense University Press, 1986); Doughty, *Evolution of US Army Tactical Doctrine*, pp. 12–19.

15. Paul Herbert, *Deciding What Has to Be Done: General William E. DePuy and the 1976 Edition of FM 100-5, Operations* (Ft. Leavenworth, KS: U.S. Army Combat Studies Institute, 1988); Doughty, *Evolution of US Army Tactical Doctrine*, pp. 19–25, 40–6.

16. John Romjue, *From Active Defense to AirLand Battle: The Development of Army Doctrine 1973–1982* (Ft. Monroe, VA: U.S. Army Training and Doctrine Command, 1984); Huba Wass de Czege and L. D. Holder, "The New FM 100-5," *Military Review*, July 1982, pp. 53–70.

17. For current U.S. Army operational doctrine, see *FM 3-0: Operations* (Washington, D.C.: Headquarters, Department of the Army, 2001). On NCW/RDO, see, for example, Arthur Cebrowski and John Garstka, "Network-Centric Warfare," *U.S. Naval Institute Proceedings* (January 1998); U.S. Joint Forces Command, *A Concept for Rapid Decisive Operations* (Norfolk, VA: Joint Forces Cmd. J9 Joint Futures Lab, 2001).

18. See, for example, John A. Nagl, *Learning to Eat Soup with a Knife: Counterinsurgency Lessons from Malaya and Vietnam* (Westport, CT: Praeger Publishers, 2002); T. X. Hammes, *The Sling and the Stone: Warfare in the Twenty-First Century* (St. Paul, MN: Zenith, 2004); Kalev I. Sepp, "Best Practices in Counterinsurgency," *Military Review*, May–June 2005, pp. 8–12; Stephen Biddle, "Seeing Baghdad, Thinking Saigon,"

Foreign Affairs, March/April 2006; Andrew Krepinevich, "How to Win in Iraq," *Foreign Affairs*, September/October 2005; Kenneth Pollack and the Iraq Working Group, *A Switch in Time: A New Strategy for America in Iraq*, Analysis Paper No. 7 (Washington, D.C.: Brookings, February 2006). For official U.S. counterinsurgency doctrine, see *FM 3-24: Counterinsurgency* (Washington, D.C.: Headquarters, Department of the Army, 2006).

19. See, for example, Tami Davis Biddle, *Rhetoric and Reality in Air Warfare* (Princeton, NJ: Princeton University Press, 2002), chs. 3–5; Charles Webster and Noble Frankland, *The Strategic Air War Against Germany* (London: Her Majesty's Stationery Office, 1961).

20. Bernard Brodie, *Sea Power in the Machine Age* (Princeton, NJ: Princeton University Press, 1943); Theodore Ropp, *The Development of a Modern Navy: French Naval Policy, 1871–1904* (Annapolis, Md.: Naval Institute Press, 1987 ed. of 1937 orig.), ed. Stephen S. Roberts; William McNeill, *The Pursuit of Power: Technology, Armed Force, and Society since A.D. 1000* (Chicago: University of Chicago Press, 1982), pp. 262–5.

21. See, for example, Till, *Seapower*; Friedman, *Seapower as Strategy*.

22. Shelford Bidwell and Dominick Graham, *Firepower: British Army Weapons and Theories of War, 1904–1945* (London: Allen and Unwin, 1985), pp. 7–60; David G. Herrmann, *The Arming of Europe and the Making of the First World War* (Princeton, NJ: Princeton University Press, 1996), pp. 59–112; Paddy Griffith, *Battle Tactics of the Western Front* (New Haven, CT: Yale University Press, 1994), pp. 48–52; Antulio Echevarria, *After Clausewitz: German Military Thinkers Before the Great War* (Lawrence: University Press of Kansas, 2000), pp. 121–81, 213–28; Jonathan House, *Toward Combined Arms Warfare: A Survey of Twentieth Century Tactics, Doctrine, and Organization* (Ft. Leavenworth, KS: U.S. Army Combat Studies Institute, 1984), pp. 7–18; John English, *On Infantry* (New York: Praeger, 1984), pp. 1–11.

23. J. B. A. Bailey, *Field Artillery and Firepower* (Oxford: Military Press, 1989), pp. 130–41; Robin Prior and Trevor Wilson, *Command on the Western Front* (Oxford: Blackwell, 1992), pp. 154–70; G. C. Wynne, *If Germany Attacks: The Battle in Depth in the West* (London: Faber and Faber, 1940; Greenwood Press rpt., 1976), pp. 168–318; Timothy Lupfer, *The Dynamics of Doctrine: Changes in German Tactical Doctrine During the First World War* (Ft. Leavenworth, KS: U.S. Army Combat Studies Institute, 1981), pp. 1–36; Bidwell and Graham, *Firepower*, pp. 61–130.

24. Bailey, *Field Artillery and Firepower*, pp. 141–52; Bidwell and Graham, *Firepower*, pp. 94–130, 139–46; Prior and Wilson, *Command on the Western Front*, pp. 311–15, 362–6; Lupfer, *Dynamics of Doctrine*, pp. 43–6; Griffith, *Battle Tactics of the Western Front*, pp. 93–100, 120–58; Bruce Gudmundsson, *Stormtroop Tactics: Innovation in the German Army, 1914–1918* (New York: Praeger, 1989); English, *On Infantry*, pp. 17–26; Gary Sheffield, *Forgotten Victory* (London: Review, 2002), pp. 221–63.

25. Stephen Biddle, *Military Power: Explaining Victory and Defeat in Modern Battle* (Princeton, NJ: Princeton University Press, 2004), ch. 3, which also treats the modern system at the operational level of war.

26. Bacevich, *The Pentomic Era*; Doughty, *The Evolution of US Army Tactical Doctrine*, pp. 12–25, 40–6; Herbert, *Deciding What Has to Be Done*; Romjue, *From Active Defense to AirLand Battle*, pp. 23–50. For current U.S. Army tactics, see, for example, *Field Manual 71-1: Tank and Mechanized Infantry Company Team* (Washington, D.C.: Headquarters, Department of the Army, 1998).

27. See, for example, Brig. Gen. David A. Deptula, *Effects-Based Operations: Change in the Nature of Warfare* (Arlington, VA: Aerospace Education Foundation, 2001); Cebrowski and Garstka, "Network-Centric Warfare;" U.S. Joint Forces Command, *A Concept for Rapid Decisive Operations*.

28. See, for example, Bard O'Neill, *Insurgency and Terrorism: From Revolution to Apocalypse* (Washington, D.C.: Potomac, 2005); Ian Beckett, *Modern Insurgencies and Counterinsurgencies: Guerillas and their Opponents since 1750* (London: Taylor and Francis, 2005); James Anthony Joes, *Resisting Rebellion: The History and Politics of Counterinsurgency* (Lexington: University Press of Kentucky, 2004); and the references in note 18 above.

29. On naval tactics, see esp. Wayne Hughes, *Fleet Tactics and Coastal Combat* (Annapolis, MD: U.S. Naval Institute Press, 2000 ed.). For accounts of illustrative tactical debates within the U.S. air force, see, for example, Mackinlay Kantor and Curtis LeMay, *Mission with LeMay: My Story* (New York: Doubleday, 1965); Eliot Cohen, director, *Gulf War Air Power Survey, Vol. II, Part I: Operations* (Washington, D.C.: U.S. Government Printing Office, 1993).

30. Russell F. Weigley, "The Political and Strategic Dimensions of Military Effectiveness," in Williamson Murray and Allen Millett, eds., *Military Effectiveness, Vol. III* (Boston, MA: Allen and Unwin, 1988), pp. 341–64; Michael Gordon and Bernard Trainor, *Cobra II: The Inside Story of the Invasion and Occupation of Iraq* (New York: Pantheon, 2006); Thomas Ricks, *Fiasco: The American Military Adventure in Iraq* (New York: Penguin, 2006).

31. Paul Kennedy, "Britain in the First World War," in Millett and Murray, *Military Effectiveness, Vol. I*, pp. 31–79; Biddle, *Military Power*, ch. 7; Stephen Biddle, "Speed Kills: Reevaluating the Role of Speed, Precision, and Situation Awareness in the Fall of Saddam," *Journal of Strategic Studies* 30:1 (February 2007), pp. 3–46.

2

The Department of Defense and the Department of State: Out of Balance and into Trouble

Stephen D. Wrage

An Improbable Balance

The Department of State and the Department of Defense (DoD) are so vastly unequal in all forms of resources that it is surprising that a rough balance of influence has historically existed between the two. These two departments are cases of inequality in the extreme, being disparate in almost every way except for their role in the policymaking process. At times, however, a severe imbalance of influence has developed, and those times have often produced policy that in retrospect has been ill considered and damaging to American interests. Moreover, the policy choices made during times of imbalance have tended to be especially injurious to the military. The uniformed services have fared best when State and Defense have enjoyed roughly equal influence in the White House or when they have at least worked together in a consultative way. When there was no balance of interest, the military has found itself cast into situations from which it has taken years to recover.

An Imbalance in Resources

The first and perhaps the most fundamental way to compare any two departments is by their budgets. Students of bureaucratic politics give the same advice that Deep Throat gave Bob Woodward: "Follow the money." In this case the money is easy to follow; the budget of the State Department is dwarfed by that of the Pentagon. According to the Office of Management and Budget (OMB), the discretionary budget authority for the Department of State in 2005 was $10.3 billion.[1] The discretionary budget authority for DoD was $401 billion,[2] or about forty times as large. With supplemental budgets over the last few years, the DoD budget has been at least sixty times larger.

A second way to compare the resources controlled by the two departments is through their personnel numbers. Again according to the OMB, the State Department has a total of thirty thousand employees.[3] DoD has a total of seven hundred thousand civilian employees, plus 2.3 million military employees in active duty, reserve, and guard units.[4] In round numbers, for every one person working for the secretary of state, one hundred people work for the secretary of defense. The disparity in human resources is suggested by the fact that "more people play in Army bands than serve in the U.S. foreign service."[5]

A third way to compare two U.S. government agencies is by the real estate they control in Washington. (It would be absurd to compare their real estate globally, because the military bases controlled by DoD are so vast in area compared to the embassies of the Department of State.) During the decades between 1888 and 1939, State and War shared quarters with the Department of the Navy in what is now called the Old Executive Office Building; however, in 1939 the War Department was granted new quarters in an area long left open because of its low-lying, unattractive location in moist air and on swampy ground west of the main centers of government.

The War Department built a plain, rectangular building and gave it the unimaginative name of the "New War Building," but they did not stay there long. In 1947, Defense left its cast-off building for State to inhabit and moved to much grander, iconic quarters across the Potomac. State reluctantly moved into the New State Building and has been there ever since. Perhaps because the building was not actually new at all, the name evolved a little from "New State" to "Main State," and so it has remained.[6] Main State is a large building that covers all but the sidewalks of two city blocks; by comparison, however, the Pentagon was originally granted a tract of land of no less than 583 acres and is now ensconced in the largest office building in the world—a single structure that encompasses thirty-four acres.[7]

A fourth way to compare two bureaucratic entities is in terms of their relationships with competing bureaucratic entities and to Congress, the White House, and their own constituencies. In 1947 the National Security Act gave State a new bureaucratic competitor in the form of the National Security Council (NSC), which took up quarters next door to the White House and placed its director, the National Security Advisor, in an office just a few yards from the Oval Office. The same act created the Central Intelligence Agency (CIA), another formidable player in policymaking activities that State had formerly performed. Defense, by contrast, grew immensely after the NSC issued NSC 68, the document that spurred the construction of what Daniel Yergin has called "the National Security State"[8] and put the United States on what Yergin has argued was a permanent war footing.

In terms of their relations with Congress and the benefits the two departments can offer to members of the House and the Senate, the difference again is one-sided in favor of Defense. First, State does not have enough natural constituents to make a difference in any district, even Maryland's eighth, which includes Bethesda and Chevy Chase, home to many of the department's employees. Defense, by contrast, has 3 million employees spread across the state and district of every senator and representative, respectively. The military services see to it that their members register to vote; the services provide voting assistance programs[9] and absentee ballot information, and they exert a good deal of informal encouragement aimed at mobilizing the military's voting power. Absentee military voters in Florida almost certainly delivered the 2000 election to George Bush (see Donald Inbody's chapter later in this book).

In addition, however, the Department of State has virtually nothing to offer a representative or senator in the way of pork to bring home to the voters. In fact, being on the House Committee on Foreign Affairs or the Senate Committee on Foreign Relations can be a liability to a legislator in the sense that it associates him or her with the granting of foreign aid, which many voters consider an objectionable giveaway to foreigners. It is almost a cliché for a legislator to say, "We've got to stop taking money away from poor Americans and sending it overseas to fill the pockets of rich foreigners!" To make matters worse, many Americans imagine that the foreign aid "giveaways" are a major portion of the U.S. budget. One survey in 1994 revealed that 46 percent of the respondents believed foreign aid was the second largest category of expenditure in the federal budget, when in fact it made up less than four-tenths of 1 percent.[10]

The Defense budget, by contrast, is a veritable cornucopia of contracts to bring home to the district, and a senator who holds a major appropriations or armed services committee post can expect to be courted by the military and can hope to see his or her state richly endowed with new projects bearing his or her name. For example, Senator John J. Sparkman of Alabama, chair of the Joint Committee on Defense Production, was able to make Redstone Arsenal in Huntsville the original home of the National Aeronautics and Space Administration (NASA), dramatically changing the cotton economy of northern Alabama. Later, Senator John C. Stennis, chairman of the Senate Armed Services Committee from 1969 to 1980, managed to remove NASA's principal rocket engine test facility from Alabama and bring it to his home state of Mississippi, where it was christened the Stennis Space Center. Though he publicly declined the honor, the navy insisted on naming an aircraft carrier and a strike group after Senator Stennis, following the practice of Admiral Hyman Rickover, who broke the tradition of naming battleships after states, cruisers after cities, and submarines after fish, and started naming them after politicians. After all, Admiral Rickover observed, "Fish don't vote."[11]

In terms of resources, then, the departments of State and Defense stand in an extremely unequal relationship. Nonetheless, a rough balance of influence between the two departments has been maintained for decades, with only intermittent periods of imbalance. It is worth considering how this balance has been sustained historically, and how it has been lost recently.

Sustaining a Balance in Influence

The first and most fundamental reason the balance has been maintained is because the roles of the two departments are complementary. Diplomacy is not effective unless it is supported by the potential for military force, and force will be used far too quickly and far too often in the absence of effective diplomacy. Effective force keeps diplomacy relevant; good diplomacy keeps war as a last resort. When the functions of the two departments fall out of balance and cease to be mutually supportive, the effectiveness of diplomacy decreases and the frequency of the use of force increases. The risks of failure for both departments substantially increase. Examples cited below will illustrate this effect.

A second reason the balance has been maintained is because astute and skillful presidents have worked to maintain it. President Franklin Roosevelt, for example, worked to keep his assertive secretary of state Cordell Hull in check and working in tandem with his secretary of war Henry Stimson. When Hull indulged his inclination to be domineering and to exclude Stimson from correspondence and from meetings, Roosevelt occasionally would reach around Hull and deal directly with undersecretary of state Sumner Welles.[12] In this way Roosevelt was able to accomplish two ends: he could keep his cabinet officers working productively *with* each other, but also set them working usefully *against* each other. That is, each would have to work consultatively with the other or risk being excluded from the policymaking process; yet each would also have to work against the other in the sense that each would have to explore, develop, and champion policy alternatives that the president could review and choose between.

A third reason why a balance has been maintained is that many secretaries of state and defense—for example, George C. Marshall (who held both posts)—exercised a reserve and self-restraint that did not inspire or require others to work to constrain their influence. By contrast, others—for example, Henry Kissinger and Alexander Haig at State or Robert McNamara or Donald Rumsfeld at Defense—effectively required that the rest of the government implement a micropolicy of containment aimed specifically at them. The measures necessary to monitor and contain the most assertive secretaries have usually been obstructive of the entire policymaking process, but such measures were necessary if the president was to be spared from falling into the trap of hearing from a single advisor and being deprived of his proper role of choosing among a number of alternatives.

A fourth major reason why the balance has endured is because when a serious imbalance did occur, the system of policymaking often functioned badly, unfortunate choices were made, and an effort to restore the balance necessarily ensued. For example, on the occasion cited above when Franklin Roosevelt chastised Secretary of State Hull for his role in leaking a scandal that drove Welles to resign, Roosevelt ostracized Hull and his department and chose to attend major wartime conferences without the counsel of representatives from his own diplomatic service.

At Yalta, for example, FDR purposely excluded representatives from Hull's State Department,[13] and at that conference he yielded vast concessions to the Soviet Union, ceding control over Poland and other parts of Central Europe and so easing the establishment of the Soviet bloc. Though much of Roosevelt's behavior may have been due to his failing health, he had also deprived himself of counselors who would have argued for more caution and resistance in dealing with Stalin. One State Department official he would likely have had at his side, if he had not been boxing out State at the time, was George F. Kennan, the chargé d'affaires in Moscow and the diplomat of his generation who probably understood Soviet intentions better than any other. The president deprived himself of his best advice and made worse decisions as a result.

One can multiply such examples. Before the Bay of Pigs invasion, President John F. Kennedy excluded or discounted diplomatic and military advisors and listened uncritically to Richard Bissell of the CIA. Bissell played on his monopoly on Kennedy's attention and guided him into committing to an intervention that the Pentagon, State, and the Joint Chiefs of Staff (JCS) all opposed. Bissell expected that the intervention might fail, but he calculated that, faced with failure, Kennedy would call in air, naval, and ground forces. Kennedy refused, and the entire invading force was killed or captured. In the assessment of Evan Thomas, "Bissell had been caught in his own web. 'Plausible deniability' was intended to protect the president, but as [Bissell] had used it, it was a tool to gain and maintain control over an operation . . . Without plausible deniability, the Cuba project would have been turned over to the Pentagon, and Bissell would have become a supporting actor."[14]

Not only Bissell but Kennedy himself had been caught in Bissell's web. By wrapping himself in a Bissell-spun cocoon that excluded the voices of others, Kennedy was left to choose among only the poor alternatives that Bissell provided to him. The result was a policy disaster that still casts a shadow on U.S.–Cuba policy, a disaster that probably emboldened Nikita Khrushchev eighteen months later when he placed nuclear-armed missiles in Cuba. By that time Kennedy had rethought and reworked the way he worked with his foreign policy advisors, and in the "ExComm" or Executive Committee he created to deal with the crisis, he made sure that he heard from a wide range of voices and that they were not impeded in the ways in which they gave him counsel.

Another example of an imbalance of influence leading to poor policy was Secretary of Defense Robert McNamara's domination of the policymaking process regarding Vietnam in the Lyndon Johnson White House. H. R. McMaster has documented the ways McNamara and his group of "Whiz Kids" were able to direct the debate and override the weak resistance of the JCS and others in 1964 and 1965 and so draw the United States deeply into an unwinnable war. McNamara himself has candidly fortified this portrayal of events in his memoir, In Retrospect.[15]

President Richard Nixon seems to have repeated many of the same errors of imbalance in permitting his national security advisor, Henry Kissinger, to monopolize access to him. In this case, other advisors became desperate enough to resort to a variety of measures. Secretary of State William Rogers resigned only to see Kissinger take over the State Department while retaining control of the NSC, making Kissinger a one-of-a-kind foreign policy czar. Secretary of Defense Melvin Laird fought back, actively spying on Kissinger and actually turning the message-intercept powers of the National Security Agency (NSA) against his colleague.[16] The JCS actually planted an agent, Navy Yeoman Charles E. Radford, in Kissinger's offices with orders to copy and smuggle top-secret documents to his bosses in the Pentagon. For fifteen months Radford worked and traveled with Kissinger and his deputy, Al Haig, and when he was unobserved, he searched desktops, burn bags, briefcases, and interoffice envelopes, surreptitiously making copies and delivering them to the office of Admiral Thomas Moorer, chairman of the Joint Chiefs of Staff (CJCS).[17] When Radford at last was discovered,

Kissinger demanded that Moorer be fired, but Nixon chose to keep the matter quiet. Nixon knew that Kissinger had secretly wiretapped his own closest aides and that he had given transcripts to Haig and to White House chief-of-staff H. R. Haldeman. And Nixon knew he had done some taping of his own.

President Gerald Ford and President Jimmy Carter worked to relieve the atmosphere of deviousness and secrecy that had infected the American foreign policy process under Kissinger and Nixon, but errors of imbalance were hard to avoid. President Carter ignored the strenuous objections of his secretary of state, Cyrus Vance, to a secret mission to rescue the hostages held in the American embassy in Teheran. Finally, Carter simply excluded Vance from subsequent discussions and went ahead with the mission when Vance was away from Washington. Desert One became the gravest foreign policy blunder of Carter's presidency, and Vance, seeing himself rendered irrelevant to the policymaking process, could only resign.

President Ronald Reagan testified that he allowed not only his State and Defense departments but even *himself* to be excluded from the policymaking process with regard to the Iran-Contra scheme. He depicted that embarrassing policy episode as having been hatched entirely from within a tiny, secret, self-funding cell of the CIA that was located inside the NSC. The result was an embarrassing series of hearings before the Senate and legal charges and convictions of major policymakers, including Secretary of Defense Caspar Weinberger and Assistant Secretary of State Elliott Abrams, followed by presidential pardons issued by Reagan's successor, President George H. W. Bush.

Regardless of the efforts of astute presidents to maintain a balance of influence between State and Defense, over time the balance has substantially shifted against State. The era is long past when, as in the Truman and Eisenhower administrations, secretaries of state such as George C. Marshall, Dean Acheson, and John Foster Dulles overshadowed secretaries of defense such as Robert A. Lovett, Charles E. Wilson, and Neil H. McElroy. Over decades, the growth of Yergin's "national security state" has enhanced the power of Defense while the multiplication of competing policy centers has weakened State, particularly in times of war. In fact, the two secretaries of defense who have decisively overmatched their contemporary secretaries of state have been McNamara, who dwarfed Dean Rusk, and Rumsfeld, who boxed out Colin Powell. The tenures of McNamara and Rumsfeld coincided with the wars in Vietnam and Iraq, making it seem that wartime can enhance the opportunities of defense secretaries to shoulder aside their diplomatic counterparts.

These episodes suggest three things. First, they suggest that the policymaking process works best when a fundamental balance between agencies is maintained— and that the balance between State and Defense is at the center of a balanced policymaking process. Second, they indicate that times of imbalance often give rise to unfortunate policy choices, many of which have had damaging consequences for the U.S. military. Third, and most importantly, they demonstrate that when a president has failed to maintain a balance among his advisors, he has found himself unable to perform his proper role of hearer of, and chooser between, the alternatives brought to him by his advisors.

Losing the Balance

The proper balance of influence between the departments of State and Defense was lost in the first six years of the George W. Bush administration. A bad policy process produced bad policy. Ill-considered—sometimes disastrous—decisions were made, and the president abdicated his role of chooser between alternatives brought to him by a well-functioning set of executive agencies. As has often been the case in the past, the U.S. military suffered its share, or more than its share, of the negative consequences of those poorly made decisions.

By 2001, a balance between State and Defense would have been very difficult to maintain in any case. From 1995 through 2000, when Senator Jesse Helms of North Carolina headed the Senate Foreign Relations Committee, the State Department had been systematically defunded and diminished, despite the best efforts of Secretary of State Madeline Albright to charm the senator and protect the department. At the same time, the more generously funded U.S. military had stepped forward and accepted new roles as they were shed by State.[18] The situation became grave enough that General John Shalikashvili, CJCS in 1999, warned against further cuts in State's funding. It is uncommon for the leader of one agency of the bureaucracy to plead that scarce funds go to a competing one. Nonetheless, he was concerned enough at the deterioration of the State Department to tell a meeting at Meridian House, "What we are doing to our diplomatic capabilities is criminal. By slashing them, we are less able to avoid disasters such as Somalia or Kosovo, and therefore we will be obliged to use military force still more often."[19]

The administration of George W. Bush might have set about rebuilding the capabilities of the State Department, and it would have if it had understood the importance to presidential power of having a balance of voices. President Bush was little interested in developing his government's diplomatic capabilities, however. Instead, he was thoroughly committed to exercising its military strengths.

President Bush took to heart the call from Charles Krauthammer, who wrote, "An unprecedentedly dominant United States . . . is in the unique position of being able to fashion its own foreign policy. After a decade of Prometheus playing pygmy, the first task of the new [Bush] administration is precisely to assert American freedom of action."[20] President Bush strongly endorsed a policy of unilateral action, preemption, and regime change even before the attacks of September 11, 2001. Such a policy implied a diminished role for an already diminished State Department. It also discounted the value of consultation and consensus seeking, both within the U.S. government and between the United States and other governments.

The impact of President Bush's unilateralism on the foreign policy process was reinforced by his preference to decide, then delegate. He repeatedly stated, "I delegate to good people." The president recently expanded on this theme in a speech in Lancaster, Pennsylvania:[21]

> I delegate to good people. I always tell Condi Rice, "I want to remind you, Madam Secretary, who has the Ph.D. and who was the C student. And I want to remind you who the adviser is and who the president is."

I got a lot of Ph.D.-types and smart people around me who come into the Oval Office and say, "Mr. President, here's what's on my mind." And I listen carefully to their advice. But having gathered the advice, I decide, you know, I say, "This is what we're going to do." And it's "Yes, sir, Mr. President." And then we get after it, implement policy.

The president may imagine that he delegates and that his appointees report to him with advice; and that he then makes decisions, and they return to their agencies and implement his intentions. That is a very incomplete view of the policymaking process, however. It omits all of the backstage struggles and the secretive give-and-take that are the essence of bureaucratic maneuvering. In fact, an effective president needs to inquire, to examine, to test, to weigh, to judge, to demand explanations and justifications, to question assumptions, to intervene, and after all that, to reassess and redirect repeatedly. In a well-functioning bureaucratic process, much of that questioning would be done for him by various pairs of bureaucratic counterparts. The State and Defense departments would keep each other's agenda in check. Lacking such a process, the burden on the president is immense, and only the most alert, vigorous, attentive, and perceptive chief executive would be equal to the task.

Again, one can compare the way Franklin Roosevelt managed his bureaucracy to the way President Bush describes his own style:

[Roosevelt's] civilian appointments reflected the demands of politics. Hull, [Harold] Ickes, [Henry A.] Wallace, and Frances Perkins spoke for particular constituencies whose support the president needed. They symbolized his political coalition, but they were not free to set policy in their individual bailiwicks. Roosevelt did not hesitate to dip down to resolve departmental issues, often structured competing lines of authority, and had no hesitation second-guessing decisions his subordinates had made. Cabinet leaders were kept on a short leash.[22]

President Roosevelt had staffed his cabinet with representatives of the constituencies that supported him. Although that meant that he constantly had to calculate the impact of his policy choices on his domestic coalition, it also meant that he could reward or sanction cabinet members by favoring or neglecting the groups they represented. President Bush, by contrast, seems to have delegated much of the selection of his cabinet and subcabinet to Vice President Dick Cheney, who made some strange choices.

Cheney, as head of transition, recommended Donald Rumsfeld at Defense. Rumsfeld was a man of extreme independence and great experience (a veteran, twenty-five years before, of that exact job), someone with huge background knowledge, a vast array of connections, considerable charisma, and a very pronounced agenda that did not necessarily jibe with the president's. Clearly, this was someone who might be very difficult to constrain.

For State, Cheney recommended Colin Powell, another person with great experience, knowledge, connections, and charisma, who might have served very well as a counterweight to Rumsfeld had he been employed in that role by the White House. Instead, the president and his close advisors, including particularly the

vice president, kept Powell at a distance from the very outset of the administration. By treating him as an outsider in the circle of his close advisors, President
Bush sacrificed Powell's usefulness as a counterbalance to Rumsfeld. By bringing
him up short in the first months of the administration and by overruling him on
pressing for negotiations between the Israelis and the Palestinians, on the Kyoto
Agreement, and on the Anti-Ballistic Missile (ABM) Treaty, President Bush
diminished his secretary of state. After Powell's highly visible role at the United
Nations (UN), where he offered "proof" of the existence of weapons of mass
destruction (WMD) in Iraq, Powell's effectiveness was nearly finished. Certainly
his capacity to counterbalance Rumsfeld was long exhausted.

National Security Advisor Condoleezza Rice is reported to have been President
Bush's personal choice, but her daughterly relationship with the president did not
position her to be a strong figure who could counterbalance or discipline a figure
like Donald Rumsfeld or George Tenet if he seemed to be overreaching. Rice was
surrounded by figures with far more experience in foreign policy than she had—
and with far more than the president had for that matter.

Cheney seems to have reserved a very strong bureaucratic position for himself.
Two acute observers of the bureaucratic process report,

> He created his own mini-NSC staff, hiring a dozen national security specialists of
> unusually high caliber. Al Gore's staff was half the size and made up almost entirely
> of mid-career military officers. This larger staff of professionals enabled the OVP, as
> the Office of the Vice President is known inside the bureaucracy, to operate essen-
> tially as an independent agency. Through his staff Cheney had input at virtually
> every level of the interagency decision-making process and then again in private as
> the president's counselor.[23]

Finally, Cheney seems to have helped install neoconservatives in a very large
number of significant posts. These include Paul Wolfowitz, Richard Perle,
Douglas Feith, John Bolton, Paula Dobriansky, Elliott Abrams, Zalmay
Khalizad, Peter Rodman, William B. Schneider, Kenneth Adelman, and his own
chief of staff, Scooter Libby.[24] As a group, the neoconservatives were not shy
about pressing a foreign policy agenda that long predated the president's own
and were likely to be impatient with any process that required consultation—
much less accommodation—with competing power centers, including the State
Department. If one were concerned about maintaining balance in a foreign
policy process, inserting neoconservatives in many high offices would be an odd
step to take. Moreover, many of the neoconservatives were vocally critical of
Colin Powell. When Paul Wolfowitz, who had been a deputy secretary of defense
in the administration of President George H. W. Bush, was asked why he was
willing to take up the same position in the administration of his son, he was
reported to have answered, "Powell."[25]

President Roosevelt's appointees "were not free to set policy in their individual
bailiwicks,"[26] yet President Bush's have been allowed great freedom from oversight, much less intervention. President Bush has made it clear that he expects his
appointees to be intensely loyal to him personally, but it is naïve to suppose that

loyalty makes oversight superfluous. The president does not seem to have concerned himself with many profoundly important measures taken by the Office of the Secretary of Defense (OSD) or to have involved himself even in very significant decisions. It is astonishing, for example, that there is no evidence that the White House was consulted or even informed before the fateful decision in May 2003 to issue Coalition Provisional Authority (CPA) Order Number 2 and disband the Iraqi military.[27]

President Roosevelt "did not hesitate to dip down to resolve departmental issues," he "often structured competing lines of authority," and he showed "no hesitation in second-guessing . . . his subordinates." He kept his cabinet officers "on a short leash."[28] By contrast, it is hard to find examples of President Bush calling his subordinates to account, even when severe problems occurred in the operations under their supervision. On the other hand, it is easy to find many instances when awards of the highest order were granted to people who were vacating their posts after severe problems. For example, the president awarded the Presidential Medal of Freedom to CIA director George Tenet, General Tommy Franks, General Richard Myers, and Ambassador Paul Bremer.[29]

The policy process created in the Bush Oval Office seems to have made it practically impossible for the president to play the elevated role of "the decider" that he quite properly desired to play. Instead of being at the pinnacle of a balanced yet vigorous process in which well-tested options are brought up to him for his consideration, he seems to have become encased in a cocoon spun by a few close advisors. He willingly allowed them to be his sources for knowledge of the outside world.[30] Inside this circle of advisors, it was very difficult for him to know, much less to guide, the actions of figures like his secretary of defense who were acting with extreme independence.

This circle of advisors proved difficult to break into, even for the most savvy bureaucratic actor with the most crucial information. One example of the impenetrability of the process surrounding President Bush was Richard A. Clarke, the administration's chief antiterrorism official and an experienced operator who had served nine years on the NSC. Clarke had to wage a consistent and focused campaign for nine months to get the cabinet officers to review his information on the al Qaeda network. That principals-level meeting finally occurred on September 4, 2001, exactly a week before the attacks.[31]

Though many critics have harshly attacked President Bush for his failure to ask the right questions, few have focused on the way that the process in which he was embedded made asking those questions difficult. Getting insight into the workings of that process and reforming it would have been still more difficult, especially when so much was happening so fast and so badly, particularly in Iraq. The president may have lost his chance to govern his own bureaucracy effectively at a very early point when he failed to maintain the balance between agencies that would have shifted the burden of preparing, testing, and justifying options downward to his staff, where it belonged. After that balance was lost, the role of the president became almost impossible to perform successfully, and damaging policy choices were practically inevitable. Since these choices involved war, the damage they did fell heavily on the U.S. military.

After the unbalanced process was established, that process would work against its own reform. That is, the dominance of Rumsfeld, together with the exclusion of Powell, would suppress the kinds of challenges State could present to Defense that might have led to useful reexamination of policies and the assumptions behind them. A second force against the reestablishment of balance was the secrecy and evasion of accountability instituted by the OVP.[32] The loyalty demanded by President Bush would also discourage expressions of doubts about policy choices, since they would be perceived as expressions of doubt about him.

Out of Balance in Iraq

The products of imbalance are obvious if one compares the decision making prior to war with Iraq in 1990 to that in 2002. Curiously, many of the same people were involved. The presidents were different, though they are father and son, and the policymaking processes they oversaw differed dramatically, although Cheney had a role in each process, first as secretary of defense and later as vice president. Powell appears twice, first as CJCS and later as secretary of state. Wolfowitz was an undersecretary of defense in 1990 and a deputy secretary of defense in 2002. Margaret Thatcher, British prime minister in 1990, had been replaced by Tony Blair, by 2002 Brent Scowcroft, the national security advisor in 1990, was replaced by Rice. James Baker, the secretary of state in 1990, does not appear in 2002, though Robert Gates, Scowcroft's deputy in 1990, returned as the secretary of defense in 2006.

In 1990 there was vigorous debate between Cheney and Baker. Cheney was impatient with sanctions; Baker wanted more time for them to work. Powell weighed into the debate, proposing that sanctions against Saddam Hussein be allowed at least two years to work.[33] In the fall of 1990, Baker worked a circuit of foreign powers, including the United Kingdom, Japan, Germany, Saudi Arabia, and the Kuwaiti exiles, gathering diplomatic support and financial contributions that would amount to more than the total cost of the war. The president consulted with congressional leaders and called Congress back from summer recess to gain their endorsement of Operation Desert Shield. In this way, he recognized the role of Congress under the War Powers Act and stimulated a debate among the American people that paralleled that in the Senate. Baker organized the effort that produced to UN Security Council Resolution 678, which authorized force to extract Iraq from Kuwait. Congress, after a serious review of the sanctions versus force question, during which two former CJCSs, Admiral William Crowe and General David Jones, counseled that sanctions should be allowed more time, at last supplied a strong endorsement of the president's plans for war.

Instead of the highly visible interagency and international exchanges of 1990, policymaking in 2002 was characterized by decisions swiftly made by closed groups in nontransparent ways. There was a concentrated campaign to sell the decisions to the public after they were made, but little openness to genuine debate over even the most important matters of peace and war. The campaign to sell the decisions quickly descended into a scare campaign in which the president's October 7, 2002, speech referred to terror, terror attacks, terrorists, and WMD over eighty times in thirty-four hundred words and climaxed with the memorable and often-repeated warning, "Facing clear evidence of peril, we cannot wait for the final proof—the smoking gun—that could come in the form of a mushroom cloud."[34] The validity of many of those frightening warnings, both those about WMD in Iraq and those about Saddam's connections to terrorist cells, has been brought into question and so, therefore, has the reliability of the president's word. This kind of destructive blunder could have been avoided and the president's word could have been protected if there had been genuine give-and-take within the president's own policymaking process.

The most interesting point of comparison between the policymaking processes in 1990 and 2002 is the fact that in 1990 the secretary of state and the CJCS were able to force the secretary of defense to examine, justify, revise, and expand his war plan. In front of the NSC, Powell, backed by Baker, conveyed the requests of U.S. Central Command (CENTCOM) commander Norman Schwarzkopf. These included two additional armored divisions, as well as "a second Army corps . . . the 1st Infantry Division, . . . a doubling of the Marine forces in the Gulf, three additional aircraft carriers, and a virtual doubling of the number of Air Force planes."[35] This is in dramatic contrast to the private process by which Rumsfeld beat down the commanders' requests for troops made in 2002 and 2003. Once war began in 1991, Cheney ceded center stage to Powell and Schwarzkopf, who together ran the televised briefings. By contrast, in 2003 Rumsfeld starred in the briefings and General Tommy Franks stood behind him as silent as a cigar store Indian.

The tragic turn of events that has taken place in Iraq since the brief, brilliantly successful military campaign of 2003 is too familiar to require repeating This essay cannot prove that a more balanced policymaking process would have produced better outcomes, but it can suggest that the president would have been better served and that the American military might have been spared terrible costs if the decision makers inside the OSD had been called on by other participants in the process to lay out, explain, and defend their choices. If that had occurred, there might not have been such a swift resort to force, brushing aside all alternatives short of war; such unyielding resistance to the force levels the leaders in the field requested; and such egregious failure to plan for postwar operations, even though extensive planning had been done by the State Department, the Future of Iraq Project at the Army War College, and the U.S. Agency for International Development (USAID), among others.[36] A vigorous debate between agencies might have spared the U.S. military many political deaths—the deaths ensuing from the failure to guard weapons caches, the failure to stop the looting of public buildings, the failure to move quickly and effectively to restore electricity and water to the populace, the failure to engage Arabists and linguists from the start, and the failure to take into account the sensitivities of the Iraqi people and the realities of Iraqi ethnic politics.

Balance Restored

Democracies are both resilient and unrelenting in the way they demand accountability of their leaders. President Bush survived what he called an "accountability moment" in 2004, but accountability arrived nonetheless after the 2006 midterm elections in the form of congressional investigations and hearings, as well as judicial proceedings against major administration figures. Rumsfeld has been replaced by Secretary of Defense Robert Gates, and Gates has worked quickly to establish a more balanced, more consultative interagency process. He did not recommend General Peter Pace for a second two-year term as CJCS, and this was the first time in forty years that an incumbent was denied reappointment. Gates also has behaved in an open and conciliatory pattern toward senators from the Democratic Party.

The U.S. military may find it difficult to rebound after the loss of life in Iraq. It will also struggle to recover from the loss of trust in the civilian leadership. "In 2006, according to a Military Times poll, almost 60 percent of servicemen and servicewomen did not believe that civilians in the Pentagon had their 'best interests at heart.'"[37] Much of this loss of trust, as well as much loss of life, might have been avoided if better patterns for decision making had been maintained.

Notes

1. See the Office of Management and Budget website at http://www.whitehouse.gov/omb/budget/fy2005/state.html. Accessed October 5, 2007.
2. See the Office of Management and Budget website at http://www.whitehouse.gov/omb/budget/fy2005/defense.html. Accessed October 5, 2007.
3. See the Office of Management and Budget website at http://www.whitehouse.gov/omb/budget/fy2005/state.html. Accessed October 5, 2007.
4. See the Office of Management and Budget website at http://www.whitehouse.gov/omb/budget/fy2005/defense.html. Accessed October 5, 2007.
5. Sarah Sewell, introduction to the University of Chicago edition of the *US Army/Marine Corps Counterinsurgency Field Manual*, p. xxx.
6. Main State is formally named the "Harry S. Truman Building," but the name is so little used that it makes a good trivia question even for the people who work there.
7. http://renovation.pentagon.mil/history-features.htm#size. Last accessed September 29, 2007.
8. Daniel Yergin, *Shattered Peace: The Origins of the Cold War and the National Security State* (New York: Houghton Mifflin, 1978.)
9. See, for example, the Air Force program at http://www.afcrossroads.com/VoteFund/Vote/default.htm, which features, along with a great deal of useful information for anyone in uniform who wants to exercise his or her franchise, a second-by-second countdown clock until the next election.
10. The only item thought to be larger was welfare. Spending on defense did not figure high in the minds of the respondents. See Charles Kegley and Eugene Wittkopf, *American Foreign Policy, Pattern and Process* (New York: St. Martin's Press, 1995), p. 252.
11. "In the 1970's, four submarines were named posthumously for important members of Congressional committees on defense spending. Since then, the Navy has named a Trident sub for the late Senator Henry Jackson and a nuclear carrier for former Representative Carl Vinson." *New York Times*, Topics of the Times, December 14, 1987, at http://query.nytimes.com/gst/fullpage.html?res=9B0DE0DC1039F937A25751C1A9619 48260. Last accessed October 5, 2007. Since 1987, when this article was written, naming ships for politicians has practically become standard practice.
12. Edward Jean Smith, *FDR* (New York, Random House, 2007), pp. 581–3.
13. Ibid., p. 583.

14. Evan Thomas, *The Very Best Men* (New York, Simon and Schuster, 1996), p. 266.

15. H. R. McMaster, *Dereliction of Duty: Johnson, McNamara, the Joint Chiefs of Staff, and the Lies That Led to Vietnam* (New York, Harper Perennial, 1998.); Robert S. McNamara, *In Retrospect: The Tragedy and Lessons of Vietnam* (New York, Random House, 1997).

16. Walter Isaacson, *Kissinger* (New York, Simon and Schuster, 1992), p. 201. Isaacson records Laird's methods:

    > When Laird took the job, he extracted from Nixon a written letter that promised he could appoint his own people to key positions. But it was not such posts as assistant secretary that most concerned him. The first thing he did was put his "own man," Vice Admiral Noel Gayler, in charge of the National Security Agency [NSA], the supersecret spy outfit that electronically intercepts satellite and other communications from around the world. When he appointed Gayler, Laird told him that he had better be loyal to him; if so, he would get his fourth star.
    >
    > Laird got what he wanted. "The NSA gave me my own copy of every back-channel message Henry sent, though I made sure he didn't know that," Laird said later. "Sometimes you have to do these things and play someone else's game against them."
    >
    > Laird even kept up with the most secret Kissinger secret of all: the private peace talks with the North Vietnamese in Paris. "Hanoi's negotiators sent very good reports, full of Henry's sniveling, back from Paris every time Henry went over there," Laird said. These cables quickly made it to Laird's desk, even though Kissinger was going to great lengths to make sure that the Pentagon and the State Department did not even know that these negotiations were under way.

17. James Rosen, "Nixon and the Chiefs," *The Atlantic Monthly*, April 2002, pp. 53–9. See also Isaacson, *Kissinger*, pp. 380–5.

18. This series of developments is told and examined in Derek Reveron, ed., *America's Viceroys: The Military and U.S. Foreign Policy* (New York: Palgrave Macmillan, 2004.)

19. Shalikashvili is quoted in Dana Priest, *The Mission: Waging War and Keeping Peace with America's Military* (New York: W. W. Norton, 2003), p. 54.

20. Krauthammer is quoted in Ivo H. Daalder and James M. Lindsay, *America Unbound: The Bush Revolution in Foreign Policy* (Washington, D.C.: Brookings Institution Press, 2003), p. 12.

21. Associated Press story by Deb Reichman which appeared in *The Miami Herald*, October 3, 2007. http://www.miamiherald.com/692/story/259307.html. Accessed October 5, 2007.

22. Smith, *FDR*, pp. 598–9.

23. Daalder and Lindsay, *America Unbound*, p. 59.

24. This list could be expanded if one included other associates of the neoconservative think tank, the Project for a New American Century. See Gary Dorrien, *Imperial Designs: Neoconservatism and the New Pax Americana* (New York: Routledge, 2004), p. 141.

25. The quotation appears in Johanna McGeary, "Odd Man Out," *Time*, September 10, 2001, p. 28.

26. Smith, *FDR*, pp. 598–9.

27. See Thomas E. Ricks, *Fiasco: The American Military Adventure in Iraq* (New York: Penguin Press, 2006), pp. 162–3. See also James Fallows, *Blind Into Baghdad: America's War in Iraq* (New York: Random House, 2006), pp. 102–4.

28. Smith, *FDR*, pp. 598–9.

29. http://www.senate.gov/pagelayout/reference/two_column_table/Presidential_Medal_of_Freedom_Recipients.htm. Accessed October 5, 2007.

30. From an interview with President Bush by Brit Hume of Fox News, September 22, 2003: HUME: How do you get your news? BUSH: I get briefed by Andy Card and Condi in the morning. They come in and tell me. . . . I glance at the headlines just to kind of a flavor [sic] for what's moving. I rarely read the stories, and get briefed by people who are [sic] probably read the news themselves. . . . [T]he most objective sources I have are people on my staff who tell me what's happening in the world." http://www.foxnews.com/story/0,2933,98006,00.html. Accessed October 5, 2007.

31. For the record of many warnings from Clarke, see National Commission on Terrorist Attacks, *The 9/11 Commission Report: Final Report of the National Commission on Terrorist Attacks Upon the United States* (New York, W. W. Norton & Company, 2004), especially the chapter titled "From Threat to Threat."

32. On Vice President Cheney's attempts to expand the powers of the executive branch and to evade accountability to Congress, see Jack L. Goldsmith, *The Terror Presidency: Law and Judgment Inside the Bush Administration* (New York: W. W. Norton, 2007).

33. On Powell and sanctions, see Michael R. Gordon and Bernard E. Trainor, *The Generals' War: The Inside Story of the Conflict in the Gulf* (Boston, MA: Little, Brown, 1995), p. 131.

34. The full text of the Cincinnati speech is at http://www.narsil.org/war_on_iraq/bush_october_7_2002.html. Accessed October 5, 2007.

35. Gordon and Trainor, *The Generals' War*, p. 153.

36. For an exploration of these failures, see Fallows, *Blind Into Baghdad*.

37. Michael C. Desch, "Bush and the Generals," *Foreign Affairs*, May/June 2007. http://www.foreignaffairs.org/20070501faessay86309/michael-c-desch/bush-and-the-generals.html. Accessed October 10, 2007.

3

More than Advice? The Joint Staff and American Foreign Policy[1]

Stephen M. Saideman

This may be a strange time to be suggesting that the Joint Staff (JS) has an influ-ence on foreign policy, given events of the past six years. After all, when Army Chief of Staff General Eric Shinseki testified to Congress that the United States would need significantly more troops for occupying Iraq than the administration had been planning for, his career ended abruptly. Critics of the Joint Chiefs of Staff (JCS) argue that the system should be rebuilt because of the JCS's historical (Vietnam)[2] and more recent (Iraq) "failures."[3]

The formal role of the chairman of the Joint Chiefs of Staff (CJCS) is to advise the president and the secretary of defense. The Goldwater-Nichols Act of 1986 shaped the position in an effort to prevent the chairman from having any execu-tive authority; the chairman cannot order troops into battle or command opera-tional forces.[4] The combatant commanders of the various Unified Commands (formerly known as commanders in chief [CINCs]) have that responsibility. The chain of command goes from the president to the secretary of defense through to the combatant commander (e.g., generals Norman Schwarzkopf, Wesley Clark, and Tommy Franks).[5] These arrangements are explored in depth in Derek Reveron's chapter in this book. Still, because of how foreign policy is made in the United States, the JS, including the chairman, have more influence than one might expect.

This chapter delineates two mechanisms through which the military can affect foreign policy. One involves the chairman; the second involves the JS's participa-tion in the interagency process. Distinguishing between the elite decision making, which involves the chairman and other members of the JCS, and the day-to-day operations of the interagency process will help to reveal how these two levels operate. Both give the military significant influence on how foreign policy is made. Through discussion of the North Atlantic Treaty Organization (NATO), this chapter will illuminate why the JS may have more influence on U.S. foreign policy when NATO is involved than in other circumstances when it is not. It will also consider some of the limitations and constraints that affect the JS, using examples from the George H. W. Bush administration. The chapter will conclude with some predictions about the future role of the JS.

The Chairman

The chairman has the responsibility of advising the secretary of defense, the president, and the National Security Council (NSC). He is appointed to the position by the president upon the recommendation of the secretary of defense.[6] The Senate must then concur in his appointment. While presidents can and do inherit a chairman from their predecessors, the overlap is not long, as the term of office, which may be renewed, is only two years. While the chairman is authorized to engage in strategic planning, evaluating preparedness, developing doctrine and training for joint operations, proposing budgets, and coordinating the requirements for the various commands, neither the president nor the NSC nor the secretary of defense must accept the chairman's recommendations.

It may seem unlikely now, but evaluations of the Goldwater-Nichols reforms before the ascendance of Secretary of Defense Donald Rumsfeld tended to assert that the chairman was becoming too powerful. "In practice," one critic said, "Goldwater-Nichols empowered the Chairman to act as a de facto equal to the Secretary of Defense and de facto commander of the Armed Forces."[7] While this might have seemed the case when Colin Powell was chairman under both George H. W. Bush and Bill Clinton, this has NOT been the case recently. Both generals Richard Myers and Peter Pace were dominated by Rumsfeld. Indeed, the contrast between Powell[8] and Myers underlines the fact that the dynamics at the top are largely personality-driven. "The chairman's power, therefore, emerges not from his authority but rather from his prestige, his respect among civilian decision-makers, and ultimately his power to persuade."[9]

The key relationship is between the chairman and the secretary of defense. They can be partners, adversaries, or superior and subordinate. Colin Powell played a larger role than other post–Goldwater-Nichols chairmen, not only because of his stature and experience, but also because the secretaries of defense considered him to be powerful, relevant, and useful. Under both Bush and Clinton, Powell provided a key voice in decisions about interventions and noninterventions abroad in places such as Panama, Kuwait, and Bosnia. Richard Myers played an almost invisible role due to Rumsfeld's personality, Rumsfeld's increased stature after 9/11, and the dynamics of the Bush administration.

The Joint Staff and the Interagency

The JS consists of officers from all of the armed services as well as a small number of civilians.[10] While working in the Pentagon is often seen as a less than desirable tour of duty,[11] working on the JS is a key career step for those seeking promotion to the highest level. In fact, working within a joint command is a requirement for promotion to general or admiral, and while there are other ways to fulfill this criterion, serving on the JS is one of the more direct ways.[12] This requirement is part of the Goldwater-Nichols Act, which sought to create better working relationships among the services and to develop senior officers who can think in terms of Joint and national interests rather than in terms of parochial service concerns. As a result, the JS officer is encouraged to think "purple" rather than blue (air force), green (army), khaki (marines), or white/black (navy).[13] The JS is supposed to offer politically neutral advice, recommending what is in the best interests of the United States, not what is best for a service or for a political party. During my time, the JS tended to be fairly moderate and multilaterally minded—at least compared to the civilians under Rumsfeld—due to the experiences of the officers on overseas assignments.

Officers and civilians in the JS's Directorate of Strategic Planning and Policy (J-5)[14] are responsible not only for advising the chairman on political-military affairs, but also for working on a daily basis with representatives from the State Department, the Office of the Secretary of Defense (OSD), the NSC, and other players in the foreign policymaking process.[15] In this process, words on paper matter, as papers, cables, and speeches are circulated among the relevant agencies to determine policy and provide those implementing policy with guidance. These documents go forward only after a consensus is reached among the relevant agencies. If no consensus is reached, the issue is sent up the respective chains of command and hammered out at a higher level. Because the time of the principals (the chairman, the cabinet secretaries) and their deputies is a scarce resource, many policy debates are conducted at lower levels, with the various actors seeking to act in accordance with the stated and perceived intentions of their superiors.

As this process is document-driven, much of the activity focuses on writing and revising documents. Indeed, once key phrases are inserted into a speech or a paper, they echo in a variety of subsequent policy discussions. In 2001 and 2002, two phrases (uttered by the president) governed all the thinking about U.S. and NATO policy in the Balkans: "In Together, Out Together" and "Hasten the Day." The first phrase refers to the idea that the United States would not abandon its allies in the various Balkan missions. This was, of course, fudged, as NATO's Stabilization Force in Bosnia became the European Union's responsibility in 2005, with the United States (and Canada) largely pulling out. The second phrase refers to the idea that while the West was and is committed to the Balkans, it would seek to accelerate the development of indigenous institutions and capacities so that NATO could leave.

Because words are so important, once an agency is given the task of writing a cable, a speech, or a policy paper and the paper is written and vetted by the agency, it is circulated among the other agencies, allowing them to propose specific additions and deletions (word-by-word changes). This process reveals two important issues for our understanding of foreign policymaking. First, the JS has a say or "chop" roughly equal to that of State and OSD. Second, the agency that writes the paper sets the agenda for the subsequent debate.

To be clear, formally the JS advises the chairman and, through him, the secretary of defense. As a practical matter, in the ordinary business of the interagency policy process, the JS frequently acts in competition with OSD and State. This is particularly true when considering policies that have a military component, such as the conduct of peacekeeping operations.[16] Thus, when documents are circulated, the JS provides input, and it can make meaningful changes as long as the other agencies are not strongly opposed. At interagency meetings, members of the JS can and do actively participate.

The person who writes the initial draft of a policy document sets the agenda for subsequent discussions and revisions. By choosing which issues to raise and what to omit, the writer shapes the contours of the debate. Members of other agencies might raise different issues or pursue different angles in the process of revising, but that first document sets the terms of the debate. Who determines who writes the first draft? In my experience, the State Department and NSC representatives usually set the agenda for interagency discussions and policy papers. Then the most relevant agency would write the paper for the topic of that meeting—Justice, if it concerned rule of law; State, if it concerned treaty issues; and the Department of Defense (DoD), if it had significant military stakes, such as restructuring the Bosnian militaries. The key here is that DoD referred to both the JS and OSD, so it was frequently left to the representatives from each to decide which one would write the first draft.

NATO and the Joint Staff

As a key international institution, NATO has the potential to strengthen the influence of the JS's impact on foreign policy.[17] It might be odd to think that an international organization would affect the role of the JS, but because of the particular nature of NATO's structure, the JS gets to set the agenda for the interagency when it comes to Euro-Atlantic military matters.

Documents governing NATO operations go through two committees before they become policy—the Military Committee and then the North Atlantic Council (NAC). The former consists of senior military representatives from each member state, while the latter consists of ambassadors from each. Both operate by consensus, so that a document is passed forward only if no country "breaks silence" and asks for changes (again, line-by-line, word-by-word substitutions). If this happens, representatives ask their respective home countries for guidance as to how to respond to requested alterations—hence the need for guidance cables. The important point here is that most issues are addressed first at the Military Committee *before* they make it to the NAC.

When the military representative calls home for orders on how to respond to the document and then to its suggested revisions, the JS (J-5) picks up the phone.[18] The J-5 officer then seeks information and opinions from the relevant parts of the military—the JS's Directorate of Operations (J-3), Intelligence (J-2), defense attachés, and/or one or more of the services—and, always, the JS Legal office. The J-5 desk officer's recommendations then go to his or her immediate superiors, and if he or she recommends a "break in silence," then the proposed guidance goes up the chain, usually to the director of the JS (a three-star officer) and perhaps above. Because the Military Committee reviews policies before the NAC does, the JS can shape the document before it reaches the NAC, and therefore before it reaches the rest of the interagency (State, OSD, NSC.). To be clear, the JS's focus here is on the military components of the relevant document.

Once a document goes to the NAC, it is then circulated among the relevant agencies back in the United States—including OSD, State, and the JS again—and a guidance cable is eventually drafted and circulated. Thus, the JS gets two shots at a NATO document, giving feedback at both stages.[19] What is important here is that the JS has a voice that is institutionalized through NATO's procedures. While OSD or State can take a strong stand on a document when it is at the NAC, the JS has an established role in shaping U.S. input before it reaches that stage.

Why is this important? The JS's influence is certainly not consistent over time, and the process discussed here suggests that its impact also varies depending on the relevant region. NATO gives it substantial influence in European affairs, but we might have expected the JS to play a smaller role in the lead-up to Iraq, even taking into account the efforts by Secretary of Defense Rumsfeld to marginalize the JS.

Constraining the Chairman and Joint Staff

Two actors play significant roles in amplifying or marginalizing the JS and its chairman. They are the secretary of defense and the president. But given that military forces are employed by combatant commanders, they can impede the JS, too. Depending upon the personalities of each, the chairman and the JS can play an enormous role in shaping major decisions, as exemplified by General Colin Powell during both the George H. W. Bush and Clinton administrations, or they can be completely sidelined, as has been true during the George W. Bush administration. Below, I first consider the constraints confronting the chairman and then consider those facing the JS.

Chaining the Chairman

The secretary of defense (SecDef) is the most important actor shaping the relevance of the JS and the chairman's role in foreign policy. This has been demonstrated recently by Donald Rumsfeld's active marginalization of generals Myers and Pace and the JS.[20] First, the SecDef has significant influence on who becomes the chairman. This was demonstrated early in the Bush administration when Rumsfeld recommended to the president Air Force General Richard Myers, who was more likely than other candidates to support Rumsfeld's vision of transformation because of his background in Space Command.[21] Similarly, Secretary of Defense Robert Gates took the unusual step of recommending that Pace not be reappointed after his first term because of the political controversy that would ensue because of Pace's presence as vice chairman and chairman when the Iraq war was conceived and executed.[22]

The SecDef can influence the chairman's access to other decision makers, despite the statutory authority given to the chairman to advise the president. In the various books on Operation Iraqi Freedom,[23] it is clear that the chairman was not invited to key meetings between the president, the SecDef, and Tommy Franks, the relevant combatant commander—or if he was at a meeting, his presence was not significant enough to mention. This is very different from the approach taken by Richard Cheney when he was SecDef in the George H. W. Bush administration. There, Colin Powell served as the key intermediary between the civilians and the combatant commander—Max Thurman of Southern Command (SOUTHCOM) during the Panama intervention and, more famously, Norman Schwarzkopf of Central Command (CENTCOM) during the first Gulf war.[24] Similarly, the SecDef can influence the chairman's access to the media. Again, recently, the chairman seemed more like a sidekick in the Rumsfeld era than an independent actor.

Most importantly, the SecDef, not the chairman, makes the decisions on whether and how to use force and on which plans to use to address a threat or engage in a conflict. The willingness of the SecDef to take advice, then, is crucial, as the chairman can influence decisions only if the SecDef is open to persuasion. While the influence of the JS as a whole depends on the structure of decision making, it is clear that the chairman's influence depends on his personality and that of the SecDef above all else.

For example, "As Chairman, Myers found Rumsfeld so hands-on that he would confide to one of his senior aides, at times, he wondered why he was even there. When they went to the White House, it had all been rehearsed. They achieved what Myers called a 'mind meld,' which meant that Myers adapted his mind to Rumsfeld's."[25] This is in significant contrast to repeated entries in Powell's autobiography where he contradicts or surprises the SecDef in his meetings with the president.

In most cases, a second actor is also quite important—the combatant commander of the relevant part of the world. This individual is directly in the chain of command, unlike the chairman, so the chairman's ability to influence policies and events depends critically on their relationship. Again, the two Iraq wars reveal a great contrast. Schwarzkopf worked closely with Powell, seeking and heeding his advice. In contrast, in his book General Tommy Franks consistently expresses contempt for the JCS.[26] He does refer to the chairman at one point as his "anchor in the Building,"[27] but this is at odds with the rest of his autobiography, in which he consistently marginalizes and denigrates the JCS and the JS. Most situations have been closer to the Powell-Schwarzkopf end of the spectrum than to the Myers-Franks end. Four-star officers tend to consider themselves as equals, with the chairman as first among his peers, so the chairman is not usually ignored.

Because the chairman's job is to give advice, his influence rides entirely on his relationships with the SecDef, the combatant commanders, and the president. If these individuals are willing—or are compelled—to listen to the chairman, then he has a great deal of power. On the other hand, if they are determined to reject the chairman's advice, or if the president and the SecDef purposely choose a compliant chairman, then the office may be largely irrelevant.

Stiffing the Staff

The JS can summon a great deal of expertise, making it an extraordinary asset to the SecDef and his staff (OSD) as they engage in policy discussions with State, the NSC, and other actors in the bureaucracy. In the interagency process and in the press, the JS and OSD are often conflated—that DoD has a certain position or the Building position is x or y. Indeed, more than a few officers in 2001 and 2002 revealed some nostalgia for the Clinton administration, because there was usually a consensus between the JS and OSD, and representatives went to interagency meetings with a "Building" position to push forward.[28] However, during the first six years of the George W. Bush administration, the JS faced a much less cooperative partner in OSD.[29] Instead of working hand in hand, the JS representatives sat on the other side of the table, both symbolically and literally, at interagency meetings, often finding more in common with State and NSC representatives.

Ironically, the bureaucratic survival strategies of OSD civilians at first enhanced the power of the JS, but this lasted for only a short time. Because the people working directly for Secretary of Defense Rumsfeld lived in fear of him,[30] they had to figure out ways to bring ideas, plans, and documents up the chain without getting blistered by the resulting heat. The first strategy was to let the JS write the documents that the interagency had asked DoD to draft. This way, the OSD reps could take these papers up their chain but disavow responsibility for the positions. For a year or so, this allowed the JS to draft policy, giving it significant agenda-setting power, even if Rumsfeld and his immediate underlings later sought to alter the ideas. As a result, a lieutenant colonel in J-5's Central and East European Division largely wrote the policies shaping America's positions on NATO's involvement in Macedonia.

Over time, Rumsfeld became aware of this tactic and directed OSD representatives to write the papers, thus weakening the JS's influence. OSD officials turned to a new survival strategy—drafting papers that would contain very unilateral, very extreme policy recommendations so, at worst, they would be only mildly admonished for their enthusiasm.[31]

Accounts of the planning of the Iraq invasion and the phase 4 (postwar occupation) indicate the JS was working with State and the NSC. However, the actual decisions to send Jay Garner, to replace him with Paul Bremer, to stand down the Iraqi army, and to fire all Ba'athists were made without the JS's input despite the obvious military issues involved.[32] Rather than building upon the JS's expertise in postconflict operations, developed during the previous ten years in Bosnia and Kosovo, Rumsfeld and OSD sought to impose their views upon reality and actively refused to include individuals within the interagency, including those from the JS, in the making of meaningful decisions.[33]

Rumsfeld pursued a second strategy to dominate the JS—burying it with snowflakes. A snowflake is a request for information made by any of the heavy-hitters in Washington—the president, the vice president, the SecDef, and representatives and senators. They are called snowflakes because they require a very quick response. Rumsfeld used these to great effect when he would sent a barrage of requests covering the most minute issues while larger, more significant policy issues were on the table. Furthermore, he would send the same snowflake again and again if he did not like the answer he received.

For instance, during my single year in the Pentagon (2001–2), I was responsible for handling the same issue three times—can the United States pull its troops out of a variety of commitments around the world? The list that came down included some very small detachments that were providing the United States with maximum political capital with minimum costs. It also raised questions about very large and important commitments to allies. The JS forwarded recommendations back to Rumsfeld, advising that we maintain most of these commitments because the net gains were greater than the net costs. Each time, Rumsfeld would send down a nearly identical question, because he did not like the advice he received. Responding to these snowflakes takes time and energy. One must draft documents, coordinate with other elements of the U.S. military (defense attachés, the staffs of various commands, military intelligence, the legal offices, etc.), and then go up the chain of the JS to the chairman. While these requests may have been sincere efforts to ask questions, they also served the purpose of distracting the JS from longer-term analyses, such as providing alternatives to current policy initiatives.

The Future of the Joint Staff

The bad news is good news—that the marginalization of the JS under the Bush administration is likely to be temporary because the dynamics were personality-driven rather than institutional. It is likely that not only Robert Gates but also the next SecDefs will rely more upon the advice of the chairman and that the JS will again be a relatively equal partner in the interagency process. In part, this is likely because the Bush administration's foreign policy efforts have been unsuccessful, particularly in terms of its use of force. One of the obvious lessons to be learned is that the military might actually have something useful to say about how force should be deployed. While civilian control of the military requires that the chairman advise the SecDef, and not the other way around, it is clear that U.S. foreign policy is better implemented when it is thoroughly vetted with all of the relevant experts involved in the process, including those who have participated in past military operations in places like Panama, Kuwait, Bosnia, Kosovo, and now Afghanistan and Iraq. Moreover, we ought to expect and certainly to recommend that the next generation of combatant commanders work with the chairman, as in the case of Schwarzkopf, rather than work around him, as in the case of Franks.

It has been a relatively implicit assumption of this chapter that the military, through the JS, can make a meaningful contribution to American foreign policy. While military domination of the foreign policy process would be a mistake, those who have expertise and high stakes in the use of force ought to have a voice at the table when U.S. decision makers consider when and how to deploy violence abroad.

In future administrations, SecDefs need to consider and build upon the advantages of the system as it is in place. To get the best advice, they should appoint senior officers not according to who is most compliant but rather according to who has excelled in working in Joint commands where leadership and coordination matter more than service loyalty. To be clear, for the chairman to be an effective advisor, the secretary not only must appoint a strong individual to that position, but also must appoint combatant commanders who are willing to give advice to—and to take advice from—the chairman and the JS.

The good news is that it is far easier to learn from dramatic failures than from subtle mistakes. The Rumsfeld regime offers a variety of lessons to the future managers of American security. Working with, rather than against, the JS is an important first step.

Notes

1. This chapter is largely based on my experience as a Council on Foreign Relations Fellow that placed me on the Joint Staff in 2001 and 2002, fostering conversations with a variety of people within the interagency. Specifically, I served in the Directorate of Strategic Planning and Policy on the Bosnia desk and worked with officers responsible for Central and Eastern Europe. I am grateful to the Council on Foreign Relations for the International Affairs Fellowship. I owe a significant debt to the men and women of the Central and Eastern Europe Division of 2001–2 for engaging in wide-ranging conversations about the interagency. Derek Reveron and Judith Stiehm provided helpful suggestions.
2. H. R. McMaster, *Dereliction of Duty: Johnson, McNamara, the Joint Chiefs of Staff, and the Lies That Led to Vietnam* (New York: Harpercollins, 1997).
3. Andrew J. Bacevich, "Joint Failure," *Boston Globe*, June 17, 2007.
4. For an excellent analysis of why the chairman has these and no other powers, see Amy Zegart, *Flawed by Design: The Evolution of the CIA, JCS, and NSC* (Stanford: Stanford University Press, 1999). The position of chairman in the U.S. system contrasts quite sharply, for instance, with that of the chief of the Defense Staff in Canada, who is the commander of the Canadian Forces. Also, for an analysis of the increased "jointness" in the U.S. military, see Peter J. Roman and David W. Tarr, "The Joint Chiefs of Staff: From Service Parochialism to Jointness," *Political Science Quarterly* 113, no.1 (1998): 91–111.
5. These commands are largely regional—NORTHCOM (North America), SOUTH-COM (South America), EUCOM (Europe and Africa), CENTCOM (Middle East), and PACOM (Pacific and Indian Ocean), but also include functional commands such as JFCOM (Joint Forces), Special Operations (SOCOM), and Strategic Command (STRATCOM). In 2008, a new regional command to be responsible for Africa (AFRICOM) is due to be stood up. For more on the combatant commanders' impact on foreign policy, see Derek S. Reveron, ed., *America's Viceroys: The Military and U.S. Foreign Policy* (New York: Palgrave Macmillan, 2004); Dana Priest, *The Mission: Waging War and Keeping Peace with America's Military* (New York: W. W. Norton, 2003).
6. I use the masculine pronoun to refer to the chairman, as the position has always been filled by a male, and it is unlikely in the near or intermediate future for this to change.
7. Christopher M. Bourne, "Unintended Consequences of the Goldwater-Nichols Act," *Joint Forces Quarterly* 18 (Spring 1998): 100.
8. Ironically, while Colin Powell was a very powerful and influential chairman, he proved to be just as ineffectual as secretary of state as Myers was as chairman.
9. Gordon Lederman, *Reorganizing the Joint Chiefs of Staff: the Goldwater-Nichols Act of 1986* (Westport, CT: Greenwood, 1999).
10. Not only army, navy, air force, and marines; the Coast Guard is also represented.

11. Officers usually look forward to the end of their time in the Pentagon for a variety of reasons, including the difficult commutes, the cost of living in the Washington area, and the fact that they are not working within the usual base community.

12. Serving in Joint positions at one of the Combatant Commands is another way to fulfill the requirement.

13. The Navy's uniform changes during the year: white in the summer and black in the winter. During my tour in the Pentagon, it was often said that the JS was the cream of the U.S. military, a distinct break from pre–Goldwater-Nichols. While this seemed a bit self-serving since it was often uttered by JS officers, in my brief experience, the JS officers seemed brighter, more open-minded, and more analytical than other officers I encountered. For concurrence, see Bourne, "Unintended Consequences."

14. The JS consists of nine directorates, but our focus is mostly on J-5, because it serves as the key element of the JS in its interactions with the policy community on issues related to foreign policy. The Directorate on Force Structure (J-8) would be more relevant if the topic were procurement, for instance. Moreover, the position of J-5 director is an important stepping stone to more powerful positions, including the director of the JS and combatant commanders of CENTCOM (John Abizaid), EUCOM (Wesley Clark), and Army Chief of Staff (George Casey). See Wesley K. Clark, *Waging Modern War: Bosnia, Kosovo, and the Future of Combat* (New York: Public Affairs, 2001), chapter 2.

15. Indeed, after Goldwater-Nichols took effect, members of the services (e.g., the Marines) complained about the power of the JS—that it was developing policy recommendations without seriously consulting the relevant services, Roman and Tarr, "The Joint Chiefs of Staff," 108.

16. Of course, the JS matters less and other agencies matter far more in other policy realms, such as financial assistance. However, given the complexity of contemporary foreign policy, the military is implicated in many issues, such as refugee returns or transitional justice.

17. Congress is another institution that greatly shapes how much influence the JS can have. See chapter 8 for more on its relationship with the U.S. military.

18. With the exception of cables to the military representative, most guidance cables originate in the State Department (and often arrive at the Pentagon late on Friday).

19. Apparently, many of the European allies find this process rather strange, as the United States will often take different stances between the two stages of the process, whereas they coordinate more closely and tend to speak with a single voice.

20. Also see chapter 16.

21. For a vivid portrayal of the process that selected Myers rather than other, perhaps less acquiescent, candidates, see Bob Woodward, *State of Denial* (New York: Simon and Schuster, 2006).

22. Usually, a chairman is renewed at least once. Pace, however, served only one term.

23. L. Paul Bremer III, with Malcolm McConnell, *My Year in Iraq: The Struggle to Build a Future of Hope* (New York: Simon and Schuster, 2006); Tommy Franks, *American Soldier* (New York: ReganBooks, 2004); Thomas E. Ricks, *Fiasco: The American Military Adventure in Iraq* (New York: Penguin, 2006); Michael R. Gordon and Bernard E. Trainor, *Cobra II: The Inside Story of the Invasion and Occupation of Iraq* (New York: Pantheon, 2006).

24. Colin Powell, with Joseph E. Persico, *My American Journey* (New York: Ballantine, 1995); and H. Norman Schwarzkopf, with Peter Petre, *It Doesn't Take a Hero* (New York: Bantam, 1992).

25. Woodward, *State of Denial*, 72.

26. The term he uses to describe them is unprintable in most places.
27. Franks, *American Soldier*, 456.
28. This might suggest that during the Clinton administration, the JS dominated the SecDef and OSD and missed that level of influence, but the actual results seem to suggest that the military did not dominate the civilians, as Clinton repeatedly intervened in places the military sought to avoid—Haiti, Bosnia, and Kosovo.
29. It is not clear yet whether the atmosphere has changed, although I suspect that it has, given the distinct personalities and reported tendencies of Rumsfeld and Gates.
30. This section is based on a series of conversations I had with OSD representatives during my time in the Pentagon. It is now widely known that Rumsfeld treated his underlings quite abruptly.
31. Conversation with a JS officer who served from 2002 to 2003.
32. George Packer, *The Assassins' Gate: America in Iraq* (New York: Farrar, Straus and Giroux, 2005), esp. ch. 4. See also Bremer, *My Year in Iraq*; Ricks, *Fiasco*; Gordon and Trainor, *Cobra II*.
33. The lockout of the Department of State, including folks such as Tom Warrick, has been highlighted in various books (Packer, Ricks, etc.) more clearly than has the marginalization of the JS.

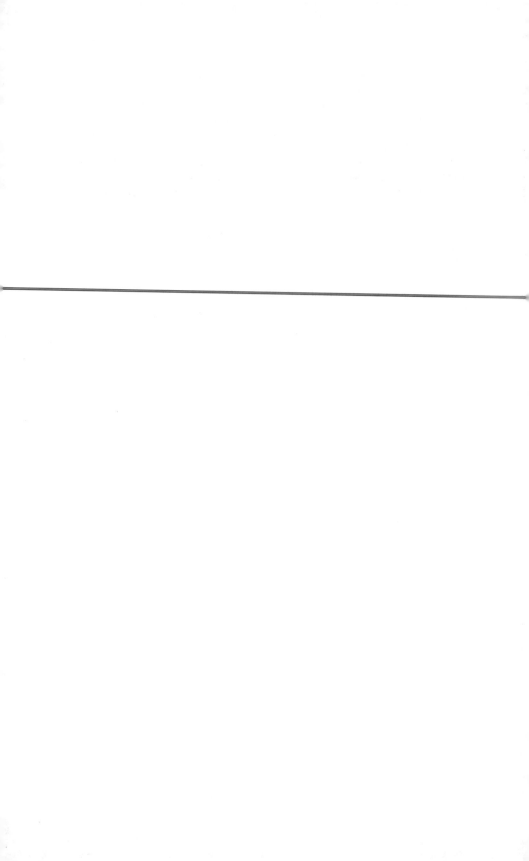

4

Military Diplomacy and the Engagement Activities of Combatant Commanders

Derek S. Reveron

Military commanders are as much policy entrepreneurs as they are warfighters, fulfilling important diplomatic roles for the United States.[1] While the State Department is America's lead foreign policy organization, the Defense Department (DoD) is frequently tasked with filling diplomatic roles. Moreover, compared with the State Department, Defense has a distinct advantage in terms of both size and resources, with an operating budget sixty times greater.[2] With its forward presence, large planning staffs, and various engagement and intelligence tools, America's military commands are well equipped for these diplomatic tasks, and increasingly welcome them. Today, they routinely pursue regional-level engagement strategies by hosting international security conferences; promoting military-to-military contacts; and providing American military presence, training, and equipment to improve regional security.

In spite of the size disparity between State and Defense, the two organizations are mainly mutually supporting. American ambassadors are the president's representatives to particular countries, and U.S. military commanders assist in formulating and implementing the president's foreign policy. Both departments advance and defend national interests. General Anthony Zinni captured the military's perspective on this: "I was asked to carry out presidential and other diplomatic missions that would normally have fallen to diplomats. I'm sure such things frustrated the State Department, but I don't think they disapproved. In fact, they were very supportive. It was more a case of, "Well, if we can't do it, at least somebody is taking care of it. If it's the CINCs [heads of US military commands], then God bless them."[3]

General Zinni's comments likely strike a nerve among some Foreign Service officers, but they have learned to deal with the military's diplomatic activities, and U.S. ambassadors ensure that the military programs support larger national security objectives within a particular country. The State Department is well aware of its congressionally limited capacity, but embassies are still the focal point for all US government activities within a particular country.

DoD's size and operational orientation does give it significant advantages in the policymaking process. For example, when President George W. Bush announced that the United States would become more strategically engaged in Africa, it was to be through the creation of a new military command—U.S. Africa Command (AFRICOM)—and not simply by increasing the budgets of the U.S. Agency for International Development (USAID) or the State Department's Africa Bureau. Yet, tellingly, this new "combatant" command will have a decidedly non-warfighting focus, as the president's vision for it suggests—"promote stability and peace by building capacity in partner nations that enables them to be cooperative, trained, and prepared to help prevent or limit conflicts."[4] Since the creation of the new command, AFRICOM has had to assure its friends and partners that this bureaucratic change is not a sign of escalation of US military involvement in Africa, but rather a way to streamline military assistance programs.

The non-warfighting roles of the U.S. military have attracted criticism from both within and outside the military itself as being contradictory to the military's warfighting ethos. For example, John Hillen writes, "To maintain the skills necessary to execute this [warfighting] function requires strategy, doctrine, training, and force structure focused on deterrence and war fighting, not on peacekeeping missions."[5] Others have questioned whether military officers have or can reasonably be expected to acquire the linguistic skills and political and cultural knowledge to operate effectively as surrogate diplomats. Nevertheless, the fact is that military forces have always fulfilled important non-warfighting roles for the United States.

Military diplomacy is increasingly common, with the primary mission being to develop relationships and form partnerships with other militaries or their governments. Reflecting on his command, General Zinni remarked, "As my experiences throughout the region in general and with [Pakistan's President] Musharraf in particular illustrate, I did not intend to sit back and say, 'Hey, my job is purely military. When you're ready to send me in, coach, that's when I go in.' When I assumed command of CENTCOM [Central Command] and had the ability to choose between fighting fires or preventing them, I chose prevention."[6] With a host of security cooperation tools, General Zinni engaged with countries in the Near East, Central Asia, and the Horn of Africa by hosting regional conferences, building strong security relationships and allied capabilities, and enhancing the education of military leaders. From a democratic perspective, it is dissatisfying that military leaders like Pervez Musharraf, Muammar Gaddafi, or Hugo Chavez rule their countries, but it is an unfortunate reality that U.S. foreign policy must contend with.

Security assistance can help fledgling democracies consolidate, fragile states avoid failure, and authoritarian states liberalize. When he conducted engagement operations in the 1980s, Admiral William J. Crowe, then commander in chief of Pacific Command, said that national leaders frequently told him that without American military presence, their achievements in democracy and development would not have been possible.[7] This is evidenced in the liberalization of countries like South Korea or the Philippines. Security is essential for economic and social development. To be sure, engagement is fundamentally different from warfighting. Engagement is about managing relationships, not command and control; it is about cooperation, not fighting; and it is about partnership, not dominance.

Non-warfighting activities do fulfill important training, basing, and operational requirements for American forces. To advance American interests, combatant commands build partners' capabilities and capacity to generate security, influence nonpartners and potential adversaries, mitigate the underlying causes of conflict and extremism, and enable rapid action when military intervention is required. Since combined operations are the norm today, U.S. forces need regular interactions with their international partners. These activities fulfill current military strategic requirements of assuring friends and allies, dissuading potential competitors, and deterring conflicts in nonlethal ways. Again, military engagement has become one tool—and an increasingly important one—in the arsenal of American "soft power."

From Coercive Diplomacy to Soft Power

Writing soon after the Berlin Wall fell, former assistant secretary of defense Joseph Nye commented, "Although the United States still has leverage over particular countries, it has far less leverage over the system as a whole."[8] Nye observed that not only was the international system changing from bipolar to unipolar, but power itself was changing. Nye predicted that lethal military power would not be enough to affect outcomes. Instead, outcomes were more likely to be affected through noncoercive measures or soft power, which Nye defines as "the ability to get what we want through attraction rather than coercion or payments."[9] This prediction bore itself out in the late 1990s when coercive diplomacy did not produce the desired effects and in the first decade of the twenty-first century in reaction to a post-9/11 U.S. foreign policy.

Consequently, the U.S. government has placed renewed emphasis on generating soft power to serve as a reservoir from which to draw nonlethal solutions to U.S. foreign policy problems. One way, among many others, is through global military engagement, which can build trust among societies. As Robert Art notes, "short of waging war or playing chicken in a crisis, then, military power shapes outcomes more by its peacetime presence than by its forceful use."[10] In addition to peacetime presence, the military engages in diplomacy and security cooperation. While military leaders have historically represented their countries abroad, this chapter traces the contemporary roots of military engagement to the 1996 National Security Strategy.

The Roots of Military Engagement

President Bill Clinton's 1996 *National Security Strategy of Engagement and Enlargement* directed the military to engage with international partners and to provide a credible overseas presence. Being forward deployed during the Cold War had demonstrated that by providing for other countries' security, the United States could advance its trade agenda, and countries protected by American security guarantees could focus on their own political and economic development.

Taking its cue from the 1996 strategy, DoD sought to codify engagement as a key element in the national military strategic outlook. Positing a new foundation of "shape-respond-prepare," the 1997 strategic defense review not only emphasized the capability to fight and win wars, but also placed "greater emphasis on the continuing need to maintain continuous overseas presence in order to shape the international environment."[11] A major goal of engagement or shaping, then, is to reduce the drivers of conflicts.

In addition to formal direction from the Clinton administration, the military's experience in Somalia, Haiti, and Bosnia-Herzegovina forced recognition that it is far more effective to prevent state failure than to respond to its aftermath. Consequently, the military stepped up its engagement efforts. A key tool the military uses is security cooperation, which is driven by the following: combating terrorism, transforming alliances and building coalitions, influencing the direction of key powers, cooperating with parties to regional disputes, deterring and isolating problem states, combating weapons of mass destruction (WMD), and realigning forward presence.

The current focus on transnational threats has been the impetus for building new partnerships. The goal of capacity building is for partners to perform missions of common interest with the United States. For example, the United States largely trained and supported African Union forces in Darfur. The benefit to the American personnel is training in new environments and building relationships with their foreign counterparts. The obvious benefits to the international participants are American training and financial assistance.

To be sure, engagement activities support overall U.S. national interests, but they also fulfill important training, basing, and operational requirements for American forces. With military sites around the world, the military has found it essential to advance American interests by building partners' capabilities to generate security, by influencing potential adversaries, by mitigating the underlying causes of conflict, and by enabling rapid action when military intervention is required.

Military Diplomacy

Epitomized by the activities of geographic combatant commanders, military diplomacy brings all instruments of power to bear to develop relationships and form partnerships.[12] "The current norm of 'been there, done that' visits should be transformed into *persistent, personal, and purposeful* contacts that yield results."[13] Military involvement in diplomacy does not obviate the role of the Foreign Service officer. Instead, "DoD's role in shaping the international environment is closely integrated with our diplomatic efforts . . . "[14] In spite of this Quadrennial Defense Review (QDR) statement, General Zinni captured the challenges of synchronizing these activities: "I never found a way to effectively join forces with the State Department to link their plans with mine. I had no way to get answers to questions like, What's the diplomatic component of our strategy? What's the economic component? How is aid going to be distributed?"[15] While not unique to CENTCOM, generating unified action through the interagency process remains a contemporary national security challenge. To overcome this, the Joint Staff (JS) established interagency coordination as a high priority, some combatant commands have created an interagency directorate (J-9 at U.S. Southern Command [SOUTHCOM]), and the newest combatant command, AFRICOM, will have a decidedly interagency orientation. Many of these activities can be characterized as security cooperation.

Security Cooperation

A key piece of these non-warfighting activities is security cooperation, which is "the ability for DoD to interact with foreign defense establishments to build defense relationships that promote specific U.S. security interests, develop allied and friendly military capabilities for self-defense and coalition operations, including allied transformation, improve information exchange, and intelligence sharing to help harmonize views on security challenges, and provide U.S. forces with peacetime and contingency access and en route infrastructure."[16]

Given its shrinking fleet and global challenges, the U.S. Navy has embraced security cooperation. Senior navy strategists Vice Admiral John G. Morgan Jr. and Rear Admiral Charles W. Martoglio wrote that "policing the maritime commons will require substantially more capability than the United States or any individual nation can deliver."[17] As such, the United States seeks partnerships with international navies to create the proverbial 1,000-ship navy, which can respond to piracy, smuggling, and other illegal activities, and protect important sea lines of communication. The chief of naval operations reinforced this message in 2007: "Wherever the opportunity exists, we must develop and sustain relationships that will help improve the capacity of our emerging and enduring partners' maritime forces."[18] Exemplified by Task Force 150 and the North Atlantic Treaty Organization's (NATO) Operation Active Endeavor, the 1,000-ship navy or Global Maritime Partnership Initiative represents an effort to promote international maritime security. Essential to a successful global maritime partnership is building partners' capabilities and capacity.

Building Military Partner Capabilities and Capacity

Building military partner capabilities is defined as "the ability to improve the military capabilities of our allies and partners to help them transform and optimize their forces to provide regional security, disaster preparedness and niche capabilities in a coalition."[19] For example, Commander Naval Forces Europe (CNE) has been developing a capability for maritime domain awareness throughout Europe and Africa. CNE has been working with NATO allies and African partners to develop a regional capability to protect trade, natural resources, and economic development. This includes establishing maritime domain awareness through the Automated Identification System, an array of coastal radar systems, and improved command and control of a naval reaction force. A program like this is a part of a combatant commander's "theater security cooperation plan" (TSCP), which serves as the primary blueprint for regional military engagement. To ensure that other federal assistance is synchronized with the TSCP, the country team prepares a "mission strategic plan" (MSP) that communicates to senior State Department officials in Washington how the mission will contribute to achieving the primary goals of American foreign policy and development assistance in that country. In coordination with the senior Defense representative, the MSP recommends cooperative defense activities and funding of programs within the State Department budget, such as International Military Education and Training (IMET), Foreign Military Sales, or Economic Support Funds, which are critical elements of the TSCP.

Augmenting military training is Foreign Military Financing (FMF), which supplies grants and loans to finance purchases of American weapons and military equipment. The State Department oversees the program, but combatant commanders manage it on a day-to-day basis. In fiscal year (FY) 2007, the FMF budget was the largest program in the State Department's international assistance account (known as the "150 account"), consuming over $4.5 billion, which is 50 percent more than the Economic Support Fund and 60 percent more than the Global HIV/AIDS Initiative.[20] Of that $4.5 billion, though, nearly 80 percent goes to two countries, Israel ($2.3 billion) and Egypt ($1.3 billion). Of the remaining 20 percent, just a few countries receive substantial assistance: Pakistan ($300 million), Jordan ($206 million), and Colombia ($90 million). The remaining $300 million is shared by sixty-six countries.[21]

In addition to FMF, IMET is an important security cooperation tool. This program, too, is funded through the 150 account, but it is implemented by DoD. From 1997 to 2004, IMET has funded sixty-six thousand participants, with a notable threefold increase from 1997, when there were 3,454 students, compared to 11,832 in 2004. Programs include attendance at U.S. professional military education institutions like the Naval War College, English-language training at the Defense Language Institute, or training activities like the basic infantry officer's course. While the training is often well received, "it is tougher to quantify how such relationships can impact policy issues and ties between the international community and the United States as those students attain higher levels of responsibility within their government in the succeeding years."[22] Yet, General Bantz Craddock, head of U.S. European Command, testified in 2007 that "IMET remains our most powerful security cooperation tool and proves its long-term value every day."[23] One major impact of IMET programs is building personal and professional relationships with people likely to rise to senior levels within their countries. As a testament to the quality of selections for the Naval War College's Naval Staff College, for example, 236 participants have attained flag rank, 102 later served as chiefs of service, five became cabinet ministers, and one became his nation's president.[24]

Resistance to Military Engagement Activities

While combatant commanders are not rogue commanders, proconsuls, or viceroys, the 1990s "shape-respond-prepare" strategy gave rise to the "superpowers don't do windows" argument. Some identified diplomatic engagement by generals Wesley Clark, Zinni, or Charles Wilhelm in the 1990s or state-building missions in Haiti, Bosnia, and Kosovo as apostasy for an organization that is supposed to fight and win the nation's wars. Largely a reaction to Clinton-era uses of the military, then presidential candidate George W. Bush said, "I'm not so sure the role of the United States is to go around the world and say this is the way it's got to be. We can help. I just don't think it's the role of the United States to walk into a country and say, we do it this way, so should you."[25] Once Bush was elected, the administration attempted to rein in engagement activities through largely symbolic acts. Engagement activities were recast as "security cooperation" to emphasize the security dimension of these activities. Secretary Donald Rumsfeld reduced these leaders' stature by preserving the title commander in chief, or CINC, for the president alone. In a largely symbolic response, these leaders reverted to their *Title 10* designations, *combatant* commanders, with an emphasis on the *combat* role they are supposed to fill.

Policy analysts also reacted negatively to what was sometimes cast as postmodern imperialism, a failure in civilian control of the military, or a major problem with the interagency process. Reacting to the preventive intent of shaping, Justin Logan and Christopher Preble found that the United States "has been overly prone to military intervention, without a proper appreciation of the costs ahead of time."[26] John Hillen raised this concern about fears of overextension: "Most Americans would agree that the United States must be active in the world, but not so active that the effort wastes American resources and energies in interventions that yield little or no payoff and undermine military preparedness."[27] Or Andrew Bacevich linked the tendency for the military to do it all with a disturbing trend within American politics that linked "a militaristic cast of mind with utopian ends," which leads to an increased propensity to use force.[28]

Echoing C. Wright Mills's findings from the 1950s, American leaders tend to define international problems as military problems, which can preclude nonmilitary solutions.[29] For example, U.S. assistance to Colombia has a decidedly military focus to combat the Revolutionary Armed Forces of Columbia (FARC) insurgency, but it has been criticized by some for lacking the correspondent development assistance to connect FARC-controlled parts of the country to the center.[30] Or when Belgrade did not sue for peace after a few days of airstrikes, a protracted airwar resulted in a real potential to develop into a major ground campaign.[31] The crucial learning point, however, is to ensure that all elements of power are synchronized in the most efficient way to achieve the desired outcome. And to date, the data suggest that U.S. military-to-military contacts are positively and systematically associated with liberalizing trends throughout the world.[32]

Inevitably, concerns about the nonwarfighting role of the military, which dwarfs other federal departments, fuels calls for interagency reform. Critics contend that if only the State Department were on equal footing with DoD, the United States would have a more balanced, less belligerent foreign policy. The effects of this imbalance were recognized by a Senate Foreign Relations Committee report: "As a result of inadequate funding for civilian programs, U.S. defense agencies are increasingly being granted authority and funding to fill perceived gaps."[33]

Consequently, DoD runs human rights initiatives, HIV/AIDS programs, and hosts conferences on natural resource management. There is also disparity with the international assistance account 150. In contrast to public perceptions, the United States does not dole out suitcases filled with cash to allies. Instead, foreign assistance typically takes the form of U.S. goods and services. The largest line item is foreign military financing. In spite of calls for budgetary reform to increase social and economic assistance, defense issues are simply more compelling for Congress. Politicians have an interest in associating themselves with ideas of patriotism and strength, so it is much easier to find advocates for exporting attack aircraft than for women's empowerment programs. The conventional wisdom on the Hill indicates that while defense spending is understood to be a matter of national security, international assistance spending sounds less urgently important to American voters.

Mitchell Thompson argues that a remedy for this political and budgetary imbalance necessarily entails "breaking the proconsulate." Thompson writes, "Our current geographic Combatant Commands should be redesigned to break their heavy military orientation, and be transformed into truly interagency organizations, under civilian leadership, and prepared to conduct the full spectrum of operations using all elements of national power within their assigned regions."[34] This call is echoed by current strategy to combat international terrorism that sees the military playing only a supporting role to other federal departments, which can counter terrorists' ideology, interdict terrorist financing, and promote development among vulnerable populations—tasks that are not core military functions.

While the reactions have been real and sometimes dramatic, efforts to reduce the non-warfighting role of combatant commanders have largely failed. In contrast to objections during the 2000 presidential election, the Bush administration could not escape from the reality that there is a global demand for U.S. engagement programs and that the military is the most capable federal department to do the engaging. In fact, Congress in the FY 2007 National Defense Authorization Act recognized this: "Civilian agencies of the United States Government lack the capacity to deploy rapidly, and for sustained periods of time, trained personnel to support . . . operations in the field."[35]

Geographic combatant commanders do offer the president an important tool of power that can be exercised in all realms: political, economic, military, social, and informational. Just as it is important to illustrate national security resolve by deploying an Expeditionary Strike Group (ESG), that same ESG can be used to deliver humanitarian assistance in stability operations or to serve as training platforms for foreign militaries. Tom Barnett, for example, has argued that DoD must embrace this mission and develop unique capabilities.[36] But, DoD can and does execute the full range of military operations with little noticeable impact on its ability to conduct major combat operations. An exercise like Cobra Gold simultaneously brings the United States, Thai, and other regional militaries closer; tests expeditionary warfare concepts; and implements humanitarian assistance programs.

Setting this aside, the military's active involvement in diplomacy does not preclude cooperation with the State Department. In fact, a combatant commander works extremely closely with his political advisor (POLAD) and the country teams where his or her engagement programs occur. With time-limited tours of duty, a combatant commander needs support from outside his or her military staff. Occasionally, there are tensions with strategic impact. "Left unclear, blurred lines of authority between the State Department and the Defense Department could lead to interagency turf wars that undermine the effectiveness of the overall U.S. effort against terrorism. It is in the embassies rather than in Washington where interagency differences on strategies, tactics, and divisions of labor are increasingly adjudicated."[37] However, both U.S. ambassadors and combatant commanders understand they need each other's cooperation. If done well, military engagement activities are coordinated with other interagency activities beginning at the national level where both the State Department and the Office of the Secretary of Defense (OSD) derive priorities and guidance from the National Security Strategy, which in turn drives theater security cooperation plans and mission strategic plans.[38] Yet an ambassador's focus on one country and a combatant commander's focus on an entire region necessitate coordination. A combatant command can serve as a regional hub of not only coordination, but also interagency and combined planning.

Outside of the United States, opinion on U.S. engagement is mixed. Majorities in thirteen out of fifteen publics polled say the United States is "playing the role of world policeman more than it should be." This is the sentiment of nearly three-quarters of those polled in France (89 percent), Australia (80 percent), China (77 percent), Russia (76 percent), Peru (76 percent), the Palestinian territories (74 percent), and South Korea (73 percent).[39]

While negative feedback to U.S. activities is substantial, negative reactions appear to be based on the mode of U.S. involvement rather than on U.S. involvement itself.[40] Publics around the world do not want the United States to disengage from international affairs, but rather to participate in a more cooperative and multilateral fashion.[41] Majorities in thirteen out of fifteen publics (Argentines and Palestinians disagreed) polled support U.S. involvement in a more cooperative and multilateral fashion through international institutions, instead of in what is perceived as irresponsible unilateralism. The United States has also learned that being a superpower does not make it a superhero that can accomplish anything it desires. Consequently, the United States has been attempting to coordinate engagement activities to more effectively confront transnational security challenges instead of trying to provide for global security alone.

Conclusion

I believe if you have these kinds of relationships they would go a long way to ensuring that we don't get into a war or get into a fight with people that we're engaged with like this.

Admiral Michael Mullen, USN[42]

Overall, the rationale for engagement activities has been based on the assumption that instability breeds chaos, which will inevitably produce military intervention. Accordingly, DoD should support other countries through security assistance programs. The military attempts to build global security through military-to-military contacts, weapons transfers, and combined training activities. Furthermore, since militaries play important roles in many societies, senior American military officers share with their counterparts a common language, one that is used by DoD to create and maintain a global set of partners essential for responding to crises.

The criticisms of this role for the military are substantial and include marginalizing the State Department, militarizing foreign policy, and diluting the military's warfighting ethos, but these engagement activities are not likely to end anytime soon. Presidents, both Democrat and Republican, find a ready tool in the military to respond to natural disasters, bolster new diplomatic friendships or long-standing allies, and share the costs of security with nearly every government in the world. Consequently, the question is not whether the military should be engaged in security cooperation activities. Rather, the question is how to structure these operations to fully include civilian agencies and organizations to ensure that broader national security objectives are attained.

Notes

1. An early version of this argument appeared as chapter 1 in Derek S. Reveron, ed., *Shaping the Security Environment* (Newport, RI: Naval War College Press, 2007).
2. In the FY2009 budget, the Defense Department baseline request was $515.4 billion with another $150 billion likely in supplementals. The State Department operating budget request was $11.2 billion . For the defense budget in detail see www.budget.mil. For the international affairs budget, see www.state.gov/documents/organization/100014.pdf.
3. Tom Clancy with General Tony Zinni and Tony Koltz, *Battle Ready* (New York: Putnam, 2004), p. 319.
4. "Africa Command [AFRICOM] will enhance our efforts to help bring peace and security to the people of Africa and promote our common goals of development, health, education, democracy, and economic growth in Africa." George W. Bush, "President Bush Creates a Department of Defense Unified Combatant Command for Africa," February 6, 2007, available at http://www.whitehouse.gov/news/releases/2007/02/20070206-3.html, accessed on April 18, 2007.
5. John Hillen, "Superpowers Don't Do Windows," *Orbis* 41, no. 2 (Spring 1997), p. 242.
6. Zinni, "Military Diplomacy," p. 14, in Reveron, *Shaping the Security Environment*.
7. William J. Crowe, Jr. "U.S. Pacific Command: A Warrior-Diplomat Speaks," in Derek S. Reveron, ed., *America's Viceroys: The Military and U.S. Foreign Policy* (New York: Palgrave Macmillan, 2004), p. 74.
8. Joseph Nye, "Soft Power," *Foreign Policy*, Autumn 1990, p. 156. "Soft power" is something that a country has that can be generated from cultural, political, and economic behavior, but it is better thought of as a by-product rather than as a raw material. Soft power is noncoercive and is not simply nonmilitary. On this point, see Joseph Nye, "Think Again: Soft Power," *Foreign Policy Web Exclusive*, February 23, 2006.

9. Joseph S. Nye, *Soft Power: The Means to Success in World Politics* (New York: Public Affairs, 2004), p. x.

10. Robert J. Art, "The Fungibility of Force," in *The Use of Force: Military Power and International Politics,* edited by Robert J. Art and Kenneth N. Waltz, 6th ed. (New York: Rowman and Littlefield, 2004), p. 4.

11. William S. Cohen, "Secretary's Message," *1997 Quadrennial Defense Review,* available at http://www.fas.org/man/docs/qdr/msg.html, accessed on April 18, 2007.

12. Military Diplomacy is defined as "the ability to support those activities and measures U.S. military leaders take to engage military, defense and government officials of another country to communicate USG policies and messages and build defense and coalition relationships." See "Joint Capability Areas Tier 1 and Supporting Tier 2 Lexicon, Post 24 August 2006 JROC," available at http://www.dtic.mil/futurejointwarfare/, accessed on December 20, 2006.

13. Joint Forces Command and European Command, Draft Military Support to Shaping Operations, Joint Operating Concept, June 5, 2007, p. 13.

14. 1997 QDR, available at http://www.fas.org/man/docs/qdr/msg.html.

15. General Toni Zinni, *The Battle for Peace: A Frontline Vision of America's Power and Purpose* (New York: Palgrave Macmillan, 2006), p. 135.

16. "Joint Capability Areas Tier 1 and Supporting Tier 2 Lexicon, Post 24 August 2006 JROC," available at http://www.dtic.mil/futurejointwarfare/, accessed on December 20, 2006.

17. "The 1,000 Ship Navy: Global Maritime Network," *Proceedings,* November 2005, p. 17. See also Admiral Mike Mullen, "What I Believe: Eight Tenets That Guide My Vision for the 21st Century Navy," *Proceedings,* January 2006.

18. Admiral Mike Mullen, "Priority Tasking Memo," March 7, 2007.

19. "Joint Capability Areas Tier 1 and Supporting Tier 2 Lexicon, Post 24 August 2006 JROC" available at http://www.dtic.mil/futurejointwarfare/, accessed on December 20, 2006.

20. U.S. Department of State, "Foreign Military Financing Account Tables," available at www.state.gov/s/d/rm/rls/iab/2007/html/60203.htm, accessed on April 4, 2006. It is important to note that military assistance for Iraq and Afghanistan are not included in this account data.

21. For a break-down by country, see http://www.state.gov/documents/organization/100014.pdf.

22. Ronald H. Reynolds, "Is Expanded International Military Education and Training Reaching the Right Audience?" *DISAM Journal of International Security Assistance Management,* Spring 2003, p. 94.

23. General Bantz Craddock, "Statement before the House Armed Services Committee," March 15, 2007, p. 11.

24. Bill Daly, "Building Global Partnerships," *Proceedings* April, 2007, pp. 44–47.

25. George W. Bush, "Excerpt of Presidential Debate October 12, 2000," available at http://www.pbs.org/newshour/bb/politics/july-dec00/for-policy_10-12.html, accessed on April 18, 2007.

26. Justin Logan and Christopher Preble, "The Case Against State's Nationbuilding Office," *Foreign Service Journal,* November 2006, p. 55.

27. Hillen, "Superpowers Don't do Windows," p. 257.

28. Andrew J. Bacevich, *The New American Militarism* (New York: Oxford University, 2005), p. 3.

29. C. Wright Mills, *The Power Elite* (New York: Oxford Press, 1956).

30. Myles R. R. Frechette, "Colombia and the United States—The Partnership: But What is the Endgame?" Le Tort Paper, U.S. Army War College, February 2007.

31. Derek S. Reveron, "Coalition Warfare: the Commander's Role," *Defense and Security Analysis* 18, no. 2 (June 2002), pp. 107–122.

32. Carol Atkinson, "Constructivist Implications of Material Power: Military Engagement and the Socialization of States, 1972–2000," *International Studies Quarterly* 50 (2006), pp. 509–537.

33. "Embassies as Command Posts in the Anti-Terror Campaign," *A Report to Members of the Committee on Foreign Relations, United States Senate,* December 15, 2006, p. 2.

34. Mitchell J. Thompson, "Breaking the Proconsulate: A New Design for National Power," *Parameters, US Army War College Quarterly,* Winter 2005–6, p. 63.

35. FY2007 Defense Authorization Act, Sec 1222, paragraph a2.

36. Thomas P. M. Barnett, *Pentagon's New Map: War and Peace in the Twenty-First Century* (New York: Putnam, 2004).

37. "Embassies as Command Posts in the Anti-Terror Campaign," *A Report to Members of the Committee on Foreign Relations, United States Senate,* December 15, 2006, p. 2.

38. Joint Publication 5-0, p. II-8. In European Command, for example, U.S. Naval Forces Europe (NAVEUR), working with the U.S. Department of State, U.S. European Command (EUCOM), and the Africa Center for Strategic Studies, led a ministerial-level conference on Maritime Safety and Security in the Gulf of Guinea. See General Bantz Craddock, "Statement before the House Armed Services Committee," March 15, 2007.

39. World Public Opinion, "World Publics Reject US Role as the World Leader," available at http://www.worldpublicopinion.org/pipa/articles/home_page/345.php?nid=&id=&pnt=345&lb=hmpg1, accessed on April 20, 2007.

40. Lisa Haugaard argues that a tarnished U.S. image in Latin America is nothing new, but reflects historical frustration with interventions and U.S. trade policy. But frustrations have been exacerbated by reductions in military assistance, disputes over the International Criminal Court, and the Guantanomo Bay detention center. See "Tarnished Image: Latin America Perceives the United States," The Latin America Working Group Education Fund, March 2006.

41. Steven Kull, "America's Image in the World," *Testimony Before House Committee on Foreign Affairs, Subcommittee on International Organizations, Human Rights, and Oversight,* March 6, 2007, available at http://www.worldpublicopinion.org/pipa/articles/views_on_countriesregions_bt/326.php?nid=&id=&pnt=326&lb=btvoc, accessed on April 20, 2007.

42. "CNO: Humanitarian Missions Essential To Relationships, Global War On Terrorism," *Navy Newsstand,* June 19, 2007. http://www.navy.mil.

5

The Undermilitarization of U.S. Foreign Policy?

John Garofano

With the United States prosecuting protracted wars in two countries and committed to a global war on a phenomenon that springs from a vast reservoir of both antipathy and potential foot soldiers, it seems clear to many analysts that U.S. foreign policy has become "militarized" in a way analogous to shifts in policy at the start of World War II or the Korean War. The concept of militarization can be defined and measured in three quite different ways, however. Perhaps the most common refers to a large and unusual proportion of resources being devoted to military operations and preparations for them. War costs today have reached $12 billion per month, and appropriations are expected to reach $760 billion for the next fiscal year.[1]

A second definition would hold that policy is militarized if national goals are inordinately concerned with military outcomes to the neglect of broader political goals. A military-centric "victory at all costs" approach, as has occasionally been taken by high-ranking soldiers and civilians in the midst of protracted conflicts, is an example of this—for example, Douglas MacArthur's desire to conquer all of Korea. A variation of this approach occurs when policy focuses inordinately and unrealistically on military power and tactics, to the exclusion of diplomatic, informational, and economic sources of power.[2]

A third version does not focus on outcomes (goals) or strategies (with a focus on means), but examines the process by which policy is made and whether or not there is overbearing influence by the military. Arguments about the militarization of policy*making* are less common than are those about goals and means, perhaps because few would argue that the process has been hijacked by the military.[3]

In a curious twist, the Iraq War has raised the issue of whether U.S. foreign policymaking is not in fact *under*militarized, particularly regarding Iraq, Afghanistan, and the war on terror. Adopting a line of argument heard during the Korean and Vietnam wars, Michael Desch claims that Secretary of Defense Donald Rumsfeld's "meddling approach contributed in significant measure to the

problems in Iraq and elsewhere."[4] Invoking what has become a de rigueur interpretation of Vietnam policymaking, Desch supports the views of H. R. McMaster's
powerful but flawed *Dereliction of Duty: Johnson, McNamara, the Joint Chiefs of
Staff, and the Lies that Led to Vietnam,* which held that in the 1960s senior military
leaders were derelict in their duty to speak truth to power and were therefore complicit in policymakers' bad decisions.[5] As a remedy, Desch argues that Washington
must return to the ideal type of civil-military relations known as "objective control,"
discussed below, in which civilian leaders set policy goals and then turn the selection of means and the execution of wartime tasks over to the military.[6]

Just how influential was the U.S. military in decision making related to Iraq?
Did civilians run roughshod over the wisdom of military leaders? Should we—can
we—return to a purported ideal in which policymakers set goals and the military
is given the freedom to achieve them as they see fit? As during the final stages of
the Vietnam War and the subsequent quarrels over who "lost" it, the views
cogently expressed by Desch are gaining in currency today. It is my belief that
Desch's indictment of decision making related to Iraq is inaccurate and that his
prescriptions for the future are impractical. I argue that objective control may no
longer be functional in today's environment, while the Vietnam narrative invoked
by critics of current policy is based on selective history.

In the next section, I explore what current discussions about civil-military relations offer regarding the "proper" role of the military in decision making about
war. In the third section, I use the Iraq war as a case study based on the evidence
available. In the fourth section, I refer to the myths of Vietnam and draw some
conclusions about Iraq and the larger issues.

Civil-Military Relations and the End of Distinct Roles

During the years of the Clinton presidency, there was considerable concern that
the general tenor of civil-military relations had reached crisis proportions. One
officer went so far as to half-caricature those relations as laying the groundwork
for a coup within a few decades.[7] Arguing in a *New York Times* article that General
David Petraeus effectively runs America's Iraq policy, Frank Rich has similarly
derided "the quaint notion that our uniformed officers are supposed to report to
civilian leadership."[8] Yet the United States has witnessed no real danger of a coup
or of the military otherwise seizing the reins of power, supporting the claim by
Samuel Huntington in his 1957 classic *The Solider and the State* that the problem
of the modern state is "not armed revolt but the relation of the expert to the
politician."[9]

In a recent article in *Foreign Affairs,* Michael Desch has argued that the relationship has moved too far in the direction of control by the politician rather than
by the military expert. As noted, Desch echoes the McMaster view of Vietnam and
finds in the current period weak-willed military officers who fail to assert their
views of what is necessary militarily to accomplish political goals. The solution,
Desch argues, "is to return to an old division of labor: civilians give due deference
to military professional advice in the tactical and operational realms in return for

complete military subordination in the grand strategic and political realms." This is, Desch claims, the operationalization of Huntington's notion of objective control. "The proper balance would give civilian leaders authority over political decisions—such as whether the United States should stay in Iraq or use force against Iran—and the military wide leeway in making the operational and tactical decisions about how to complete a mission."[10]

Desch contrasts Huntington's "objective control" with the thesis of Eliot Cohen's *Supreme Command,* which President Bush reportedly read over his 2002 summer vacation, and concludes that "it would have been far better for the United States if Bush had read Huntington's *The Soldier and the State* rather than Cohen's *Supreme Command.*" Cohen critiques Huntington's objective control, arguing that in critical instances civilian intervention in military operations has been necessary to achieve the desired outcome.[11] Writing prior to General Petraeus's September 2007 testimony before Congress, Desch suggested that Petraeus had learned from Vietnam and that "hopefully, he will speak candidly" to his civilian masters and ... they will listen to him.[12]

Objective control, indeed the very concept of "civil-military relations," presumes two distinct spheres of activity. Huntington enshrined the notion of distinctness in *The Soldier and the State,* arguing that after Napoleon, politics and military science had each become so advanced and complex that the necessary expertise could no longer be found in one person. The effective division of labor between Otto von Bismarck and Helmuth von Moltke symbolized the new dichotomy. Huntington quotes Field Marshal Wavell:

> Interchangeability between the statesman and the soldier passed forever, I fear, in the last century. The Germans professionalized the trade of war; and modern inventions, by increasing its technicalities, have specialized it. It is much the same with politics, professionalized by democracy. No longer can one man hope to exercise both callings, though both are branches of the same craft, the governance of men and the ordering of human affairs.[13]

From this Huntington concluded that the ideal military man was conservative in strategy, in the sense of heeding military science's eternal principles, and neutral vis-à-vis politics, which was beyond the scope of the military. "Politics undermines their professionalism, curtailing their professional competence, dividing the profession against itself, and substituting extraneous values for professional values."[14] The statesman must respect the integrity of the military profession, while also exerting guidance. "Civilian control exists when there is this proper subordination of an autonomous profession to the ends of policy."[15]

New Environment, New Relationship

Some analysts, beginning with S. E. Finer, have rejected the notion of two distinct spheres.[16] In less frequently quoted passages, Huntington himself noted that the two spheres would overlap in several areas, including the military's responsibility "to represent the claims of military security within the state machinery," to serve in an advisory function, and to execute all politically legitimate decisions, even those that run contrary to the best military judgment. "The top military leaders of the state inevitably operate in this intermingled world of strategy and policy." Huntington also agrees with Carl von Clausewitz that "the art of war in its highest point of view becomes policy, but, of course, a policy which fights battles instead of writing notes."[17] Thus, Huntington seems to envision a convergence of perspectives at the highest levels within each sphere, as well as a potential overlap in actual functions.

The problem is that the ideal division of labor prescribed by Huntington, long adopted legally and normatively in the United States, and almost universally supported by scholars and analysts, is no longer plausible in practice or useful in theory. Huntington, Wavell, Bismarck, and Moltke were probably all correct that both military affairs and politics had undergone revolutions requiring a greater degree of expertise than ever before. But in the early twenty-first century, narrowly defined "political" or "military" expertise is not necessarily the most valuable currency for an effective leader, civilian or military. Rather, two kinds of abilities have become paramount.

The first is the ability to integrate across fields of expertise. Soldiers and civilians require unparalleled breadth and depth of knowledge about social and international dynamics. This includes an understanding of the world's religions, political systems, demographics, societal structures, laws and norms affecting the use of force during war and occupations, and economic development, to name just a few of the areas bearing on current roles and tasks of U.S. soldiers and civilians overseas. All of this must be combined as well with an understanding of what military power can accomplish; the differences among air, land, sea, and hybrid forms of military power; current and changing capacities in surveillance and intelligence; and budgetary and other limitations.

The Allies were little concerned with civilian casualties from aerial bombardment prior to the D-Day invasion of France. Today, plans for intervention or invasion must take into account international norms regarding civilian casualties, tribal and ethnic relations in an intervening state, the pool of indigenous talent ready to assume leadership, the utility and limitations of the military for providing security and building a society, and the role of various actors in constructing a market economy and a democratic form of government—among other tasks.

The magnitude of these intellectual demands should be compared to pre–Operation Iraqi Freedom failures to grasp the much simpler analysis regarding how and how hard Saddam Hussein would respond to an invasion. The questions of how hard he would fight, how he would use his Scud missiles, whether he had weapons of mass destruction (WMD) and whether he would use them, and whether he would attack Israel—all of these fundamentally political considerations had major implications for the kinds of forces the United States would need and for how long the battle would last. They involved understanding the outlook and power relations of a relatively small number of people operating within a simple command structure. The fact that we got so many assumptions wrong is not heartening.[18]

These knowledge requirements are reinforced—and in some cases compounded—by the structure of the policymaking process. The national security machinery remains rooted in the legal and normative structure devised in 1789, with some modifications made in 1947. The effect is that a small number of individuals are responsible for a wide range of policy choices.

This fact relates to the second kind of intellectual and policy ability suggested above—namely, an appreciation of the linkages among grand strategy, theater strategy, and military operations and tactics. Abu Ghraib reminds once again that the lowest level of action can have strategic consequences; moreover, the ability to communicate within and across borders has created a fundamental change in the interconnectedness among strategic arenas. If a combatant commander makes comments about his goals in a region, they could tip off (or mislead) actors about actual U.S. policy. In another scenario, a combatant commander could terminate a conflict based on his understanding of the operational picture only, excluding wider theater and political concerns. During termination of the first Gulf war at Safwan, both the commander on the ground and his superiors in Washington seemed not to appreciate the wider political and regional implications of such tactical issues as whether Saddam should be allowed to retain the use of certain kinds of aircraft.

The post–Cold War policy of actively expanding the sphere of democratic governments and of capitalism gravely increases the demands on high-ranking soldiers and civilians. When this involves forceful regime change, they are expected to understand not only highly complex social structures and economies, but also how to build and sustain them. Even for the most modern of countries, the task is formidable and is fraught with overlapping civil and military knowledge and functions. From the military significance and political challenges of putting an army division in Turkey at the start of the Iraq war, to decisions on using force in specific neighborhoods within Iraq, the realm of military operations and the realm of civilian political choices that are amenable to the kind of specialization necessary for objective control are dwindling.

Supreme Commander of Allied Forces Dwight D. Eisenhower's orders to invade Europe read: "You will enter the continent of Europe and, in conjunction with the other Allied Nations, undertake operations aimed at the heart of Germany and the destruction of her Armed Forces."[19] In their simplicity, they represent the era of objective control, in which political masters can set goals and hand off responsibility and decision-making powers to the military. That era is over.

The Iraq War: "Undermilitarized"?

The initiative for planning a possible invasion of Iraq came from the president with the support—not entirely uniform—of his primary national security advisors. Immediately after the September 11, 2001, attacks, there was near unanimity that Afghanistan and the Taliban should be the first targets of U.S. military might, as demonstrated by the 4-0-1 straw vote among the president's advisers at Camp David on November 21.[20] The president simultaneously asked Secretary of

Defense Rumsfeld about war plans for Iraq. Rumsfeld had the Joint Staff (JS) ask U.S. Central Command (CENTCOM) general Tommy Franks for a "commander's estimate," including the current war plan and what he thought he could do to improve upon that plan, which called for seven months to move a force of five hundred thousand to the theater before military operations could begin.[21] The secretary of defense said that action against Iraq could come "as early as April or May" of 2002.[22]

The parameters of the nature, timing, and size of an actual deployment to Iraq—using a much smaller force, more rapidly deployed, with the aim of getting to Baghdad quickly and then rapidly turning over the reins of government to some coherent, effective force—were set between November 2001 and the summer of 2002. Rumsfeld felt that the plans left by General Anthony Zinni were too slow and too big and that they did not fit the administration's new defense policies. But the commander in the field, General Franks, enthusiastically supported Rumsfeld's perspective. As he told the secretary of defense, "This is not 1990. The Iraqi military today is not the one we faced in 1991. And our own forces are much different. We see that in Afghanistan."[23]

At the president's ranch on December 28, 2001, Franks briefed what he had of his new plan, listing seven lines of operations against nine vulnerabilities in Saddam's regime. The plan recognized the limited role of conventional force in shifting Iraqi public support away from the regime, and stressed information operations. He discussed various levels of international support and time lines, having war as a feasible option within four to six months (or April to June 2002). Rumsfeld probed and prodded, clearly leaning towards a lighter force and more rapid movement.[24]

This process was repeated until Franks briefed the sixth version of the plan on February 7, 2002, calling for ninety days of preparation and the movement of three hundred thousand troops and equipment (including a corps through Turkey), forty-five days of bombing, and ninety days of combat operations. According to Woodward, the reaction was "Wow!" as in, how much could be done with so few troops in so little time.[25] Franks mentioned that phase 4 (reconstruction) operations still required much work.[26] In an August 5 briefing to the National Security Council (NSC), Franks introduced a new hybrid concept to distinguish it from the previous version, shrinking the preparatory phase dramatically to sixteen days for establishing an air bridge, eleven for transporting initial forces, sixteen days of airstrikes and Special Forces operations, 125 days of decisive combat operations, and stability operations of an unknown duration. There was perfunctory discussion of troop levels necessary for phase 4.

It was at this meeting that Powell said that the United States would then "own" Iraq. The president's recollection is that he, as president, remained focused on the duty to provide security for the United States. Powell was being tactical, the president said, while "my job is to be strategic. Basically what [Powell] was saying was, was that if Saddam was toppled by military [invasion], we better have a strong understanding about what it's going to take to rebuild Iraq."[27] The exchange and the president's recollection of it are telling. The president was honoring the tradition of delegating to his Defense (and State) Department the details of executing orders just as the objective control theory would have it.

Civilians failed to insert themselves into military planning for postcombat operations, and military leaders did not comprehend the political aspects of phase 4.

On August 6, 2002, Franks ordered his commanders to make the transition to his latest plan of attack.[28] The plan was subject to "one of the most elaborate simulations any combatant command had ever conducted" later that fall at the Joint Operations Center in Qatar. Exercise Internal Look 03 convinced Franks that he could dramatically compress the time frames of several phases of the battle campaign using speed, maneuver, and "the overwhelming 'mass of effect' of a smaller force." In Franks's view, the result was "a true revolution in warfare."[29]

One can get the sense from the push for an ever-compressed time frame and plans for an ever-lighter force that civilian policymakers ran roughshod over their military subordinates. But in his memoirs, published just as progress in the war began to stall and violence escalated, Franks portrays himself as being fully committed to the war plan. He was in agreement, too, with the overall defense philosophy of the administration, and saw himself in opposition to those "Title 10 motherfuckers," the chiefs of staff of the army and air force, the chief of naval operations, and the commandant of the Marine Corps, who, by virtue of the way the services are funded, constantly do battle over missions and the budgets that will support them.[30] Franks reportedly told Rumsfeld that micromanaging the war "ain't going to work. You can fire me. I'm either the commander or I'm not, and you've got to trust me or you don't."[31]

Franks has been criticized for misinterpreting information, listening only to good news, and fostering an atmosphere in which demoralized subordinates provided ill-informed "SWAG," or "scientific wild-assed guesses."[32] The kind of analysis done by military leaders in key planning and intelligence positions was probably more influential than was civilian pressure. In other words, the problem was not an undermilitarized process, but rather the military advice itself. Franks made fundamental conceptual errors, according to an internal army study. The first was in never grasping the fact that taking a capital does not equate with a lasting victory.[33] Second, in a strong parallel to Vietnam, senior military leaders did not have convincing alternatives to what was a notably unclear intelligence picture. Thomas Ricks claims there was widespread concern in the summer of 2002 about three issues: whether Saddam had WMD; the danger of urban warfare; and the postwar occupation. "Yet for all those doubts, only one top officer really deeply objected to the entire war plan. That was [Lt. Gen. Gregory] Newbold, who as the Joint Staff's director of operations was aware of almost everything of significance going on in the U.S. military, and to the classified information it was receiving." This did not include the president's Daily Briefings, but "I think I had one hundred percent other than that," Newbold claimed.[34]

A third problem was that there were fundamentally two different intelligence analyses. The civilian branch concluded that Saddam had WMD and that the postwar situation would be benign, while some military were, at the least, skeptical. Some planners were also concerned that the force cap that seemed to hinder operations in Afghanistan was being imposed, via the process of negotiation at the highest levels between senior military and civilian leaders, in Iraq. Conflicting assessments were never reconciled, however. "Instead, the planning process attempted to achieve a compromise between these competing outlooks."[35]

In late November, Franks requested three hundred thousand troops immediately. Rumsfeld rejected this, stating that it would run counter to diplomatic efforts. "We're going to dribble this out slowly, so that it's enough to keep the pressure on for the diplomacy but not so much as to discredit the diplomacy." Rumsfeld approved each deployment order, causing displeasure among some army brass.[36] But again in a strong parallel to Vietnam, there was no clear "military" answer to the prodding and pushing represented by Rumsfeld. Colin Powell had boots-on-the-ground experience and years of Pentagon and White House work. Whereas after the initial briefings he had reached out informally to Franks to warn him not to accept fewer troops than he needed, Powell eventually felt better about the plan, even taking a harder line towards Saddam when he testified before the Senate Budget Committee on February 12. His deputy, Richard Armitage, also a retired officer with experience in Vietnam, went out of his way to show that the department was on board with a policy stance that could lead to war sooner rather than later. [37]

Furthermore, the conceptual basis of such postwar planning as was done by the military was problematic. Eclipse II, the army's plan for phase 4 operations, was based on three false assumptions, according to an Army War College study: large numbers of Iraqi security forces would support the occupation; the international community would provide extensive in-country support; and an Iraqi government would quickly be established and gain legitimacy. A 2005 Rand study concluded similarly that "post-conflict stabilization and reconstruction were addressed only very generally, largely because of the prevailing view that the task would not be difficult."[38] More to the point, perhaps, is the fact that the army has traditionally considered postwar governance as a requirement entirely separate from war itself and also as a responsibility of civilian agencies.[39]

"A lot of folks say the military rolled over" for Rumsfeld. "We didn't. We did the best we could," said one officer in the planning shop.[40] Later, Franks acknowledged that "we had First Armored and First Cav in the flow. . . . Don Rumsfeld did in fact make the decision to off ramp the First Cavalry Division."[41] But General John Keane thought the greatest failure may have been that throughout the senior military leadership, there was no consideration of a possible guerrilla war. "This was not just an intelligence community failure, but also our failure as senior military leaders, including myself."[42] To reiterate, however, even the critics were unclear on what would result after the war. As General Anthony Zinni put it, "We have lit a fuse, and we don't know what's at the other end—a nuke, a hand grenade, or a dud."[43] As in Vietnam, few felt entirely confident in their predictions or even in their concerns. This may explain why the State Department, with two former military officers at the top, did not press harder for acceptance of their postwar plans.

It is true that General Eric Shinseki's February 2003 statements to Congress suggested that "several hundred thousand" troops might be needed. Also, Paul Wolfowitz famously claimed that an estimate of several hundred thousand troops was "wildly off the mark," and that around thirty-four thousand troops would be needed by August 2003. Pentagon spokesman Lawrence Di Rita, ex-navy, claimed at the time that thirty thousand troops would remain in Iraq after 120 days.

Yet as prescient as Shinseki seems in retrospect, no extensive analysis has surfaced to support his statements, which were dragged out of him by Senator Carl Levin only after repeated questioning. Furthermore, the numbers game is a questionable exercise in straight-line extrapolation from very different environments, an exercise in which others also participated. Former secretary of defense William Perry held that for Bosnia, the Pentagon used a formula of one soldier for every 50 Bosnians, suggesting a need for approximately 560,000 troops or about 300,000 if we exclude the population of the Kurdish north. Before his February 25, 2003, testimony, he tasked army historians to research the number of troops needed after other conflicts. The Army's Center for Military History concluded about 260,000 would be needed. If extrapolations were made based on the number of insurgents, perhaps millions of troops would be needed. One PowerPoint slide produced by the office that Franks had created for postwar planning, Joint Task Force IV, noted that based on the army's experience in Bosnia and Kosovo, the situation in Iraq would require 470,000 troops. The work of this cell was roundly criticized, however, as being naïve, unrealistic, and more "like a war college exercise" than serious planning.[44] It is not difficult to see, in any case, that claims based on very different historical cases might not have sufficient punch to alter existing assessments. Another problem was that General Shinseki seemed to focus on humanitarian concerns, which did not materialize and were in addition to the more critical society-building tasks that the United States eventually faced in Iraq.[45] It is by no means clear that more troops would have contributed to these tasks. After the Office of the Secretary of Defense (OSD) leaked the name of his replacement fifteen months before his scheduled retirement, there were poor relations and a lack of communication between General Shinseki's office and OSD. When Shinseki and other members of the Joint Chiefs of Staff (JCS) met with the president during the winter, Shinseki's criticism was muted and focused primarily on lines of communication and other issues relevant to major combat operations.

This is not to downplay the fact that General Shinseki was, in retrospect, probably more accurate than other policymakers and military leaders. A major conference at the National Defense University, which brought together some seventy regional and military experts, concluded that occupying Iraq would be the most daunting foreign policy task since containing the Soviet Union.[46] A major Rand study completed in the summer of 2005 confirmed that General Franks had a "fundamental misunderstanding" of the military's role in postwar Iraq.[47] But the weakness of his protests, their emphasis on humanitarian and policing concerns, and the simple extrapolation logic suggest that the general's dismissal is not clear evidence of a causal chain running from civilian bullying through military dereliction to policy failure. And other military leaders did not adequately develop alternatives.

"Silence of the Lambs" and "Dereliction of Duty" or Uncertain Warriors?

In summarizing the performance of senior military leaders on Iraq, Michael Desch invokes Vietnam and H. R. McMaster's *Dereliction of Duty* thesis, while Thomas Ricks, in *Fiasco*, characterizes it as "the Silence of the Lambs." This theme has a long heritage dating at least to Harry Summers's classic *On Strategy* and his later work on the first Gulf war, down through McMaster's *Dereliction*, which has been "required reading" in the U.S. officer corps for years, to current critics like Desch and Andrew Bacevich. Bacevich's recent skewering of General Petraeus for playing "politics—of the wrong kind," following the latter's testimony before Congress in September 2007, also invokes the lessons of Vietnam.[48]

The storyline in *Dereliction* is that a lack of moral courage on the part of senior military leaders and lies on the part of political leaders led to a disastrous policy in Vietnam. President Lyndon Johnson and Secretary of Defense Robert McNamara are said to have at times ridden roughshod over the objections of the JCS or, at other times, to have kept the truth from them and to have prevented them from airing their views—views that would have led to better policy and to victory. The actual history of civil-military relations during the Vietnam period were not as dysfunctional as depicted, however, and we should learn from this that current relations might, too, not be what they seem. Meetings between civilian and military leaders, for example, were regular—hundreds of them from 1964 to 1968—and frank. The larger problem was that the military was unable to make a convincing case for a strategy other than the limited war advocated by civilian policymakers. In particular, they were unable to pierce the argument that a major vertical and horizontal escalation of the U.S. war effort would inevitably be met with a larger opposing force and a wider war geographically, that the battlefield could not be sealed, and that the chances of a conflict with China and possibly the Soviet Union would be much greater and potentially catastrophic. Furthermore, when pressed, the military accepted and often advocated even limited action to halt the potential falling dominoes.

General Harold. K. Johnson, the chief of staff of the army, is quoted by Harry Summers as saying, in his later years, that he would go to his Maker knowing his lack of moral courage had prevented him from speaking truth to power.[49] But shortly after Vietnam, in perhaps a less nostalgic mood, Johnson was clear that he and his counterparts were wary of taking military action that could lead to a wider, longer war. "No one wanted the Chinese to come moving out of South China." Furthermore, he stated that in the Vietnam case, he and his counterparts "were all guilty of an unstated assumption that when the United States committed itself, that the enemy would go scampering off."[50] Other emerging documentary evidence shows the extent to which the military lacked a clear and convincing alternative. General William C. Westmoreland's weekly reports, General Harold K. Johnson's initial recommendations, internal war games, formal strategic estimates, and major summits (e.g., the April 1965 Honolulu Conference) revealed commonly held misunderstandings about the conflict, across the civil-military spectrum.[51]

In the Iraq case, we do not know the extent to which the chairman of the JCS fulfilled his duties, as laid out in Section 153 of Title 10 of the U.S. Code, as the president's principal military advisor. But the combatant commander was intimately involved, as the Goldwater-Nichols Act of 1986 had envisioned. It is doubtful that Franks conceded on the biggest issues, though he may have been subject to persuasion, and his views aligned with those of his civilian masters. The military did not, in any case, provide or recommend an alternate solution that would have guaranteed victory.

Nevertheless, the myth of "dereliction" in Vietnam buttresses current critiques about both senior military leaders and civilian policymakers. It suggests to some that the military should be left alone and be allowed to fulfill the goals set by policymakers as they see fit, as the theory of objective control would have it if taken to its logical extreme. But what was required for Iraq was not greater leeway for the military's views about how to conduct the war, but greater understanding on the part of civilian policymakers about military power and what it could and could not accomplish, particularly with respect to the relatively complicated social, political, and economic goals on the ground. Similarly, there was a need for greater understanding on the part of senior military leaders about the real—and ultimately overriding—political realities in Iraq, in the region, and at home. Objective control is not a solution. Greater understanding on the part of both civilians and the military is. This is not a new task, but it is one that is likely to become more and more difficult to achieve in the future.

Notes

1. Congressional Research Service, "The Cost of Iraq, Afghanistan, and Other Global War on Terror Operations Since 9/11," July 16, 2007.
2. See William C. Martel, *Victory in War: Foundations of Modern Military Policy* (New York: Cambridge UP, 2007), esp. chs. 5 and 12.
3. Andrew Bacevich's *The New American Militarism: How Americans are Seduced by War* (New York: Oxford UP, 2005) is an important contribution on the militarization theme.
4. Michael C. Desch, "Bush and the Generals," *Foreign Affairs* (May/June 2007), p. 97.
5. H. R. McMaster, *Dereliction of Duty: Lyndon Johnson, Robert McNamara, the Joint Chiefs of Staff, and the Lies that Led to Vietnam* (New York: Harper Collins, 1997).
6. Desch, "Bush and the Generals," pp. 97–108.
7. Peter Feaver, *Armed Servants: Agency, Guardians, and Civil-Military Relations* (Cambridge, MA: Harvard UP, 2003), chs. 1 and 6 survey this literature thoroughly.
8. Frank Rich, "Who Really Took Over During That Colonoscopy?" *New York Times*, July 29, 2007, WK10.
9. Samuel Huntington, *The Soldier and the State: The Theory and Politics of Civil-Military Relations* (Cambridge, MA: Harvard UP, 1957), p. 20.
10. Desch, "Bush and the Generals," p. 97.
11. Eliot Cohen, *Supreme Command: Soldiers, Statesmen ,and Leadership in Wartime* (New York: The Free Press, 2002).
12. Desch, "Bush and the Generals," pp. 107–108.
13. Huntington, *Soldier and State*, p. 70 and note.
14. Huntington, *Soldier and State*, p. 71.
15. Huntington, *Solider and State*, p. 72.
16. Samuel Finer, *The Man on Horseback: The Role of the Military in Politics* (London: Pall Mall, 1962). See also Morris Janowitz, *The Professional Soldier* (New York: The Free Press, 1964); Yehuda Ben-Meir, *Civil-Military Relations in Israel* (New York: Columbia UP, 1995).
17. Huntington, *Solider and State*, p. 73.

18. Gregory Hooker, *Shaping the Plan for Operation Iraqi Freedom*, Military Research Paper No. 4 (Washington, D.C.: Washington Institute for Near East Policy, 2005).
19. Dwight D. Eisenhower, *Crusade in Europe* (New York: Doubleday, 1948), p. 225.
20. Bob Woodward, *Plan of Attack* (New York: Simon and Schuster, 2004), p. 26. Rumsfeld abstained, while Wolfowitz voted to invade Iraq, making the argument that there was between a 10 and 50 percent chance that Saddam was involved in the 9/11 attacks.
21. Woodward, *Plan of Attack*, pp. 1–5.
22. Ibid., pp. 38–43.
23. General Tommy Franks, *American Soldier* (New York: Regan Books, 2004), p. 333.
24. Ibid., pp. 335–40; Woodward, *Plan of Attack*, pp. 54–63.
25. Woodward, *Plan of Attack*, p. 101; see Franks, *American Soldier*, pp. 369–77.
26. Woodward, *Plan of Attack*, pp. 101–102.
27. Ibid., p. 152.
28. Woodward, *Plan of Attack*, pp. 147–52.
29. Franks, *American Soldier*, p. 416.
30. Woodward, *Plan of Attack*, p. 118.
31. Ibid., p. 6.
32. Ricks, *Fiasco, pp.* 32–5.
33. Ibid., pp. 70–1.
34. Ibid., p. 40.
35. Gregory Hooker, *Shaping the Plan for Operation Iraqi Freedom: The Role of Military Intelligence Assessments* (Washington, D.C.: Washington Institute for Near East Policy, 2005), xi.
36. Woodward, *Plan of Attack*, pp. 233–4.
37. Ibid., pp. 117–19.
38. Ricks, *Fiasco*, pp. 110–11.
39. On military planning and doctrine for postwar situations see Nadia Schadlow, "War and the Art of Governance," *Parameters* (Autumn 2003), pp. 85–94.
40. Ricks, *Fiasco*, p. 38.
41. Michael Gordon and Bernard Trainor, *Cobra II: The Inside Story of the Invasion and Occupation of Iraq* (New York: Pantheon Books, 2006), p. 529.
42. Ibid., pp. 568–9.
43. Zinni speech to 1st Marine Division, November 2002, in Ricks, *Fiasco*, p. 67.
44. Ricks, *Fiasco*, pp. 79–80.
45. Ibid., p. 97.
46. Woodward, *State of Denial*, pp. 129–30.
47. Michael Gordon, "Army Buried Study Faulting Iraq Planning," *New York Times*, February 11, 2008.
48. Andrew Bacevich, "Sychophant Savior," in *The American Conservative*, October 8, 2007, at http://www.amconmag.com/2007/2007_09_24/article2.html.
49. Harry Summers, *On Strategy II: A Critical Analysis of the Gulf War* (New York: Dell, 1992), p. 54.
50. Oral History of General Harold K. Johnson, May 21, 1973, p. 37.
51. See John Garofano, "Deciding on Military Intervention: What is the Role of Senior Military Leaders?" *Naval War College Review* 52:2 (Spring 2000), pp. 54–7.

6

Military Intervention and International Law

Isaiah Wilson III[1]

During the first decade of the twenty-first century, military force has occupied a central place in American foreign policy as the nation has confronted new threats, opportunities, and responsibilities resulting from globalization and other geopolitical shifts in the international environment.[2] Questions about whether and how to intervene militarily have become more important than ever.

Since the end of the Cold War, and certainly since the shock of 9/11, the United States has found itself faced with a "Goldilocks" dilemma—how to find that "just-right," or ethically just and legally right, answer to the operational questions of the day—that is, how to project and exercise military power in a manner that is effective, but just and lawful.

Recent U.S. interventions, particularly those related to "the war on terror," have come under increasing international scrutiny. Indeed, the United States is at risk of becoming a pariah in the eyes of many members of the international community, who perceive some U.S. actions as violations of international law and convention.

This chapter examines recent U.S. military interventions against three sets of criteria: (1) domestic, (2) international laws, and (3) international conventions—both standing and newly emergent.

The relationship between codified and conventional international law concerning right and proper intervention policy and practice is important for at least three reasons: (1) its effect on the perceived legitimacy or illegitimacy of intervention practices, (2) the preservation of the concept of the rule of law, and (3) the legitimacy of the nation-state international system itself.

International Law

Legal rules about the use of military force are a relatively recent development. Prior to the adoption of the United Nations (UN) Charter in 1945, international law imposed few binding constraints on the use of arms. In the nineteenth and early twentieth centuries, countries were bound only by their own choice and domestic law. Even then, they were bound only to those rules to which they were a signatory, either through formal treaty or through a consistent pattern of behavior that over time gave rise to what is today referred to as "customary international law."

The UN serves as the modern-day repository of the laws, norms, and rules defining right and just international intervention. The preamble to the UN Charter—an international treaty ratified by 192 countries—gives as the dominant and defining purpose of international intervention a determination to "save succeeding generations from the scourge of war."[3]

Customary international law is an unwritten body of rules that derives from a combination of state practices (precedents) and what is known as *opinion juris*, governments' beliefs that their conduct is obligated by international law. Again, this body of law is based on consent. Every action a state takes in accord with conventional international law validates and reinforces it. Still, a state may elect not to follow that law.

The second kind of international law derives from treaties—contracts that are entered into by two or more countries with the intent of creating binding rights and obligations and that are registered with a third party, typically the UN secretary-general.[4] For example, Article 2(4) of the UN Charter limits rightful intervention as follows:

> All Members shall refrain in their international relations from the threat or use of force against the territorial integrity or political independence of any state, or in any other manner inconsistent with the Purposes of the United Nations.[5]

Consistent with the "Purposes of the United Nations" are special rules (*jus cogens* rules), which include prohibitions on genocide, slavery, and torture.[6] Overall, the ordinary meaning of Article 2(4) is clear: the use of force across borders is not permitted, with the jus cogens rules as exceptions along with two additional exceptions: (a) authorization by the UN Security Council and (b) the dominant doctrine of self-defense, the latter stipulated in Article 51 of the Charter:

> Nothing in the present Charter shall impair the inherent right of individual or collective self-defence if an armed attack occurs against a Member of the United Nations, until the Security Council has taken measures necessary to maintain international peace and security.[7]

In addition to customary law governing recourse to force, there are rules relating to the application of force. The four Geneva conventions of 1949 are treaties that establish what has come to be regarded as the Law of War, Law of Armed Conflict, and/or International Humanitarian Law. International humanitarian law establishes specific categories of individuals—combatants and noncombatants—and sets rules for their protection, as well as defines the legal and rightful actions they can take. This law prescribes a bright dividing line between the protected person (namely, noncombatant civilians and special-category military personnel such as medics) and lawful combatants (e.g., soldiers). There is no discussion of any third category such as unlawful enemy combatants.

Traditional Norms Related to Armed Intervention

Over the centuries, Western philosophers and theologians have developed criteria for differentiating just from unjust wars. These criteria originated in the fourth-century writings of St. Ambrose and St. Augustine and were further developed by St. Thomas Aquinas in the thirteenth century and by a variety of other writers up through the present day. The Treaty of Westphalia (1648) codified many of the just war principles. This may have been as important as its other primary function, the establishment of the nation-state as the primary actor on the world stage and the agreement that it, the nation-state, would enjoy sovereignty.

Recent Challenges to International and Traditional Law

The post–Cold War period has proven to be a period of widespread ethnic-religious-cultural conflict that neither states nor nonstate actors have been able to contain. The interventions in Somalia in 1992 and 1993, and in Rwanda's genocide in 1993 and 1994, are two examples of a failure to resolve conflict through intervention.

Since 9/11, the international community has had to confront the rise of transnational terrorists. It has also been challenged to accommodate developing norms and obligations related to such things as human security, self-determination, and human rights.

As a hegemon of the prevailing international system, the United States is not merely a player on the stage of international affairs; it also shapes and defines the system. What it does and how it does it matter—for better or worse.

U.S. military interventions since 1989 have fostered changes in the international system. They have challenged traditional norms, principles, rules, and decision-making procedures that have provided stability to the system for the past sixty years. In particular, U.S. interventions have challenged what was once considered inviolable—territorial sovereignty.

An Emergent Norm

While the 1990s have seen a decline in interstate wars, there has been a rise in internal conflicts, and, importantly, an increase in the internationalization of these internal conflicts. In fact, the defining feature of many of the military interventions of the 1990s—Somalia, the Balkans, Haiti, Rwanda, Kosovo, East Timor, and others—has been intervention against sovereign states on behalf of citizens and communities within those states. Thus, the inviolability of state territorial sovereignty has unraveled, in part through a combination of changes in the international security system, but also at the hands of interveners among whom the United States was a lead participant.

Indeed, it has become apparent that the United States has had a profound effect on the destabilization of the international system and that it has challenged the traditional legal and normative international regimes that have defined the obligations—and limits—of right and just intervention for a half century.

Recently, the United States claimed an exemption to Article 2(4) prohibitions. It has asserted the right to preemptive or "anticipatory military action"—as demonstrated in the 2003 intervention/invasion of Iraq. U.S.-led interventions in Grenada (1983) and Panama (1989) were at least implicit assertions of a right to intervene militarily to restore democracy. The UN Security Council's establishment of no-fly zones in northern and southern Iraq (1991) and during the Kosovo War (1999–2000) are also precedents for a justification on the grounds of universal humanitarian rights.

In 1998 and 2001, the United States invoked self-defense to justify military action in Afghanistan and Sudan following terrorist attacks against U.S. targets. These military interventions have also had a significant effect on the norm of state sovereignty.

The Goldilocks dilemma facing the United States and the international community today involves reconciling these new justifications for intervention with the traditional norms that focused on checking territorial aggressions by asserting near-absolute state sovereignty. It is unclear whether or not U.S. actions will establish new norms for intervention by other powers or whether the past twenty years will be considered a historical anomaly. One thing that is for certain is that the United States has simultaneously been challenging other countries' sovereignty and reinforcing its own sovereignty—for example, by withdrawing from treaties like the Anti-Ballistic Missile (ABM) Treaty or refusing to sign new ones (e.g., the Mine Ban Treaty, the Kyoto Protocol, or the Rome Statute of the International Criminal Court).

Reconsidering the Case of (for) Iraq

Is the current Iraq war a legal war? Was it an ethical and just intervention? This is not only an important question for the international state system; it is also important to the morale of troops prosecuting the war. Troops need to believe that their duties are right as well as important.

There are three traditional bases for the use of force: self-defense (which may include collective self-defense); averting an overwhelming humanitarian catastrophe; and authorization by the Security Council acting under Chapter VII of the UN Charter.

Force may be used in self-defense if there is an actual or imminent threat of an armed attack. Force must also be necessary—that is, the only means of averting an attack. Further, it must be a proportionate response. In a letter of advice[8] given to former British prime minister Tony Blair, dated March 7, 2003, then Attorney General Lord Goldsmith described regime change in Iraq as a disproportionate response to Saddam Hussein's alleged failure to disarm, and illegal in the eyes of international law. Goldsmith stressed that in terms of legality, "regime change could not be the objective of the military action." Lord Goldsmith acknowledged the United States' argument for recognition of a broader doctrine of a right to use force to preempt a future grave and growing danger, but voiced his opinion to Blair that if what the United States sought implied more than a right to respond proportionately to an imminent attack, such a doctrine did not exist and such use of force would not be recognized in international law. This view may represent the bulk of world public opinion.

Force may be used where it is authorized by the UN Security Council acting under Chapter VII of the UN Charter. The key question here was whether resolution 1441 had the effect of providing such an authorization. Many legal scholars question whether UN RES 1441 was an adequate authorization for this intervention.[9]

The lawfulness of the military action in Iraq also depends on the question of proportionality. According to many legal experts, force used pursuant to the authorization in resolution 678 would have to:

- have as its objective the enforcement of the cease-fire contained in resolution 687 (1990) and subsequent relevant resolutions;
- be limited to what is necessary to achieve that objective; and
- be a proportionate response to that objective—that is, securing compliance with Iraq's disarmament obligations.

In this sense, the military action taken to remove Saddam Hussein could be deemed legal if and only if it could be demonstrated that it was a necessary and proportionate measure for securing the disarmament of Iraq. While it is still a point of debate, many argue that "regime change" could not rightly be the objective of military action.

The Legal Rightness and Ethical Justness
"In the Wake of War" ~ Jus Post Bellum[10]

President Bush's May 1, 2003, declaration of the end of hostilities in Iraq and UN Security Council resolution 1483 of May 22, 2003, made the United States and the United Kingdom (UK) the belligerent occupants of Iraq subject to a host of obligations. These derived from the four Geneva conventions of 1949, the 1907 Hague Regulations on land warfare, U.S. Army Field Manual 27-10 (1956) or its British equivalent, the humanitarian provisions of Additional Protocol I of 1977 to the four Geneva conventions of 1949, and the customary international laws of war.

In effect, the United States and the UK pledged to the Security Council that "the States participating in the Coalition would strictly abide by their obligations under international law, including those relating to the essential humanitarian needs of the people of Iraq."[11] This, as Rear Admiral (U.S. Navy chaplain) Louis V. Iasiello has noted, adds up to new obligations for an intervention force (the "belligerent occupant"):

> From war's inception (jus ad bellum) and throughout its prosecution (jus in bello), the goal of all should be the establishment of a just and lasting peace. Therefore, the long-term consequences of even a justified use of force require that just intention extend into the post bellum stage, thus demanding our consideration of a third category of just war theory (jus post bellum). As recent events in Afghanistan and Iraq attest, nations must fight wars with a war-termination vision and plan carefully for the post-conflict phase.[12]

The state of affairs in Iraq at the time of this writing (fall 2007) is a tragic testament to the fact that this proposition is increasingly proving relevant.

The Future of Military Intervention and International Law and Ethics

The United States has come to the conclusion that today's problem is not powerful states but weak states and the instability that emanates from them. In the 2002 National Security Strategy, President George W. Bush turned realism on its head—"America is now threatened less by conquering states than we are by failing ones."[13] The problem is that while military intervention has proven to be an effective instrument for regime change, it has not always been able to create a strong and stable state.

Since the formal articulation of the Bush Doctrine,[14] the United States has been waging a "War on Terror." Unfortunately, in war-torn societies, U.S. actions have sometimes done as much to decrease security and stability as to increase them. This makes it imperative that the United States consider and evaluate the sometimes *pyrrhic*[15] nature of its past, recent, and ongoing interventions.

Conclusion

In some noteworthy instances, U.S. actions have failed the nation's (and "Westphalia's") long-standing tests. On the other hand, global security realities and new norms may call for military intervention not only to help failing and failed states but also—by restoring/imposing order—to protect local populations and fledgling democracies from their own militaries and security forces, as well as from external forces.[16]

It appears that resolute and effective international interventions may sometimes be necessary to ensure the protection of societies and human security worldwide. However, grave questions about the legality and legitimacy of such actions arise when sovereignty is violated. The international community is damned if it does intervene and damned if it does not. The imperative of finding a new "just-and-right" solution to the Goldilocks dilemma of maintaining established international law and norms in the face of new calls for military intervention could not be more clearly evident.

Appendix

Table 6.1   U.S.-Led Intervention in Iraq, 2003 to Present: Legal and Just?

	U.S.-led Intervention in Iraq	Implications "beyond" Iraq
Legal Grounds?	■ Legal, if considered as an extension of the 1990 Gulf War intervention; Questionable legality, if considered as a unique military intervention. ■ Violation of 1907 Hague Convention (Opening of Hostilities) ■ Violation of Nuremburg Charter (Crime against Peace)	■ The "customary" nature of international law and convention should be considered by the United States even when written and codified law fails to outright prohibit unilateral interpretations of the law and unilateral actions and practices based on these interpretations. As the leader of the nation-state-based international order, the United States should consider the "spirit of the laws" and its responsibilities to the security of the international system as well as its own national security interests.
Grounds of Jus ad Bellum? (six criteria)	1. *Legitimate Authority?* Weakness of U.S. claim as the primary legitimate authority (at best, fifth or sixth in hierarchy of legitimacy—unanimous international commitment, UN decision, UN Security Council decision, other regional or international alliance) 2. *Public Declaration?* Met by President Bush statement on 19 March 2003 for Saddam Hussein to 'stand down' 3. *Just Intent?* Questionable. Debate tilts on question of "imminence" of the threat ('clear and present threat versus a 'grave and growing' danger) 4. *Proportionality?* Questionable, based on traditional criteria of proportionality which imply a "response-based" determination 5. *Last Resort?* Questionable and ambiguous 6. *Reasonable Hope of Success?* Questionable and ambiguous	■ Could there be more legitimacy to be gained by the United States in its own unilateral actions by proceeding through supranational bodies of legal and ethical decision making? ■ In a globalized (and information-based) world environment, is there a "broader General Public" to which leaders of nation-states must declare their intent to intervene? ■ Have technological advances in the instrumentality of war once again outpaced and outmoded the capacity of nation-states to "command and control" intervention practices holding them obedient to normative and legal rules and requirements for "just intervention"? If so, is there a new legitimate need to reconsider the adequacy of a rule-set governing international intervention that is still based on a prohibition on interventions short of a clear and imminent threat? ■ If jus post bellum obligations are increasingly justifying international interventions, what relevance does the traditional criterion of "Last Resort" have on postmodern-age intervention? ■ If jus post bellum obligations now dominate, how must "success" be reconsidered?
Grounds of Jus in Bello?	A mixed record	

Notes

1. The views expressed in this article are the author's own, and do not reflect the policies or judgments of the Department of Defense, the U.S. Army, the United States Military Academy, the National War College, or any other government organization.

2. For relevant strategic assessment studies, see The Development, Concepts and Doctrine Centre (DCDC), *Strategic Trends Programme, 2007–2036*, United Kingdom Ministry of Defence, 3rd ed., 2007; Stephen J. Flanagan, Ellen L. Frost, and Richard L. Kugler, "Challenges of the Global Century: Report of the Project on Globalization and National Security," *Institute for National Strategic Studies (INSS)*, National Defense University, 2001; Christopher J. Bowie, Robert P. Haffa, Jr., and Robert E. Mullins, "*Future War: Future War:* What Trends in America's Post-Cold War Military Conflicts Tell Us About Early 21st Century Warfare," Analysis Center Papers, Northrop-Grumman Corporation, January 2003; *The Global Century: Globalization and National Security*, National Defense University, available at http://www.ndu.edu

3. Charter of the United Nations available at http://www.un.org/aboutun/charter/, accessed October 8, 2007.

4. Michael Byers, *War Law: Understanding International Law and Armed Conflict* (New York: Grove Press, 2005), 4.

5. UN Charter, as cited in Inis L. Claude, *Swords into Plowshares* (New York: Random House, 1964), pp. 419, 427–429.

6. Byers, *War Law,* p. 6.

7. Ibid., p. 7.

8. Marie Wolfe, "The Legality of War: Regime Change Is No Basis for War, Remember?" *London Independent*, April 29, 2005.

9. For example, according to University of Illinois law professor Francis Boyle, the U.S. war in Iraq fails the legal war test on several counts, including the following: (a) it is in violation of the customary international laws of war set forth in the 1907 Hague Convention on the Opening of Hostilities to which the United States is still a contracting party, as evidenced by paragraphs 20, 21, 22, and 23 of U.S. Army Field Manual 27-10 (1956); (b) the war against Iraq constituted a Crime against Peace as defined by the Nuremberg Charter (1945), the Nuremberg Judgment (1946), and the Nuremberg Principles (1950), as well as by paragraph 498 of the U.S. Army Field Manual 27-10 (1956).

10. A major source document used in this consideration of jus post bellum principles is "Jus Post Bellum: The Moral Responsibilities of Victors in War," by Rear Admiral Louis V. Iasiello, Chaplain Corps, U.S. Navy, *Naval War College Review* 57, no. 3/4 (Summer/Autumn 2004).

11. Louis V. Iasiello, *Naval War College Review*, September 22, 2004.

12. Ibid., p. 39.

13. Office of the Chairman of the Joint Chiefs of Staff, *The National Military Strategy of the United States of America*, (Washington, D.C.), March 27, 2002.

14. Term attributed to the tenets of U.S. security policy speaking to no safe harbor to terrorist organizations and the legitimacy of preventive war and preemptive attacks in light of "grave and growing dangers" to national security as opposed to traditional "clear and present danger" (imminent danger) triggers.

15. A reference to King Pyrrus's campaign against the Romans. Under Pyrrus's leadership, the Hellenic city-states successfully defeated the "weaker" Roman foe in nearly every battle, yet in spite of these victories, the Greeks lost the wider war against the Romans. This led King Pyrrus himself to state, "Another victory like this and we will be completely undone."

16. Paul Collier, *The Bottom Billion: Why the Poorest Countries are Failing and What Can Be Done About It* (New York: Oxford University Press, 2007), pp. 124–134.

7

Problem Definition in Foreign and Security Policy

Russell A. Burgos

Paratroopers from the army's 82nd Airborne Division patrolled the streets, warily checking windows after reports of gunfire, looting, and anarchy. The "presence patrols," one officer told a reporter, were intended to demonstrate to local residents that the U.S. government was actively undertaking measures to promote their security and to bring stability to their city. Though the streets were in New Orleans's French Quarter, they could just as easily have been in Baghdad's Adhamiya district. In spite of the distance between the two cities and the fact they are embedded in quite different political contexts, they shared an important quality—both were defined as *military* problems and so required *military* solutions.

Since the end of the Cold War, security scholars and practitioners have debated the use of armed forces for missions that do not involve their core function—to close with and destroy other armed forces. While some policymakers called for a conservative approach to the use of American military power based upon a careful calculation of the national interest (often called the "Powell Doctrine" after then chairman of the Joint Chiefs of Staff [JCS] Colin S. Powell), others sought to apply military instruments of power to an increasing range of nontraditional missions. As former secretary of state Madeleine K. Albright put it, what was "the point of having this superb military you're always talking about if we can't use it?"[1] These competing views reflect a tension inherent in any decision to use force: While military professionals carry out the missions, civilian elites *define* what the missions will be.[2] That tension leads to an analytical puzzle: How do political elites decide that the military is the appropriate institution for one policy problem or another? Such decisions are often controversial. Since comparatively few civilian policymakers are vested in the nuances of strategic and operational arts, they tend to see problems and opportunities in political terms, yet in colloquial American political discourse, there are few things worse than "playing politics" with questions of security policy.

In this chapter, I join recent calls for scholars of security policy to apply to that puzzle an analytical paradigm more familiar to scholars of public policy.[3] The "problem-definition paradigm" treats security policy as public policy—no less subject to political challenge, compromise, and bargaining than any other kind of policy. Political elites seek to define and redefine problems in specific ways so that they can implement their own favored solutions for those problems. To understand that definitional process, we must analyze the strategic use of language in security policymaking. We can explain the decision to apply military force, rather than some other instrument of national power, by looking at the ways in which security policy problems are defined by political elites.

Traditional theories of international relations deny that language matters in the "high politics" of war and peace. There, the decision to use force is a function of the structure of the international system, systemic "rules of the game," and a country's capabilities and position in the system. Though analytically tidy, the empirical record calls that logic into question—the United States has often used military force when neither its survival nor its vital interests were at stake.[4] Jutta Weldes argues that interests are not fixed, but are "historically contingent and culturally specific."[5] *Interests* and *problems* are interests and problems because someone in power says they are. In other words, particular actors base their definitions of interests upon particular interpretations of events at particular times. Therefore, scholars should analyze how policymakers define what constitutes an appropriate occasion for the use of force. The decision to deploy military power is an artifact of the way a problem is defined.

Consider the problem of international terrorism. To many policymakers today it seems obvious that the United States should use military force to *defeat* terrorism, but that was not always the case. For thirty years prior to 9/11, the United States treated terrorism as a social and law enforcement problem—it was something to be "controlled," not defeated.[6] Since 9/11, however, terrorism has been redefined as a military problem—as something to be defeated, not controlled. Redefining the problem redefined the solution. There is, in short, a necessary relationship between the rhetorical framing of security problems and the solutions that are proposed to meet them. The problem-definition paradigm seeks to unpack that relationship analytically. At its core is a dynamic interaction between policy ideas and political institutions, a two-level game in which political elites first compete to define the meaning of some event in the international system and then compete to enact their preferred policy for that event.[7]

The first game is inherently *ideational*—it is based upon competing understandings of what does or does not constitute a threat to American security. The second game is inherently *institutional*—it is "political" (in the colloquial sense of the term) and depends not only upon the fact that the military has the institutional capacity to perform a wide range of missions, but also upon the coalition-building, bargaining, and compromise we expect to see in domestic policymaking. It treats foreign and security policy as *politics*—competition by actors with varying endowments of power to direct the instruments of the state to some end of their choosing. Those engaged in this competition very likely have differential power endowments—some are in power and some are out of power. Those in power seek to defend a policy status quo in which they are vested, while those out-side of power seek to challenge and replace it. Therefore, we can analyze security policy change as competition between groups—those that have *situational* power, or the power to control the instruments of state, and those that seek *definitional* power, or the power to impart meaning to events in world politics.

Problem Definition and Policymaking

There is a large body of research on problem definition in public policy.[8] Here I provide only a brief introduction to key terms and concepts and illustrate them with a case study. Scholars trace the paradigm to E. E. Schattschneider's observa-tion that "the definition of alternatives is the supreme instrument of power."[9] In other words, the goal is to define what politics will be *about*—what the state will (or will not) do about some problem. As the sociologist Robert Merton put it, "The same . . . condition will be defined by some as a social problem and by others as an agreeable and fitting state of affairs."[10] Those with situational power have an obvious advantage. Scholars of social movements, for example, note how difficult it is for minorities or other "outsiders" to get politicians to attend to issues that concern them. Those who wish to change the policy status quo must therefore acquire definitional power—they must, in other words, be able to define what policy will be about.

Instead of rational choices based upon objective evaluations of the international system, security policies are "constructed"—that is, produced by rhetorical strategies that define some problem as being of Type A rather than of Type B. The specific definition matters because every problem definition carries with it a prescription for one solution rather than another.[11] In fact, this paradigm might more accurately be called "solution promotion," because the objective of those who seek to redefine policy is not simply to name a problem, but to name the solution. The dynamics of security policy change hinge, therefore, on *how* challenges to U.S. security are defined and *by whom*—those who prefer a more assertive American presence in the international system, for example, will tend to define more things as being "military" problems.

Terms. The *policy agenda* consists of those issues that have attracted government attention; some are enduring (e.g., highways and taxation), while others come and go as events dictate. The agenda also includes the solutions (or *policies*) the government has defined as appropriate for those issues. *Agenda setting* is a "pre-decisional process" of political *contestation* by different groups to define those problems and solutions.[12] That contestation takes place through the use of language and *symbols*.[13] The strategic use of such symbols is *framing*, or imparting meaning to the outside world. Limiting access to the agenda is one goal of a *policy monopoly*, which controls both the "political understandings concerning the policy of interest" and the "institutional arrangements" that are "responsible for policymaking."[14] The goal of a *policy entrepreneur* is to break that monopoly and institutionalize his or her preferred policy solution in its place. The principal actors in the process of foreign and security policymaking are the president and his leading civilian and military advisors; members of Congress associated with the armed services and foreign affairs committees; foreign affairs analysts at Washington, D.C.-based think tanks; and commentators in the national media.[15]

Process. Assume there exists some *policy status quo* in the United States' strategic interaction with some other country and assume that there are policy entrepreneurs outside of government who are dissatisfied with that status quo. To redirect policy, they must first redefine the meaning of the interaction by demonstrating the superiority of their understanding of the problem (definitional power). They must then build alliances with elites in government who can carry their new definition into political debates over the policy status quo and, ultimately, redirect the instruments of state applied to that interaction (situational power). Scholars refer to the second step as "venue shopping"—a "dual strategy of presentation of images and the search for a more receptive political" environment for those images—and both the ideational and institutional games are necessary for explaining policy change.[16] According to the political scientist Jeffrey Legro, a policy is "ripe" for being overturned when the expectations it creates about world order are no longer borne out by events in the international system—when it no longer "fits" with what observers see happening around them.[17] However, the principal challenge for scholars is not to show that other policy ideas existed "out there," but to explain both why political actors adopted a particular set of ideas and why those ideas prevailed in the public sphere.[18] A problem-definition analysis does both.

From a problem-definition perspective, foreign and security policy is no different from domestic policy. Traditional theories of international relations assume that, in an anarchic international system, the state is always at risk. But the greater a state's range of capabilities—diplomatic, economic, and military—the greater the range of potential strategies it has for managing that risk. Why, then, turn to military instruments of power? If some elites prefer military power—for ideological or instrumental reasons—they may well seek to redefine an increasing number of problems as being "military problems." To do so, they engage in the politics of problem definition. This was the case with U.S. policy towards Iraq during the 1990s. Containment, the policy status quo, was an inherently diplomatic approach to managing regional stability. A group of policy entrepreneurs—known (somewhat incorrectly) as the "neoconservatives"—preferred a more assertive policy aimed at ousting Saddam Hussein. That preference was embedded not only in their particular understanding of the regime, but also in a particular set of beliefs about the utility of military power. The remainder of this chapter will illustrate the process described above and will show how the "Iraq Problem" was redefined in the 1990s.

The Rhetorical Construction of the Iraqi Threat

After Saddam's defeat in 1991, American policymakers assumed that the Iraqi military would overthrow him, as it had done with past leaders who failed in military adventures.[19] Muddling through the costs, benefits, and likely outcomes of a more assertive U.S. policy in the Persian Gulf, the George H. W. Bush administration chose containment largely because it was there—containment was, in essence, an accidental strategy.[20] However, once containment became the status quo for promoting regional security, both George H. W. Bush and Bill Clinton committed themselves to it. The United States would not overtly seek to topple Saddam, assuming instead that if economic sanctions bit hard enough, someone in Iraq would undo him. Memoirs from the George H. W. Bush administration are remarkably consistent on this point—U.S. policymakers had neither the political mandate nor the political will to overthrow, occupy, and recreate the Iraqi state.[21] As then Secretary of Defense Dick Cheney put it several years later, "Saddam is just one irritant [in] a long list of irritants in that part of the world."[22]

However, some lower-ranking administration officials in the departments of Defense and State and hawkish journalists in the national media rejected the reasoning behind containment, including "neoconservatives" like Richard Perle and Paul Wolfowitz. Unlike traditional balance-of-power realists, they rejected containment as being both strategically and morally flawed and inappropriate for a Great Power like the United States.[23] Perle and Wolfowitz, along with journalists like Jim Hoagland, A. M. Rosenthal, and William Safire, were among the first political elites to call for Saddam's ouster and would comprise the core of a group of policy entrepreneurs who sought to redefine Iraq policy during the 1990s.[24] Their strategy, as predicted by problem-definition analysis, was to refocus the Iraq policy debate on their construction of Saddam's regime as a clear and present danger to U.S. security, requiring Saddam's ouster for its successful resolution.

From 1991 to 1997, proponents of regime change waged a media campaign, publishing scores of editorials and essays challenging the utility and efficacy of containment and painting a dire picture of Saddam's regime. Because their editorials were printed in the nation's most influential newspapers—the *New York Times* and the *Washington Post*—regime change gradually acquired a veneer of legitimacy and enhanced the policy entrepreneurs' definitional power. Their rhetorical strategy was to simultaneously challenge the legitimacy of Clinton administration policy towards Iraq (attacking both containment and Clinton) and promote the notion that "only" regime change would "solve" Saddam's growing threat to U.S. security.[25] Instead of focusing on systemic structure or Iraq's traditional goal of regional hegemony, they focused on regime type; Saddam was the problem, not Iraq.

Regime change resonated as an idea in part because it was premised upon a simple causal logic: Saddam is the problem, get rid of Saddam, problem solved. One reason the Clinton administration struggled to defend containment was that—despite the assumptions of policymakers in the first Bush administration—in practice the strategy was remarkably complex. Containment depended upon sustaining support for the weapons inspections and sanctions regimes within the United Nations (UN) Security Council, which meant that American security policy was effectively subject to the preferences of three veto players—China, France, and Russia—whose interests were seldom aligned with those of the United States. The strategy floated on a complex diplomatic web—bilateral relations with each Security Council member, the UN, Gulf Arab states, and, of course, Iraq. Any one of those strategic interactions was sufficient to undermine the strategy, and by 1997 all were in play. Proponents of regime change challenged the appropriateness of subjecting American security to the votes of "foreigners," and could point to the recurring series of Saddam's challenges to his "box" as evidence that containment was strategically insufficient.

In 1994, Saddam made a visible show of again threatening Kuwait, deploying forty thousand troops to his southern border. In 1995, his son-in-law, Lieutenant-General Kamel Hussein, defected to Jordan and made the startling announcement that Iraq was secretly *expanding* its weapons of mass destruction (WMD) program in spite of UN sanctions, lending credence to claims that containment would not put an end to Saddam's ambitions.[26] In 1996, Saddam successfully ousted regime opponents, including Ahmed Chalabi's Iraqi National Congress, from the so-called northern safe haven where they were operating under U.S. protection. And in 1998, the UN weapons inspections functionally came to an end, leaving Saddam's presumed WMD program unchecked. What was known about that program at the time disturbed both supporters of containment and supporters of regime change.

From 1991 to 1994, the International Atomic Energy Agency (IAEA) had discovered, and dismantled, a formerly unknown nuclear weapons program—thus validating claims that Saddam could secretly reconstitute such programs.[27] By 1995, UN teams searching for biological and chemical weapons concluded that Iraq still had active programs.[28] Iraqi officials admitted to producing a number of weaponized toxins, including nineteen thousand liters of botulinum toxin, eight thousand liters of anthrax, and two thousand liters of aflatoxin. Iraqis also admitted to having produced four tons of VX nerve agent and thirty-nine tons of VX chemical precursors in violation of the sanctions regime.[29] In other words, despite seven years of sanctions, there was evidence that containment was not achieving its intended goals.

As Legro's model would predict, because containment no longer "fit" events in the material world, the Iraq problem was ripe for redefinition. Policy entrepreneurs took every opportunity to do so. Not only did the *New York Times*, the *Wall Street Journal*, and the *Washington Post* regularly print their essays, but so too did conservative magazines like the *National Review*, the *American Spectator*, and the *Weekly Standard*. With titles like "We Must Lead the Way in Deposing Saddam," "Overthrow Him," and "Crank Up Now to Bury Saddam," these articles made no attempt to disguise their strategic objectives. Clinton, they argued, was "retreating" from Saddam, and containment lacked the power, the aggressiveness, and even the causal logic necessary to prevent such a retreat.[30] Like Neville Chamberlain at Munich, Clinton was giving the strategic initiative to Saddam. This campaign so successfully redefined Iraq policy that the Clinton administration itself adopted its rivals' language simply because it so dominated the policy discourse.

For example, by 1994, neoconservatives, hawkish journalists, and Republicans started dismissing containment's tit-for-tat coercive retaliation as "mere pinpricks" that had no effect on Saddam's strategic calculations or capabilities.

That pejorative term "pinprick" became so closely identified with containment that Secretary of Defense William Cohen and General Anthony Zinni, the commander of U.S. Central Command (CENTCOM), both used it in Senate testimony, promising that there would be "no more pinpricks" on their watch. Though the administration dispatched its foreign policy leaders on a talking tour to defend containment—the United States would maintain containment "for as long as it takes," Albright said, because it was the "best" strategy available—their case was substantially weakened by their own adoption of rival claims about the seriousness of the Iraqi threat.[31] In November 1997, for example, Cohen claimed that Saddam had enough anthrax to "kill millions" and that he could "quickly reconstitute" such programs even if attacked by the United States. He later sat for a television interview to discuss the possibility that Saddam "could kill everyone on Earth with his chemical weapons arsenal."[32] By accepting rival definitions of the problem and rival claims about the nature of the Iraqi threat, the Clinton administration itself made much of the case for replacing containment.

Once proponents of regime change successfully redefined the Iraqi threat, they turned their attention to acquiring situational power by playing to the Republican majority on Capitol Hill and moved debate from the editorial pages to Congress. In other words, they achieved the venue access necessary for redefining policy. Republicans on Capitol Hill, eager to score points against President Clinton, adopted regime change and began promoting it in a series of symbolic legislative acts and carefully constructed public hearings designed to bring as much discredit upon containment as possible.[33] The hearings made little pretense of being objective forums for policy analysis; witness lists were heavily slanted in favor of regime-change proponents. For example, on October 8, 1998, the House's Committee on International Relations held hearings titled "The Foreign Policy of the Clinton Administration," and the only witnesses were Republicans or neoconservatives—L. Paul Bremer III, John R. Bolton, Kim Holmes of the Heritage Foundation, Peter Rodman of the Nixon Center, and Representative Ben Gilman of New York, a leading proponent of ousting Saddam. As was true of other hearings held to "evaluate" Clinton's Iraq policy, the day's message was dire—Saddam was "winning" and only a significant policy change would turn back the threat to U.S. security.

Republican legislative activity, while often symbolic and not always successful, simply added to the impression that the ground was shifting away from containment. Senate Concurrent Resolution 71 urged the president to develop a "policy aimed at *definitively ending* the threat to international peace and security posed by the government of Iraq and its weapons of mass destruction programs (emphasis added)."[34] Senate Resolution 179 demanded that Clinton "devise a long-term plan . . . for the removal of Saddam Hussein." House Resolution 3599 sought to ban contributions to the International Monetary Fund (IMF) unless Iraq was denied access to all IMF programs. House Joint Resolution 125 declared Iraq to be in "material breach" of Security Council Resolution 687, a legal maneuver that, if taken literally, would have ended the 1991 cease-fire, effectively restarting Desert Storm. New York Representative Benjamin Gilman later introduced House Resolution 4655, the Iraq Liberation Act, resolving that "it should be the policy of the United States to support efforts to remove the regime headed by Saddam Hussein from power in Iraq."[35] The House passed the measure on October 5, and Senate Majority Leader Trent Lott called for quick approval as "a strong demonstration of Congressional support for a new policy toward Iraq—a policy that overtly seeks the replacement of Saddam Hussein's regime."[36] Carefully constructed hearings, legislative action, and a constant rhetorical drumbeat in favor of regime change, coupled with events in Iraq and the sudden resignation of the leading U.S. weapons inspector in Iraq, lent credence to the new construction of Iraq as a clear and present danger.

The Apotheosis of Scott Ritter

In January 1998, Iraq demanded that all Americans be removed from UN Special Commission (UNSCOM) weapons inspection teams, accusing them of espionage; instead, the UN simply withdrew all teams. Secretary-General Kofi Annan brokered a deal in February that would permit a limited return of the inspectors but that would also preserve Iraq's "dignity," causing outrage in Republican circles.[37] Annan's "sell-out" proved that containment could do nothing to forestall an Iraqi victory over the West, they said.[38] A. M. Rosenthal, executive editor of the *New York Times*, accused Clinton of avoiding "what [he] knows is the *only solution*: the overthrow of Saddam" (emphasis added).[39] And if final proof were needed for those still sitting on the fence in terms of changing policy, it came in the form of a public repudiation of containment by an unlikely figure, William "Scott" Ritter. Ritter, a Marine Reserve major, had the reputation of being one of the UN's toughest inspectors. With no obvious political affiliation or ambition, he became the poster child for regime change in Iraq.

Ritter publicly resigned from UNSCOM on August 26, 1998, claiming that he had been "on the doorstep" of Saddam's secret WMD program and charged that the UN secretary-general and the Clinton administration "stymied" his teams.[40] Ritter essentially claimed that Clinton and Annan were conspiring to move Iraq off the foreign policy agenda, creating only the "illusion of arms control."[41] Clinton's policy, he declared, was a "sham that will almost certainly play right into Saddam Hussein's hands."[42] According to Ritter, the Clinton administration so desperately wanted to maintain containment that Albright, National Security Advisor Samuel Berger, and others deliberately undermined the inspectors for fear they would discover valid reasons for going to war. Facing impeachment, the argument went, Clinton did not want to risk further political jeopardy by confronting Saddam resolutely. Rhetoricians use the term "synecdoche" to describe those phrases we commonly use to represent some larger concept—"the White House," for example, is a synecdoche for a president or a presidential administration. For those who wanted to redirect Iraq policy, "Scott Ritter" instantly became a synecdoche for what they said was Clinton's failure to stop the growing Iraqi threat.[43]

House Speaker Newt Gingrich used Ritter's resignation to launch what the *Washington Post* called "a concerted Republican attack on the Clinton administration's Iraq policy."[44] Again, the administration helped make its rivals' case for them.

Rather than engaging the substance of Ritter's charges, the White House and its congressional supporters attacked him personally, virtually ensuring that Republicans would take his charges even more seriously.[45] CBS News reported that the Federal Bureau of Investigation (FBI) had been ordered to open an espionage investigation against Ritter after he first met with reporters.[46] Senate Democrats challenged his competence for rendering judgments on the high politics of security policy, with Senator Joseph Biden scolding "Scotty-boy" for thinking "above [his] pay grade." Albright dismissed Ritter as simply being too obtuse to "get" the "big picture."[47] That strategy, like Ritter's resignation, was made-to-order for those promoting regime change. A *New York Times* editorial denounced the administration's strategy of trying to "discredit and intimidate Scott Ritter" as "repugnant," and George Will described the administration's response as a "low, dishonest moment in our nation's life." In the *Washington Post*, Biden was compelled to write a public apology for attacking Ritter; the hawkish columnist Charles Krauthammer, another regime-change proponent, lambasted the administration for "trashing" Ritter after he "blew the whistle" on "Albright's surrender to Saddam"; and Fred Hiatt, editor of the *Post*'s editorial pages, lamented Ritter's "betrayal" as a "new low" even for the "Clintonites."[48]

By the end of 1998, the politics of containment were in tatters. Those seeking to redefine Iraq as a clear and present danger, requiring a new, military-centered response, could point to the empirical record to support their contention that Saddam had the upper hand and could secretly reconstitute WMD. Rather than review containment's efficacy or engage the substance of its opponents' case, the Clinton administration chose instead to defend the policy by attacking critics and by attempting to co-opt their arguments by incorporating the central tenets of their case into their justification for containment. Proponents could muster an impressive array of statistics, media and UN reports, and congressional testimony by "experts" to demonstrate the merits of their case—Iraq was a threat, containment was failing, and only the use of military power to oust Saddam could ensure American security. The president was unable to defend containment even within his own party. Liberal Democrats attacked it for punishing ordinary Iraqis for Saddam's crimes, while hawkish Democrats joined Republicans in claiming it was not tough enough. Nebraska Senator Bob Kerrey told a journalist, "We've got to change [our] objective in Iraq and say that we're going to try to replace this dictatorship with a democracy."[49] Fellow Democrat John Kerry not only supported a public declaration of regime change as U.S. policy, but also proposed that the United States covertly deploy special operations forces throughout Iraq to hunt down Saddam. It was time, he said, to "go beyond mere containment."[50] Scott Ritter symbolized the ideational shift, and in October 1998 the Congress passed the Iraq Liberation Act, publicly signaling the policy change from containment to regime change.

The change in definition was accompanied by a changing institutional focus. In containment, coercion was subordinated to economic and diplomatic initiatives—military power enforced economic statecraft. Had Saddam complied with the UN's demands for weapons accountability, containment would have been brought to an end peacefully. Regime change, on the other hand, was a much more assertive strategy, requiring a much more assertive use of American military power. Diplomacy was subordinated to coercion, rather than vice versa. The change was reflected in the rhetoric of policymaking as well. Instead of trying to *contain, manage,* or *keep* Saddam *in a box,* the United States would *attack, confront, deny, destroy, eliminate, force, knock out, oust, overthrow, remove, sack,* or *take out* Saddam.[51] The objective of regime change was not diplomatic—it was military. Redefining the problem redefined the solution.

Conclusion: From Problems to Policies

In this chapter, I have made a case for analyzing the way elites define and debate problems in American security policy. From 1991 to 1998, a group of policy entrepreneurs successfully redefined Iraq policy by constructing an Iraqi threat so significant that the policy status quo, containment, was "certain" to fail to contend with it. As problem-definition theorists hypothesize, the seeming disconnect between events in the empirical world, combined with changes in the way the Iraq problem was described, led to a change in policy. The regime-change policy resonated with many political elites not only because it challenged the Clinton administration's approach to Iraq, but also because it played to a belief in the viability of American military power that characterized conservative discourse in the 1990s. Containment was a diplomatic strategy backed by the occasional use of military power; regime change would be an inherently military policy that happened to seek a diplomatic goal.

When scholars analyze why policymakers choose military—as opposed to diplomatic, economic, or informational—instruments of power, they would do well to look at how those policymakers defined the problems they faced. In 1998, the "Iraq problem" was redefined from being a diplomatic irritant to being a national security threat, and regime change replaced containment as declaratory U.S. policy. By 2000 that definition was embedded in elites' understandings of what Iraq meant for U.S. security. While one cannot claim that the Iraq Liberation Act "caused" the 2003 invasion, it is clear that the process of contesting and redefining what Iraq meant in elite political discourse created the necessary foundation for those who promoted the ouster of Saddam as an appropriate response to the new threats faced by America after September 11.

Notes

1. Colin Powell with Joseph E. Persico, *My American Journey* (NY: Random House, 1995), 576.
2. See William Ruger's chapter in this volume (chapter 15).
3. Howard H. Lentner, "Public Policy and Foreign Policy: Divergences, Intersections, Exchange," *Review of Policy Research* 23, no. 1 (2006): 169–81; Michael J. Mazarr, "The Iraq War and Agenda Setting," *Foreign Policy Analysis* 3, no. 1 (January 2007): 1–23.
4. Richard F. Grimmett, *Instances of Use of United States Armed Forces Abroad, 1798–2007,* Congressional Research Service Report RL32170, September 12, 2007.
5. Jutta Weldes, *Constructing National Interests: The United States and the Cuban Missile Crisis* (Minneapolis: University of Minnesota Press, 1999), 97.

6. John W. Amos II and Russel H. S. Stolfi, "Controlling International Terrorism: Alternatives Palatable and Unpalatable," *Annals of the American Academy of Political and Social Science* 463 (September 1982): 69–83.
7. Robert D. Putnam, "Diplomacy and Domestic Politics: The Logic of Two-Level Games," *International Organization* 42, no. 3 (Summer 1988): 427–60.
8. The best introductions are David A. Rochefort and Roger W. Cobb, ed., *The Politics of Problem Definition: Shaping the Policy Agenda* (Lawrence: University Press of Kansas, 1994); John W. Kingdon, *Agendas, Alternatives, and Public Policies* (New York: HarperCollins, 1984); Roger W. Cobb and Charles D. Elder, *Participation in American Politics: The Dynamics of Agenda-Building* (Baltimore, MD: Johns Hopkins University Press, 1972).
9. E. E. Schattschneider, *The Semi-Sovereign People: A Realist's View of Democracy in America* (New York: Holt, Rinehart and Winston, 1960), 68.
10. Robert K. Merton, "Epilogue: Social Problems and Sociological Theory," in *Contemporary Social Problems*, ed. Robert K. Merton and Robert Nisbet (New York: Harcourt, Brace and Jovanovich, 1966), 786.
11. Aaron Wildavsky, *Speaking Truth to Power: The Art and Craft of Policy Analysis* (New Brunswick, NJ: Transaction Publishers, 1979).
12. Cobb and Elder, *Participation in American Politics*, 12.
13. Murray Edelman, *The Symbolic Uses of Politics* (Champaign: University of Illinois Press, 1966).
14. Frank R. Baumgartner and Bryan D. Jones, *Agendas and Instability in American Politics* (Chicago: University of Chicago Press, 1993).
15. Donald E. Abelson, *Do Think Tanks Matter?: Assessing the Impact of Public Policy Institutes* (Montreal: McGill-Queen's University Press, 2002).
16. Baumgartner and Jones, *Agendas and Instability*, 36.
17. Jeffrey Legro, *Rethinking the World: Great Power Strategies and International Order* (Ithaca, NY: Cornell University Press, 2005).
18. Sheri Berman, "Ideas, Norms, and Culture in Political Analysis," *Comparative Politics* 33, no. 2 (January 2001): 231–50.
19. Phebe Marr, *The Modern History of Iraq*, 2nd ed. (Boulder, CO: Westview Press, 2005), 133–5.
20. P. Edward Haley, *Strategies of Dominance; The Misdirection of U.S. Foreign Policy* (Baltimore, MD: Johns Hopkins University Press, 2007), 53–7.
21. George H. W. Bush and Brent Scowcroft, *A World Transformed* (NY: Alfred A. Knopf, 1998), 489; James A. Baker III, *The Politics of Diplomacy: Revolution, War and Peace, 1989–1992* (New York: G. P. Putnam and Sons, 1995), 435; Powell, *My American Journey*, 490; H. Norman Schwarzkopf with Peter Petre, *It Doesn't Take a Hero* (New York: Linda Grey/Bantam, 1992), 497.
22. "Frontline: The Gulf War," Public Broadcast System, http://www.pbs.org/wgbh/pages/frontline/gulf/oral.
23. Michael C. Williams, "What is the National Interest: The Neoconservative Challenge in I. R. Theory," *European Journal of International Relations* 11, no. 3 (2005): 307–37.
24. Russell A. Burgos, "Origins of Regime Change: *Ideapolitik* on the Long Road to Baghdad, 1993–2000," *Security Studies*, forthcoming; Andrew Flibbert, "The Road to Baghdad: Ideas and Intellectuals in Explanations of the Iraq War," *Security Studies* 15, no. 2 (April–June 2006): 310–52.
25. Jim Hoagland, "Crank Up to Bury Saddam," *Washington Post*, January 21, 1993; William Safire, "Unfinished Business," *New York Times*, March 29, 1993.
26. Daniel Williams, "U.S. Questions Top-Level Iraqis, Saddam Calls Defectors 'Judas,'" *Washington Post*, August 12, 1995.

27. Kenneth Katzman, "Iraq: Weapons Threat, Compliance, Sanctions, and U.S. Policy," *Congressional Research Service Report* IB92117, December 10, 2002.

28. John Barry and Gregory L. Vistica, "The Hunt for His Secret Weapons," *Newsweek*, December 1, 1997, 32.

29. "Iraq: Ready to Play Ball? Interview with Richard Butler," *Newsweek*, June 22, 1998.

30. Jim Hoagland, "Retreat on Iraq," *Washington Post*, February 11, 1998; George Melloan, "Another Defeat for an Ad Hoc Foreign Policy," *Wall Street Journal*, November 17, 1998.

31. Thomas W. Lippman, "Albright Says U.S. Is Adamant about Maintaining Sanctions against Saddam's Iraq" *Washington Post*, March 27, 1997.

32. John F. Harris, "Cohen Cites Iraqi Ability on Weapons," *Washington Post*, November 17, 1997; "Larry King Live," Cable News Network, November 25, 1997.

33. James M. McCormick, Eugene R. Wittkopf, and David M. Danna, "Politics and Bipartisanship at the Water's Edge: A Note on Bush and Clinton," *Polity* 30, no. 1 (Autumn 1997): 133–49.

34. United States Congress. Senate. S.Con.Res. 71, "Resolution Condemning Iraq's Threat to International Peace and Stability," 105th Cong., 2nd sess., January 28, 1998.

35. United States Congress. House of Representatives. "105 H.R. 4655, An Act to Establish a Program to Support a Transition to Democracy in Iraq," 105th Cong., 2nd sess., September 29, 1998.

36. Trent Lott, "Establishing a Program to Support a Transition to Democracy in Iraq," *Congressional Record* 144 (October 7, 1998), 139.

37. Frank Gaffney, Jr., "Handwriting on the Iraqi Wall," *Washington Times*, April 21, 1998.

38. Hoagland, "Retreat on Iraq"; Melloan, "Another Defeat."

39. A. M. Rosenthal, "A Package for Saddam," *New York Times*, February 10, 1998.

40. Judith Miller, "American Inspector on Iraq Quits, Accusing U.N. and U.S. of Cave-in," *New York Times*, August 27, 1998.

41. Miller, "American Inspector."

42. Scott Ritter, "Saddam's Trap," *The New Republic*, December 21, 1998.

43. William Safire, "Diddled Again," *New York Times*, November 16, 1998.

44. Barton Gellman, "Gingrich Opens Fire on White House's Iraq Policy," *Washington Post*, August 29, 1998.

45. Barton Gellman, "Senate Democrats Attack Ritter," *Washington Post*, September 4, 1998.

46. Miller, "American Inspector."

47. Eric Schmitt, "U.N. Arms Inspector Who Quit is Told He Can't Make Policy," *New York Times*, September 4, 1998.

48. "A Dangerous Poker Game With Iraq," *New York Times*, October 4, 1998; Joseph Biden, "I Meant No Disrespect," *Washington Post*, September 19, 1998; George F. Will, "The Illusion of Arms Control," *Washington Post*, September 3, 1998; Charles Krauthammer, "Enough," *Washington Post*, October 8, 1998; Fred Hiatt, "The Betrayal of Scott Ritter," *Washington Post*, September 6, 1998.

49. National Broadcasting Co., Inc., "Meet the Press," March 1, 1998.

50. Chris Black, "In Congress, Some Want End to Iraqi Threat," *Boston Globe*, February 28, 1998.

51. Russell A. Burgos, "The Apotheosis of Scott Ritter: The Rhetorical Construction of Iraq's WMD Threat," paper presented at the annual meeting of the American Political Science Association, Chicago, IL, August 2007.

Part 2

The Military and Government Institutions

8

The Military and Congress

Michael F. Morris

Ask any visitor to Washington, D.C.—two of the most recognizable landmarks in the city are the Capitol and the White House. The branches of government represented by these two distinctive buildings—the legislative branch and the executive branch, respectively, each of which has responsibility for the military—capture what is special about America. As designed by the framers of the Constitution, the checks and balances that support the principle of civilian control of the military set the United States apart, both historically and today.

The U.S. Constitution establishes the basic relationship between the military and the civilian government. Beginning with the opening paragraph, the founding fathers made clear their intent to "provide for the common defence" through the creation and sustainment of a military force. Article II, Section 2 establishes executive control of the military by stating that "the President shall be Commander in Chief of the Army and Navy of the United States." Article I, Section 8 grants Congress the power to carry out a number of important functions associated with the armed forces, including the power to declare war, to "raise and support armies," "to provide and maintain a Navy," and "to make Rules for the Government and Regulation of the land and naval Forces . . ."[1] This division of power and responsibility is crucial to understanding the relationship between the armed forces and the elected government.

The Congress

Over the years, many members of Congress have served in the armed forces, but the percentage of representatives and senators who have served in the military has fallen steadily since 1973[2] (see Jeremy Teigen's chapter in this book). This might seem unusual given that the American public consistently places more trust in the military as an institution than it does in Congress.[3] Whatever the reason for this decline, the end result is that a growing number of legislators lack personal understanding of the experience, demands, and culture of military service.

National security matters generally enjoy bipartisan support in Congress. Neither party wishes to be perceived as not "supporting the troops," particularly in a time of war. Members of Congress who serve on defense-related committees often cooperate on legislation—with differences being the exception rather than the norm. That said, the most recent conflict in Iraq has generated a struggle in Congress, as legislators debate and argue over nearly every aspect of the war, from political objectives to strategy to troop levels. "Often bipartisan, sometimes acrimonious" might best describe the current congressional view toward defense issues. The regular defense budget has enjoyed bipartisan support (see Daniel Wirls's chapter in this book). Deliberations over budgets for the war have been more acrimonious.

Military affairs are managed by a relatively small cadre of individuals who serve in the offices of members of Congress and on congressional committee staffs. In member offices, they are responsible for monitoring governmental affairs across a wide range of agencies and issues, often related to the committee assignments or interests (personal or constituent) of the representative or senator. A staff member responsible for military affairs often carries the title of "military legislative assistant" (MLA). In other offices, the chief of staff or legislative director might handle those duties, particularly if the congressperson has one or more committee assignments related to the military. Committee staffs are more specialized and, generally, more experienced. Working under the direction of the committee chairperson or the ranking committee member, they are often responsible for drafting legislation related to authorization or appropriation for the Department of Defense (DoD). They sometimes have military or civilian experience within the DoD, and they often serve for relatively long periods of time. These staffers are often acknowledged experts and work closely with the DoD.

Two types of congressional committees oversee defense matters: authorizing committees (the House and Senate Armed Services committees) and appropriations committees (the House and Senate Appropriations committees, and specifically the Defense subcommittees). Subcommittees are organized along functional lines. The House Armed Services Committee has seven subcommittees: Readiness; Seapower and Expeditionary Forces; Air and Land Forces; Oversight and Investigations; Military Personnel; Terrorism and Unconventional Threats and Capabilities; and Strategic Forces. On the Senate side, the Armed Services subcommittee structure is similar, with one exception: the Senate does not have a subcommittee devoted solely to oversight and investigations.

The House and Senate committees annually produce a defense authorization bill and a defense appropriations bill. Next, the House and Senate versions of the two authorization bills and the two appropriations bills are reconciled into single "conference reports." This sometimes delicate process—known as "conferencing"—results in two pieces of legislation: one to authorize the DoD and one to appropriate funds for its operation. Each conference report is returned to both houses for passage. If passed by both houses, they are then sent to the president.

In the case of the authorizing legislation, the final product of this sometimes lengthy process is the National Defense Authorization Act (NDAA). It contains statutory law and guidance for a variety of issues, such as procurement; research and development (R&D); operations and maintenance (O&M); personnel authorizations, policy, and compensation; acquisition matters; and readiness and management issues.

Not surprisingly, the NDAA is of great importance to the DoD. It can produce dramatic changes in department policies and practices, affecting major weapons systems acquisition and personnel recruitment and retention. The NDAA can mandate new reports or studies (e.g., the annual DoD report on the "Military Power of the People's Republic of China"), or it can change the process or focus of existing studies (e.g., the Quadrennial Defense Review [QDR]). It can also dramatically affect the resources available to the DoD and the military services and thus impact the number of military personnel on active duty and the number and location of bases at which they serve. Accordingly, secretaries of defense regularly communicate their priorities to the committees early in the legislative process and work with committee members and their staffs in an attempt to shape or influence the NDAA.

While budget figures are included in the authorizing legislation, the NDAA does not appropriate funds. That role is reserved for the Appropriations committees. Both the House and the Senate Appropriations committees are divided into subcommittees according to the governmental functions for which they are responsible. The Appropriations subcommittees in each chamber are organized in identical fashion. Two subcommittees have great significance for the military: Defense appropriation; and Military Construction, Veterans Affairs, and Related Agencies. Because the DoD bill is by far the largest appropriations bill passed by either chamber, it draws a great deal of attention and generates a large number of amendments. The appropriations process is extended and, in some ways, complicated by the occasional use of "emergency" supplemental appropriations. These additional appropriations are typically used to fund unforeseen or unbudgeted needs facing the DoD, such as costs relating to Operation Iraqi Freedom, an unexpected rise in fuel prices, or fluctuations in currency exchange rates.

The annual Defense Appropriations Act defines spending limits and time frames within which the department must operate. It appropriates money for O&M, procurement, military personnel, R&D, and a host of other purposes. Occasionally, directive language regarding policy is included in the appropriations act, but fiscal matters are the focus of the legislation.

The Role of the DoD

Appropriations can be understood as the final product in an extended planning, programming, and budgeting process that begins with the military services' budget requests to the Office of the Secretary of Defense (OSD). While decisions about appropriations for personnel matters are important, much of the debate concerns long-term weapons systems acquisition programs. Examples include the navy's Littoral Combat Ship, aircraft such as the Joint Strike Fighter, and land force programs such as the army's Future Combat System. Thus, for hundreds of officers, enlisted members, and civilian employees, assisting Congress is their primary duty; it is a secondary duty for hundreds more. This assistance to both authorizations and appropriations committee members and their staffs can take a variety of forms, including answering policy questions, resolving constituent issues, addressing budget concerns, or even assisting with travel.

One DoD staff organization is devoted to congressional matters associated with the two authorizing committees, the House Armed Services Committee and the Senate Armed Services Committee. This legislative affairs staff coordinates with the authorizing committees on legislative matters, maintains liaison offices on both the House and Senate sides of the Capitol, and prepares senior service leaders for testimony before House and Senate committees. Legislative affairs staffers may also travel with members of Congress and their staffs on domestic and international fact-finding trips. These trips allow members of Congress and their assistants to see the U.S. military in action, both in the United States and in a deployed environment. These trips, often called "Codels" (for congressional delegations) or "Staffdels" (for staff delegations), offer numerous opportunities for personal contact between the military and elected officials and their staffs.

A second, separate support staff, tasked with the same functions as noted above, is devoted to congressional matters associated with the two Appropriations committees. The separate nature of this staff helps to ensure that the members of both the appropriating and authorizing committees have unimpeded access to support services, especially since the legislative process for the authorization and appropriations bills are often simultaneous.

Additionally, all of the military services offer selected mid-level officers the opportunity to serve as a Legislative Fellow. This academic experience lasts one congressional year and allows officers to temporarily "detach" from their service responsibilities and serve as congressional staff members. While the services do not place officers in specific member or committee offices, most of the Fellows seek—and find—positions in offices with defense responsibilities. Upon completion of the fellowship, these officers return to their respective services with a deeper appreciation of the complexities of both the congressional environment and the legislative process.

The Congressional-Military Relationship

Because the relationship between Congress and the armed forces shapes thousands of important DoD decisions and programs—affecting millions of DoD members and employees and, ultimately, the national security of the United States—the quality of the relationship between the military and Congress has grown increasingly important. As the military budget increases and as military missions expand, the requirements for congressional oversight, involving communications, reports, briefings, and hearings, also expand.

The oversight function mandated by the Constitution can be complicated. At times, the division of power and responsibility between the executive and legislative branches of government has created difficult situations for military leaders as they have sought to respond to the sometimes different interests and viewpoints of the Congress and the president. Also, the influence of partisan politics can play a role in the relationship between the military and Congress. Congressional members have, on occasion, appeared to use hearings on military readiness or service budgets to make politically charged or politically motivated statements. Conversely, military leaders have run afoul of the administration by making impolitic, though truthful, statements during testimony that were later contradicted by senior defense officials. For example, in February 2003, Army chief of staff General Eric Shinseki testified before the Senate Armed Services Committee that, in his judgment, the number of soldiers required to be mobilized as the administration considered going to war in Iraq would be "something on the order of several hundred thousand soldiers." In rapid succession, Deputy Secretary of Defense Paul Wolfowitz and Secretary of Defense Donald Rumsfeld publicly contradicted the general's estimate, characterizing it as considerably higher than they believed would be necessary; Secretary Rumsfeld called it "far from the mark." General Shinseki found himself caught between a Senate committee asking for his professional military judgment and his civilian leaders who found his judgment inconsistent with the administration's assessments.[5]

Sometimes congressional interests complicate matters for the military and result in decisions that seem to work at cross-purposes to national security. One example involves the American Service-members' Protection Act of 2002 (ASPA), a law intended to protect U.S. service members from prosecution by the International Criminal Court. Section 2007, subsection (a) of the Act states that "no military assistance may be provided to the government of a country that is party to the International Criminal Court."[6] Military assistance has been interpreted to include attendance by officers from other countries at U.S. professional military education institutions. The purpose of the act was to pressure countries to waive their right to prosecute U.S. service members (generally known as an Article 98 waiver). Many countries chose to do so; others did not. The outcome of the ASPA is that members of the U.S. military are prohibited from developing key personal relationships with officers from selected countries that could—and some would argue, should—be sought as strategic partners. Further, other countries have used this as an opportunity to fill the void left by this policy by inviting officers to attend their schools. Similar examples could be cited; for instance, those related to troop strength limits in certain countries, and the "Armenia genocide" resolution.

Congressional reporting requirements have proliferated in recent years. Congressional committees, eager to assert their rightful influence on the activities of the DoD, now require hundreds of reports on a wide variety of subjects, ranging from the well known (e.g., Army general David Petraeus's "Report to Congress on the Situation in Iraq," made public September 10, 2007) to the more obscure (e.g., the DoD's renewable energy strategy). While these reports provide an opportunity for increased understanding on both sides of the congressional-military relationship, they do exact a cost from both the members of the military and the civilians in the DoD who prepare the reports and the congressional staff members who receive them. Admiral William J. Crowe Jr., former chairman of the Joint Chiefs of Staff (JCS) in the administrations of Ronald Reagan and George H. W. Bush, lamented both the cost and the lack of usefulness of the multitude of reports required by Congress.[7] He noted that approximately six hundred reports were required annually in 1993. The number has been reduced over the years, but Congress is a great consumer of staff reports.

In addition to reports, there are a number of other modes of contact between Congress and the DoD. These include meetings between senior DOD officials and congressional staffers (and occasionally congressional members themselves) to discuss ongoing legislation. Some of these contacts are initiated by the DoD—for example, to request the reprogramming of appropriated funds or to inform members of Congress about issues of importance to the services or to the DoD. Other contacts are initiated by representatives, senators, or congressional staffers. These include requests for briefings on the department's budget requests (often resulting in a series of meetings sometimes called "staffer days"); requests for information or action on constituent complaints; and sometimes even calling members of the department, both civilian and military, to testify before Congress.

Hearings are a centerpiece of the congressional-military relationship. While hearings may occur anytime Congress is in session, they tend to occur early in the legislative cycle, typically from February through June. Hearings can be called by full committees or by subcommittees. Hearings may be open to the public or closed, depending on the sensitivity or classification of the material. They can be fairly specific with regard to topic (e.g., military recruitment and retention), or focused on a broader, more general set of issues (e.g., readiness or the posture of the service's budget submission). Senior civilian and military leaders are the typical witnesses, although committees have asked junior members of the military and civilians—and occasionally even spouses—to appear and testify.

An important aspect of the relationship between the military and Congress that is linked to both national security and partisan politics is the interests of constituents within a congressperson's state or district. At times, both national security and the political interests of the member or of his or her local constituents are well served; at other times, that relationship is unclear.

Because the presence of military bases, units, weapons systems, facilities, and personnel can represent political power, members of Congress typically work very hard to protect those interests. At home, these efforts can take the form of visits by the congressperson to the installations in his or her state or district, communication with local commanders, and recognition of military members winning installation or service-wide awards. Other activities might include unit openings or closings, the opening of new facilities, and the christening or commissioning of a new naval vessel. Members of Congress may also establish relationships with local military affairs committees, which are often found in communities near military installations. These interactions serve as reminders of the importance of the relationship between the armed forces and the civilian public they serve.

In Washington, the efforts can take the form of attempting to influence appropriations or authorization legislation to benefit state or district installations. In the legislative process, members from both parties and from both houses may take the opportunity to request that funding be set aside for specific projects or needs in their respective states or districts. If their requests are signed into law, they become binding on the department or service. For example, representatives may attempt to win approval for the construction of new facilities or for the renovation or repair of existing ones. Other examples of congressional inserts include provisions to fund defense-related work at businesses or firms within a particular state or district. For example, members of Congress may attempt to add provisions requiring the DoD to fund specific research, procurement, or training at military installations, centers, colleges and universities, or research institutions in their state or district. Previous provisions have directed funding to such organizations as the Lithographic and Alternative Semiconductor Processing Techniques Center, the Department of Energy's Pittsburgh Energy Technology Center, and the Army High Performance Computing Research Center. Such funding provisions are notable, as the language mandates that funds be spent "only for" such items. This language prevents the DoD from redirecting such appropriations to other purposes.[8]

This is not to imply that these provisions, widely known as "earmarks," are always unwelcome by the military. In many cases, they are very welcome. New training equipment, a renovated maintenance facility, or a lengthened and improved runway may greatly benefit both the people and the mission at an installation—and contribute to national security in the process. But while these provisions are sometimes additions to the funding for the services, at other times no additional funding is provided, and the law requires that the money be drawn from the existing funding, a condition known as paying for the provision "out of hide." In these cases, the funding required to carry out a specific provision is then unavailable for the purposes originally intended. While the total of these "earmarks" is not great in relative terms, they may be 2–3 percent of the DoD appropriation.

In addition to inserting provisions into legislation, members of Congress can also work directly with the DoD to attempt to keep or assign units, missions, weapons systems, or personnel to installations within their jurisdiction. Often the member of Congress and the military service join forces to ensure a mission remains at a post or station. They can also expend considerable effort to maintain basing or production of a weapon system within their state or district. For example, Representative Norm Dicks, a Democrat representing Washington's Sixth District, has been especially successful in promoting his district's interests in defense legislation. His advocacy played a part in the fiscal year (FY) 2007 defense appropriations bill, which included several billion dollars in spending for Boeing and Raytheon programs in the Tacoma area, including the air force's C-17 airlifter and the navy's F/A-18G electronic attack aircraft.[9] In the Senate's FY 2008 defense appropriations bill, Senator Trent Lott, Republican from Mississippi, touted $9 billion in impact from defense program funding, for such programs as the DD(X) future navy destroyer ($2.8 billion, produced in Pascagoula); the lightweight 155 mm Howitzer ($584 million, produced in Hattiesburg); and the C-130J Hercules aircraft ($918 million, the fuselage of which is built in Meridian). Senator Lott is quoted in one of his office's press releases as stating,

> Mississippians are always interested in the defense appropriations process as our state is home to numerous military bases and defense contractors. From this perspective, our state is again well represented in this defense measure. As our military's mission in the War on Terror continues, I urge Congress and the President to finish this bill quickly and get this funding and equipment to the dedicated military personnel who're responsible for protecting our freedom.[10]

In some circumstances, however, the relationship between Congress and the military can be adversarial. Maintaining bases, installations, weapons, and people costs an enormous amount of money. Sometimes, the services believe it is in their best interest to relocate missions, units, and hardware from one place to another. When such a decision means that an installation in a congressperson's state or district may lose assets—creating associated economic impact on the local community—some members take measures to attempt to change the service's position. These attempts may include such tactics as putting a hold on other pieces of legislation important to the DoD or the service, mobilizing local efforts to influence the DoD or service leaders, influencing or holding up consideration of that service's officer promotion lists, or even writing prohibitions against mission changes into law. For example, the air force faces serious budget issues, due in part to congressional mandates to keep and maintain older aircraft that, in the service's view, should be retired. The funding required to maintain an aging fleet should, the air force contends, be invested in newer, more modern aircraft with lower maintenance costs. Such conflicts can escalate and disrupt the working relationship between service leaders and members of Congress.

A special case of this tension over military presence in a state or district is found in the Base Realignment and Closure Commission, (BRAC)an independent body that is chartered to impartially consider the closing of U.S. military installations; however, even after the BRAC makes its recommendations and those recommendations are approved by Congress and the president, the execution of those recommendations can still prove contentious.

Members of Congress often intervene with the military on behalf of individual constituents. All the services receive correspondence from members of Congress requesting consideration (or, in some cases, reconsideration) of various individual concerns, including assignments, pay or benefits, awards and decorations, family issues, problems with medical care, or even recognition for service during previous conflicts. If possible—within the bounds of equity, service guidelines, and the law—service officials attempt to remedy any harm done to service members. At other times, however, no harm was done or nothing can be done to change the circumstances. However, it is understood that service members always have an unquestioned right to appeal to their member of Congress.

The Senate, in particular, has a special role to play regarding the military services. The Senate Armed Services Committee, on behalf of the Senate and in its "advise and consent" role mandated by the Constitution, takes action on lists of officers recommended by the service secretaries and the president for promotion (including general and flag officers). They also approve reassignment of those senior officers to other duties, and approve their retirement in grade.

Challenges

How well do the military services and Congress communicate with each other? Is there increasing understanding between them? Do the people in the two institutions work effectively together? These critical questions are considered each day by leaders in the Pentagon and in the Capitol. The answers, important in peacetime, become even more important in time of war. So what can be done to raise the level of cooperation between the two sides of the Potomac?

First, leaders must ensure that all involved keep the nation's best interests at heart. Parochialism and self-interest may have their place in other areas, but national security remains one area of concern that demands bipartisanship. This has been the tradition in both Congress and the Pentagon, and it must remain so.

Second, members of the military and congressional staffers need to understand the differences between their institutional cultures. Neither is perfect; nor is one right and the other wrong. Each contributes, in its own way, to achieving national security for the United States. Mutual respect and understanding are an absolute necessity.

Third, leaders and staff members in both organizations can commit themselves to open and transparent communication. Of course, this requires trust, which is usually already a part of the relationship. In those instances in which trust might be lacking, it is especially important that the views of all are heard and considered.

The relationships between the leaders and staffs of Congress and the military services—despite their cultural and professional differences—are generally cooperative and collegial. In today's rapidly changing security environment, an effective Congressional-Defense partnership remains a cornerstone of American security—just as the framers of the Constitution envisioned.

Notes

1. US Constitution, Article 2, Section 2, and Article 1, Section 8. An electronic transcript of the U.S. Constitution can be accessed at http://www.archives.gov/national-archives-experience/charters/constitution_transcript.html, accessed October 20, 2007.
2. "Membership of the 110th Congress: A Profile," CRS Report for Congress, December 15, 2006.
3. Gallup Poll, Trust in Public Institutions, available at http://www.pollingreport.com/institut.htm, accessed February 16, 2008.
4. For a thorough treatment of the legislative process, see Walter J. Oleszek, *Congressional Procedures and the Policy Process*, 4th ed. (Washington, D.C.: Congressional Quarterly Press, 1996).

5. Eric Schmitt, "Pentagon Contradicts General on Iraq Occupation Force's Size," *New York Times*, February 28, 2003. Available at http://www.globalpolicy.org/security/issues/iraq/attack/consequences/2003/0228pentagoncontra.htm, accessed October 19, 2007.

6. Text of the American Service-members Protection Act of 2002. Available at http://www.state.gov/t/pm/rls/othr/misc/23425.htm, accessed October 20, 2007.

7. William J. Crowe, Jr., *In the Line of Fire* (New York: Simon and Schuster, 1993), p. 238.

8. *Making Omnibus Consolidated Appropriations for Fiscal Year 1997*, Conference Report to Accompany H.R. 3610, September 28, 1996, pp. 939–941.

9. Rep Norm Dicks website, article regarding FY 2007 defense appropriations bill "FINAL DEFENSE BILL ADDS NAVY OVERHAUL FUNDS, MORE C-17s AND F/A-18G ELECTRONIC AIRCRAFT." Available at http://www.house.gov/dicks/news/defensefy07conf.htm, accessed October 19, 2007.

10. Website for Senator Trent Lott, R-MS, regarding impact for Mississippi in the FY 2008 Senate Defense Appropriations Bill. Available at http://lott.senate.gov/public/index.cfm?FuseAction=PressOffice.PressReleases&ContentRecord_id=9592ca65-802a-23ad-4f13-478bf04f8aa5&Region_id=&Issue_id=, accessed October 19, 2007.

9

Hidden in Plain Sight: The Bush Military Buildup

Daniel Wirls

Introduction

The attacks of September 11, 2001, not only triggered a declaration by the George W. Bush administration of a "Global War on Terror" (GWOT), but also facilitated, under the cover of that conflict, a military buildup separate from the funding for that war. The buildup—one of the largest increases in military spending in the country's history—is one of the most important legacies of the Bush presidency, yet one of the less understood and least controversial. The politics of war protected and obscured its size and significance.

From 2000 to 2008, defense spending increased by 66 percent, and President Bush's request for fiscal year (FY) 2009 would take that to 77 percent.[1] That might not seem like a lot for a nation at war, were it not for the fact that these figures do not include the nearly $650 billion separately appropriated since 2002 to cover the costs of the wars in Iraq and Afghanistan. Even by the end of Bush's first term in office, the U.S. military budget (adjusted for inflation and without the war funding) was above the average for the years of the Cold War and was rapidly approaching 50 percent of the world's military expenditures. With it the United States has been developing and buying a vast array of weapons—such things as the Future Combat System for the army and the F-22 fighter for the air force—as part of an arms race with itself. At $75.7 billion, the Pentagon's 2007 budget for research and development (R&D) alone was more than double the entire budget for the Department of Homeland Security.[2]

The Bush administration took power with plans for a more assertive national security policy, backed by a transformed and rearmed military, all of which would require substantial increases in military spending. Prior to 9/11, however, the administration seemingly lacked the necessary political leverage to bring this to fruition. The 9/11 attacks and the wars that followed not only displaced other issues and conflicts, but even masked central aspects of national security policy.

September 11, 2001, provided the political cover to implement a buildup without debate, a buildup to furnish the martial muscle for a new grand strategy premised on unprecedented military superiority.

Bush and Military Spending Before 9/11

During the election campaign of 2000, the Republican Party, presidential candidate Bush, and conservative elites, some of whom would become key figures in the Bush administration, criticized the Clinton administration's military policies and budgets. While vague about budgetary implications, they argued for strategies, pay increases, and programs such as ballistic missile defense that all implied a significant increase in spending.[3] Overall, however, national security was a relatively minor issue during the campaign. Despite the invocation of Ronald Reagan's policy of "peace through strength," the Republicans could not replicate, amid the relatively placid and prosperous times, the kind of public concern about national security that had helped them gain power two decades earlier.

Once in office, Bush's first budget proposed a modest increase in military spending of $14.2 billion, or 4.8 percent over 2001, in line with other increases since 1999.[4] This was characterized as a down payment toward a major transformation of the military that had been in a strategic and structural holding pattern since the end of the Cold War. The new strategy was to be announced as part of a major review by Defense Secretary Donald Rumsfeld. According to Secretary Rumsfeld, however, some things could not wait, and in late June 2001 he announced a large increase in the military budget just proposed by the Bush administration: another $18.4 billion to be added to the earlier increase for a total of $32.6 billion, or 11 percent over 2001. Bush proudly announced that this would be "the largest increase in military spending since Ronald Reagan was the president and commander-in-chief."[5]

By late summer 2001, the Bush administration had not presented the promised review and justification for the increases in military spending augured by the additions to the 2002 budget. Although Rumsfeld had previewed elements of the "new strategy" over the summer, the congressionally mandated Quadrennial Defense Review (QDR) was to be the vehicle for the new strategy's public release in early September.[6]

The QDR was "largely completed before the September 11, 2001 terror attacks on the United States."[7] Besides the "foreword" by the secretary of defense and some brief references to the attacks and their implications, the QDR read like the justification for the kind of robust military budgets the Bush administration had wanted prior to the attacks. As Rumsfeld noted, "Even before the attack of September 11, 2001, the senior leaders of the Defense Department set out to establish a new strategy for America's defense that would embrace uncertainty and contend with surprise" as it "sought to set the conditions to extend America's influence."[8]

An analysis of the 2001 QDR is beyond the scope of this chapter. The central point for our purposes is that, predating 9/11, the QDR and its central concepts of transformation, dissuasion, a shift from threat-based to capabilities-based planning, and an expanded two-war requirement certainly implied a far more aggressive strategy and a more expensive military complex, even if some critics also saw some old conceptual wine being poured into new bottles and a lack of detail about what implementation would mean, and particularly about what transformation would entail.[9] Dissuasion, however, was a new and rather demanding doctrine. Dissuasion made it official U.S. policy to be so strong and so superior in military capabilities as to discourage others from even trying to compete, by convincing them not even to spend the money, do the research, or build the weapons that would be necessary to undertake a military operation against the United States or its vital national interests.[10]

A great unknown of the presidency of George W. Bush is what its policies would have been absent 9/11. How far could Bush have increased military spending without a clear and present danger abroad, especially amid a rapidly ballooning deficit that was created in part by the tax cuts that were his top priority after taking office? We cannot answer this question. It certainly appeared as though Congress was more than ready prior to 9/11 to go along with the 4.8 percent increase originally planned for the 2002 budget. But the additional $18.4 billion tacked on that summer was not considered by Congress before 9/11; in fact, the Defense Appropriations bill was taken up by the House Appropriations Committee on the day of the attacks. Delays followed, and it was not until late November that Congress debated the bill, which finally got through the Senate on December 7.

What did 9/11 change? The short answer is that while very little changed in actual military policy and planning, politically everything changed. There was no longer any need to justify the new strategies and budgets. In fact, the Bush administration was able to spend even more than it had hoped for on the military, even though most of the spending was essentially unrelated to the nascent war on terror. September 11 rendered the QDR politically irrelevant as it simultaneously turned it into material reality.

The political impact of 9/11 was quickly demonstrated by congressional action. Amid the expressions of outrage and calls for justice and vengeance, a frequently voiced sentiment on the floor of the House and Senate was that Congress would do what it would take to fund the incipient conflict. Just days after 9/11, Democratic Senator Joe Lieberman said that Congress's job was to "lock arms in support of the commander in chief," but that someday in the future "we're going to need to talk about funding and how it's carried out."[11] That day would never come.

Changes in Proposed Military Spending After 9/11

Aside from the supplemental budgetary requests to meet the emergency of 9/11 and the military response to it (including operations in Afghanistan), the Bush administration did not reveal the impact that the QDR would have on the bottom line until it submitted its FY 2003 budget request in February 2002. By this time, major combat operations in Afghanistan were (temporarily) over, but the president had declared a GWOT; had labeled Iraq, Iran, and North Korea an "axis of evil"; and had begun the campaign that would lead to war with Iraq.

During his 2002 State of the Union address, Bush also made an easy and imprecise political link between "this war" and military spending:

> It costs a lot to fight this war. We have spent more than a billion dollars a month—over $30 million a day—and we must be prepared for future operations. . . . My budget includes the largest increase in defense spending in two decades—because while the price of freedom and security is high, it is never too high. Whatever it costs to defend our country, we will pay.[12]

President Bush did not explain that the costs of the war were being handled by emergency supplemental appropriations separate from the regular budget requests. Seventeen billion dollars for the war on terror had been appropriated in 2001; another $14 billion was requested for 2002; and nearly $70 billion would be required for 2003. The "largest increase" in two decades referred to the military budget *independent* of the costs of the war. This means that the FY 2003 budget request reflected almost exclusively new spending over and above the costs of the GWOT. It represented what the Bush administration apparently had planned to do regardless of 9/11.

The proposed changes to the military budget were substantial (Figure 9.1). Bush made rather modest projections for military spending increases in his pre-9/11 budget for 2002, estimating only a 16.4 percent increase from 2001 to 2006 (2.7 percent per year). The FY 2003 request was radically different. With an average annual increase of 7.3 percent, the military budget would grow 44 percent in six years, a cumulative addition of $332 billion dollars to the pre-9/11 plans for the defense budget. These projections proved quite accurate, as we shall see. Even as $500-plus billion in war supplementals were added, the increases in military spending, apart from the war, followed the path laid down in the 2003 request.

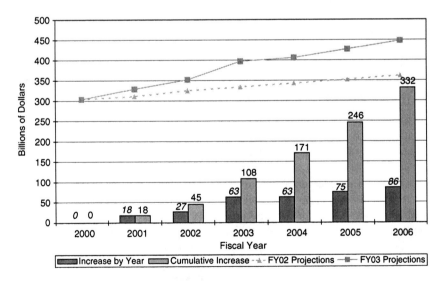

Figure 9.1   Projections of Military Spending before and after September 2001

No Shock, No Awe: The Buildup, 2001–2008

The wars and the military buildup grew simultaneously as the administration, with the support of Congress, was able to exceed its revised projections for the regular defense budget while war spending quickly exceeded the largest prewar estimates (Figure 9.2).[13] Yet the politics of war would obscure the size of the buildup by concentrating congressional and public attention on the Iraq conflict. This simultaneous expansion of the war budget and the regular military budget was aided, as we shall see later, by the fact that war continued to be funded by supplemental appropriations bills, which were not subject to the regular budget process and spending restrictions. Tough choices could be evaded. Money for the war was not in direct competition with money for research, development, and procurement of new weapons systems that were largely unrelated to the war.

Within a few years, the Bush administration's total military spending reached and then exceeded the peak spending (adjusted for inflation) of the Cold War era, including the Korean War, the Vietnam War, and the Reagan buildup (Figure 9.3).[14] Attention, however, remained focused on the costs of the Iraq war. Little notice was given to the fact that the regular defense budget was growing nearly 7 percent a year between 2001 and 2008. In effect, Bush was combining a Vietnam War with a Reagan buildup. In conjunction with the tax cuts of 2001 and 2003, the rapid rise in military spending was making a substantial contribution to the return of large deficits and an increase in the national debt from about $5.6 trillion in 2000 to about $9 trillion in 2007. As a percentage of the economy, military and war spending combined grew from 3 percent to just over 4 percent of gross domestic product (GDP) over the same period. Four percent was still a historically low figure for the defense burden. While in no way a measure of what should be spent on national security, the relatively low percentage helped politically and was often

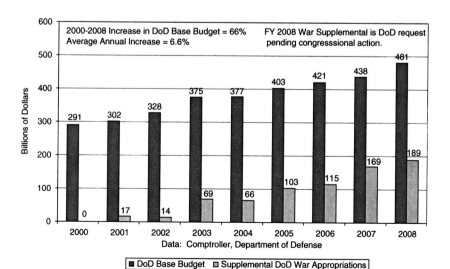

Figure 9.2   Defense Spending versus War Appropriations

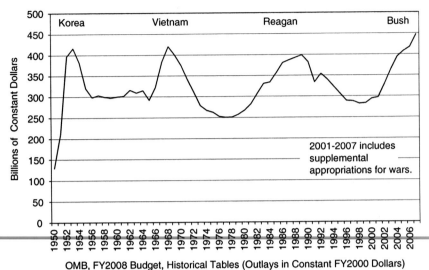

Figure 9.3   Military Spending (Outlays) in Constant Dollars, 1950–2007

cited by the Pentagon and the administration as an alternative perspective on how much the United States was spending.[15]

Despite the size of the supplemental appropriations and the regular defense budgets, a common perception, at least until early 2007, was that there was not enough money for the war, and the Pentagon seemed willing to foster this belief. As one skeptical reporter wrote, "Amid one of the greatest military spending increases in history, the Pentagon is starved for cash."[16] Little was done by Congress or by anyone else to unravel this paradox, despite the obvious contradiction and implausibility. Another measure of the scale of the buildup separate from the war is the amount of money spent per uniformed personnel *excluding* the war supplementals. In 2006 the Pentagon was spending nearly $350,000 for each man and woman on active duty and reserve, about $100,000 more per capita than in 2000, or a 40 percent increase.[17] Much of this was accounted for in the substantial increases in the budgets for R&D and procurement. Funding for R&D doubled between 2000 and 2007, increasing from $37.6 billion to over $75 billion. Procurement went up by nearly 57 percent from about $52 billion to $81 billion. Expenditures for personnel and for operations and maintenance (O&M), by stark contrast, increased only 13 percent. Much as Reagan had done, Bush was funding a rather capital-intensive buildup that focused on the development and production of a vast array of weapons.

Under Ronald Reagan, architect of the largest peacetime buildup in American history, the military budget doubled from 1980 to 1985. As noted earlier, defense spending—separate from war funding—increased by two-thirds from 2000 to 2008. In eight years President Bush did not match the percentage increase achieved by Reagan, but his buildup—with seven years of increases and an eighth on the way—was more sustained than any of his predecessors, whether at war or peace. As we shall see, one major difference is that Reagan's buildup was subject to vigorous opposition from Congress and the public. Bush's, by contrast, was hidden in plain sight.

Few Americans were aware of the fact that behind the war spending were significant and sustained increases for programs and activities unrelated to, or largely unrelated to, the GWOT, but supporting administration doctrines and policies requiring unprecedented global military superiority. Even as the war became increasingly unpopular and the Democrats took control of Congress in 2007, the FY 2008 budget process revealed how little had changed politically.

"This is a huge number," said House Speaker Nancy Pelosi, presumably referring to the nearly $650 billion that the administration was requesting for FY 2008 to fund both the Pentagon's regular budget and the war. As the administration was asking for several large appropriations all at once, there were several figures that might be considered "huge." First, there was the extra $100 billion war supplemental for FY 2007 (to supplement the $70 billion already appropriated). Next was the $142 billion war supplemental for FY 2008. And last, but certainly not least, was the $481 billion for the Pentagon's regular budget, a 10 percent increase over its 2007 funding. Altogether, the president was asking for nearly three-quarters of a trillion dollars, and this did not include the Department of Homeland Security. Even these extraordinary numbers failed to pierce the shroud that had all but enveloped the massive military buildup that proceeded apart from, and in addition to, the war on terror. These astronomical figures generated little outrage or even inquiry. Instead, Democrats were quick to note, "We clearly want to make sure our troops have everything they need."[18] Senate Majority Leader Harry Reid averred that "Democrats pledge that our troops will receive everything they need to do their jobs."[19]

Spending for the war was vaulting past the half-trillion-dollar mark on its way to exceeding the total real spending on the nearly ten years of the Vietnam War. Yet, at the same time, the regular defense budget was increasing by over 10 percent. War spending and the military budget were increasing independently and by leaps and bounds. This is another indication of just how much the politics of 9/11 were alive and well despite the sea change in the fortunes of war and the tide of public opinion. The new Democratic majority, joined by an increasing number of disillusioned Republicans, would concentrate on changing policy in Iraq. Yet it did so while "supporting the troops," and that meant that neither the Pentagon budget nor the supplemental war appropriations were seriously questioned or challenged.

Emergency Supplemental Funding and the Backdoor Buildup

By the summer of 2007, supplemental funding for the GWOT had reached over $550 billion. Despite criticisms of the use of putatively emergency supplemental appropriations and despite recommendations (including one from the Iraq Study Group) that the administration integrate war spending into the regular military budget, the practice continued.[20] In 2006, senators John McCain and Robert Byrd authored an amendment to the 2007 defense authorization bill; the amendment mandated that future war funding be made part of the regular budget process. Although Bush signed the bill with the McCain-Byrd amendment, he did so with a signing statement specifying that he could, in effect, ignore it.[21] The main purpose of this chapter is to show the size of the military buildup separate from the war funding. A second important point, however, is that the supplemental war funding also became part of the buildup.

Even before passage of the McCain-Byrd amendment, evidence had emerged that the supplemental requests were taking advantage of the politics of war to exceed what was required for ongoing operations in Iraq and Afghanistan. Reports showed that some of the funding for procurement and research involved weapons systems and equipment that either were inappropriate or, in some cases, would not be available for several years—things that should have been in the general defense budget and that in no way qualified for emergency or supplemental spending. The army's Modularity Program, which was included in supplemental requests for FY 2005 and FY 2006, is an example of a regular modernization/transformation program that was funded via emergency supplemental requests.[22]

Such additions were sanctioned and encouraged in October 2006 when Deputy Secretary of Defense Gordon England sent a memo to the services announcing the expansion of supplemental funding to include efforts outside of Iraq and Afghanistan. This raised concerns that virtually anything even tangentially related to the GWOT could now be funded through emergency supplemental appropriations.[23] A congressional staffer concluded that the services "are using the availability of the supplementals to finance virtually all of the shortfalls they can identify."[24]

The latitude taken by the administration is demonstrated by "replacement of old equipment with new models—actions historically subject to the normal budget review process."[25] For example, the 2007 supplemental contained money for twenty-two new C-130J Hercules cargo planes. It also included a $400 million request for two F-35 fighters, which will not be ready for combat for at least three years. Another $300 million was requested for seven of the new (and controversial) V-22 Osprey transport planes, another system that is arguably not ready for deployment, let alone war. There was even considerable money for the R&D of such things as a new unmanned aerial vehicle.[26] While new or nonexistent items were being purchased, much of the existing equipment was being modernized and upgraded with new technology rather than simply being restored to its previous condition. Budget documents indicate that the M1A1 Abrams tank would receive an "unspecified systems enhancement program." The army and the marines in particular came to view the supplementals as essential to their plans for modernization and transformation.[27]

Whether this use of the supplemental process is an abuse or not, the result is a backdoor addition to the military buildup. Before 9/11, emergency supplementals composed, at most, a few percentage points of total defense spending. In 2007 about 23 percent of military spending was in the form of supplemental funding.[28] In particular, the supplemental appropriations beef up the capital-intensive aspects of the military budget. Procurement and R&D have composed over 20 percent of the supplementals since 2005 and could reach 30 percent with the 2008

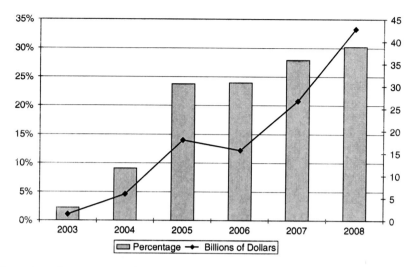

Figure 9.4   Procurement and R&D in Supplemental War Appropriations

supplemental (Figure 9.4). That 30 percent translates into $42.8 billion for pro-curement and R&D—more than the entire defense budgets of all but a few nations. Even ignoring the direct evidence that the supplementals contain new, non-war procurement, it is self-evident that the United States is not expending or degrading nearly $43 billion worth of equipment in Iraq and Afghanistan.

The extraordinary thing is that this backdoor buildup was proceeding at the same time as the regular Pentagon budget—particularly procurement and R&D—was increasing rapidly. In effect, projects that could not be advanced with 7 percent growth each year in the regular military budget were wedged into the supplementals. Congressional resistance was negligible, given the solid partisan support for the administration and the fear of being perceived as not "supporting the troops."

The Pork Barrel of National Security

However frustrating the "emergency" supplemental process might have been for some members of Congress, it eased the burden on most members by allowing them to evade decisions about what and what not to fund, which would have been harder to do if the money for the backdoor buildup was reflected in the official budget. Further, there was another factor affecting funding—the protection of parochial interests. Among other examples, the near rejection by Congress of Rumsfeld's cancellation of the army's Crusader program illustrates how difficult it was to cut programs that conflicted with transformation and war funding.[29] Despite the media glare that accompanies a war, Congress remained adept at the relatively quiet distributive politics that function so well in flush times.

One might think that a national emergency on the order of 9/11 and the GWOT would bring some discipline to congressional military spending. Indeed, it has been argued in the academic literature that a certain level of responsibility characterized congressional handling of military spending during much of the Cold War, as opposed to the years immediately after its end.[30] Yet, as we have seen, Congress did almost nothing to oversee—let alone control—military spending after 9/11. A significant increase in so-called military earmarks provides further evidence of congressional complicity. The term *earmarks* (sometimes called "member projects") refers to items that are added by members of Congress and that were not requested by the administration or by the relevant bureaucracy and that typically "target benefits to a particular company, organization or locality."[31] Earmarks are commonly associated with pork barrel spending.

Post-9/11 military earmarks ranged from the relevant to the ridiculous. The relevant category included changes in the funding for existing weapons or programs. For example, during the FY 2007 appropriations process, Senator James Talent of Missouri led an effort to add $2.1 billion for ten C-17 cargo planes, a program important to his state but that the Pentagon wanted to discontinue. Ridiculous items for a military appropriations bill included $1.2 million for prostate cancer research backed by Alaska Senator Ted Stevens.[32]

Relevant or ridiculous, earmarks in defense appropriations bills shot up with the Bush buildup. According to studies by the Congressional Research Service, the dollar value of military earmarks rose steadily from 2000 to 2006, increasing by 54 percent, about 10 percent above the increase in the regular (nonwar) defense budget.[33] The number of earmarks grew by 186 percent, from 997 in 2000 to 2,847 in 2006. Increasing from 2.28 percent to 2.36 percent of total defense appropriations, earmarks can be seen as insignificant or substantial, typically the former because they constitute such a small percentage of the total budget. However, at $9.43 billion dollars (in 2006), such add-ons collectively exceed the annual spending on any individual weapons system (e.g., the F-22 fighter or a new aircraft carrier) and even the total annual spending on the Ballistic Missile Defense (BMD) program, which consists of many individual elements and contracts.[34]

A recent and award-winning study of Congress showed how earmarks or pork barrel projects are used to build legislative majorities for legislation that benefits the general public.[35] This perspective on pork has little to say, however, about congressional action on recent military appropriations. The post-9/11 military appropriations bills have not needed earmarks to gain legislative support. In fact, the reverse has been true. The massive money trains were leaving the legislative station unimpeded; elected officials got on board; and there was plenty of room. Military spending bills attracted little scrutiny and few negative votes as earmarks were loaded aboard.

The Bush Buildup in Historical Perspective

As we have seen, the Bush administration was planning for significant increases in military spending before 9/11, but lacked political leverage in the form of a credible threat. The Republican Congress seemed ready to support some of the administration's plans for military transformation and recapitalization, which included fabulously expensive programs such as BMD and the F22 fighter, but there is every reason to doubt that they could have sustained a major buildup in the absence of 9/11. Largely because of the way the Bush administration interpreted those attacks for the American public and the world, an immediate war and the longer term equivalent of the Cold War were launched. The United States was commencing a war not only against specific actors (al Qaeda and the Taliban) implicated in the attacks but also against terrorism in general, and it was to be fought anywhere, much like the Cold War against communism.

It is not surprising then that the Bush military buildup shares political and material parallels with buildups of previous administrations. Prior to the Bush presidency, the last three periods of major increases in military spending came under Harry Truman during the Korean War, Lyndon Johnson during the Vietnam War, and Ronald Reagan as part of the Cold War; two as a direct consequence of war and the other in the absence of war.[36] As noted earlier, the regular defense budgets of the Bush administration emphasized capital-intensive investment in procurement and R&D versus spending on ongoing O&M or pay.

The Vietnam War produced, as one might suspect, a rather labor-intensive increase in military spending (Figure 9.5). Even during an era with conscription and, therefore, low labor costs, and with a war that was consuming considerable equipment, personnel costs outpaced procurement and research. Not surprisingly, O&M shot up dramatically in comparison to procurement and R&D. Compare this with the Reagan peacetime buildup, which was radically capital-intensive. Procurement and R&D doubled in real terms as the Reagan administration sought first and foremost to modernize most major weapons systems.

All indications were that prior to 9/11, the Bush administration planned a similar capital-intensive buildup (the essence of "transformation"), such that even if they could not match the scale of the Reagan-era increases, they could mirror its major goal of next-generation rearmament. In many ways the administration

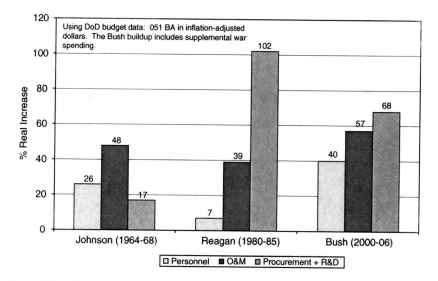

Figure 9.5   Comparing Military Buildups

did just that, as we have seen. The massive spending on the various post-9/11 conflicts, especially the Iraq War, shifted the balance back toward personnel and operations. Labor had become generally more expensive, with an all-volunteer and more skilled armed services competing against a fairly successful economy, and the war prompted even higher pay and extensive use of such things as reenlistment bonuses and payments to civilian contractors. At the same time, though, American warfighting had become more capital-intensive because of a higher ratio of costly weapons and equipment per uniformed personnel. It might be expected, therefore, that GWOT expenses would be more capital-intensive than expenses incurred during the Vietnam War. Nevertheless, it is remarkable that when GWOT spending is combined with the regular defense budgets, procurement and R&D went up 68 percent from 2000 to 2006 and still significantly outpaced personnel (40 percent) and O&M (57 percent). Again, under the cover of war, the Bush administration has pushed hard for projects that have little, or even nothing, to do with fighting and winning the struggles of the first decade of the twenty-first century—or even a long-term struggle with terrorism.[37]

This is not just about dollars; it also speaks to the politics of defense policy. In stark contrast to the military buildup of the Bush years, the military buildup of the early 1980s became one of the principal controversies of the early Reagan presidency. Reagan's military spending and programs spawned a large peace movement even though the nation was not at war. Centered on opposition to his nuclear weapons programs and strategy, this movement converged on the nuclear freeze proposal as a positive alternative to Reagan's policies. Perhaps I should rephrase things: Reagan's military buildup faced a peace movement at least in part *because* the nation was not at war. Despite public concern about the decline of American might and influence in the 1970s, for many Americans, the threat was elusive—the Russian bear had not seemed particularly dangerous for many years, and there were no troops in harm's way.[38] Instead, many Americans were confused and alarmed by the combination of hawkish (and sometimes cavalier) rhetoric about nuclear conflict and programs that would seemingly make such conflicts more likely.

The point is that Reagan's buildup, despite initial support, never had leverage from external events to justify or sustain it. In fact, many moderate Democrats and even Republicans in Congress criticized the waste, fraud, and abuse that accompanied the huge infusion of defense spending. They rallied around a banner of "military reform," a nonpartisan package of reforms aimed at ensuring that U.S. defense dollars were not wasted.[39]

Bush's buildup, on the other hand, was made possible by the crisis of 9/11. The impact of the global war on terror was to silence virtually all opposition to a militaristic response. What opposition did finally arise was focused on the threat of war against Iraq—and then on the actual war once it started. The buildup, which proceeded rapidly, went all but unnoticed. Consequently, this buildup without debate does not require elaborate explanation. In the wake of 9/11, no politician could afford even the perception that he or she did not support the troops while the nation was at war, even if much of the money had nothing to do with a war on terror. Potential opposition in Congress was stymied. Also, as I have indicated, a cynical bargain has been at work as well. Members of Congress might be queasy about the war, but the military buildup through the regular budget spreads billions of dollars across the land. The price of the war is alleviated by the benefits it produces in states and districts far and wide.

The elections of 2006 did little to disrupt this buildup without a debate. The Democrats came to power as opposition to the war grew, but they have had a tough enough time endgaming Iraq without undermining their fragile credibility on defense; all the more reason to turn a blind eye to the overall military budget, no matter how large and how arguably unjustified it is. A year later, when the president released his FY 2009 budget proposal, a few headlines and editorials took note of the fact that the request for Pentagon funding (not counting any separate appropriations for the war) would take military spending to its highest level since World War II and exceed the rest of the world's defense expenditures combined. Those stunning facts disappeared, however, amid the news of a faltering economy and the contest for the presidential nominations. The size and merits of the Bush buildup, or its relation to a post-Iraq national security policy, failed to penetrate the debates and primaries for both parties. In fact, one could be forgiven for concluding from the candidates' rhetoric that defense spending was too low. Insofar as the subject was mentioned at all, the frontrunners among the Republicans all endorsed higher military budgets and the Democrats talked about having to rebuild our armed forces in the wake of the war. The costs and consequences of the Bush buildup remained unquestioned and unexplored.

Not long after the attacks of 9/11, the nation learned that for the administration the crisis was not really about al Qaeda and Afghanistan, but about Iraq. In some important ways, it was not about Iraq either, but about rearmament and unprecedented military superiority. Long after the price of Iraq became apparent to many Americans, the size and purpose of the military buildup remained hidden in plain sight, even as they prepared to select the next president.

Notes

1. These percentage increases are based on figures from the DoD Comptroller for Pentagon base funding (051). The Pentagon's base budget does not include some components of total military spending, including the portion of the Department of Energy's budget that is for nuclear weapons. This is, therefore, a rather conservative measure of the increase.
2. It was also about 1.5 times the size of the military budget for the United Kingdom (UK).
3. The Republican vision of national security can be found in their 2000 platform: http://www.cnn.com/ELECTION/2000/conventions/republican/features/platform.00/#1. One example from the first presidential debate typifies candidate Bush's critique and position: "If we don't have a clear vision of the military, if we don't stop extending our troops all around the world and nation building missions, then we're going to have a serious problem coming down the road, and I'm going to prevent that. I'm going to rebuild our military power. It's one of the major priorities of my administration" (http://www.debates.org/pages/trans2000a.html). Also, in a refrain from the campaign trail, Bush would tell the "men and women in uniform" that "help is

on the way." "George W. Bush Holds Campaign Rally in Grand Rapids, Michigan," *CNN News*, http://transcripts.cnn.com/TRANSCRIPTS/0011/03/se.04.html. For the rather more far-reaching views of the Project for a New American Century, whose membership included Dick Cheney, Donald Rumsfeld, and Paul Wolfowitz, see http://www. newamericancentury.org/statementofprinciples.htm.

4. "A Blueprint For New Beginnings: A Responsible Budget for America's Priorities," http://www.whitehouse.gov/news/usbudget/blueprint/budtoc.html.

5. Quoted in Mary H. Cooper, "Bush's Defense Policy," *CQ Researcher*, September 7, 2001.

6. "Testimony Before the Senate Armed Services Committee: Defense Review Strategy," June 21, 2001, www.defenselink.mil/Speeches/Speech.aspx?SpeechID=377.

7. *Quadrennial Defense Review Report*, Department of Defense, September 30, 2001, v.

8. Ibid., iii.

9. For example, there were few details about transformation as far as either the new programs that would constitute it or the old programs that might be cut to afford and make room for it are concerned. Michael E. O'Hanlon, *Defense Policy Choices for the Bush Administration*, 2nd ed. (Washington, D.C.: Brookings Institution, 2002), 11–13; Michael Vickers, "The 2001 Quadrennial Defense Review, the FY 2003 Defense Budget Request and the Way Ahead for Transformation: Meeting the 'Rumsfeld Test,'" Center for Strategic and Budgetary Assessments, http://www.csbaonline.org/.

10. *Quadrennial Defense Review Report*, 12; *National Security Strategy of the United States of American*, September 2002, 30.

11. Quoted in Karen Foerstel and David Nather, "Beneath Capitol's Harmony, Debate Simmers Patiently," *Congressional Quarterly Weekly*, September 22, 2001, 2188.

12. http://www.whitehouse.gov/news/releases/2002/01/20020129-11.html.

13. The figures for the military (050) budget authority come from the Office of Management and Budget (OMB), while the supplementals come from the Congressional Budget Office (CBO). Official sources (OMB, Department of Defense [DoD], General Accounting Office [GAO], Congressional Research Service [CRS]) provide somewhat inconsistent figures for the war supplementals. The numbers for 2001–2007 from each source add up to nearly the same total of between $548 billion and $560 billion. But there are some discrepancies, including in what fiscal year to count some of the spending. For example, some sources include $25 billion in Title IX "bridge" funding as part of 2004's totals because the money was made available to spend in FY 2004, though it was passed as part of the FY 2005 Defense Appropriations Act.

14. In real (2000) dollars, military spending during the Korean War peaked at $416 billion, during Vietnam at $420 billion, and during the Reagan buildup reached $399 billion. By 2005, total military spending reached $420 billion, and would continue rising for at least three more years. Budget data from the OMB.

15. For one of many examples, see Defense Secretary Gates's testimony before Congress on the 2008 budget: Jim Garamone, "Gates: Historical Context Important When Considering Budget Requests," *Armed Forces Press Service*, February 7, 2007, http://www. defenselink.mil/news/newsarticle.aspx?id=2966. The Heritage Foundation even started a campaign called "Four Percent for Freedom" based on the premise that it represented the minimum the nation should commit to national security, http://www.heritage. org/Research/NationalSecurity/Misc/4percent.cfm.

16. Tim Weiner, "A Vast Arms Buildup, Yet Not Enough For War," *New York Times*, October 1, 2004, C1 and 2.

17. This calculation includes active guard and reserve. Data from the Department of Defense, OMB, and CBO.

18. Nita Lowey, a Democrat on the House Appropriations Committee. Lowey and Pelosi quoted in Michael Abramowitz and Lori Montgomery, "Bush to Request Billions for Wars," *Washington Post*, February 3, 2007, 1.
19. Senator Harry Reid, Press Release, February 2, 2007, http://reid.senate.gov/newsroom/record.cfm?id=268452.
20. *The Iraq Study Group Report*: 59–60, http://www.usip.org/isg/iraq_study_group_report/report/1206/index.html; Bryan Bender, "Iraq Panel Assails Bush Use of 'Emergency' War Budgets," *Boston Globe*, December 8, 2006, www.boston.com.
21. "President's Statement on H.R. 5122, the 'John Warner National Defense Authorization Act for Fiscal Year 2007,'" http://www.whitehouse.gov/news/releases/2006/10/20061017-9.html.
22. Christian Lowe, "'Two Sets of Books': U.S. Army, Marines Tap Emergency Funds for Long-Term Changes," *Defense News*, February 14, 2005, www.defensenews.com. See also testimony by Stephen M. Kosiak before Congress: *The Global War on Terror (GWOT): Cost Growth and Estimating Funding Requirements: Hearing before the United States Senate Budget Committee*, 110th Congress, February 6, 2007.
23. *In the October 25, 2006*, memo, England wrote, "By this memo, the ground rules for the FY'07 Spring Supplemental are being expanded to included the (Defense) Department's overall efforts related to the Global War on Terror and not strictly to Operation Enduring Freedom and Operation Iraqi Freedom." Memo quoted in James Rosen, "House Committee Prepares to Examine Iraq War Costs," *McClatchy Newspapers*, June 8, 2007, http://www.mcclatchydc.com/staff/james_rosen/story/ 15381.html.
24. Gopal Ratnam and William Matthews, "DoD Loosens Supplemental Rules," *Defense News*, November 6, 2006, www.defensenews.com.
25. Julian E. Barnes and Peter Spiegel, "Controversy over Pentagon's War-Spending Plan," *Los Angeles Times*, November 29, 2006, www.latimes.com.
26. These examples are from, David S. Cloud, "Bush's 2008 Budget Request Doubles Spending on Replacing Military Equipment," *New York Times*, February 6, 2007, 19; and Brian Bender, "Weapons That Aren't Ready Dot Bush's War Budget," *Boston Globe*, February 8, 2007, http://www.boston.com/news.
27. Christian Lowe, "'Two Sets of Books': U.S. Army, Marines Tap Emergency Funds for Long-Term Changes," *Defense News*, February 14, 2005 [www.defensenews.com].
28. My calculation of about 23 percent is based on the $163 billion total of the two FY 2007 supplementals.
29. Pat Towell, "Crusader's Friends on Capitol Hill Keep White House Scrambling," *CQ Weekly Online*, May 18, 2002, 1326–7, http://library.cqpress.com/cqweekly/weeklyreport107-000000438708.
30. Eugene Gholz and Harvey M. Sapolsky, "Restructuring the U.S. Defense Industry," *International Security* 24, no. 3 (Winter 1999–2000): 5–51.
31. Jonathan Allen, "Earmark Reform: The First Battle Is to Define the Term," *The Hill*, January 25, 2006, http://www.hillnews.com/thehill/export/TheHill/News/Frontpage/012506/earmark1.html.
32. David D. Kirkpatrick, "Earmarks Find Way into Spending Bill," *New York Times*, September 30, 2006, 10.
33. Congressional Research Service, "Earmarks in Appropriation Acts: FY1994, FY1996, FY1998, FY2000, FY2002, FY2004," March 17, 2004, and "Earmarks in FY2006 Appropriations Acts," March 6, 2006.
34. The FY 2006 BMD budget was about $8.8 billion.
35. Diana Evans, *Greasing the Wheels: Using Pork Barrel Projects to Build Majority Coalitions in Congress* (New York: Cambridge University Press, 2004).

36. Kennedy produced a two-year burst in military spending that resulted in a 15 percent real increase from FY 1961 to 1963, with almost all of the increase coming in 1962, but real decreases in FY 1964 and 1965 reduced military spending to a rather modest 8 percent increase over five years.
37. What weapons might be useful or essential in a long-term war against terrorism is debatable, of course. But most of the big-ticket programs (the F-22, the Joint Strike Fighter, Ballistic Missile Defense, much of the navy's ship-building program) are about conflicts with nation-states. In fact, there is some level of recognition that the buildup is a solution in search of a problem; that the DoD needs, as one critical commentator puts it, "a 'peer' competitor like China worthy of our weaponry. We have the hammer. Now all we need is the right nail." Major General Robert Scales, U.S. Army (Ret.), "Transformation," *Armed Forces Journal*, March 2005, 22–7.
38. In fact about the only troops in harm's way were those killed by a suicide car bomb attack while in Lebanon on a peacekeeping mission in 1983. Two hundred forty-one American military personnel died, including 220 marines, on October 23.
39. For analysis of the nuclear peace movement and the military reform movement, see Daniel Wirls, *Buildup: The Politics of Defense in the Reagan Era* (Ithaca, NY: Cornell, 1992).

10

Invoking Military Credentials in Congressional Elections, 2000–2006[1]

Jeremy M. Teigen

Ostensibly, members of the military are politically confined to the barracks, away from policymaking decisions in the United States. Nevertheless, the words of uniformed personnel carry special weight in the public forum of American politics, whether they are the words of enlisted men and women appealing for redress or subtle policy signals from members of the Joint Chiefs of Staff (JCS). In an environment where the president conditions his decision to deploy either more or fewer troops in Iraq upon field commanders' judgments, and where retired officers' opinions are routinely employed to legitimate policy preferences on Capitol Hill, we should not be surprised if military credentials feature prominently in electoral politics. Currently serving members of the military are legally precluded from participating in public political discussion, but the invocation of previous military service in the electoral arena is a recurring phenomenon in U.S. elections (see Kathleen Mahoney-Norris's chapter in this volume). Veterans have run for high political office since the beginning of the republic, waving their military service as a banner; however, the limited scholarly attention to the phenomenon means we are uncertain about its influence on voters and election outcomes.

Of those obtaining a major party nomination to run in presidential elections, thirty-seven have been military veterans; indeed, swells of veterans entering politics followed each of the nineteenth-century conflicts as well as World War II. Men such as George Washington, Andrew Jackson, Ulysses Grant, and Dwight Eisenhower were former generals whose military reputation engendered a successful presidential bid. Theodore Roosevelt, John Kennedy, George McGovern, George H. W. Bush, Bob Dole, and John Kerry also employed their wartime heroism to bolster their electoral appeal. Indeed, many candidates seeking all levels of political office use previous military service in their campaigns.

This fact suggests that men and women with military experience engender a special appeal among voters. The possibility that military service helps candidates win elections was informally quantified in a foxhole during the Normandy invasion in 1944. When asked what he was doing there by Captain Stuyvesant Wainwright II, who later became a congressman from New York, Major Strom Thurmond, later an eight-term senator and presidential candidate, replied, "Captain, being in on this here D Day is goin' to be worth 250,000 votes back home."[2]

In the campaign season preceding the 2006 congressional midterm elections that would shift control from Republicans to Democrats, a number of veterans from the conflicts in Afghanistan and Iraq ran for Congress as Democrats. These "Fighting Dems," such as Tammy Duckworth and Joe Sestak, used their military service to demonstrate their competence in defense policy and insulate themselves from the traditional claim that Democrats are soft on defense, hoping to gain the military credibility enjoyed by Republicans. By using their military experience to craft a campaign theme, they sought to provide cover for the Democrats' criticisms of the conduct of the wars in Iraq and Afghanistan. Despite the recurring efforts of veterans to brandish their service records, it is unclear whether military service helps in an election, and if it does, by how much. Sestak won, but Duckworth did not.

To find out if being a veteran actually translates into votes, this research analyzes recent congressional elections to evaluate three theories. First, I look at the assertion that military service helps candidates appeal to voters. I quantify the electoral gain from military service after controlling for the usual factors that influence election outcomes. While previous scholarly attention to this topic has been rare, there is no shortage of evidence that campaigners and candidates believe military service helps garner votes. Candidates of all kinds emphasize issues related to their own personal record and background.[3] Military veterans regularly highlight their military experience in their campaign biographies.

Second, it is important to consider party differences related to military service. Since Vietnam, the Republican Party has enjoyed ownership of issues related to national defense, security, and war, an advantage solidified during the 1980s (see Donald Inbody's chapter in this volume). Voters have judged the Republican Party to be more competent on military issues than their Democratic rivals.[4] Citizens may use a candidate's military service as an information shortcut that fosters belief in a candidate's knowledge about security and defense issues, as well as in his or her leadership capacity.[5] Thus, a Democratic candidate can use his or her military résumé to attempt to blunt the advantage Republican candidates have on security issues. Recent congressional elections provide an excellent example to parse the military service question. It is difficult to imagine military service helping congressional Democratic candidates at another time if it did not help them in 2006.

The third question about the nature of veterans' potential electoral advantage relates to whether challengers or incumbents benefit more. Incumbent politicians have the benefit of name recognition, and voters are likely to judge them based more on track record than biography. Hypothesizing that positive biographical information about candidates would help candidates who are less familiar to voters, this effort estimates the effect of military service on electoral outcomes by contrasting challengers and incumbents.

Discovering whether past military service affects election outcomes has other policy implications as well. While congressional veterans mirror nonveterans in terms of most domestic policy preferences, veterans in Congress vote differently than their nonveteran peers on matters of war.[6] The proportion of veterans serving in important leadership positions, including those in Congress, may affect the nature of American foreign policy. Specifically, veterans in Congress are more reluctant to begin conflicts, but more likely to increase their intensity once conflict has begun.[7] Another study showed no measurable differences between veterans and nonveterans among senators regarding arms treaty ratification votes.[8]

Candidates and Military Service

Scholars have investigated veterans' candidacies in several ways. One study showed that the winners of U.S. presidential elections who outpaced their party's support, in so-called surge elections, were almost all popular former generals with well-known military experience—for example, Andrew Jackson, William Henry Harrison, and Dwight Eisenhower.[9] Others have looked to congressional contests. One way to ask whether veterans have electoral appeal is to ask if they are overrepresented in Congress. Both chambers of Congress were flush with veterans after World War II; specifically, there were only ninety-five veterans in Congress in 1941, but there were 323 veterans by 1959. Somit and Tanenhaus investigated this postwar veteran boom and concluded that voters were ambivalent about veteran candidacies in the early 1950s.[10] Nevertheless, both parties' leaders were keen to nominate veteran candidates because of a belief in their electoral attractiveness. Somit and Tanenhaus's initial answer to the first question—whether veterans gain more votes—was negative, despite veterans' overrepresentation in the legislature. They explain the disproportionately high number of veterans in Congress by pointing to party elites who nominated the candidates rather than voters' preferences.

Bianco and Markham calculated Congress's veteran composition as if it were demographically reflective of the veteran population, and found that in the 1990s, for the first time since the early 1900s, veterans were *underrepresented* in Congress. They argued that simple generational replacement does not explain the decrease in veterans on Capitol Hill. Instead, they suggest, the end of conscription in 1973 had a critical effect on young people destined for life in elite political circles. Since the 1990s, military veterans have become a rarity among federal legislators.[11]

There has been occasional attention paid to the military service of presidential candidates recently as well. Scrutiny surrounded the apparent preferential treatment given to both vice presidential candidate Dan Quayle in 1988 and presidential candidate George W. Bush in 2000 and 2004. Both had influential fathers, and both performed their service in the National Guard rather than in Vietnam-bound units during the draft era. Critics labeled Bill Clinton a draft dodger during the 1992 election campaign because of his lack of service and his attempts to avoid it. In 2004, John Kerry became the first Vietnam veteran to obtain a major party presidential nomination. His navy service, coupled with his antiwar activities after his return, created a complicated legacy for a presidential campaign. His memorable salute opening his acceptance speech was followed by a series of "Swift Boat" advertisements that attempted to refute Kerry's positive claims about his service.[12] Many, including senior strategists working within the Kerry campaign, believe that the slow response to these widely seen negative advertisements seriously harmed Kerry's support.[13]

In a prelude to the 2006 congressional elections, Ohio held a special House open-seat election in a strongly Republican district in the summer of 2005. Paul Hackett, the Democratic nominee, exceeded expectations and almost beat the Republican.[14] An Operation Iraqi Freedom veteran, he made criticizing Bush's conduct of the war and touting his own military service central to his campaign, and the national media followed the race closely. In 2006, the Fighting Dems repeated this pattern of Democrats using their service as a platform to criticize President Bush and the Republican-controlled Congress on the conduct of the war in Iraq. This loose group of Democratic candidates consisted of military veterans running with an antiadministration position. The assumption was that just as "only Nixon could go to China," only veterans possessed the credibility to highlight missteps by the administration in Iraq. The 2006 congressional election cycle is of particular concern for this analysis, not only because it represents the Democratic takeover of both chambers, but also due to the salience of veteran candidates generated by the Fighting Dems. The group enjoyed repeated media coverage, typically featuring individuals such as Tammy Duckworth, a helicopter pilot who had lost her legs during combat in Iraq.[15]

Data Analysis and Findings

This analysis uses general election data from U.S. House of Representatives elections (2000–2006) to evaluate the electoral bonus of military service. The best barometer with which to measure the electoral appeal of military service is the percentage of the two-party vote that candidates win. While House elections are not generally competitive, because of advantageously drawn district boundaries and the advantages of incumbency, there is variation in the candidates' share of the major party ballots. Rather than take random subsamples of races as Somit and Tanenhaus did, this analysis uses data for all the candidates in the 2000–2006 House elections.[16] Somit and Tanenhaus, as well as Bianco and Markham, examine the proportion of members of Congress with military experience, which provides a rough measure of the electoral appeal of candidates' military service. However, their analysis is limited by their inattention to losing candidates. By collecting biographical information on incumbents seeking reelection, open-seat challengers, and challengers seeking to unseat incumbents, this study offers a more thorough assessment of how much veteran status helps political aspirants at the polls.

While there are many duties, posts, and ranks within the military, this study codes candidates dichotomously, as either nonveterans or veterans. Collecting biographical data on congressional candidates involved using multiple sources.[17] Some congressional races featured candidate military service more prominently than others. For example, Kansas Republicans nominated a navy pilot, Adam Taff, who had enforced the no-fly zone over Iraq and who was a civilian airline pilot flying on September 11, 2001. Vietnam veteran Darryl Roberts made his service— and the "duty and honor" it bestowed—central to his campaign for Oklahoma's Fourth District.[18] Republican primary voters selected Operation Desert Storm veteran Rebecca Armendariz Klein to take on an incumbent in 2004 in one of the newly drawn districts in Texas, and her military service was central to most of her campaign literature. In 2006, attention centered on the sixty-odd Democratic candidates for the House with military experience.

Campaigns today exhibit overwhelming prima facie evidence that candidates and campaigns believe that past military service attracts voters. Even though the proportion of veteran representatives in the legislature is lower than it has been in the past, there is no shortage of contemporary candidates who refer to their military service. Candidates trumpet their service when they have it, and barring that, borrow it from proxies if they can vis-à-vis the service of a family member or their ties to veterans in their community. Table 10.1 presents the average Democratic vote share in the four permutations of races in terms of veteran status: neither candidate a veteran, Democratic candidate a veteran, Republican candidate a veteran, or both candidates veterans. In the aggregate, military service increases vote share in most contexts. For example, in 2004, Republicans in the House with service records performed, on average, 9 percent better than their Republican colleagues in districts featuring no veterans. The ability of Democratic candidates with military service to outperform nonveteran Democratic candidates is distinctly less impressive than Republican veterans across the time series, but it is especially anemic in 2006. Average Democratic vote share in races with a Democratic veteran and a Republican nonveteran was less than in races without any veterans. While the Democrats retook the chamber from Republicans by increasing their seat total by thirty in a year in which the president's approval ratings flagged they cannot credit their success on the individual electoral performances of the Fighting Dems. It was a Democratic year, but not because of the Democratic veterans' performance.

Table 10.1 Mean Two-Party Democratic Vote Share by Candidates' Military Service, House Elections 2000–2006

	2000		2002		2004		2006	
	GOP Nonvet	GOP Vet	GOP Nonvet	GOP Vet	GOP Vet	GOP Nonvet	GOP Nonvet	GOP Vet
Dem Nonvet	54.8	44.4	51.7	42.0	53.3	44.3	60.1	52.8
	(239)	(100)	(250)	(103)	(248)	(96)	(255)	(77)
Dem Vet	59.0	48.1	59.9	53.8	51.3	51.5	52.0	52.6
	(63)	(25)	(55)	(19)	(64)	(19)	(70)	(25)

Source: Barone et al., *Almanac of American Politics* (see note 17).
Note: Number of cases is in parentheses.

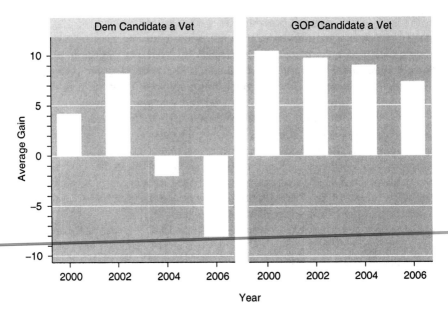

Figure 10.1   Average Veteran Advantage in Vote Share, House Elections, 2000–2006

Figure 10.1 demonstrates the relative overall performance of each party's veterans, separated to depict the deviation from the baseline state of no veterans in the race. The baseline, or zero, refers to the average vote share when neither of the candidates is a veteran, as seen in Table 10.1. For example, the average Democrat's vote share in 2000 with no veterans in the race was 54.8 percent (note that the baseline for each election year is different). The first bar represents the gain or loss of the average Democrat's vote share when considering races with one veteran in the race on the Democratic side, compared to races without veterans. In 2000 and 2002, mean Democratic performance in contested races increased when Democrats nominated a veteran to run against a nonveteran Republican; but in 2004 and 2006, Democratic veterans did worse than their nonveteran Democratic peers overall. For Republican veterans, the situation is more consistent. In each of the four years considered here, average performance of veteran Republicans exceeded that of nonveteran Republicans by 7 to 10 percent.

Though the aggregate percentages in Table 10.1 and Figure 10.1 offer a straightforward picture of the overall performance of veterans running for office, a multivariate model disentangles the effect of veteran status from related factors that affect election outcomes (incumbency, campaign spending, etc.). The model regresses the two-party Democratic vote share on the veteran status of both candidates along with other factors that affect election outcomes (see Table 10.2). Empirical evidence demonstrates that Democratic candidates with military service received 1.7 percent more of the vote share in contested 2002 races than Democratic nonveterans did. In 2006, Republican veterans enjoyed a commensurate advantage over Republicans without service. In 2000 and 2004, veterans from neither party benefited at the polls from their previous military service at a statistically significant level.

Table 10.2 Democratic Vote Share in House Elections, 2000–2006

	Contested Elections					All Elections				
	2000	2002	2004	2006	Pooled	2000	2002	2004	2006	Pooled
Dem Vet	0.449	1.707	0.259	-0.772	0.423	2.343	4.824	2.250	0.095	2.450
	(0.704)	(0.811)*	(0.654)	(0.642)	(0.359)	(1.048)*	(1.044)*	(1.125)*	(0.948)	(0.525)*
GOP Vet	-0.244	-0.699	-0.232	-1.337	-0.681	-2.486	-3.248	-2.173	-4.002	-3.016
	(0.614)	(0.664)	(0.587)	(0.595)*	(0.317)*	(0.920)*	(0.861)*	(0.993)*	(0.903)*	(0.466)*
Observations	367	352	363	370	1452	426	427	427	422	1702
Adj. R²	0.92	0.91	0.93	0.92	0.92	0.87	0.89	0.86	0.87	0.87

Source: Barone et al., *Almanac of American Politics* (see note 17).

Note: Ordinary least square analysis. Standard errors in parentheses (* $p \leq .05$). Controls include the previous election's Democratic vote share, incumbency, district partisanship measured by the Republican presidential candidate's overall percentage of the vote in the previous election, the share of the district that is white, the region, the year, and the spending and gender of both candidates.

The columns of Table 10.2 denoting "All Elections" present the results of the model considering all House races. The electoral power of previous military service grows when uncontested races, along with the more numerous contested races, are considered. For Democrats, the advantage is between 2 and 5 percent, and for Republicans, it is between 2 and 4 percent. The differences between the two sets of estimates, the contested versus the uncontested data, are evidence of a veteran effect among unopposed incumbents. In other words, if incumbents lacking challengers have successfully scared off potential contenders, veteran incumbents are especially fearsome to would-be aspirants. Comparing the estimates of the contested models to those that include unopposed races suggests that veteran status helps incumbents as much or more than it helps challengers.[19]

Discussion: Elections and Previous Military Service

This analysis used data to evaluate three questions about the intersection of previous military service and congressional elections: (1) Do political candidates receive more votes because they served in the armed forces? (2) After 9/11, do Democrats benefit more at the polls from military service than Republicans by using military service to counteract the traditional Republican advantage on defense issues? (3) Do challengers benefit more from military service than incumbents? In contrast to the conventional wisdom, results show that the effect of previous military service is substantively small and that it does not manifest in every election. Regarding partisan differences, Democratic candidates who touted their veteran status in 2002 benefited only slightly in terms of vote share, while Republicans in the same position did not. However, the advantage soon disappeared, even as aggregate Democratic strength intensified. Despite explicit attempts to cast Democratic veterans returned from Iraq and Afghanistan as a vanguard to take control of the legislature in 2006, it was actually Republican veterans who benefited more on Election Day than Democratic veterans. Other things being equal, Republican veterans did about 1.3 percent better in terms of vote share than Republican nonveterans did.

Tammy Duckworth in Illinois, Joe Sestak in Pennsylvania, and Eric Massa in New York are three prominent examples of Democratic challengers who employed their military service to obtain credibility in their criticism of the administration's conduct of the war in Iraq (and their respective Republican opponents). Sestak beat his opponent, though Duckworth and Massa lost by slim margins in competitive races. Overall, when comparing the electoral performance of the Fighting Dems in 2006, they did not fare as well as their nonveteran peers, even when controlling for important factors such as campaign spending and district partisanship. As the Bush administration's control of the situation in Iraq continued to deteriorate in 2006, the prominence of these Democratic candidates with military service may have helped nationalize the congressional elections. Their candidacies may have supported Democrats overall, but they did not help the veteran candidates individually.

The last hypothesis sought to establish whether previous military service had a distinctive effect among incumbents as opposed to challengers. Incumbents use name recognition, federal projects and money spent in the district, legislative efforts, and constituency service to make their case to voters, and hence should not need to rely heavily upon personal prepolitical biography to impress the electorate. The empirical results point to a different conclusion, however. Given the results in Table 10.2, there is little evidence that military service helps challengers, and modest evidence that it assists incumbents.

What is the significance of the small advantage enjoyed by Democratic veterans in 2002 and Republicans in 2006? In most House races, changing the outcome by 2 percent in either direction would not alter the outcome. However, national party organizations pour resources into the handful of close, open-seat races because gaining even a 1 percent vote share can make a difference. Having a veteran on the ballot can be a small but inexpensive advantage. There were five contests in 2006 in which the Democrat won the election over a nonveteran Republican by a margin smaller than the 1.3 percent bonus a given Republican could expect to gain from previous military experience. However, these cases are not common. Military service is obviously not essential for electoral victory; if it had a robust impact on elections, there would be 535 veterans on Capitol Hill. It is unreasonable to expect the effect of candidate biography to rival the effects of issues, incumbency, partisanship, and campaign spending. Given that there are somewhere between 190,000 and 250,000 two-party votes cast in a House election, and that veterans at their most appealing could only hope to attract 1.7 percent more than normal, three to four thousand more votes is all one could expect in a given House race. Hence, Senator Thurmond's speculation about the electoral lift from military service is a bit of South Carolina hyperbole.

There are several plausible explanations for the gulf between the degree to which political elites, such as campaign strategists and candidates, believe military service increases candidate appeal and the minor degree to which it actually does. One interpretation might be that military service potentially benefits only presidential candidates because of the obvious connection between the military and the president's role of commander in chief. Another possibility might stem from a measurement problem. The imprecision of the military service variable in this analysis may overly homogenize the concept of military service. A former supply clerk at Fort Dix and a Congressional Medal of Honor winner would appear identically in this study, but could yield very different campaign benefits.

Given the reality that the electoral effect of military service is minimal and inconsistent, why do we view military service positively in campaigns if its effects are slight and sporadic? Why do campaign websites, candidate biographies, television advertising, and media coverage focus heavily on the military service of congressional candidates? As Somit and Tanenhaus found with party elites in the 1950s, there is an apparent, widespread, and enduring perception that military service aids candidates at the ballot box. One reason may be the amount of trust the public has had for the military as an institution since the end of conscription and the war in Vietnam.[20] Another reason may be that military service does not hurt candidates' chances: with the notable exception of the Democrats in 2006, the evidence indicates that military service helps, if only slightly. Finally, invoking martial themes and the military institution by trumpeting one's own past military service may inadvertently blur the civil-military divide by infusing military imagery into partisan contests, but it is hard to fault office seekers for using their service in a popular institution to demonstrate their service to their country and their military experience.

Notes

1. The author thanks Derek Reveron, Judith Stiehm, Daron Shaw, Kent Jennings, David Leal, Bruce Buchanan, Brian Roberts, Julie George, Rich Holtzman, Neal Allen, Ken Kollman, Gary Segura, Bill Bianco, Peter Feaver, Seth McKee, Susan Hangen, and Brian Arbour for helpful comments. Anika Wouters and Scott Stripling assisted obligingly with data collection.

2. Cited in Arthur T. Hadley, *The Invisible Primary* (Englewood Cliffs, NJ: Prentice-Hall, 1976), p. 3.

3. Patrick J. Sellers, "Strategy and Background in Congressional Campaigns," *American Political Science Review* 92, no. 1 (1998).

4. Helmut Norpoth and Bruce Buchanan, "Wanted: The Education President: Issue Trespassing by Political Candidates," *Public Opinion Quarterly* 56, no. 1 (1992); John R. Petrocik, "Issue Ownership in Presidential Elections, with a 1980 Case Study," *American Journal of Political Science* 40, no. 3 (1996).

5. Samuel L. Popkin, *The Reasoning Voter* (Chicago: University of Chicago Press, 1991).

6. Modest evidence of selected domestic policy distinctions are reported by William T. Bianco and Jamie Markham, "Vanishing Veterans: The Decline of Military Experience in the U.S. Congress," in *Soldiers and Civilians: The Civil-Military Gap and American National Security*, ed. Peter D. Feaver and Richard H. Kohn (Cambridge: MIT Press, 2001).

7. Christopher Gelpi and Peter D. Feaver, "Speak Softly and Carry a Big Stick? Veterans in the Political Elite and the American Use of Force," *American Political Science Review* 96, no. 4 (2002).

8. C. James Delaet, Charles M. Rowling, and James M. Scott, "Politics Past the Edge: Partisanship and Arms Control Treaties in the U.S. Senate," *Journal of Political & Military Sociology* 33, no. 2 (2005).

9. Charles Sellers, "The Equilibrium Cycle in Two-Party Politics," *Public Opinion Quarterly* 29, no. 1 (1965): 2.

10. Albert Somit and Joseph Tanenhaus, "The Veteran in the Electoral Process: The House of Representatives," *Journal of Politics* 19, no. 2 (1957).

11. Norman Ornstein, "The Legacy of Campaign 2000," *Washington Quarterly* 24, no. 2 (2001): 102.

12. Coverage of John Kerry's service in Vietnam is elaborated in Douglas Brinkley, *Tour of Duty: John Kerry and the Vietnam War* (New York: William Morrow, 2004). More details about the role it played in 2004 are described in Jeremy M. Teigen, "Veterans' Party Identification, Candidate Affect, and Vote Choice in the 2004 U.S. Presidential Election," *Armed Forces & Society* 33, no. 3 (2007).

13. For example, Robert Shrum, *No Excuses: Concessions of a Serial Campaigner* (New York: Simon and Schuster, 2007).

14. James Dao, "Republican Edges out Iraq Veteran for Congress," *New York Times*, August 2, 2005.

15. For example, Gwyneth K. Shaw, "From Soldiers to Politicians," *Baltimore Sun*, April 18, 2006; John Whitesides, "Iraq War Vets Entry US Political Fray," *Washington Post*, February 3, 2006.

16. Vermont's single district, from 2000–2004, and all of Louisiana's seven districts are omitted from the analysis because of incomparability. Vermont's incumbent, Bernie Sanders, was an independent, and Louisiana voters participate in a unique balloting system that holds the primary and general elections simultaneously.

17. For incumbents, see Michael Barone, Richard E. Cohen, and Grant Ujifusa, *The Almanac of American Politics, 2006* (Washington, D.C.: National Journal, 2005). For incumbents and challengers, see the 2004 American National Election Study "Auxiliary File" (Ann Arbor: University of Michigan, Center for Political Studies [Producer and Distributor]), the Library of Congress' Minerva website (http://memory.loc.gov/cocoon/minerva/html/minerva-home.html), as well as Associated Press candidate biographies on Lexis-Nexis.

18. Barone et al., *Almanac of American Politics*, p. 1318.

19. Models of veterans' electoral attractiveness that include uncontested races have provisos, particularly that the Democratic vote share be manipulated to generate a hypothetical weak challenger, that vote share be clumped around the extreme ends of the variable's range, and that the gender and spending of the counterfactual challenger be imposed rather than measured.

20. David C. King and Zachary Karabell, *The Generation of Trust: Public Confidence in the U.S. Military since Vietnam* (Washington, D.C.: AEI Press, 2003).

11

Presidential Image and the Military

Brendan J. Doherty

In January 1951, in the midst of an unpopular war in Korea and facing a sagging economy at home, presidential aide George Elsey wrote an internal White House memorandum advocating that President Harry Truman hold events at military bases in order to improve his image and promote his programs. Elsey reasoned that such events would allow Truman to make the case to the American people, "in his own words, rather than filtered through the Washington press corps," about why the Korean War was worth fighting. After reluctantly making one such trip to Aberdeen, Maryland, Truman refused to do any similar events, declaring them to be "gimmickry."[1]

Presidential practices in this regard have changed dramatically in the more than fifty years since Elsey made his proposal. Presidents of both parties now regularly travel to speak at military installations and before members of the armed forces. Most famously, on May 1, 2003, President George W. Bush landed in a flight suit on the deck of the USS *Abraham Lincoln* off the coast of California. He then addressed the nation from the deck of the aircraft carrier and, in front of a large banner proclaiming "Mission Accomplished," declared an end to major combat operations in Iraq.[2] While President Truman and some of Bush's contemporary critics may have considered this to be "gimmickry," this dramatic event provided memorable images that captured the attention of the American people and allowed the president to communicate directly to a national audience about his views on the Iraq War.

As commander in chief, the president wields extraordinary power, both militarily and politically. In recent years, the military has become an integral part of presidential image-making, allowing the nation's chief executive to project strong leadership by emphasizing his role as commander in chief. Presidents now regularly travel to military settings, and their message is often intended for a much broader audience than the uniformed men and women before them. Through the systematic examination of presidential public events in domestic military settings from 1977 through 2004, I discuss the military as a source of political strength for the president and its evolving role in burnishing the president's public image.

First, I consider the nature of presidential image-making and the military's role in it, and then I analyze the dynamics of presidential military events over time, within term, by political party, and in relation to other patterns of presidential travel. I then focus on the military context of each presidency, the personal military background of each president, and the dynamics of presidential military events in election years to further elucidate the relationships between presidential image and the armed forces.

Presidential Image-Making

Presidents have long invested substantial effort in crafting their public image. In his classic work on presidential power, Richard Neustadt argued that a president's public prestige is a critical resource that can enhance or erode his bargaining position in Washington.[3] Samuel Kernell contended that recent presidents regularly "go public" in an attempt to communicate directly with the American people and enhance their public standing. This in turn strengthens their hand in their dealings with Congress.[4] These academic assessments have been echoed by political actors. Patrick Caddell, a top aide and pollster to then president-elect Jimmy Carter, declared in a 1976 transition memo that "it is my thesis that governing with public approval requires a continuing political campaign."[5] In 1997, an adviser to President Bill Clinton asserted, "A President doesn't just need a majority on Election Day. The President needs a majority every day of the week behind every bill that he has."[6] In order to build and sustain such support, presidents often communicate directly with the public in an effort to portray themselves as strong and effective leaders.

Military venues can be particularly effective settings in which to project such an image, as they emphasize the president's role as commander in chief, and thus as the principal defender of the nation. While in many other democracies the roles of head of state and political leader fall to two individuals, in the United States they are combined into one president. As such, the chief executive must project an image of national unity, filling the role played by a constitutional monarch in many countries. But he—and someday she—also serves as the head of a political party that requires him to advance a partisan agenda and pursue electoral success. The second role is likely to divide the country rather than unite it. Thus, the aggressive pursuit of partisan goals can jeopardize a president's effectiveness as a unifying leader.[7]

Scholars have documented the effect on a president's standing of so-called rally events, in which a president's popularity surges in the face of an international crisis. In such situations, presidents are given wide leeway to act in what they see as the best interests of the country, and enjoy broad, if temporary, bipartisan support.[8] Given this, it is no wonder that presidents might seek to hold events before military audiences where they can tout their role as a strong, unifying, national leader.

Not incidentally, appearances before a military audience also ensure that the president will receive a positive reception. As the president sits atop the military chain of command, the members of the armed forces are obliged to greet their commander in chief respectfully and enthusiastically, regardless of whether they agree with his political positions. Presidents relatively unpopular with the military receive the same positive response from the troops as those who engender strong support from the men and women in uniform.

Recent presidents have paid close attention to the visual backdrops of their public events. While presidents throughout the television age have used this medium to reach out to the American people, Reagan aide Michael Deaver has been credited with the careful selection of speech settings and with perfecting "the 'photo op,' which positioned the former actor in visually irresistible locations where troublesome reporters' questions could not intrude: atop the Great Wall of China, on the beach at Normandy for the 40th anniversary of D-Day or in front of a construction site as the president announced the latest government report on housing starts."[9] Events with the military often provide stirring images of the commander in chief thanking uniformed men and women. Often, troops appear onstage with the president and are shown in photographs of the speech with American flags waving in the background.

Making Sense of Presidential Image and the Military

In order to analyze presidential image and the military, I constructed a dataset of domestic presidential events at military installations or on vessels outside of the Washington, D.C., area from 1977 through 2004 by examining the *Public Papers of the Presidents of the United States.* This study covers a twenty-eight-year period that encompasses five presidencies—those of Jimmy Carter, Ronald Reagan, George H. W. Bush, Bill Clinton, and the first term of George W. Bush. As I am primarily interested in the dynamics of presidential military travel, events in or near Washington, D.C, are excluded. Presidents hold many events in the Maryland and Virginia suburbs of the nation's capital. As they are only a few miles from the White House, trips there are not comparable to other types of presidential travel. Thus, events at the Pentagon, Arlington National Cemetery, Fort Myer, Andrews Air Force Base, Bethesda Naval Hospital, and other DC-area military locations are not included in this study. Events in Maryland and Virginia outside of suburban Washington, however—including those at the United States Naval Academy and the Aberdeen Proving Grounds in Maryland, as well as those in Newport News, Norfolk, and Quantico, Virginia—are considered in this analysis.[10]

Presidents in this study held three types of events in these military settings. Of the 196 presidential military events, 79.1 percent of them were appearances where the president was clearly speaking to the troops. Another 9.2 percent of these events were exchanges with the press in a military setting. These incidents are included in this study because they are often the only record of a president interacting with the troops on a given day. For example, on April 28, 1980,

President Carter spoke with reporters at the Brooks Army Medical Center at Fort Sam Houston in Texas after visiting troops who had been wounded in the attempt to rescue American hostages in Iran. This represented an important action taken by the president in his role as commander in chief and certainly garnered media attention, even though he did not make a major public address on a military base that day.

Finally, 11.7 percent of the events in this study were held in military settings before an audience that did not clearly include members of the armed forces. For example, on April 22, 1997, President Clinton stood alongside federal and local officials in the Enlisted Club at Grand Forks Air Force Base in North Dakota to discuss floods that had devastated that area. Additionally, on December 10, 2004, President Bush addressed United Service Organizations (USO) volunteers at Fort Belvoir in Virginia as they prepared care packages to send to the troops overseas. In both instances, it was not clear if members of the armed forces were in the audience, but it seems prudent to include these events in a study of the president's efforts to craft his public image in military venues.[11]

Patterns of Presidential Military Events

Presidents have a great deal of discretion in deciding when and where they travel, as they allocate one of their scarcest resources—their time. Such decisions are taken quite seriously, and a tremendous amount of effort goes into preparing for every presidential move. An advance team lays the groundwork for each presidential trip, coordinating details that range from security to public relations. At least three helicopters—one bearing the president, and two providing security and serving as decoys—ferry the president from the White House to Andrews Air Force Base, where he boards Air Force One. Accompanying the president is a large entourage that includes support planes carrying personnel and military and communications equipment, and cargo planes bearing armored vehicles, the president's limousine, and at times his helicopter, Marine One. In short, moving the president and what has been called his mobile White House around the country requires no small amount of investment of time, money, and political effort.[12] Patterns of presidential travel in general, and of presidential military events in particular, can reveal a great deal about a president's priorities.

Presidential military events are tremendously varied. Presidents address the troops before they deploy overseas and welcome them home when they return. They visit the wounded and make remarks at memorial services. Presidents regularly speak at the several service academies, christen newly constructed ships, speak to military communities across the country, and land briefly at military installations on their way to far-flung destinations, such as stopovers in Hawaii or Alaska on a journey to Asia.

As figure 11.1 illustrates, levels of presidential military events increased dramatically between the beginning of the Carter administration in 1977 and the conclusion of George W. Bush's first term in 2004. Bush's first-term total was two-and-a-half times as great as that of Carter a quarter century earlier, and

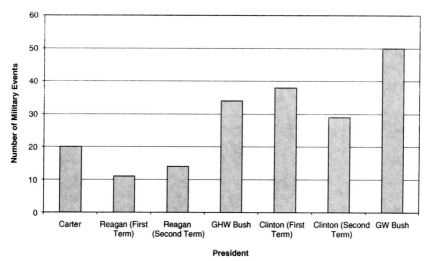

Source: Public Papers of the Presidents of the United States

Figure 11.1   Presidential Military Events by Presidential Term, 1977–2004

Table 11.1   Presidential Military Events by President and Year of Term, 1977–2004

President	Year of Term				Total
	1	*2*	*3*	*4*	
Carter	4	8	4	4	20
Reagan (First Term)	3	3	2	3	11
Reagan (Second Term)	2	6	3	3	14
GHW Bush	10	5	12	7	34
Clinton (First Term)	7	9	11	11	38
Clinton (Second Term)	6	5	9	9	29
GW Bush	14	11	15	10	50
Total	46	47	56	47	196

Source: Public Papers of the Presidents of the United States.

nearly four times larger than the average number of military events that Ronald Reagan held in each of his two terms in office. With the exception of Reagan and a slight drop during Clinton's second term, the rise in military events has been fairly steady over the course of this period.

Table 11.1 reveals that in the aggregate, levels of presidential military events were relatively even within presidential terms, with a spike in the third year, when the Persian Gulf War began during President George H. W. Bush's term and when the Iraq War commenced during his son's administration. Looking at individual presidents within terms, only George W. Bush achieved double-digit levels of military activity in each of his four years, and his totals are the highest of any president in three of the four years of his term. On average, there is very little difference in the level of military activity by political party, as Reagan's low totals

Table 11.2   Presidential Military Events as a Percentage of all Presidential Public Events outside of Washington, D.C., Maryland, and Virginia

President	Presidential Military Events	All Presidential Events Outside of Washington, DC, Maryland, and Virginia	Percentage
Carter	20	384	5.2%
Reagan (First Term)	11	345	3.2%
Reagan (Second Term)	14	237	5.9%
GHW Bush	34	599	5.7%
Clinton (First Term)	38	630	6.0%
Clinton (Second Term)	29	624	4.6%
GW Bush	50	726	6.9%
Total	196	3545	5.5%

Source: Public Papers of the Presidents of the United States.

are balanced out by the Bushes' higher numbers. Democrats in this study averaged 29 military events per presidential term, while Republicans held 27.25 events, on average, in each four-year term.

What proportion of presidential travel is composed of events in military settings? Table 11.2 details the number of military events outside of the Washington, D.C., area in relation to the number of all presidential public events outside of Washington, D.C.; Maryland; and Virginia.[13] As presidential military events became more frequent over the period of this study, presidential public events overall grew substantially as well. The percentage of military events has thus not grown as dramatically, rising from 5.2 percent under Carter to 6.9 percent under the second President Bush. The lowest percentage belongs to Reagan during his first term.

Any explanation of presidential attention to the military must take into account the individual circumstances of each president. Reagan held the fewest military events and total events of the presidents in this study. This is likely due, at least partially, to his relatively advanced age when he was inaugurated as president, as well as to his lengthy recovery from the assassination attempt on his life in Washington, D.C., in March 1981. At the other end of the scale, George W. Bush's high numbers and percentage of military events seem to be naturally explained by the attacks of September 11, 2001, which put the United States on a wartime footing for the rest of his term. I now turn to some of the contextual factors that further elucidate patterns of presidential military events.

The Military Context

Do the frequency and intensity of military engagements during a presidency correspond to a president's tendency to hold events in military settings? While this explanation is intuitively appealing and surely accounts for some levels of presidential military events, two pieces of evidence suggest that the story is more complicated. First, a review of Louis Fisher's comprehensive study of presidential war powers indicates that actual military engagements do not seem to relate directly to the number of presidential military events for two of the five presidents in this study.[14]

Under President Carter, the only military endeavor initiated by the president was the failed attempt in 1980 to rescue the American hostages held in Iran. Reagan held far fewer military events than did Carter, in spite of the fact that he initiated military action on several occasions. First, he sent marines to Lebanon as part of a peacekeeping mission from 1982 through 1984. He then sent American troops to the island of Grenada in 1983 and launched air strikes against Libya in 1986. Toward the end of his term, Reagan substantially increased the U.S. military presence in the Persian Gulf in response to a 1987 Iraqi missile strike upon the USS *Stark* that killed thirty-seven Americans.[15]

The administration of George H. W. Bush was marked by several major military operations—first, the 1989 deployment of eleven thousand additional troops to Panama, joining the thirteen thousand American troops already stationed there, and the removal of General Manuel Noriega from power. Second, in 1990, in response to Saddam Hussein's invasion of Kuwait, Bush commenced a troop buildup in the Middle East, and in 1991 U.S. forces moved into Kuwait and expelled the Iraqi forces in the first Gulf War. Finally, in the closing days of his term, Bush authorized the deployment of U.S. peacekeeping forces to Somalia.[16]

President Clinton authorized a large number of military actions during his term as president. He continued and extended the military operations in Somalia, which lasted until 1994. He authorized air strikes against Iraq in 1993, 1996, and 1998, and sent troops to Haiti in 1994 to help stabilize the country upon the return of President Jean-Bertrand Aristide. In Bosnia, Clinton first ordered airstrikes in 1994 as part of a North Atlantic Treaty Organization (NATO) operation; and in 1995 he sent in ground troops as part of a peacekeeping force, the start of a troop presence that would continue throughout the remainder of his presidency. Clinton launched airstrikes against targets in Afghanistan and Sudan in 1998, and in 1999 he authorized U.S. forces to conduct airstrikes against Yugoslavia as part of a NATO operation.[17]

President George W. Bush, in response to the attacks of 9/11, sent U.S. forces into Afghanistan to topple the Taliban regime and subsequently invaded Iraq in 2003 to remove Saddam Hussein from power. Military operations in both countries continued throughout his term in office, leading to the highest levels of sustained military activity during the period of this study.[18]

These snapshots of military activity reveal two things. First, for Carter and Reagan, there does not seem to be a direct connection between levels of military activity and numbers of presidential military events. But for both Bushes and for Clinton, there does appear to be a general correspondence between their high levels of military activity and their frequent appearances in military venues. This rough measure helps to explain, in particular, the tendency of George W. Bush to appear before the military frequently.

But can we say that George W. Bush's high levels of presidential military events are due solely to the events of 9/11? Figure 11.2, which depicts the number of

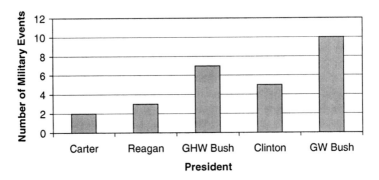

Source: Public Papers of the Presidents of the United States

Figure 11.2   Presidential Military Events before September 11 of the President's First Year in Office

military events held by each president before September 11 of their first year in office, suggests that there is more to the story. Examining this seven-and-a-half month stretch reveals that George W. Bush placed greater emphasis on military events than did other presidents in this study, even before the United States was attacked. Bush held ten events in this period, followed by his father, who appeared seven times in domestic military settings. Clinton, Reagan, and Carter registered five, three, and two events, respectively. Bush's higher levels of pre-9/11 activity suggest a propensity to focus on the military even in the absence of the influence of the terrorist attacks during his first year in office.

The Personal Context

To what extent do personal factors relate to levels of presidential military activity? Are presidents with stronger personal ties to the military more likely to associate more frequently with military personnel in their public events? A brief review of the backgrounds of the five presidents in this study suggests that this, too, is an imperfect indicator of presidential military events.

The first three presidents in this study all served on active duty in the military. Carter was a 1946 graduate of the United States Naval Academy, and subsequently served for seven years on active duty in the navy.[19] Reagan served in the army's Officer Reserve Corps beginning in 1937, served on active duty from 1942 through 1945, and subsequently continued to serve in the Reserve Corps until 1953.[20] George H. W. Bush joined the navy in 1942 on his eighteenth birthday and served as a naval aviator in World War II.[21]

In contrast to their predecessors, neither Clinton nor George W. Bush served on active duty in the military, and both had to answer pointed questions during their election campaigns about their efforts to avoid the Vietnam War. Clinton never served in the armed forces at all, and was dogged by accusations that he was a draft dodger. Bush did serve in the Texas Air National Guard, but was hounded by allegations both that his father's connections kept him from serving on active duty in Vietnam and that he did not fulfill the obligations of his National Guard service.[22]

Thus, while the first three presidents in this study all had undisputed records of military service, they each held fewer presidential military events than did the two final presidents in this study, both of whom were accused of using connections to avoid serving in the Vietnam War. Perhaps these two presidents, the only commanders in chief in the post–World War II era not to have served on active duty, felt inclined to assert themselves more actively and more visibly in an effort to effectively lead the nation's armed forces.

The Electoral Context

If presidents hold events with the military at least in part to bolster their standing with the public, it is fair to question whether presidents seek direct electoral gain from their association with the armed forces. A good deal of recent scholarly and journalistic attention has focused on what has been labeled a permanent campaign for the presidency. According to this view of presidential governance, "the line between campaigning and governing has all but disappeared, with campaigning increasingly dominant,"[23] and the techniques and strategies of presidential campaigning are applied throughout the course of a president's term. Viewing presidential actions through the lens of the permanent campaign leads one to ascribe calculating, election-related motivations to much of what presidents do, and it raises the question of whether or not electoral concerns are related to levels of presidential military events.

One piece of evidence suggests that the answer is no. While presidents might seek to build their credentials as leaders through an association with the military, a review of presidential military events in campaign years indicates that they do not actively do so in the months preceding Election Day. In 1980, Jimmy Carter did not hold a domestic event with the military outside of the Washington, D.C., area after July 10. In 1984, Ronald Reagan held his final such event of the year on May 30. In 1992, George H. W. Bush did hold one event at a naval air station in Louisiana in October, within a month of the election, but he spoke there to a group of law enforcement officials, and not to a military audience. Before that, his last military event was on August 6. In 1996, Bill Clinton's last domestic military event before the election took place on July 23. And in 2004, George W. Bush did speak with troops about to depart for Iraq at an Air National Guard base in Maine on September 23, but he made brief remarks on the troops' plane and did not hold a public rally. Aside from this instance, his final domestic military event before the election took place on June 18.

All five presidents, then, largely avoided holding domestic military events outside of the Washington, D.C., area in the months leading up to their reelection bid. Perhaps they actively sought not to use the military as an audience and backdrop in the heat of an election campaign. Whether they did so in order to avoid politicizing the military or because holding military events would come at the expense of campaign events with the general public, given the scarcity of the president's time, is beyond the scope of this study. While presidents might hope to reap indirect electoral benefits from frequent association with the military, over the twenty-eight year period of this study, they did not seek to do so directly as Election Day drew near.

Conclusions

It is clear that presidential practices have changed substantially since the time of Harry Truman. In contrast with Truman's refusal to promote his message and programs at military installations, recent commanders in chief have embraced the opportunity to do so. These events provide presidents with a friendly and supportive audience. They are often carefully staged to project the image of the president as a strong, unifying leader—not just to the audience with the president that day, but to the public at large.

Over the twenty-eight-year period of this study, the levels of presidential military events have risen dramatically. But the proportion of military events relative to overall presidential public events has held relatively steady, as presidents have become more publicly active in other settings as well. While there are substantial differences within each political party, on average, Democrats and Republicans have held comparable levels of presidential military events.

The military context of each president's term does not explain the varying levels of events that presidents have held with the military. The three most recent presidents all did command substantial military operations throughout their terms and held correspondingly high numbers of events in military settings. But this pattern does not hold for Presidents Carter and Reagan. Carter held more presidential military events, but less military action occurred under his watch, while for Reagan the situation was the reverse.

Although George W. Bush's high levels of presidential military events are surely in part explained by the country's military engagements following the attacks of 9/11, examination of military events in the first year of each president's term reveals that Bush outpaced his counterparts in his military events even before the country was attacked, suggesting a tendency to speak in military venues independent of the effects of the attacks of 9/11.

There appears to be an inverse relationship between a president's personal record of military service and his levels of public presidential activity, as the first three presidents in the study, all of whom served on active duty, exhibited lower levels of public military activity than did their successors, both of whom did not serve on active duty and dealt with lingering controversies over the manner in which they avoided service in the Vietnam War.

Direct electoral considerations appear to have been kept separate from presidential military events, as each president in his reelection campaign steered entirely, or almost entirely, clear of these sorts of events in the lead-up to Election Day. While some candidates likely sought to benefit indirectly from their association with the men and women in uniform, the lack of events in the heat of the election campaign indicates that, in this respect, the lines between campaigning and governing have not been blurred.

This initial survey of presidential image-making and the military has addressed a number of questions, and its findings raise several more. What themes do presidents sound when they speak in military settings? Do such appearances engender positive news coverage and associations in the mind of the public? Would analysis of geographic patterns of presidential military appearances help to better understand presidential strategy? How do patterns of presidential military events relate to presidential popularity?

While President Truman might view the activities of his successors as gimmickry, presidential military events have become an accepted and important element of the public presidency. Presidents now routinely address the troops and, at the same time, directly address the American people. By analyzing the dynamics of these events, we can better understand the role of the military in modern presidential leadership.

Notes

1. George Elsey (White House aide to President Truman), interview with the author, September 2006.
2. *Public Papers of the Presidents of the United States*, 1977–2004 (Washington, D.C.: United States Government Printing Office), http://www.presidency.ucsb.edu/ws; http://www.gpoaccess.gov/pubpapers/index.html; http://www.reagan.utexas.edu/archives/speeches/publicpapers.html; http://www.bushlibrary.tamu.edu/research/paper.html; http://www.clinton6.nara.gov; http://www.whitehouse.gov/news.
3. Richard E. Neustadt, *Presidential Power and the Modern Presidents* (New York: Free Press, 1990).
4. Samuel Kernell, *Going Public: New Strategies of Presidential Leadership*, 3rd ed. (Washington, D.C.: CQ Press, 1997).
5. Joe Klein, "The Perils of the Permanent Campaign: Can the Public Live with an Administration That Is Cutting Corners and Ignoring the Details?" *Time*, October 30, 2005, http://www.time.com/time/columnist/klein/article/0,9565,1124237,00.html (accessed April 28, 2006).
6. Kernell, *Going Public*, v.
7. Fred I. Greenstein, *The Hidden-Hand Presidency: Eisenhower as Leader* (New York: Basic Books, 1982); Thomas E. Cronin and Michael A. Genovese, *The Paradoxes of the American Presidency*, 2nd ed. (New York: Oxford University Press, 2004).
8. Kernell, *Going Public*.
9. Patricia Sullivan, "Reagan Image-Maker Changed American Politics," *Washington Post*, August 19, 2007, A1.
10. Since this study focuses exclusively on military events outside of the Washington, D.C. metropolitan area, from this point forward, the term "presidential military event" will be used for such events.
11. *Public Papers*.
12. Mike Allen, "On the Way to the Fundraiser; Stopovers Let Bush Charge Taxpayers for Political Trips," *Washington Post*, May 20, 2002, A1; Mike Allen, "Bush Capitalizes On Travel Bargain; President Uses Air Force One for Price of 1st Class." *Washington Post*, March 5, 2004, A21; Charles R. Babcock, "Campaigning via Air Force One: Public Foots

Much of Bill," *Washington Post*, December 31, 1991, A15; Charles R. Babcock, "Flying Political Class on Air Force One; Commercial Rates Make Every Trip an Incumbent Advantage," *Washington Post*, October 19, 1992, A19; Dana Milbank, "The Cost of Presidential Travel Is Anyone's Guess," *Washington Post*, October 29, 2002, A19; Ellen Nakashima, "White House Travel Bill: $292 Million; Republican Senator Says Clinton's Air Transport Expenses Are 'Exorbitant,'" *Washington Post*, August 18, 2000, A2; Edward Walsh, "U.S. Spent Over $100,000 on Trip Carter Postponed," *Washington Post*, November 9, 1977, A2.

13. The first two columns in table 11.2 are drawn from slightly differing sets of presidential activities. As previously explained, the military events studied include all events outside of the Washington, D.C., metropolitan area. The data on all presidential public events, which are drawn from another study by the author (Brendan J. Doherty, "The Politics of the Permanent Campaign: Presidential Travel and the Electoral College, 1977–2004," *Presidential Studies Quarterly* 37 (2007): 748–772), include no events in Maryland and Virginia. In spite of the fact that the two columns display slightly different groups of events, the percentages displayed in the third column still give a good sense of the proportion of military events relative to overall presidential public events.

14. Louis Fisher, *Presidential War Power*, 2nd ed. (Lawrence: University Press of Kansas, 2004).

15. Ibid.

16. Ibid.

17. Ibid.

18. Ibid.

19. *Public Papers*, 1978.

20. Ronald Reagan Presidential Library, "Military Service of Ronald Reagan," http://www.reagan.utexas.edu/archives/reference/military.html, accessed September 20, 2007.

21. *Public Papers*, 1991.

22. Walter V. Robinson, "Bush's Guard service: What the Record Shows" *Boston Globe*, February 5, 2004, http://www.boston.com/news/politics/president/articles/2004/02/05/bushs_guard_service_what_the_record_shows/ (accessed September 20, 2007).

23. Norman Ornstein and Thomas Mann, eds., *The Permanent Campaign and Its Future* (Washington, D.C.: American Enterprise Institute and the Brookings Institution, 2000), vii.

12

Partisanship and the Military: Voting Patterns of the American Military

Captain Donald S. Inbody, USN (Ret)

Who Wins the Soldier Vote?

The controversy over the overseas military absentee ballots in the 2000 election revolved around a single assumption: military voters identify predominantly as Republicans and tend to vote for Republican presidential candidates. Left unasked in the news coverage was whether that assumption was true and, if so, why. The military, particularly the enlisted ranks that make up about 85 percent of the military population, are overrepresented by minorities who traditionally identify with the Democratic Party. Despite that, anecdotal and empirical evidence suggests a Republican bias in party identification, although likely not to the extent imagined by some sources.

A survey of military personnel conducted by the *Military Times* in 2004 found that 60 percent of its respondents identified as Republican, 13 percent as Democrat, and 20 percent as independent. Though the survey was not scientifically conducted and junior enlisted personnel were underrepresented, the finding of a Republican bias in the military had been corroborated by other data. The article listed 73 percent as planning to vote for George W. Bush, while 18 percent said they would vote for John Kerry, a 4:1 margin in favor of the Republicans. This article appears to be a principal source of claims about the heavy "Republicanism" of the military. However, these data appear to overstate the Republican bias, especially with respect to enlisted party identification and likely voting behavior.[1]

Historical Background: From Apolitical to Republican

The identification of military personnel with the Republican Party dates back to the post–Civil War years. Founded in 1866, the Grand Army of the Republic was formed by Northern veterans whose goal was to ensure appropriate pensions for veterans and widows of veterans. Growing to a maximum size of nearly half a million members, the organization strongly supported the Republican Party, claimed it had saved the Republic, and condemned the Democratic Party as Copperheads, traitors who were against the war and who would have permitted the Southern states to secede from the Union.

While support for the Republican Party by active duty military personnel and veterans is apparently strong today, this has not always been the case. The relative partisanship of military personnel during the latter nineteenth and early twentieth centuries is unclear, but by the 1930s, officers like George Marshall openly questioned whether it was ethical for a military officer even to vote for a presidential candidate, let alone campaign for him.[2]

The apolitical nature of the military was common through the 1940s, with voting among officers usually under 30 percent. The voting rate was even lower during the war years of 1942–1945. It remained low until the early 1950s, when participation began a gradual climb, but it reached only 40 percent by 1956.[3] While he ultimately became president, General Dwight Eisenhower apparently never voted while on active duty, believing that the military should maintain a strict distance from politicians.[4]

One reason why military personnel were not voting may have been that they were stationed at remote bases or overseas and had limited access to mail. Also, being stationed overseas can tend to cause an individual to pay less attention to electoral matters at home. Some have argued that military personnel have not had and do not have a difficult time voting.[5] However, numerous studies conducted since the 2000 election show that both civilians and military personnel living overseas have a more difficult time casting absentee ballots than do voters in the United States. Evidence from studies on absentee balloting in California found that compared to non-overseas absentee ballots, overseas ballots were twice as likely to not be returned and three times more likely to be challenged.[6]

Beginning in World War II, Congress has placed great emphasis on ensuring that military personnel have an opportunity to vote. The Soldier Voting Act of 1942 granted military personnel the right to request federal "war ballots."[7] The Federal Voting Assistance Act of 1955 gave assistance to American civil servants overseas, as well as recommended that states make it easier for other Americans overseas to be able to vote in state and even local elections.[8] In 1975, Congress passed the Overseas Citizens Voting Rights Act,[9] which repealed and updated the Federal Voting Assistance Act of 1955. Since then, the Uniformed and Overseas Citizens Absentee Voting Act of 1986 updated the earlier acts of Congress and ensured certain rights for all overseas citizens—especially those in the military— to enjoy an unrestrained ability to vote.[10] The Federal Voting Assistance Program was established within the Department of Defense (DoD) and is required to report to Congress on the effectiveness of the program following each election. Voting participation within the military has increased dramatically since the inception of the program: sixty-nine percent of all military personnel voted in 2000, and 79 percent voted in 2004, which was substantially higher than the national turnout of 64 percent.[11]

The Republican Party assumes that it will receive a strong majority of the military vote. While the Democratic Party insists that it also represents the military community, there is a suspicion that a mobilization of the military vote will not favor Democratic candidates. The war in Iraq and dissatisfaction with the performance of the current Bush administration may provide the Democrats some room to gain ground, but actions of the Democratic Party in the 2000 elections in Florida, heavily publicized remarks by former presidential candidate John Kerry, and the September 2007 MoveOn.org advertisement accusing General David Petraeus of "betraying" the United States suggest there is still some distance to go. In a *Washington Post* article, Peter Feaver commented that "despite an extraordinary effort to woo the military, the Democrats still have not overcome their traditional tone-deafness when it comes to civil-military relations."[12] In the mid-1970s, about 60 percent of officers identified as independents. Starting in about 1976, a gradual increase in Republican Party identification began and continued throughout the rest of the twentieth century.[13]

Why Care?

The total number of Americans participating in the military by serving on active duty has always been small, even in times of major war. America has traditionally maintained some distrust of the military, and fears of a large standing army predated the American Revolution. Just less than one-half of 1 percent of the U.S. population is currently on active duty, which is the lowest percentage since 1940.[14]

With fewer and fewer American citizens having direct contact with the military, the issue of a widening gap in political behavior between those who serve in the military and the rest of the American citizenry who are being served becomes a concern. Fewer and fewer public officials and even fewer members of the press have military experience. In 1999, 33 percent of the members of Congress (43 senators, 136 representatives) were veterans, compared to almost three-quarters in 1976. By 2006, the proportion was 29 percent (35 senators, 121 representatives). The November 2006 election sent some new veterans to Congress, but the total remaining in Congress declined further, dropping to 24 percent (29 senators, 101 representatives).[15] By comparison, 12.75 percent of the U.S. population (eighteen and over) are veterans.[16] Thus, veterans remain vastly overrepresented in Congress compared to the population as a whole.

Recent studies point to a growing cultural gap between the military and civilians. Still, while there appears to be some discomfort about the gap, few are predicting serious problems as a result.[17] The principal concern is whether the gap creates dysfunction between the civilian authority and senior military officers. This gap is explored in depth in chapters 16 and 17, by Mackubin Owens and Kathleen Mahoney-Norris, respectively.

Over the past three decades, and certainly since the end of the Vietnam War, public confidence in the military has remained high, usually exceeding that of nearly all other government and public institutions. With the introduction of the

All Volunteer Force (AVF) in 1973 and with fear of conscription eliminated as a motivating factor for negative views, public confidence in, and expectations of, the military have climbed. A consistently high level of support has been maintained across all segments of the population, including even those populations less likely to enlist and serve.[18]

There is an interesting difference between political leaders who are veterans and those who are not in terms of how best to use military force. Political leaders who are veterans appear to be more reluctant to use military force than nonveterans. Still, once the decision has been made to use force, veteran political leaders are more likely to place fewer restraints on the use of force than are nonveteran leaders. This appears to be the pattern not only in recent years, but across American history.[19]

Given how close recent elections have been, military voters can have a decisive effect on outcomes, especially since they vote disproportionately for the Republican Party. Further, military personnel tend to be concentrated in certain states, but not necessarily in areas where military bases are located. Instead, they appear to concentrate in states with favorable tax laws. Many of the states with the highest percentages of military voters, such as Florida, Virginia, California, and Maryland, do not have the highest concentrations of military bases. Instead, favorable or nonexistent state income-tax laws appear to influence military personnel in choosing their home of record. In fact, fifteen of the twenty-one states with the highest percentage of their voting population in the military either have no state income tax or otherwise exempt some military personnel from paying state income tax. Thus, local and state laws can make a difference in terms of how much of the military population votes in each state, and these laws may have played a part in bringing Florida to such prominence in the 2000 presidential election.[20]

Demographic Changes and Political Ramifications

The fact that military personnel tend to vote for Republican candidates is inconsistent with the overall demographics of American voter behavior. The American military is predominantly male (85 percent), while the American population is nearly evenly divided between males and females.[21] Both the United States and the military are predominantly white, but while the American population is, as of 2005, about 25 percent nonwhite, the military is presently 38 percent nonwhite.[22] Thus, the American military is disproportionately made up of males and minorities.

In 2000, the demographics of the American military were even more disproportionately made up of minorities, with 37.5 percent being nonwhite. While women made up only about 15 percent of the active duty force, there was a notable difference in representation of white women and black women. Tables 12.1 and 12.2 provide details for enlisted and officer personnel.

If the various demographic subgroups in the military (white males/females, black males/females, other males/females) voted similarly to the corresponding subgroups in the general population, there would be a strong Democratic vote. Table 12.3 displays the compiled results of how the voting might look in that case.[23]

Table 12.1   Active Duty Enlisted Demographics by Race and Gender

| Ethnicity | Active Duty Enlisted, 2000 (%) | | |
	Males	Females	Total
White	55.2	7.3	62.5
Black	17.2	5.2	22.4
Other	12.9	2.2	15.1
Total	85.3	14.7	100.0

Source: Office of the Undersecretary of Defense, Personnel and Readiness, Population Representation in the Military Services, table B-25. Retrieved June 10, 2005, from http://www.dod.mil/prhome/poprep2000/html/appendixb/b_25.htm. Totals may not add to 100 percent due to rounding.

Table 12.2   Active Duty Officer Demographics by Race and Gender

| Ethnicity | Active Duty Officer, 2000 (%) | | |
	Males	Females	Total
White	72.94	10.82	83.76
Black	6.0	2.06	8.06
Other	6.8	1.38	8.18
Total	85.74	14.26	100.0

Source: OSD, P&R, Population Representation in the Military Services, table B34. Retrieved June 2005 from http://www.dod.mil/prhome/poprep2000/html/appendixb/b_34.htm. Totals may not add to 100 percent due to rounding.

If the military population voted as the corresponding demographic groups did in the general population, the vote in the 2000 presidential election would have favored Gore by a ratio of nearly 1.2:1. Officers would have favored Bush over Gore by a slight 1.06:1 ratio. Enlisted personnel would have favored Gore by a ratio of nearly 1.3:1. However, it does not appear that such was actually the case.

How Did They Vote?

No valid data exist as to actual voting patterns of American military personnel. Title 18 of the U.S. Code, passed by Congress on June 25, 1948, prohibits any polling of any member of the armed forces to ask them how they voted or will vote in the future. The law does not, however, prohibit other types of polling, including those seeking information on party preference or political attitudes. Because of the law, as well as individual service policy restrictions, scientific polling of military personnel about political topics, particularly polling of enlisted personnel, has been rare and limited.[24]

The best data available on how military personnel might vote is a study conducted by the Triangle Institute for Strategic Studies (TISS) in 1998 and 1999.[25] The TISS data, summarized in Table 12.4, show how military personnel identify with the political parties.

Table 12.3 2000 Election Simulation–U.S. Military Vote Expected Result Based on 2000 ANES (American National Election Studies)

Expected 2000 Result Officer

	Gore	Bush	Other	Total	Gore	Bush	Other
White Male	58,451	81,832	7,014	147,297	39.68%	55.56%	4.76%
White Female	11,875	9,236	733	21,844	54.36%	42.28%	3.36%
Black Male	10,896	1,211	0	12,107	90.00%	10.00%	0.00%
Black Female	4,060	102	0	4,162	97.56%	2.44%	0.00%
Other Male	6,866	6,294	572	13,732	50.00%	45.83%	4.17%
Other Female	1,853	926	0	2,779	66.67%	33.33%	0.00%
Total	94,002	99,600	8,319	201,921	46.55%	49.33%	4.12%

Expected 2000 Result Enlisted

	Gore	Bush	Other	Total	Gore	Bush	Other
White Male	252,626	353,676	30,315	636,617	39.68%	55.56%	4.76%
White Female	45,763	35,593	2,825	84,181	54.36%	42.28%	3.36%
Black Male	179,299	19,922	0	199,221	90.00%	10.00%	0.00%
Black Female	58,170	1,454	0	59,624	97.56%	2.44%	0.00%
Other Male	74,325	68,131	6,194	148,650	50.00%	45.83%	4.17%
Other Female	16,853	8,426	0	25,279	66.67%	33.33%	0.00%
Total	627,035	487,203	39,334	1,153,572	54.36%	42.23%	3.41%

Expected 2000 Result Total

	Gore	Bush	Other	Total	Gore	Bush	Other
White Male	311,077	435,508	37,329	783,914	39.68%	55.56%	4.76%
White Female	57,638	44,829	3,558	106,025	54.36%	42.28%	3.36%
Black Male	190,195	21,133	0	211,328	90.00%	10.00%	0.00%
Black Female	62,230	1,556	0	63,786	97.56%	2.44%	0.00%
Other Male	81,191	74,425	6,766	162,382	50.00%	45.83%	4.17%
Other Female	18,705	9,353	0	28,058	66.67%	33.33%	0.00%
Total	702,331	577,451	47,653	1,327,435	52.91%	43.50%	3.59%

Source: American National Election Studies. Stanford University and University of Michigan. http://www.electionstudies.org

Table 12.4 Party Identification from TISS Data

Party ID	Republican	Democrat	Independent
Never served	34.6%	43.7%	21.6%
Enlisted	53.1%	27%	19.8%
Cadet/Midshipman	62.0%	13.6%	24.4%
Officer	67.1%	12.3%	20.6%

Source: Peter Feaver and Richard H. Kohn, 1999. "Survey on the Military in the Post-Cold War Era," Triangle Institute for Strategic Studies, Duke University.

Table 12.5 shows how party identification in the population as a whole converts to actual voting in the 2000 election.

The overall military voter turnout rate for the 2000 election was 69 percent. This compares favorably to a 51.3 percent turnout for the general American

Table 12.5 Vote by Party ID (% Total)–ANES 2000

	Democrat	Independent	Republican	Total
Gore	24.2	6.2	4.6	35
Bush	7.5	9.2	24.2	41
Other	2.1	1.7	0.8	4.6
None	4.6	5.8	1.7	12.1
Don't know	1.7	3.8	2.1	7.5
Total	40	26.7	33.3	100

Note: This table was developed by condensing strong Democrats, weak Democrats, and Independent-leaning Democrats into a single category: "Democrat." The same was done for Republicans. The Independent category is the Independent–Independent category from the ANES study.

Table 12.6 Estimated U.S. Military Vote, 2000 Presidential Election

Officers	Gore		Bush	
	Vote	Pct Vote	Vote	Pct Vote
Republicans	18,833	11.70%	98,501	61.18%
Democrats	15,026	9.33%	4,644	2.88%
Independents	9,650	5.99%	14,351	8.91%
Total	43,509	27.02%	117,496	72.98%
Enlisted	Gore	Pct Vote	Bush	Pct Vote
Republicans	84,144	9.37%	44,5321	48.99%
Democrats	188,436	20.73%	58,244	6.41%
Independents	52,990	5.83%	78,801	8.67%
Total	326,570	35.93%	582,366	64.07%
Total Military	Gore	Pct Vote	Bush	Pct Vote
Republicans	103,977	9.72%	543,822	50.83%
Democrats	203,462	19.02%	62,888	5.88%
Independents	62,641	5.85%	93,151	8.71%
Total	370,080	34.59%	699,862	65.41%

Source: Calculated by the author using data from Department of Defense and the TISS study.
Note: Percentages reported on this table are of those who are estimated to have voted for either the Democratic or Republican candidate, with the other candidates omitted.

population. Based on all available data, Table 12.6 shows an estimate of how American military personnel voted in the 2000 election.[26]

The Officer Corps

Actual results are easiest to obtain for officer personnel. Multiple studies have determined that officers identify as Republican at a much higher rate than the general population. Such identification has been a growing trend for nearly three decades and is well documented by Holsti's Foreign Policy Leadership Project

(FPLP) studies beginning in 1976.[27] The TISS data show that active duty officers identify as Republican at a much higher rate (63.9 percent) than do either the civilian veteran (46.2 percent) or nonveteran (30.3 percent) groups. Among active duty officers, 66.6 percent self-identify as conservative or somewhat conservative, while only 31.7 percent of civilian nonveterans identify as conservative.[28]

Accepting the TISS data from 1998 and 1999 as approximating the attitudes of military officers as a whole, we find that the expected result is much different from the actual result. The expected result predicts 49.33 percent Republican and 46.55 percent Democrat, for a 1.06:1 Republican bias; however, the actual result is 65.41 percent Republican and 34.59 percent Democrat, or about 1.89:1 Republican to Democrat. Thus, we know that factors not predicted by patterns in the general population are at work creating a strong Republican bias among military officers.

One possible factor is the apparent tendency of Republican-identifying high school seniors to go on to college, while Democrat-identifying high school seniors tend to enroll in higher education at a lower rate. Seniors who indicated that they intended to enroll in college were also generally quite low in terms of their propensity to enlist out of high school.[29] Since essentially all officers are college graduates, this would bring an obvious trend toward Republican identification.

Enlisted Personnel

Enlisted personnel identified 2:1 Republican over Democrat. The respondents who had never served reported 1.26:1 Democrat over Republican.[30] Although sufficient reliable data on enlisted personnel are not available, these admittedly thin data do reinforce anecdotal evidence. Enlisted personnel, being more likely minority and less likely college-educated than the officer corps, are less likely to identify with the Republican Party than are officers.

However, while the expected result predicts 42.2 percent Republican and 54.4 percent Democrat, for a 1.29:1 Democratic bias, the actual result is 64.1 percent Republican and 35.9 percent Democrat, or about 1.8:1 Republican to Democrat. As with the officer corps, factors not predicted by patterns in the general population are at work creating a strong Republican bias among enlisted personnel.

The Monitoring the Future (MTF) surveys of high school seniors provides a good look at eighteen-year-olds who have a high propensity to enlist in the military. These surveys indicate that high school seniors who identify as Republican tend to go on to college at a higher rate than those who identify as Democrats. Those with a propensity to enlist directly into the military following high school predominantly identify as Democrats. This would suggest that the enlisted personnel in the American military should also identify as Democrats.

The MTF team contacted some of the high school seniors after several years of service and found an increase in "Republicanism." This pattern was stronger the longer the individuals were in the service. The authors of the MTF studies found that the differences in party identification and attitude appeared to be primarily due to the initial self-selection process of deciding to enlist, but that some socialization while in service may have had a limited effect as well.[31]

Feaver and Gelpi show that socialization after enlistment may be at least as important as the selection factor postulated by the MTF data. In their research, they found that veterans, regardless of party identification, tended to have political views more closely aligned with active duty military personnel than with the nonveteran civilian population.[32] These data, when combined with older research such as psychologist Theodore Newcomb's classic Bennington Studies, suggest that socialization of young people in the presence of strong leadership may well permanently alter political views.[33]

Discussion and Conclusions

The American military identifies as Republican more than does the general American population. In 1999, about 55 percent of all military personnel tended to identify with the Republican Party compared to 28 percent of the overall population. Multiple studies have confirmed that the officer corps is strongly Republican, but little research has been conducted with enlisted personnel. It is not surprising that white males in the military are substantially Republican in party identification, as that is true of the same demographic subgroup in the total population. Given that the military population is predominantly white, even if less so than the overall population, more highly educated, and of higher socioeconomic status than the general population—all categories exhibiting a tendency to identify as Republican—such identification is unsurprising.[34]

Enlisted personnel in the American military are less likely to identify as Republican and to vote for Republican candidates than are officers. Given the higher minority representation within the enlisted ranks relative to both the officer corps and the American population in general, it is not surprising that enlisted personnel are not as strongly Republican as officers are. However, why enlisted personnel have a Republican bias at all is less clear and deserves more detailed research.

Explanations for the pattern of enlisted personnel party identification and voting may be related to the findings that those who have a propensity to enlist, regardless of their demographic subgroup and party identification, already have a tendency to have a high regard for the military. However, there is little to suggest that a high regard for the military will translate into a particular party preference. While enlisted personnel are less likely than officers to identify as Republican and to vote for Republican presidential candidates, they remain more Republican than the general population. A more powerful explanation, based on Feaver and Gelpi's work and supported by Newcomb's Bennington Studies, is the socialization effect of working with and under strong leaders with strong political ideas. The *Military Times* data suggest that senior enlisted (E-6 and up), as well as officers, tend to identify strongly as Republicans. It is also possible that once having enlisted in the military, they may tend to identify with the political party that is perceived to have best understood their role and their specific circumstances. This last explanation appears to be the weakest.

It would appear that officers will identify as Republican about 8:1 over Democrat and will vote Republican over Democrat by a margin of about 1.9:1.

Enlisted personnel identify as Republican about 1.8:1 over Democrat and vote at about the same ratio. Taking into account that officers make up only 15 percent of the military population, the overall ratio of Republican to Democratic voting is about 1.8:1. Arguments that the Republicans had a 4:1 or 5:1 advantage are apparently not true, at least not in terms of actual voting behavior.

While essentially all of the military population is eligible to vote, and with a 70-plus percent voting rate, it might appear that the military vote would be a powerful, influential bloc. However, even by adding the 1.1 million Reserve and National Guard personnel to the 1.2 million on active duty, 2.3 million is less than 2 percent of the more than 122 million who voted in the last presidential election. It would be a rare case, if one can be imagined at all, where the military vote alone would decide any election, particularly a national vote. Florida in 2000 may have been that rare case.

Notes

1. Gordon Trowbridge, "Who You Chose for President and Why," *Army Times*, October 11, 2004. In the article, the author explained, "Unlike most public opinion polls, the *Military Times* survey did not randomly select those to question. Instead, subscribers with e-mail addresses on file were sent an invitation. That means there is no statistical margin of error for the survey—so it's impossible to calculate how accurately the results reflect the views of *Military Times* readers."
2. Forrest C. Pogue, *George C. Marshall: Education of a General, 1880–1939* (New York: Viking, 1963).
3. Paul Van Riper and Darab B. Unwalla, "Voting Patterns among High-Ranking Military Officers," *Political Science Quarterly* 80, no. 1 (March 1965). There are no reliable data on enlisted voting percentages during this time, but they are assumed to be generally low, based on returns of absentee ballots. See R. Michael Alvarez, Thad E. Hall, and Brian F. Roberts, "Military Voting and the Law: Procedural and Technological Solutions to the Ballot Transit Problem" (working paper, Institute of Public and International Affairs, University of Utah, Salt Lake City, 2007, 3, http://www.ipia.utah.edu/workingpapers.html (accessed May 15, 2007).
4. Carlo D'Este, *Eisenhower: A Soldier's Life* (New York: Henry Holt, 2002). Asked in an online interview if it were true that Eisenhower never voted, D'Este replied, "As far as I know it is true. There is certainly no record of him voting during the period I covered. Like most of the military, he was apolitical and he had actually a great contempt for politicians like most of the career officers did." http://discuss.washingtonpost.com/wp-srv/zforum/02/destes053002.htm (accessed November 27, 2006).
5. Diane Mazur, "The Bullying of America: A Cautionary Tale about Civil-Military Relations and Voting Reform," http://www.law.ufl.edu/faculty/publications/pdf/mazur3.pdf (accessed September 28, 2007).
6. Alvarez, Hall, and Roberts, "Military Voting and the Law," 4.
7. Public Law 712–561.
8. 42 U.S.C. 1973cc, et seq.
9. 42 U.S.C. 1973dd, et seq.
10. 42 U.S.C. 1973 ff through ff-6.
11. Federal Voting Assistance Program, Seventeenth Report, October 2005. Seventy-two percent of overseas personnel, including those in Hawaii and Alaska, voted; and

76 percent of personnel within the continental United States voted. The survey is conducted for DoD by the RAND Corporation. These numbers are self-reported and so may be inflated to some extent.

12. Peter D. Feaver, "Whose Military Vote?" *Washington Post,* October 21, 2004, A23.

13. Ole R. Holsti and J. N. Rosenau, *American Leadership in World Affairs: Vietnam and the Breakdown of Consensus* (London: Allen and Unwin, 1984); Ole R. Holsti, *Public Opinion and American Foreign Policy* (Ann Arbor: The University of Michigan Press, 1996); Ole R. Holsti, "A Widening Gap between the U.S. Military and Civilian Society: Some Evidence, 1976–96," *International Security* 23 (Winter 1998): 5–42; Ole R. Holsti, "A Widening Gap between the U.S. Military and Civilian Society: Some Further Evidence, 1998–99" (paper presented at a conference on "Bridging the Gap," Triangle Institute for Security Studies, Chapel Hill, North Carolina, July 1999).

14. Bartholomew H. Sparrow and Donald S. Inbody, "Supporting Our Troops? U.S. Civil-Military Relations in the Twenty-First Century (paper prepared for the annual meeting of the American Political Science Association, Washington, D.C., September 2005). Including the National Guard and Reserves produces slightly higher percentages, but the trend is the same—a gradual but steady decline in personal participation in the American military.

15. For data on House members who are veterans, see http://veterans.house.gov/vetlink/vetsincongress.html. Data on Senate members were compiled by the author from multiple sources.

16. U.S. Census Bureau, 2006, http://factfinder.census.gov/servlet/GRTTable?_bm=y&-geo_id=01000US&-_box_head_nbr=R2101&-ds_name=ACS_2006_EST_G00_&-format=US-30 (accessed September 12, 2007). The 2000 census reported 26,549,704 veterans and a total U.S. population eighteen and older of 208,130,352, or 12.75 percent veterans. Counting the entire 2000 population of the United States (281,421,906), the percentage of veterans is 9.4 percent.

17. Pearl S. Buck et al., *New Evidence of the Militarization of America* (Washington, D. C.: National Council Against Conscription, 1949). In 1948, fearing a rise of militarization in the United States, the National Council Against Conscription (NCAC) warned that America could not remain democratic if the trends toward militarization were not checked. A year later the NCAC, with the endorsement of Pearl S. Buck, Albert Einstein, Louis Bromfield, and others, published this pamphlet. One recent notable exchange of articles voicing concern over whether the apparent civil-military cultural gap was dangerous was begun by Charles Dunlap, "The Origins of the American Military Coup of 2012," *Parameters,* Winter 1992–1993: 2–20. The theme was taken up by Richard Kohn, "Out of Control," *National Interest* (Spring 1994), and quickly responded to by Colin Powell, John Lehman, William Odom, Samuel Huntington, and Richard Kohn, "Exchange on Civil-Military Relations," *National Interest* (Summer 1994). Concluding that the military was not out of control was Deborah Avant, "Are the Reluctant Warriors Out of Control: Why the U.S. Military is Averse to Responding to Post-Cold War Low-Level Threats," *Security Studies* 6, no. 2 (Winter 1996/97): 51–90.

18. Paul Gronke and Peter D. Feaver, "Uncertain Confidence: Civilian and Military Attitudes about Civil-Military Relations," in *Soldiers and Civilians: The Civil-Military Gap and American National Security,* ed. Peter D. Feaver and Richard H. Kohn (Cambridge, MA: MIT Press, 2001), pp.132–135.

19. Peter D. Feaver and Christopher Gelpi, *Choosing Your Battles: American Civil-Military Relations and the Use of Force* (Princeton, NJ: Princeton University Press, 2004). Also see Thomas E. Ricks, "The Widening Gap between the U.S. Military and U.S. Society," *Atlantic Monthly,* July 1997, 66–78, and Holsti, "Widening Gap," 1999.

20. Stephen E. Frantzich, "Taxation without Representation" (unpublished case study, 1991). My thanks to Professor Frantzich for providing his case study and data. Normally, military personnel maintain voting residency based upon their residence when first entering the military service. With no action being taken, they will remain residents and eligible to vote in their original hometown until they are discharged. However, it is possible to change residency, depending on various state laws, to any state.
21. The American Community Survey reports that in 2005, 49 percent (141,274,964) of the American population was male and 51 percent (147,103,173) of the population was female.
22. American Community Survey. In 2005, the survey reported 215,333,394 whites in the American population, or 74.6 percent of 288,378,137.
23. Data were available for the various demographic subgroups constituting our "other" category, but the numbers were so small that they were found to make little difference in the final result.
24. Lieutenant General Walter Ulmer, USA (Ret.), and Dr. T. Owen Jacobs, working at the Center for Strategic and International Studies, conducted a survey of about ten thousand enlisted personnel as recently as 2000. Nearly all of the respondents were army personnel because of restrictions imposed by the other service headquarters. The data are useful in surveying attitudes about military life and desire to remain on active duty, but no questions were asked about political matters. My thanks to General Ulmer and Dr. Jacobs for locating and providing the data and making them available to me.
25. Feaver and Kohn, *Soldiers and Civilians*.
26. The author conducted an election simulation using data from multiple sources, including the American National Election Study for 2000 and the Triangle Institute for Strategic Studies. Full details of methodology are available upon request.
27. Holsti, "Widening Gap," 1998; Holsti, "Widening Gap," 1999.
28. Feaver and Kohn, *Soldiers and Civilians*, pp. 28, 33.
29. Jerald G. Bachman et al., "Who Chooses Military Service? Correlates of Propensity and Enlistment in the United States Armed Forces," *Military Psychology* 12 (Spring 2000): 1–30, and David R. Segal, Mary Senter, and Mady Wechsler Segal, "The Civil-Military Interface in a Metropolitan Community," *Armed Forces and Society*, 4, no. 3 (1978); David Segal et al., "Attitudes of Entry-Level Enlisted Personnel: Pro-Military and Politically Mainstreamed," in Feaver and Kohn, *Soldiers and Civilians*, pp. 163–212. My thanks to Jerald Bachman for calling this to my attention.
30. The TISS data contain little information on active duty enlisted personnel. It does, however, contain data for some 111 individuals who had some military enlisted service. While this is clearly not enough data from which to draw conclusive findings, it is suggestive and seems to be consistent with other findings.
31. David R. Segal et al., "Propensity to Serve in the U.S. Military: Temporal Trends and Subgroup Differences," *Armed Forces & Society* 25 (Spring 1999): 407–427.
32. Feaver and Gelpi, *Choosing Your Battles*.
33. Theodore M. Newcomb. *Persistence and Change: Bennington College and Its Students after Twenty-Five Years* (New York: Wiley, 1967).
34. Feaver and Kohn, *Soldiers and Civilians*.

13

The Military, the Courts, and the War on Terror

Kenneth E. Harbaugh

On June 26, 2006, the U. S. Supreme Court issued what was hailed by many as a groundbreaking decision on the limits of executive power. In *Hamdan v. Rumsfeld*, a plurality of justices ruled that the military commissions proposed by the president for trying accused terrorists were illegal, because Congress had not explicitly authorized such measures. In a dissenting opinion, Clarence Thomas wrote the following:

> The plurality's willingness to second-guess the Executive's judgments in this context . . . constitutes an unprecedented departure from the traditionally limited role of the courts with respect to war and an unwarranted intrusion on executive authority.[1]

With those words, Justice Thomas appealed to a centuries-long tradition of granting the other branches of government the widest possible latitude in areas where a compelling government interest is at stake. This practice is known as *judicial deference*; it is frequently applied when judges must deal with issues involving the defense of the nation.

The term *military deference* is often used to describe situations in which courts do not question military judgments. In a strict legal sense, however, military deference does not exist. The military is not its own branch of government, and thus cannot be deferred to. Service members are routinely used to help argue government cases, but the military itself has no direct constitutional claim to judicial deference and must depend on the agency of Congress or the president. Military deference, then, is more accurately described as deference to the legislature, the executive, or, in some cases, both.

Courts can never abdicate their duty to defend the Constitution, but arguments based on military necessity may weaken (though never eliminate) certain fundamental rights. For example, certain policies allow the military to legally discriminate against women and homosexuals, and First Amendment rights granted to military personnel are not as strong as those afforded civilians (specific examples are discussed below). The Supreme Court itself has acknowledged that constitutional protections may be diluted in situations involving the military: "Congress [cannot] disregard the Constitution when it acts in the area of military affairs . . . but the tests and limitations to be applied may differ because of the military context."[2]

This chapter explores the tension between the military and the courts. It examines the historical foundation of deference, its ongoing rationale, and its implications for both the courts and the military. Our ultimate query is, What role *should* the courts play in setting limits on military policies set forth by the executive and legislative branches?

The Constitutional Foundations of Judicial Deference

Judicial deference toward the military is no historical accident. Justice Thomas's admonition in *Hamdan* was a direct appeal to the nation's foundational document. Whereas the Constitution grants both Congress and the president power over military affairs, it gives the judiciary no explicit authority. Indeed, the Constitution says very little about the judiciary at all, except to describe in general terms what types of cases may fall under its jurisdiction. Notably absent from the text itself is the concept of judicial review. This notion, which maintains that judges have the last word as to what is "constitutional," arose years after the document's drafting,[3] and survives to this day as the most significant assertion of judicial power.

When historical comparisons are drawn between judicial review and judicial deference, the differences are stark. Judicial deference draws its support from the clearly delineated responsibilities of the other branches, while judicial review is largely a product of constitutional interpretation. Nevertheless, the role of the judiciary as the final arbiter of constitutional issues has gained such popular acceptance that it has become a permanent feature of the national psyche. When courts defer to the other branches today, it is seen as a departure from the established order of things, regardless of what the constitutional text explicitly says about the powers of the three branches.

With respect to national defense, the Constitution grants Congress the power to declare war, to raise and support a military, and to issue regulations for its governance. Command of those forces is vested in the president alone. At the time of the Constitution's drafting, the nation was still weak, and the entire American project labored under potentially existential threats from abroad. The framers believed that the nation required a single chief executive to act decisively in times of military crisis, but that such authority needed to be checked against potential abuse.[4] Thus, Congress has the power to declare war, but the president is responsible for waging war.

Even with the advent of modern warfare, this need for balancing has not diminished. During the Korean War, Supreme Court justice Robert Jackson eloquently characterized the distribution of power between the legislature and executive: "While Congress cannot deprive the President of the command of the army and navy, only Congress can provide him an army or navy to command."[5] Yet Jackson's insight is perhaps more ironic than even he intended. As a judge, his role in adjudicating matters relating to national defense is entirely ambiguous. The Constitution clearly sets forth the military responsibilities of Congress and the president, yet says nothing about the role of the courts.

Judicial Deference in Practice

While judicial deference has deep historical roots, it has long been defended on pragmatic grounds as well. Courts that rely upon military judgments regularly cite, as a practical justification, their own lack of expertise. Judges, so the argument goes, do not possess the necessary experience to rule on military matters. Even when a particular issue raises controversy and disagreement within the military itself—as was the case when a number of military lawyers objected to the creation of military tribunals for suspected terrorists—the judiciary is rarely presented with a complete picture of military expert opinion. Rather, the branch of government making its case before the court draws upon those military arguments most likely to bolster its position. As previously discussed, when the judiciary defers to military judgments, it is in fact deferring to the other branches and not to the military itself.

One of the paradigmatic instances of judicial deference to the legislature occurred in 1986, with a challenge to the congressionally approved uniform regulations prohibiting the conspicuous wearing of religious items. In *Goldman v. Weinberger*, a Jewish officer sued the air force to be allowed to wear a yarmulke in uniform. In rejecting his argument, the Court distinguished between constitutional rights of civilians and those of uniformed personnel: "Our review of military regulations challenged on First Amendment grounds is far more deferential than constitutional review of similar laws or regulations designed for civilian society."[6] The Court went on to say that it is "ill-equipped to determine the impact upon discipline that any particular intrusion upon military authority might have," and that "appropriate military officials . . . are under no constitutional mandate to abandon their considered professional judgment."[7] As a result of *Goldman*, the military remains one of the few institutions left in America that maintains a legal ban on the wearing of religious items.

In matters relating to military governance, courts often resort to the legislative deference seen in *Goldman*. Examples include the laws against women serving in frontline combat roles and those prohibiting gays from serving openly. For operational issues, however, courts may defer to the president. In the most famous (and notorious) example, *Korematsu v. United States*, the Supreme Court affirmed the constitutionality of an executive order that led to the relocation of over 110,000 Japanese-Americans during World War II. The Court refused to assert a strong defense of constitutional rights, because "military authorities feared an invasion of our West Coast and felt constrained to take proper security measures, [and] because they decided that the military urgency of the situation demanded that all citizens of Japanese ancestry be segregated from the West Coast . . ."[8] The military's assessment of the risk was accepted at face value, even though not a single documented act of espionage or sabotage by a Japanese-American ever occurred.[9]

While the judiciary's own lack of expertise is most often cited as the practical basis for deference, there is an underlying philosophical rationale. Unlike the executive and legislative branches of government, federal courts enjoy no direct claim of popular support. Judges must be confirmed by the Senate, but they are not elected by the people. The courts' relative lack of democratic legitimacy compared to the other branches is especially significant when judges are handed the task of refereeing disputes between the executive and the legislature. In an attempt to stay above the fray of politics, courts are sometimes wary of asserting their own position too aggressively. The judiciary possesses a long institutional memory, and is deeply conscious of the risks of political struggle.[10] In the end, the power of courts depends on the respect they command from the public, which derives entirely from their perceived *moral* virtue.[11] Any attempt to engage in politics, especially when challenging the *democratic* legitimacy of the other branches of government, risks undermining the only real authority that courts have.

The Implications of Judicial Deference

When judges defer to the military, fear of error must weigh heavily on their minds. A mistake from the bench could have dire consequences for the nation. But many other high-stakes issues come before courts without judges having firsthand experience with the issues involved. In the case of abortion rights, for example, nine *male* justices delivered the definitive ruling. The decisions mandating desegregation of public schools also impacted millions of lives, yet few of the ruling judges ever served on school boards or worked as teachers. Both of these legal conflicts marked turning points in the life of the nation, yet few judges had personal experience with the matters at hand. Still, they asserted their opinions with a confidence rarely seen in cases involving the military. What, then, sets military issues apart?

For the vast majority of judges today, the military seems entirely alien. It exists as a society unto its own. It is fundamentally undemocratic, and insular by nature. It possesses a tradition and culture necessarily separate from the nation at large. It is unique among institutions of government for operating its own legal system, which includes its own criminal code. John Paul Jones wrote in the eighteenth century, "Whilst the ships sent forth by the Congress may and must fight for the principles of . . . republican freedom, the ships themselves must be ruled and commanded at sea under a system of absolute despotism."[12] The extraordinary leeway afforded the military is allowed by the Constitution.[13] Judges know this, and some are undoubtedly influenced by it.

This is not to suggest that the military operates above the law. Today in Iraq and Afghanistan, and indeed everywhere American forces are deployed, the Uniform Code of Military Justice (UCMJ) imposes a strict legal order over U.S.

military personnel, albeit one that is separate from that binding the rest of the nation. The UCMJ empowers commanders to maintain order and discipline in ways not available to civilian bosses, and establishes its own rules for trying crimes committed by uniformed personnel. But while the military's legal code may be distinct from the system that binds every other American, it is by no means autonomous. The UCMJ is a product of congressional lawmaking, and judicial oversight of all military legal matters rests ultimately with the Supreme Court.

On policy decisions, the military is granted a flexibility unimaginable elsewhere in government. There are times when military leaders, including the commander in chief, must act on intuition alone. Yet courts, by their very nature, are uncomfortable with the very idea that important decisions might not rest on hard evidence. In his *Korematsu* dissent, Justice Jackson wrote, "Defense measures will not, and often should not, be held within the limits that bind civil authority in peace. No court can require such a commander in [wartime] to act as a reasonable man [for] he is not making law in the sense the courts know the term."[14]

Another significant factor contributing to the tendency of courts to defer to military judgments is the military's claim to moral authority. No other institution, least of all the judiciary, is routinely commanded *by the government* to sacrifice its own members in defense of the nation. When rationalizing a questionable policy, this moral standing goes a long way. Regulations that might otherwise fail to meet standards of constitutionality, such as the prohibition against wearing religious items (seen in *Goldberg*), are often defended successfully on the grounds that good order and discipline are essential to maintaining warfighting effectiveness. Few other institutions can appeal to such noble purpose when justifying their actions.

On the federal bench today, there is a dearth of military experience, especially among newer appointees. This makes the task of adjudicating military policies much more difficult. Judges with no military experience are not only susceptible to insinuations of moral superiority, but also ill-equipped to understand how the military really operates. The trend toward a bench devoid of veterans is almost certain to continue. In confirmation hearings, military service is considered a nonissue. At elite law schools, from which the judiciary draws a disproportionate number of judges, veterans are exceedingly rare. Even the government's own database of judges' professional biographies pays scant attention, if any, to their military service.

On the Supreme Court today, only one member has served in a significant military capacity.[15] Justice John Paul Stevens saw combat as a naval officer during World War II. Yet even though his time in uniform was more than sixty years ago, it almost certainly prepared him to adjudicate military matters with some degree of confidence. Justice Stevens is renowned, at least among court observers with military backgrounds, for his self-assured challenges to government claims of military necessity. In Israel, where almost every judge has served in uniform, the Supreme Court is far more aggressive in asserting itself against the military.[16] To be sure, Israel and the United States have different legal environments. But Israeli judges understand their military from firsthand experience. They are not mystified by its culture, and are not easily influenced by claims of moral superiority.

Partly as a result, Israeli courts have a far more robust tradition of challenging the military.

None of this is to say that American judges should all hail from military backgrounds, or that such experience automatically leads to confidence on the bench. In general, however, judges who understand the culture of the military and who, by their service in uniform, are immune to the suggestion of moral superiority are better equipped to challenge claims of military necessity.

The War on Terror and the Role of the Courts

For those prosecuting the war on terror, the legal landscape is still very much unsettled. A number of cases regarding the limits of executive and congressional powers are making their way through the courts. Some, like *Hamdan*, have already been decided. But several rulings that at first glance seem to establish clear constitutional guidelines appear, upon closer inspection, as deliberately vague. Recall that in *Hamdan* the Court determined military commissions, as originally envisioned, to be simply *illegal*. No judgment was offered as to their *constitutionality*. In other words, the Court left the door wide open for lawmakers to authorize the president's proposal. Congress took full advantage of this by swiftly passing the Military Commissions Act.[17]

One of the most significant issues yet to be resolved is jurisdiction. How far should the judiciary, and the Constitution itself, reach? In *Rasul v. Bush*, the Court asserted jurisdiction over Guantanamo.[18] This aspect of the ruling came as no surprise to many legal analysts. But the Court left open the possibility that its jurisdiction might extend to anywhere American military forces operate. A decision along these lines would have seismic implications for those waging the present war. Might a future court require that enemies on distant battlefields be afforded the same constitutional rights that U.S. citizens enjoy?

Some commentators have raised the specter of American soldiers being forced to read captured terrorists their rights or to provide them with an attorney. Indeed, military lawyers are more involved than ever before in advising field commanders on the legality of certain combat operations.[19] American courts could, in theory, assert jurisdiction over any action by U.S. forces in the war on terror, even those that take place on the far side of the world. Yet anyone familiar with the history and current practice of judicial deference will dismiss such fears as alarmist. The tradition runs far too deep.

Aharon Barak, president of the Israeli Supreme Court from 1995 to 2006, has more experience in dealing with terrorism than most American judges are ever likely to have. Now retired from the bench, he has written at length about the responsibility of courts in democracies under threat from extremism. "The court's role is to ensure the constitutionality and legality of the fight against terrorism. It must ensure that the war against terrorism is conducted within the framework of the law. This is the court's contribution to democracy's struggle to survive."[20] Whereas Clarence Thomas grants almost unqualified deference to the executive, as evinced by his dissent in *Hamdan*, Barak maintains that claims of military necessity cannot go unchallenged, *especially* in wartime. "Even when the artillery booms and the Muses are silent, law exists and acts and decides what is permitted and what is forbidden, what is legal and what is illegal."[21]

The opposing views of Thomas and Barak suggest an extreme dichotomy. There is, however, a middle ground. The most noteworthy is one articulated by Justice Jackson in his *Korematsu* dissent. He argued against the government, but he was deeply troubled that the Court was adjudicating the matter at all. "I do not suggest that the courts should have attempted to interfere with the Army in carrying out its task [of relocating Japanese-Americans]. But I do not think they may be asked to execute a military expedient that has no place in law under the Constitution."[22]

Justice Jackson would have preferred to leave military decisions alone, neither lending the Court's moral weight to a potentially unconstitutional act, nor challenging an interest the military deemed necessary. His reasoning is especially compelling in a time of war. He writes, "A military commander may overstep the bounds of constitutionality, and it is an incident. But if we review and approve, that passing incident becomes the doctrine of the Constitution. There it has a generative power of its own, and all that it creates will be in its own image."[23]

In the end, the judiciary's only real power lies in its own moral legitimacy and the respect it commands from the public. Courts, unlike the president, cannot command an army. Nor can they ensure their own funding. That is left to Congress. Ultimately, the judiciary's ability to affect military actions is dependent upon the moral character of the military itself. Jackson perceives this dilemma with perfect clarity: "If the people ever let command of the war power fall into irresponsible and unscrupulous hands, the courts wield no power equal to its restraint."[24]

In *Hamdan*, the Court refused to assert its own position, instead requiring the president to seek congressional approval for military commissions. The power of the executive was checked against the power of the legislature. For what was hailed as a triumph for judicial oversight, the ruling hardly qualifies as ground-breaking. The result was not surprising, however, to those with some grasp of the historical foundations of deference, its pragmatic rationales, and its underlying motivations. Of course, no amount of understanding can predict with surety how future courts may rule. Judges may be less inclined to accept the military's expertise, or more confident in asserting their own authority. But one thing is certain. So long as there are wars to fight, the American legal system will always have a special, if at times uneasy, relationship with the military that protects it.

Notes

1. *Hamdan v. Rumsfeld*, 126 S. Ct. 2749, 2826 (2006) (Thomas, C., dissenting).
2. Id. at 67.
3. In *Marbury v. Madison*, 5 U.S. 137 (1803), the Court asserted that it retains ultimate authority to determine whether actions or policies of the executive and legislative branches are permitted by the Constitution. This case established the notion of judicial review, which survives today virtually unchallenged.

4. Following America's victory over the British in the Revolutionary War, many American lawmakers were wary of funding a standing army, citing concerns that it might be used oppressively as the British army had been. Still, many of those advocating a defense dependent entirely on state militias recognized the importance of having a single commander in chief in times of crisis.

5. *Youngstown Sheet & Tube Co. v. Sawyer*, 343 U.S. 579, 644 (1952) (Jackson, J., concurring).

6. *Goldman v. Weinberger*, 475 U.S. 503, 507 (1986).

7. Id. at 507–8.

8. *Toyosaburo Korematsu v. United States*, 323 U.S. 214, 223 (1944).

9. In 1983, Korematsu's conviction was overturned in a federal court. In 1988, the U.S. government issued a formal apology to Japanese-Americans victimized by the internment policy, and in 1990, began awarding reparations to camp survivors and their families. In 1998, Fred Korematsu was personally awarded the Presidential Medal of Freedom. See Josh Dubow, "Japanese-American Who Fought Internment Dies," AP wire report, March 31, 2005, http://sacunion.com/pages/california/articles/3653.

10. For example, in *Worcester v. Georgia*, 31 U.S. (6 Pet.) 515 (1832), the Supreme Court issued a decision that was effectively ignored by the executive. The Court, led by Chief Justice John Marshall, ruled that the Cherokee nation was not bound by the laws of the state of Georgia and that only the federal government had authority over Indian affairs. President Jackson, who disagreed with this ruling, remarked, "[T]he decision of the Supreme Court has fell still born." He is often apocryphally reported to have said, "John Marshall has made his decision; now let him enforce it!" See Mr. Justice Adrian Hardiman, Supreme Court of Ireland, "Transparency and Accountability in the Enforcement of Judicial Decisions" (paper presented at the 12th International Judicial Conference, Bucharest, Romania, May 19–21, 2004, http://www.internationaljudicialconference.org/PDF/12/Hardiman.pdf).

11. Popular opinion surveys show that judges consistently rank among the most trusted members of society. Interestingly, several independent polls rank judges as slightly less trustworthy than military officers (pollsters themselves, however, generally place near the bottom). See, for example, *The Gallup Poll Honesty and Ethics List,* http://www.gallup.com. See also *The Harris Poll*® #61, August 8, 2006, http://www.harrisinteractive.com/harris_poll/index.asp?PID=688.

12. John Paul Jones, in a letter to the Naval Committee of Congress, September 14, 1776. See Harbaugh, Kenneth, "Transforming the Civil-Military Divide." *Proceedings* (United States Naval Institute, May 2004), 46.

13. The Constitution explicitly allows certain fundamental rights to be abridged in times of military necessity. For example, Article I, Section 9 states that the writ of habeas corpus can be suspended in "Cases of Rebellion or Invasion [when] the public Safety may require it." The Fifth Amendment protects the right to trial by jury, but carves out an exception for "cases arising in the land or naval forces, or in the Militia, when in actual service in time of War."

14. *Korematsu*, 323 U.S. at 244.

15. Justice Stevens served in the navy during World War II. Justice Anthony Kennedy served briefly in the Army National Guard (California), and Justice Samuel Alito served in the Army Reserves. See http://www.whoserved.com/supremecourt.asp.

16. See Seidman, Guy I., "Judicial Administrative Review in Times of Discontent: The Israel Supreme Court and the Palestinian Uprising." *Israel Affairs*, forthcoming, http://ssrn.com/abstract=856307.

THE MILITARY, THE COURTS, AND THE WAR ON TERROR

17. See *The United States Military Commissions Act of 2006*, Pub. L. No. 109–366, 120 Stat. 2600 (Oct. 17, 2006). The military commissions established by this act are functionally very similar to those proposed by the president prior to the Supreme Court's ruling in *Hamdan*. In particular, the act undermines habeas corpus rights of the accused (see Richard Epstein, "The MCA Denies Habeas and Due Process, Opening Argument, February 2007," http://www.openingargument.com/index.php?name=Home&file=article&did=115). However, the constitutionality of the act, and of the commissions themselves, is currently being challenged in federal court.

18. Guantanamo is not a state or territory of the United States, but a U.S. military installation operated under a lease with Cuba according to treaty terms agreed to by the United States and Cuba in 1903. See "Agreement between the United States and Cuba for the Lease of Lands for Coaling and Naval stations," the Avalon Project, Yale Law School (February 23, 1903), http://www.yale.edu/lawweb/avalon/diplomacy/cuba/cuba002.htm.

19. Rules of engagement, which set preconditions for the use of force, are of particular concern. Military lawyers are not only deeply involved in the writing of these rules, but are often consulted by operational commanders while missions are in progress. Anecdotal evidence abounds of military lawyers being asked to "sign off" on proposed military strikes, especially against high-value targets where a significant probability of civilian casualties exists.

20. Aharon Barak, "A Judge on Judging: The Role of a Supreme Court in a Democracy." *116 Harv L Rev* 16, no. 160 (2002).

21. Aharon Barak at 160, citing H.C. 2161/96, *Rabbi Said Sharif v. Military Commander*, 50 (4) P.D. 485, 491.

22. *Korematsu*, 323 U.S. at 248.

23. *Korematsu* at 246.

24. *Korematsu* at 248.

14

The Ethics of Interrogation: Torture and Public Management

James P. Pfiffner

A lthough some military officers obviously saw harsh interrogation techniques and torture as essential in the wars in Afghanistan and Iraq, many in the military believe that the use of torture threatens the professionalism of the American military and puts U.S. forces in danger of being tortured if they are captured. Torture is illegal under international and U.S. law, yet political guidance after the 9/11 terrorist attacks resulted in a limited number of U.S. personnel perpetrating torture and using harsh interrogation techniques at Guantanamo Bay, Cuba; Bagram Air Force Base in Afghanistan; and Abu Ghraib prison in Iraq. The evidence comes from a range of sources, including the International Committee of the Red Cross and Amnesty International, as well as the personal accounts of interrogators, victims of torture, and the U.S. military itself.[1] This chapter examines the basis for this behavior, the efficacy of it, and the political guidance that gave rise to these unlawful techniques.

The Ticking Time Bomb Scenario

In the popular TV show *24*, intrepid terror fighter Jack Bauer foils fictional attempts to commit evil deeds that can only be stopped if the hero extracts information about the impending calamities and stops them before they occur. Most of the time he is forced to resort to coercive interrogation and torture (and the torture is often graphically depicted) to get the bad guy to cough up the information, which leads to the saving of innocent lives in the nick of time. Bauer is always the patriotic hero, and his brutal means are depicted as necessary to save the day.

The American public may be convinced that such situations are often encountered by U.S. law enforcement, counterterrorism personnel, and military officers, but the reality is that they are very rare. Even the creator of the show, Bob Cochran, concedes, "Most terrorism experts will tell you that the 'ticking time bomb' situation never occurs in real life, or very rarely. But on this show it happens every week."[2] The show is so compelling that the dean of the U.S. Military Academy at West Point, Brigadier General Patrick Finnegan, went to see its creators in California to ask them to portray interrogation situations that more closely reflect reality. Military cadets were so enamored of the show that it was difficult to get them to accept the professional military doctrine that follows the U.S. rule of law and the laws of war. Finnegan said , "I'd like them to stop. They should do a show where torture backfires."[3]

The most convincing argument that torture may be necessary is the "ticking time bomb" scenario featured on 24, and blanket condemnations of torture are often countered with this type of hypothetical situation.[4] In such a case, the argument goes, torture is necessary in order to save innocent lives.[5] However, there is a chain of premises upon which such a scenario rests. First, there must be good intelligence that a planned attack exists and that the bomb is currently ticking. Second, the "right person" must be captured. Third, the captive must have detailed knowledge of the attack. (Terrorist cells typically practice good operational security.) Fourth, torture must be the best way to extract accurate information. (Many experienced interrogators argue that civil treatment is more effective, and note that a captive might say anything to stop the pain or might deliberately deceive the interrogators.) Fifth, the captive must divulge the information quickly to allow an imminent attack from taking place. (Hurried interrogations do not necessarily produce the best information, and they can result in unintended death of the detainee.) Finally, the information obtained must be actionable, and the means to prevent an attack must exist.

If any one of these premises is absent or incorrect, or if the problems cited exist, torture will not solve the problem. Thus, even if one posits that torture might be justified in order to save innocent lives—as in the simple and rare version of the ticking bomb scenario—most torture scenarios are ruled out. The further a situation is removed from the ticking bomb scenario, the less torture is justified. Some argue that even if no ticking bomb is found, the lives of soldiers may be saved if intelligence about an adversary's location is discovered through torture. This type of argument, however, can be made in almost any combat situation. Enemy captives might conceivably have information that might help, and torture might be justified by any nation in any armed conflict. Consequently, this kind of justification of torture to extract tactical information is precisely the reason that rules of warfare banning torture have developed over the centuries, and why the United States is a party to the Geneva conventions. The generally accepted rules of warfare forbid torture and provide for the humane treatment of enemy captives. Without these rules, all armed forces would be vulnerable to torture if captured by the enemy; therefore, all sides have long had a stake in banning the use of torture.

The Efficacy of Torture

One of the key assumptions of the ticking bomb scenario is the capacity to get a person to divulge crucial information to save innocent lives. While there is a wide range of interrogation techniques—from friendly trickery to the most extreme infliction of pain—the results are mixed.[6] Approaches that work with some people do not work with others. Even if people are forced to talk, they may not tell the truth. They may say whatever it takes to stop the pain. Willie J. Rowell, an Army Criminal Investigation Division (CID) agent for thirty-six years, is dubious about torture's efficacy. "They'll tell you what you want to hear, truth or not truth."[7]

The army field manual on interrogations stated (before revisions in 2006), "Army interrogation experts view the use of force as an inferior technique that yields information of questionable quality. The primary concerns, in addition to the effect on information quality, are the adverse effect on future interrogations and the behavioral change on those being interrogated."[8] In testimony before Congress in March 2005, Porter Goss, director of the Central Intelligence Agency (CIA), said, "As I said publicly before, and I know for a fact, that torture is not—it's not productive. . . . That's not professional interrogation. We don't do torture."[9] The army field manual was revised in 2006, and harsh techniques to obtain intelligence continue to be forbidden. The Bush administration, however, granted more leeway to the CIA for interrogations. They can use harsher methods, but what those methods are has not been made public.

Several British detainees at Guantanamo said that they were tortured in order to force them to admit that they went to Afghanistan to fight a holy war and that they were in a video of Osama bin Laden in 2000. They denied that they had been involved in these activities, but said that they confessed to stop the pain and ill-treatment. They were finally exonerated when British Intelligence produced proof that they were not in Afghanistan at the time the video was made.[10] Thus, even if one posits that torture might be justified in a very limited number of scenarios, there is much professional opinion and empirical evidence that torture is not necessarily effective in gaining accurate and timely information.

Behavioral Dimensions of Torture

In the wake of the publication of the Abu Ghraib photographs and other accounts of the abuse of prisoners, many citizens asked, "How could these acts have been committed by U.S. soldiers?" Part of the answer is that most human beings are heavily influenced by their immediate social setting. U.S. military training includes army doctrine on the legitimate uses of violence and on the provisions of the Geneva Accords with regard to prisoners; the Accords prohibit torture. What then, went wrong? How could U.S. soldiers commit the terrible acts that have been recorded in photographs and reported throughout the world? Several behavioral science experiments help to explain the dynamics of human behavior in institutional settings.

In trying to understand how the Holocaust could have occurred in Germany in the 1930s and 1940s, scholars have offered a number of explanations. Sadly, it has become clear that the actions necessary to exterminate Jews in large numbers were carried out in part by ordinary people (military and civilian), and not merely by Nazi party members or SS forces. One of the insights of Hannah Arendt is what she described as "the banality of evil," that ordinary people doing what they saw as their jobs and duties were capable of contributing to heinous acts. In *Unmasking Administrative Evil*, Guy Adams and Danny Balfour explain how public administrators can contribute to evil acts simply by conscientiously performing their assigned duties. Their argument is that large-scale evil is often masked; that is, perpetrators see themselves as merely doing their duty conscientiously and do not believe they are doing anything wrong. Their acts cumulatively, however, can result in an evil outcome, as in the Holocaust.[12]

In the 1960s, Yale University psychologist Stanley Milgram designed an experiment that intended to show that Americans would not be as compliant as were Germans when asked to inflict pain on other human beings. In his experiment the subject was told that he was participating in an experiment about the connection between electrical shock and memory. The subject was supposed to deliver a shock to a person (in reality, an actor) in the next room every time an incorrect response was given. The shocks were calibrated from 15 volts to 450 volts, and as the supposed voltage of the shocks was increased, the actor expressed increased pain. If the subject hesitated to administer the next level of shock, the experimenter, with the help of a white lab coat and the voice of scientific authority, prompted the subject to apply the shock despite the screams of pain from the actor in the next room. Ninety-nine percent of the subjects were willing to administer the "strong" shock of 135 volts, and 62 percent were willing to go to the "XXX" category of 435 and 450 volts.[13]

This classic experiment demonstrated that ordinary Americans, with their individualistic cultural values, were not so different from Germans. One of the lessons of this experiment is that Americans would go much further than was predicted (by Milgram) along a path of inflicting pain when it appeared to be sanctioned by science and authority.

Another classic experiment on the malleability of Americans' behavior was conducted at Stanford University in the 1970s. The purpose of the experiment was to examine the effect of adopted roles in organizational behavior. The experimenters selected what they determined to be twenty-two normal undergraduate men and randomly assigned them to be either jailors or prisoners in a simulated prison set up in the basement of the psychology building. The "ground rules" were that the prisoners would be treated as prisoners, but would not be subject to any inhumane treatment. The experiment had to be terminated after six days rather than the planned two weeks because of the brutality and mistreatment by the "guards."

Again, this experimental evidence illustrates how seemingly ordinary and normal people can easily be led to commit inhumane behavior. In this case the conditions were only an imagined "prison" environment. The "guards" knew the "prisoners" were guilty of nothing but were acting a part. The experimenters concluded, "In less than a week, the experience of a 'prison' environment undid (temporarily) a lifetime of learning; human values were suspended, self-concepts were challenged and the ugliest, most base, pathological side of human nature surfaced. We were horrified because we saw some boys ('guards') treat other boys as if they were despicable animals, taking pleasure in cruelty."[14]

Given these classic experiments, we should not be surprised that good, normal, young, military men and women would be capable of inhumane behavior. Indeed, their behavior may have been aggravated because they were guarding prisoners of a different racial/cultural background who they may have believed had been guilty of attacks on U.S. forces. This is why rules, regulations, and strict adherence to standard operating procedures are so important in military prisons. Systematic training must overcome the immediate environment.

The Importance of Leadership

In large organizations, and particularly in the military, leadership is essential. Effective leadership can harness a large organization to work effectively toward a goal, and poor leadership can result in a competent organization being unable to act effectively. With respect to torture, if its unjust use is to be avoided, strong leadership is necessary. In the case of U.S. torture during the war on terror, leadership throughout the chain of command failed. The chain created the conditions under which torture occurred. As the war in Afghanistan proceeded, a substantial number of prisoners were captured, and the United States needed a place to imprison them and to interrogate members of al Qaeda who might have knowledge about future attacks. The naval station at Guantanamo Bay on the island of Cuba was chosen because it was isolated from the mainland; and while it was clearly under U.S. control, the administration argued that it was not U.S. territory and thus did not fall under the jurisdiction of U.S. courts (a legal argument that has since been rejected by the U.S. Supreme Court). (Kenneth Harbaugh's chapter in this book provides the larger legal context for this.)

On January 25, 2002, the White House counsel, Alberto Gonzales, wrote a memo to President Bush, arguing that the Geneva conventions for the treatment of prisoners of war and other captives did not apply to al Qaeda captives. He reasoned that the war on terrorism was "a new kind of war" and that the "new paradigm renders obsolete Geneva's strict limitations on questioning of enemy prisoners."[15] Secretary of State Colin Powell objected to Gonzales's reasoning and replied in a memo dated January 26, 2002, in which he argued that the drawbacks to not applying the Geneva conventions outweighed the advantages because "it will reverse over a century of policy . . . and undermine the protections of the law of war for our troops, both in this specific conflict and in general; it has a high cost in terms of negative international reaction. . . .[and it] will undermine public support among critical allies."[16]

Despite Powell's memo, President Bush signed a memorandum on February 7, 2002, that stated, "Pursuant to my authority as Commander in Chief . . . I determine that none of the provisions of Geneva apply to our conflict with al Qaeda in Afghanistan or elsewhere throughout the world because, among other reasons, al Qaeda is not a High Contracting Party to Geneva." The president also noted, "Of course, our values as a Nation, values that we share with many nations in the world, call for us to treat detainees humanely, including those who are not legally entitled to such treatment."[17] The president's decision led to the expansion of interrogation techniques that were used at Guantanamo via Secretary of Defense Donald Rumsfeld's decisions[18] about allowable interrogation techniques, and also via the "migration" of those techniques to Iraq, which, unlike Guantanamo, the United States considered to be covered by the Geneva conventions.[19]

In addition to the decisions about harsh techniques that were allowable during interrogations, administration lawyers produced analyses that defined torture very narrowly and argued that the president's authority as commander in chief of the armed forces allowed him to ignore laws meant to forbid torture. On August 1, 2002, Assistant Attorney General Jay S. Bybee, head of the Office of Legal Counsel (OLC), signed a memorandum dealing with what would constitute torture under Title 18 of the U.S. Code (criminal law), which applied the Convention Against Torture and Other Cruel, Inhuman or Degrading Treatment or Punishment to the United States.[20] The OLC memo construed the definition of torture narrowly: "We conclude that for an act to constitute torture, it must inflict pain that is . . . equivalent in intensity to the pain accompanying serious physical injury, such as organ failure, impairment of bodily function, or even death." This narrow definition would allow a wide range of brutal actions that do not meet the exacting requirements specified in the memo. The memo specifically excludes from torture "cruel, inhuman, or degrading treatment or punishment," some examples of which are specified: wall standing, hooding, noise, sleep deprivation, and deprivation of food and drink. But the memo did specify that some practices—such as severe beatings with clubs, threats of imminent death, threats of removing extremities, burning, electric shocks to genitalia, and rape or sexual assault—would be torture. Later, when Judge Advocate General (JAG) officers in the Pentagon learned about the memo, they objected to the loosening of the restraints on torture.

After six months of experience at Guantanamo following the traditional rules, military officials became frustrated because of their inability to extract what they considered valuable intelligence. According to one military official, "We'd been at this for a year-plus and got nothing out of them," so it was concluded that "we need to have a less-cramped view of what torture is and is not."[21] Major General Michael B. Dunlavey forwarded the requested changes and justified them by arguing that the normal field manual techniques "have become less effective over time."[22] His request was forwarded to Secretary Rumsfeld by Defense Department (DoD) general counsel William J. Haynes II on November 27, 2002, with the recommendation that seventeen new techniques in several categories be authorized.[23] In December 2002, Secretary Rumsfeld approved additional techniques that could be used against detainees who refused to talk.[24]

In 2004, former secretary of defense James Schlesinger headed an independent panel, appointed by Secretary Rumsfeld, which was tasked with finding the cause of the incidents at Abu Ghraib.[25] The Schlesinger Report concluded, "It is clear that pressure for additional intelligence and the more aggressive methods sanctioned by the Secretary of Defense resulted in stronger interrogation techniques."[26] Some of the techniques approved at Guantanamo violated the Geneva conventions (e.g., stress position, up to thirty days of isolation, and removal of clothing).[27] Most of the techniques did not amount to torture, though some of them were harsh and might amount to torture, depending on the intensity and application (e.g., thirty-day isolations, sensory deprivation, twenty-hour interrogations, and noninjurious physical contact).[28] According to the *Wall Street Journal*, techniques that were used included deprivation of food, deprivation of sleep (for up to ninety-six hours), deprivation of clothing, and shackling in stress positions.[29] The problem, of course, is that in the actual practice of interrogations, as was evident at Guantanamo Bay and Abu Ghraib, guards and interrogators can get carried away and move beyond the boundaries specified in the legal memoranda. Ensuring that this does not happen is the obligation of those in leadership positions.

Despite the use of additional interrogation techniques at Guantanamo, no ticking time bomb plots were discovered (that we know of), though some useful intelligence was obtained. According to some defense officials, of the approximately six hundred men imprisoned at Guantanamo, only one-third to one-half of the inmates seemed to be of value.[30] The harsh interrogation practices, however, had meanwhile been exported to Abu Ghraib and used there, despite the fact that the war in Iraq was covered by the Geneva Agreements, as the administration admitted. General Geoffrey Miller, who was in charge of interrogation at Guantanamo, was assigned to Abu Ghraib to improve intelligence collection. General Janice Karpinski, who had been in charge of Abu Ghraib, said that Miller was sent to "Gitmo-ize" Abu Ghraib.[31]

In addition to official memoranda and executive directives, leadership was also provided through public statements by high-level officials. Even if low-level perpetrators of torture do not directly hear the statements, the impact of authoritative public statements is far-reaching. Mid-level officials in the administration and in the military take the statements seriously as expressions of policy and of the attitudes of top officials. They then pass down the chain of command the directives and the attitudes conveyed in public statements. In this case, leadership conveyed the administration's point of view concerning detainees and permissible treatment of them.

President Bush, in talking about the detainees at Guantanamo, declared, "They're dangerous and they're still around, and they'll kill in a moment's notice."[32] Vice President Cheney said, "These are the worst of a very bad lot. . . . They are very dangerous. They are devoted to killing millions of Americans, innocent Americans, if they can, and they are perfectly prepared to die in the effort. And they need to be detained, treated very cautiously, so that our people are not at risk."[33] On January 27, 2002, Secretary of Defense Rumsfeld said just before he left for Guantanamo, "These are among the most dangerous, best trained vicious killers on the face of the earth. And that means that the people taking care of these detainees and managing their transfer have to be just exceedingly careful for two reasons. One, for their own protection, but also so these people don't get loose back out on the street and kill more people. This is a very, very serious business and it ought to be treated in that manner. . . . They are not POWs, they will not be determined to be POWs."[34]

Statements like these, coming from those who were the most authoritative government officials and who should have been the most knowledgeable about the war on terror, were almost certain to dispose U.S. personnel in charge of the detainees to treat them as if they were complicit in the 9/11 atrocities and were actively seeking to kill scores of American civilians. In combination with official changes in policy, these kinds of statements helped to create the conditions under which torture was conducted.

Some of the U.S. captives were guilty of supporting al Qaeda and of resisting U.S. forces in Afghanistan and Iraq. The reality, however, was that not all of the prisoners held at Guantanamo were in fact enemy belligerents or had information that the U.S. could use to prevent future attacks. Indeed, Major General Michael Dunlavey, who was in charge of investigations at Guantanamo, estimated that up to half of the prisoners did not possess any intelligence of value to the United States.[35]

One of the reasons that many prisoners were of little intelligence value and may not have participated in hostilities toward the United States was the way in which they came to be captives of the United States. In Afghanistan, U.S. forces depended on Afghan locals to capture and interrogate suspected hostile forces. This dependency was compounded by the substantial bounties placed on the heads of U.S. enemies. The United States offered $5,000 for each Taliban member and $20,000 for each al Qaeda member brought into U.S. custody, and Secretary Rumsfeld said that leaflets advertising these offers were "dropping like snowflakes in December in Chicago."[36] With incentives like these, it does not take much imagination to figure out that some Afghanis would relish not only giving up their tribal enemies, but also profiting from doing so.

In 2002 there were so many prisoners arriving from Afghanistan of little intelligence value that Major General Dunlavey actually went to Afghanistan to "chew us out" in the words of one U.S. officer. Dunlavey complained that many of those sent to Guantanamo were "Mickey Mouse" types in terms of their military or intelligence value. Some U.S. personnel in Afghanistan then tried to alleviate the problem by drawing up a list of fifty-nine detainees who were innocent, who were not dangerous, or who had little intelligence value. Nevertheless, the danger of making even one mistake was so high that all fifty-nine ended up being sent to Guantanamo. Once in Guantanamo, it was very difficult to get out. Indeed, a U.S. spokesperson in the Pentagon denied the presence of any detainees who should not have been in Guantanamo: "All are considered enemy combatants lawfully detained in accordance with the law of armed conflict."[37]

Conclusion: The Consequences of Torture

It is notable that the justifications of, and pressure to use, torture came from civilians in the Bush administration who did not have significant military experience. The highest-level person who objected to the use of these methods was Secretary of State Colin Powell, who had had a professional military career and had seen combat in Vietnam. In addition, many in the JAG Corps of the army objected to the suspension of the Geneva conventions and the use of harsh interrogation methods. They favored the traditional policies that U.S. forces had taken toward captured enemies from the time of George Washington until the wars in Afghanistan and Iraq. It is further notable that military personnel brought "torture scandals" to light and helped put an end to them.[38]

It is important here to note that torture of prisoners has probably happened in most wars in which the United States has participated. What is different about the war on terror is that the president of the United States, by suspending the Geneva conventions in February 2002, established a policy that set the conditions that led to the torture of prisoners. In addition, President Bush threatened to veto the Detainee Treatment Act of 2005, which forbade torture and which was sponsored by John McCain (who was tortured as a POW in Hanoi). When the bill passed Congress with veto-proof majorities, the president, in signing the bill, issued a signing statement declaring that he would enforce the law only when it did not interfere with his own constitutional prerogatives, which he did not specify. The next year, in arguing for passage of the Military Commissions Act of 2006, President Bush argued that "the program" of harsh interrogation methods used by the CIA was essential to U.S. security in the war on terror.

President Bush's perspective stands in stark contrast to the statements by former generals Charles C. Krulak and Joseph P. Hoar when they wrote the following:

> Any degree of "flexibility" about torture at the top drops down the chain of command like a stone—the rare exception fast becoming the rule. . . . This has had disastrous consequences. . . . This war will be won or lost not on the battlefield but in the minds of potential supporters who have not yet thrown in their lot with the enemy. . . . This way lies defeat, and we are well down the road to it. . . . Before the president once again approves a policy of official cruelty, he should reflect on that.[39]

Notes

1. See, for instance, Antonio M. Taguba, "Article 15-6 Investigation of the 800th Military Policy Brigade" (February 26, 2003) , in *The Torture Papers: The Road to Abu Ghraib* ed. Karen J. Greenberg and Joshua L. Dratel (New York: Cambridge University Press, 2005), pp. 405–465; "Report of the International Committee of the Red Cross (ICRC) on the Treatment by the Coalition Forces of Prisoners of War and Other Protected Persons by the Geneva Conventions in Iraq During Arrest, Internment and Interrogation" (February 2004), in Greenberg and Dratel, *Torture Papers*, pp. 383–404, http:/www.globalsecurity.org (accessed July 12, 2004); Major General George R. Fay, Investigating Officer, "Investigation of the Abu Ghraib Detention Facility and 205th Military Intelligence Brigade," in *The Abu Ghraib Investigations*, ed. Steven Strasser (New York: Public Affairs, 2004), pp. 109–171; LG Anthony R. Jones, "AR 15-6 Investigation of the Abu Ghraib Detention Facility and 205th MI Brigade." reprinted in Greenberg and Dratel, *Torture Papers*, pp. 991–1018.
2. Jane Mayer, "Whatever It Takes," *New Yorker*, February 19 and 26, 2007, 66–82, 68.
3. Ibid., 72.
4. Another variation on this scenario is a case, reported by Mark Bowden, in which a young boy was kidnapped, tied, and gagged and then hidden by the kidnapper. When the kidnapper was captured by the police, he would not reveal where the boy was.

The police thought the boy might still be alive and threatened to bring in an interrogator to torture the man to get him to reveal the location of the boy (the man revealed the location, but the boy was dead). A reasonable person might conclude that torture was justified in this instance. See Mark Bowden, "The Dark Art of Interrogation," *Atlantic Monthly,* October 2003, http://www.theatlantic.com (accessed July 29, 2004).

5. For an insightful analysis of the logic of the ticking bomb scenario, see Vittorio Bufacchi and Jean Maria Arrigo, "Torture, Terrorism and the State: A Refutation of the Ticking-Bomb Argument," *Journal of Applied Philosophy* 223, no. 3 (2006): 355–373; David Luban, "Liberalism, Torture, and the Ticking Bomb," *Virginia Law Review* 91, no. 6 (October 2005): 1425.

6. See the detailed analysis of interrogation methods by Bowden, "Dark Art," http://www.theatlantic.com (accessed July 30, 2004).

7. Seymour M. Hersh, "Torture at Abu Ghraib," *The New Yorker,* May 10, 2004, 47. See also, Tim Golden and Don Van Natta Jr., "U.S. Said to Overstate Value of Guantanamo Detainees," *New York Times,* June 21, 2004, 1.

8. See. 4A3, Current Doctrine. The relevant portions of the Army Field Manual 34–52 are attached to Secretary Rumsfeld's Memorandum for the Commander, U.S. Southern Command; Subject: Counter-Resistance Techniques in the War on Terrorism (S) (April 16, 2003). They were revised in 2006 and explicitly rule out torture.

9. Douglas Jehl, "Questions Left By C.I.A. Chief on Torture Use," *New York Times,* March 18, 2005, 1, A5.

10. Vikram Dodd and Tania Branigan, "Questioned at Gunpoint, Shackled, Forced to Pose Naked, British Detainees Tell Their Stories of Guantanamo Bay," *The Guardian,* August 4, 2004, TruthOut.org (accessed August 9, 2004).

11. Hannah Arendt, *Eichmann in Jerusalem: A Report on the Banality of Evil* (New York: Viking, 1963).

12. Guy B. Adams and Danny L. Balfour, *Unmasking Administrative Evil,* rev. ed. (Armonk, NY: M. E. Sharp, 2004).

13. Stanley Milgram, *Obedience to Authority* (New York: Harper and Row, 1974). See the detailed description of the experiment and its implications in Adams and Balfour, *Unmasking Administrative Evil,* pp. 36–39, from which this description is taken.

14. C. Hanley, C. Banks, and P. Zimbardo, "Interpersonal Dynamics in a Simulated Prison," *International Journal of Criminology and Penology* 1 (1974): 69–97. See the detailed description of the experiment and its implications in Adams and Balfour, *Unmasking Administrative Evil,* pp. 27–29, from which this description is taken.

15. Memorandum for the President (January 25, 2002), from Alberto R. Gonzales; Subject: "Decision RE application of the Geneva Convention on Prisoners of War to the Conflict with al Qaeda and the Taliban." According to *Newsweek,* the memo was "actually" written by David Addington, Vice President Cheney's legal aide. Daniel Klaidman, "Homesick for Texas," *Newsweek,* July 12, 2004, 32. Gonzales has been criticized in the press for saying that the "new paradigm" renders the Geneva limitations "quaint." But the context of his use of the word "quaint" is not as damning as excerpting the word makes it seem. The end of the sentence reads: ". . . renders quaint some of its provisions requiring that captured enemy be afforded such things as commissary privileges, scrip (i.e., advance of monthly pay), athletic uniforms, and scientific instruments." Whether this is a fair representation of the Geneva requirements is a separate issue.

16. Memorandum to: Counsel to the President and Assistant to the President for National Security Affairs, from: Colin L. Powell (26 January 2002); subject: Draft Decision Memorandum for the President on the Applicability of the Geneva Convention to the

Conflict in Afghanistan," pp. 2, 4. The memo is printed in Greenberg and Dratel, *Torture Papers*, pp. 122–125. Many of the memoranda and oral directives included statements that detainees were to be treated "humanely" despite the more aggressive interrogation techniques to which they could be subjected. The problem was that if the detainees were in fact treated humanely, it would be more difficult to extract information from them. Thus, these statements must have been considered to be pro forma, while the overall thrust of the directives was that detainees were to be subject to more aggressive interrogation techniques that were outside the Geneva Convention limits.

17. The White House, Washington, Memorandum of February 7, 2002, signed by President Bush.
18. See Golden and Natta Jr., "Guantanamo Detainees," 1, A12, A13. Memorandum for Commander USSOUTHCOM; Subject: Counter-Resistance Techniques (January 15, 2003), signed by Secretary Rumsfeld. Memorandum for the Commander, U.S. Southern Command; Subject: Counter-Resistance Techniques in the War on Terrorism (S) (April 16, 2003), signed by Secretary Rumsfeld. Printed in Greenberg and Dratel, *Torture Papers*, p. 239.
19. See *Final Report of the Independent Panel to Review Department of Defense Detention Operations* (herein after, the Schlesinger Report), in Strasser, *Abu Ghraib Investigations*, pp. 7, 34, 35.
20. In a memo from Assistant Attorney General Jay S. Bybee to Alberto R. Gonzales, counsel to the president, "Re: Standards of Conduct for Interrogation under 18 U.S.C., sections 2340 and 2340A, August 1, 2002," reprinted in Greenberg and Dratel, *Torture Papers*, pp. 1, 6, 15, 24, 28. According to *Newsweek*, the memo was written in close consultation with White House lawyers. Klaidman, "Homesick for Texas," 32.
21. Quoted in Jess Bravin, "Pentagon Report Set Framework for Use of Torture," *Wall Street Journal*, June 7, 2004, *WSJ* website.
22. Memorandum for Commander, United States Southern Command; Subject: Counter-Resistance Strategies (October 11, 2002); signed Michael B. Dunlavey.
23. Action Memo for: Secretary of Defense; From: William J. Haynes II, General Counsel; Subject: Counter-Resistance Techniques (November 27, 2002). On this memo, Secretary Rumsfeld wrote by hand, "However, I stand for 8–10 hours a day. Why is standing limited to 4 hours?" This penned comment by Rumsfeld trivializing the use of stress positions must have been intended as either a glib joke or a serious question. In either case it is unworthy of the Secretary of Defense. If he was serious, it demonstrates an amazing lack of familiarity with the stress techniques used by interrogators, which often involved standing in awkward and painful positions for long periods of time in the context of little food, little sleep, terror of dogs, and disorientation due to combinations of these techniques. If he did not, in fact, understand this, he was naïve. If it was a joke, it was made in poor taste for the official of the United States Government who authorized the series of techniques that led to the abuses of Abu Ghraib. A photocopy of the memo is contained in Greenberg and Dratel, *Torture Papers*, p. 236.
24. See Golden and Natta Jr., "Guantanamo Detainees," 1, A12, A13.
25. Schlesinger Report.
26. Schlesinger Report, p. 33.
27. Schlesinger Report, p. 72, for specification of techniques used at Guantanamo and Afghanistan.
28. According to a DoD handout to the press on June 22, 2004, category II techniques that were actually used at Guantanamo included isolation, deprivation of light, 20-hour

interrogations, and forced grooming. Those approved but not used included hooding, removal of clothing, use of dogs, and noninjurious physical contact.

29. Bravin, "Pentagon Report."
30. Golden and Natta Jr., "Guantanamo Detainees," p. 1, A12, A13. See also Seymour Hersh, *Chain of Command* (New York: Harper Collins, 2004), pp. 2–3.
31. Schlesinger Report, p. 8. See also Mark Marzzetti, Julian E. Barnes, and Edward T. Pound, "Inside the Iraq Prison Scandal," *U.S. News and World Report*, May 24, 2004, 22. See also Interview by Leon Wordon, "Newsmaker Interview: Brig. Gen. Janis Karpinski," *Signal Newspaper of Santa Clara, CA*, July 4, 2004, Truthout.org (accessed July 10, 2004).
32. Donna Miles, "Bush: Guantanamo Detainees Receiving Humane Treatment," Department of Defense, American Forces Press Service, June 20, 2005, http://www.defenselink.mil/news/newsarticle.aspx?id=16359 (accessed April 2, 2005). Although this statement was made in 2005, it represents the tone of President Bush's attitude since 9/11. His attitude toward detainees might even have softened because in 2005 it had been demonstrated that many detainees were innocent and posed no threat to the United States.
33. Fox News, "Rumsfeld: Afghan Detainees at Gitmo Bay Will Not Be Granted POW Status," January 28, 2002, http://www.foxnews.com/story/0,2933,44084,00.html.
34. News conference of Secretary of Defense Rumsfeld, January 27, 2002, http://www.defenselink.mil/transcripts/2002/t01282002_t0127enr.html.
35. Tim Golden, "Administration Officials Split Over Stalled Military Tribunals," *New York Times*, October 25, 2004, A1. Joseph Margulies, *Guantanamo and the Abuse of Presidential Power* (New York; Simon and Schuster, 2006), p. 65.
36. Quoted in Margulies, *Guantanamo*, p. 69.
37. Greg Miller, "Many Held at Guantanamo Not Likely Terrorists," *Los Angeles Times*, December 22, 2002, http://www.latimes.com/la-na-gitmo22dec22,0,2294365.story.
38. See Taguba, "Article 15-6 Investigation," the "Taguba Report," Part I, Sec. 2, No. 5, in Greenberg and Dratel, *Torture Papers*, pp. 405–465. Fay, "Investigation," pp. 109–171. Jones, "AR 15-6 Investigation," pp. 991–1018.
39. Charles C. Krulak and Joseph P. Hoar, "It's Our Cage, Too: Torture Betrays Us and Breeds New Enemies," *Washington Post*, May 17, 2007, A17.

Part 3

The Military and Civil Society

15

Civilian Means of Control

William Ruger

For more than two hundred years, the threat of a military coup has been all but nonexistent in the United States. The country has been truly fortunate that the norms and institutions of civilian control of the military have been so strong as to prevent such an event. However, a state's safety from coups is hardly an adequate measure of healthy civil-military relations. Indeed, military influence on political outcomes can quietly erode or threaten civilian control even within the framework of a liberal democratic order. Still, few would argue that the military should never influence policy outcomes. Instead, we recognize that the military, as experts in "the management of violence," should have a voice in the councils of war as well as on the seemingly more mundane issues that affect military institutions.[1] However, it is important to consider when, to what extent, and how the military should influence policy decisions.

This chapter has two purposes. First, it will describe the various arguments concerning what healthy civil-military relations look like and how the state can ensure effective civilian control. Second, it will discuss some critical issues in American civil-military relations today.

Healthy Civil-Military Relations

Since the end of the Cold War, the problematic state of American civil-military relations has been regularly bemoaned.[2] As Mackubin Owens and Kathleen Mahoney-Norris discuss later in this book, Secretary of Defense Donald Rumsfeld's leadership style and decisions provoked negative responses from active and retired officers. Of course, this current "crisis" is relative to either the perceived glory days of the past or to some ideal type. Indeed, most critics of our current civil-military relations admit that we are far from a state of emergency. However, there is a palpable unease among many scholars of civil-military relations concerning the health of that relationship and, thus, the health of the republic.

What would healthy civil-military relations entail? This question is important not only as a way to establish a baseline for measuring the current state of affairs but also in order to assess the various normative theories concerning civilian control. In short, we must know our destination before we know which route is best. Unfortunately, as Don Snider and Miranda Carlton-Carew point out, "except for the most obvious cases there is no consensus in the recent literature as to what constitutes 'good' civil-military relations or 'effective' civilian control of the military."[3]

Instead, a variety of competing definitions for good civil-military relations have been offered.[4] The most common approach of those studying civil-military relations outside of the United States is to focus on coups as the prime indicator of good or bad civil-military relations. Though a lack of coups (or the threat of them) is a necessary condition for good civil-military relations, most scholars of the American situation consider it to be an insufficient measure. It is considered far too low a bar for a liberal republic founded on the principle of the rule of law and with a historic wariness of standing armies.

Rather, a number of scholars focus on the extent to which civilians get what they want in the realms of policymaking and policy implementation. For example, Samuel Huntington holds that effective civilian control means "the minimizing of military power" relative to civilians such that the military is a politically neutral body (while also maximizing "the likelihood of achieving military security").[5] Michael Desch believes that good control exists when civilians prevail "when civilian and military preferences diverge."[6] He considers this favorable not only for domestic reasons (to preserve democracy and domestic liberty), but also for national security reasons. Likewise, Kenneth Kemp and Charles Hudlin argue that effective civilian control exists when two requirements are satisfied: (1) the ends of policy are set by civilians, and the military determines only what the proper means to achieve these ends are; and (2) civilian leaders draw the line between ends and means.[7] Richard Kohn points out that when we discuss effective civilian control, "we are talking about who calls the tune in military affairs in the United States today." In other words, "the best way to understand civilian control, to measure its existence and evaluate its effectiveness, is to weigh the relative influence of military officers and civilian officials in decisions of state concerning war, internal security, external defense, and military policy."[8]

The starkest variant of this position, but with some important differences, is found in Peter Feaver's work. He holds that sound democratic civil-military relations require that civilian leaders are always obeyed, "even when they are wrong about what is needed for national security." In other words, "civilians have a right to be wrong." Of course, both Feaver and the others make room for military leaders to advise their civilian superiors. However, once the final decision has been made, the military should "execute those orders faithfully" and leave it to the electorate to ultimately judge the wisdom of those orders.[9] This position rules out military attempts to influence policy by way of what Richard Betts called "indirect negative advice" about the use of force (i.e., overinflating the costs of military action so as to undermine support for it), "end-runs," and "foot-dragging."[10] Moreover, Feaver—though not Desch—holds that good civilian control can be undermined by officers resigning in protest, since "it threatens to hold the civilian principal hostage to the preferences of the military agent."[11]

Still other scholars equate healthy civil-military relations with the maintenance of civilian values. For example, Allen Millett holds that civilian supremacy in policymaking is not enough and that "civilian control requires that the armed forces do not dominate government or impose their unique (however functional) values upon civilian institutions and organizations."[12] Likewise, Charles Dunlap marries this concern to Kemp and Hudlin's criteria to stress civilian control of priorities and policy and the dominance of liberal democratic values. In fact, Dunlap considers the last of these to be so important as to trump the former since "civilian control may be damaged when the influence of the armed forces extends into areas that endanger liberties or the democratic process, *even when that expansion is sanctioned by the civilian leadership*" [italics in the original].[13] Millett goes even further by arguing that military policy must be consistent with society's basic values, with only limited compromises for discipline and fighting effectiveness.[14]

In quite a different direction, some focus on the level/frequency of conflict and "comity" between civilian leaders and the military; on whether they "like and respect one another"; or on the relative closeness between civilian views, experiences, and culture and those of the military.[15] In terms of the latter, many scholars have become chagrined at the "gaps" between the military and civilian elites. They argue that healthy civil-military relations necessitate that those gaps be narrowed.[16] As for reduced conflict, mutual respect, and comity, Rebecca Schiff's work stands out. In her "concordance theory," Schiff argues that the "three partners" of civil-military relations—"the military, the political elites, and the citizenry—should aim for a cooperative relationship" in order to avoid military intervention.[17]

For others, good civil-military relations are evinced by good outcomes.[18] Usually this yardstick focuses on military success. Therefore, victory in World War II signified that civil-military relations were sound; defeat in Vietnam proved the opposite. However, this standard can be used off the battlefield as well. Thus the debate on gays in the military or gender integration is suggestive of good or bad civil-military relations depending on your view of the matter and of what you believe is required normatively for the health of the republic and/or democratic values. An example of this approach comes from Eliot Cohen. In addition to military subordination, Cohen stresses the importance of civilian intervention into the military sphere in order to achieve victory in war—even at the cost of significant friction with the military.[19]

How to Get Effective Civilian Control

The literature on civil-military relations is replete with theories or frameworks for providing healthy civil-military relations and solving what Feaver calls the classic "civil-military problematique."[20] These theories basically fall into three categories or schools of thought. Much of the difference among these schools concerns the extent of civilian intervention into what has traditionally been defined as the military sphere. In what has been described as objective civilian control, civilians rely on the autonomy and professionalization of a neutral, apolitical military. Subjective control and its kindred theories rely on making the military more like society, particularly with regard to its interests and values, in order to control it. Finally, assertive control focuses on using institutional arrangements and individual intervention to ensure civilian superiority. Although the dividing lines between these schools of thought are artificial (with some scholars exhibiting features of more than one school), this categorization does capture meaningful differences in how to guarantee civilian control.[21]

Objective Civilian Control

The dominant theory of civilian control is objective civilian control. It is most closely identified with Samuel Huntington's *The Soldier and the State*. Huntington and the theory he espoused are the touchstones in the field of civil-military relations.

Objective control works by creating an autonomous professional military that is "a tool of the state" rather than an active political participant.[22] According to objective control theory, autonomy and professionalization will cause the military to be "politically sterile and neutral" and "ready to carry out the wishes of any civilian group which secures legitimate authority within the state."[23] Civilians can thus best maintain their grip on the military by recognizing that there is "an independent military sphere" and respecting the divide between the civilian and military spheres as well as the division of labor during crises and wartime. In other words, objective civilian control limits the authority of the military to "military matters"—but also requires self-limiting by civilians who stay out of certain realms deemed to be within the expertise of the military, such as the operational and planning realms during wartime. As Eliot Cohen notes, objective control would be achieved by "isolating soldiers from politics, and giving them as free a hand as possible in military matters."[24]

In practice, objective control would relegate military leaders to positions as mere advisors and instruments. They would simply advise their civilian superiors about the military means by which to meet political ends as determined by civilians (including grand strategy and the decision to go to war) and then faithfully carry out the civilians' wishes. Objective control would also mean that the civilian leadership would be enjoined from attempting to make the military a "mirror" of the state or of the society in terms of its membership, interests, or principles.[25] Moreover, the military would be given substantial freedom to determine what is necessary to accomplish its tasks. In short, civilians would have to avoid trespassing into the military sphere, as doing so would compromise its autonomy and professionalism.

Many students of civil-military relations have followed in Huntington's footsteps and should be considered part of the objective control school of thought.[26] It is also worth noting that objective civilian control is particularly popular in military circles.[27] However, there are "thick" and "thin" versions of this theory. Huntington's approach might be described as thick: one gets the sense that he and his followers believe the strong division of labor between civilians and the military should be relatively impermeable. Thin versions, such as those espoused by Desch, leave substantial—but exceptional—room for civilian intervention in what would normally be the military realm, and vice versa. (He even allows limited room for the military to act politically.)

In particular, Desch argues that civilian leaders should not simply "rubber-stamp military policies, even in the tactical or operational realms." But they should do so only when they are able to give "a compelling political reason for ignoring these military recommendations."[28] Desch also suggests that the political layer is appropriately permeable by the military during the run-up to war. While some might argue that civilian control entails civilians setting even the terms of military influence on the policymaking process, he argues that "the military has a right and a duty to be heard. After all, soldiers are the experts in fighting wars—and it is their lives that are ultimately on the line." Moreover, Desch thinks that resignation—despite its reverberations in the political realm—is an appropriate action by military officers even if their central concern is only that "their advice is being ignored."[29]

The virtue of the thin approach is that it avoids eviscerating the initial delegation decision while preserving a tight connection between political ends and military means that Carl von Clausewitz showed to be the key to real victory. The danger of the thin approach is that hubris or incompetence could lead civilians to overreach into the military realm and forego the advantages of relying on expert counsel. It could degenerate into "assertive control" (discussed below). The best hope for mitigating this problem is virtue and humility on the part of political leaders. On the other hand, the problem with thick objective control is that it could allow for a disjuncture between political ends and military means.[30]

Subjective Civilian Control, Fusionism, and Concordance Theory

Subjective control and its kindred theories attempt to affect the quality of civilian control by blurring, but not destroying, the distinctions between the military and civilian realms. As Huntington explains, it comes in many forms but essentially achieves its ends "by civilianizing the military, making them the mirror of the state."[31]

Morris Janowitz is the leading scholar associated with this school of thought. He saw the solution to civil-military relations, partly due to the changed nature of warfare, as requiring a "constabulatory force" led by a particular type of professional officer. This officer would share civilian values and be "given a candid and realistic education about political matters." Control would occur as a consequence of shared values, civilian oversight, and the military's deep "sense of self-esteem and moral worth."[32]

Similarly, fusionism and concordance are attempts to control the military by eroding the differences between the two traditional spheres and merging their responsibilities. These theories are premised on the notion that "it had become impossible to maintain the distinction between political and military functions at the highest level of government."[33] Concordance, in particular, relies on a fairly lax standard for healthy civil-military relations—namely, cooperation among the principle components of government. Specifically, Rebecca Schiff argues that cooperation gained through "dialogue, accommodation, and shared values or objectives among the military, the political elites, and society" will keep the military from intervening in politics.[34] For all of these types of subjective control, oversight, personnel selection and recruitment, and education are critical mechanisms to the desired end.

Assertive Civilian Control

The most serious challenger to objective control, thick or thin, is assertive civilian control.[35] Instead of relying on autonomy and military professionalism, assertive control utilizes institutional mechanisms and individual civilian interventions to aggressively maintain civilian dominance in the crafting, shaping, management, and implementation of military policy. Indeed, assertive control specifically challenges the virtues of military autonomy, particularly during wartime. While objective control is often the military's preferred method of control, assertive control is frequently the preference of civilian officials, including those within the current Bush administration.[36]

Institutional arrangements designed to buttress civilian control have a long pedigree and have been utilized frequently by both democratic and nondemocratic regimes. Not surprisingly, many scholars and policymakers find these arrangements particularly compelling solutions to the problem of civilian control. The most common has been to legally restrict, limit, or divide military power.[37] Other mechanisms include formal (and aggressive) civilian oversight of the military. For example, Peter Feaver's work applying principal-agent theory to civil-military relations—what he calls "agency theory"—highlights the importance of using civilian monitoring mechanisms and punishment to get the military to "work" rather than "shirk."[38] Monitoring includes contract incentives, screening and selection controls, "fire alarms," institutional checks, "police patrols" (e.g., the civilian secretariat and the Office of the Secretary of Defense [OSD]), and outright revision of the initial delegation. In terms of punishment, this would include more restrictive monitoring, budget cuts, firing/retirement/discharge, and the use of legal and extralegal action against an individual officer.[39] However, Feaver does not argue for a one-size-fits-all combination of these approaches; instead, "the optimal mix of monitoring mechanisms is the one that minimizes the incentives and opportunity for the agent to flout the principal's wishes, at the least cost to the principal and while preserving the efficiencies of specialization that come with delegation."[40] Feaver's prescriptions are more general than specific. Nonetheless, they are significantly different in emphasis from the other theories under review here.

During wartime, assertive control theorists stress the particular importance of civilian intervention into the military realm. As Eliot Cohen argues in *Supreme*

Command, civilian leaders must engage in an "unequal dialogue" with military leaders in which they "coax or bully, interrogate or probe" while treating "military advice as just that—advice, not a course of action to be ratified with no more than formal consideration."[41] Unlike objective control, "civilian restraint in inter-rogating, probing, and even in extremis, dictating military action" is a pruden-tial decision, not a principled one—and thus is not critical for healthy civil-military relations. Indeed, such principled restraint could be dangerous if it prevented the achievement of political ends and "removed oversight and control from those whose job most requires it."[42] In short, civilians should frequently take *military* matters into their own hands in order to properly control the mili-tary and dictate outcomes.

Liberal Objective Control: Separation, Norms, and Responsibilities

A liberal democracy should enjoy civil-military relations that allow for civilian dominance. Indeed, as Feaver correctly observes, civilians even have "a right to be wrong."[43] This is consistent with democratic theory's central proposition that the people should rule. In the United States, this principle is enshrined in the Constitution. In practice, it means that the elected representatives of the people, the president and the Congress, make policy and are obeyed by those who are tasked with implementing it.

However, the purpose of the social contract—and the Constitution—is more than the mere creation of a system of procedures for governance. Central to the liberal democratic tradition is the notion that government is created to protect the rights of the parties to that contract. Therefore, we want more than mere civilian control. We also want the purpose of government to be realized: the security of our rights. This desire for security requires that civilians determine the desired balance between security and risk (since absolute security is impossible) and cre-ate a grand strategy to guide military policy.[44] In addition, civilians should delegate military force to a group of individuals who become experts in the management of violence and who employ it on behalf of the state when necessary. These experts also advise civilians on military policy, especially on how to use force but, impor-tantly, not on whether to use force. In peacetime, they advise about strategy, force planning, end-strength, platforms, and organizational policy; in wartime, they advise about operations and tactics.

Liberal regimes require more than civilian decision making and military secu-rity from enemies, both foreign and domestic. They also want liberal values to flourish within society. Therefore, healthy civil-military relations entail avoiding "militarism" in the civilian sphere. This requires that military influence in terms of formal advice or in terms of norms and practices be limited to the military realm.[45]

Avoiding Militarism

So how do we achieve civilian dominance and military security while also main-taining a liberal society and avoiding creeping militarism? I find the answer given by Huntington and his students not far off the mark. Indeed, this discussion flows largely from his contribution and might be called "liberal objective control"—a modified form of his classic approach.

The first, and most important, requirement is a moral commitment by the military to civilian authority. This is a critical aspect of Huntington's "professionalism" which needs to be emphasized, and which Finer and others understand to be essential to preventing military intervention.[46] In the American case, this would include a due reverence for the Constitution, which enshrines and specifies civilian command.

This norm requires, as Kemp and Hudlin outline, not just a positive commitment to obey, but a negative duty to "avoid other kinds of political involvement as well."[47] It would include self-restraint in a number of areas. Of course, it would bar open partisan activity. But more importantly, it would also forbid attempts to influence policy or public opinion. Of course, this would exempt private advice solicited by civilian leaders, including Congress, on matters within the purview of the officer as military expert. Nonetheless, it would forbid quite a lot of political activity that one regularly sees today. For example, this commitment, if honored, would have prevented Colin Powell as chairman of the Joint Chiefs of Staff (JCS) from attempting to directly or indirectly influence American foreign policy in the immediate post–Cold War era. It would also have restrained Richard Myers from publicly trumpeting the Bush administration's policies in Iraq. It would even keep members of the military—including those in the enlisted ranks—from writing op-eds (even if they are right) or from making an "Appeal for Redress" (even if legal) about things outside of their competence to judge, such as whether and how long the state should fight wars.[48] It might also suggest that military education be oriented less toward creating a politically savvy cohort of officers and more toward inculcating the propriety of being neutral advisors who should exercise due restraint in the field of politics.[49] Of course, such behavior will require a great deal of virtue on the part of military men and women. But as David Hendrickson wisely notes, "There is no substitute for better motives."[50]

There is one critical exception to this norm of neutral obedience: politically motivated resignation when obedience is believed to severely threaten the obligation of a soldier to his or her "men" and to the Constitution he or she is sworn to defend. The rule for military officers when they disagree with their civilian superiors is that they should "salute and obey." They should understand, as General George McClellan accurately noted, that "the remedy for political errors, if any are committed, is to be found only in the action of the people at the polls."[51] However, in extreme situations, resignation is acceptable.[52] It is acceptable because following orders in such cases will provide little solace to the soldiers in harm's way about whom officers have a duty to care. Given the military leader's dual duty to his masters and his troops, there has to be some means for officers to react.

The second means of achieving good civilian control is some separation of the professional military from politics and society. Autonomy, in classic objective control theory, helps ensure military subordination by giving the military room to be a professional, politically neutral institution committed to the state.[53] It also makes the military more effective at meeting the security demands of the state.

Rather than a laboratory for social change or another front in domestic political battles, the autonomous military can be structured optimally with both eyes on the requirements of war. Moreover, the military can orient itself completely toward external threats, which not only makes it more effective as a fighting force (and thus at providing security) but also keeps it from threatening liberal values and civilian control.[54]

Autonomy also allows for the maximization of the positive benefits of the initial delegation decision, which assumes that "there are certain kinds of decisions that the military is especially competent to make."[55] In other words, experts are allowed to make decisions on matters they understand best. As part of this separation, civilians would be wise, as Desch points out, to give the military "wide leeway in making the operational and tactical decisions about how to complete a mission."[56]

Separation, indeed some isolation, is also good for preventing militarism, creeping or otherwise. With the military kept on post or at the front—and out of domestic politics—military values will not compete with civilian ones. Of course, this separation is likely to lead to the creation of a particular military class that might be heavily tilted toward one ideological or partisan persuasion. However, this should not be a worry, given the proper ethic as well as the military's external orientation and professionalism.

Finally, the third key feature of proper civilian control is the responsibility of civilian leaders to act appropriately and in a self-limiting fashion that respects the military as professional experts. This entails a duty to avoid interference in the military sphere unless there is a particularly convincing reason to do otherwise.[57] For example, civilians should be cautious about insisting that women be allowed in combat roles in order to satisfy normative or political demands before the military effects of such a policy can be determined. However, there are exceptions to this rule. Racial integration of the military, for example, was an appropriate intervention for normative, domestic, and foreign policy reasons—as well as for its benefits in terms of military effectiveness. Likewise, civilian "meddling" in the operational and tactical realms is acceptable as long as civilian leaders give a "compelling political reason for ignoring these [military] recommendations."[58] Civilian leaders should also resist using the military for internal security or for domestic missions such as relief efforts. While such uses may seem sensible on a case-by-case basis, they are likely to threaten military effectiveness in providing external security, military subordination, and liberal values.[59]

Congress and the president also have a responsibility to avoid using the military as part of their institutional or partisan battles. It is unseemly and dangerous to politicize the military. This means that neither the White House nor anyone else should "encourage" a military leader to enter political battles over current policy. Lawrence Korb speculates that this may have occurred in 2004 when General David Petraeus wrote an op-ed piece about Iraq for the *Washington Post*.[60] Civilian leaders should also resist using the military for cheap photo-ops. Yet, as Brendan Doherty's earlier chapter in this book suggests, they do.

Political leaders also have a responsibility to pick good military leaders who are selected for their virtues and expertise rather than for their political views or willingness to publicly support government policy. If Fred Kaplan's recent characterization of General Peter Pace is correct, this is exactly the kind of yes-man that good leaders should avoid.[61] Instead, civilians should seek out those who will offer candid advice and who can be trusted not to "shirk" when they disagree. Secretary of Defense Robert Gates seems to have understood this given that he noted that "healthy" civil-military relations start with those in his office "creating an environment in which the senior military feel free to offer independent advice not only to the civilian leadership in the Pentagon but also to the President and the National Security Council."[62] Moreover, civilians should not punish those who are candid, though the military should advise its superiors discreetly and without stepping over the admittedly gray line into political debate.[63] In fact, some suggest that advice on the most potentially politically explosive subjects should be private rather than public.[64]

Finally, civilian leaders should behave in a fashion that lends respect and legitimacy to the government. This includes acting as moral exemplars. This will help buttress the military's normative commitment to civilian control, and it has been shown to reduce military intervention in politics.[65]

This emphasis on norms and duties is not to say that certain specific institutional arrangements (besides separation) will not augment civilian control on the margins. Maintaining interservice rivalries, for example, has the potential to support civilian control by dividing the military and increasing the likelihood of multiple views being heard during the advisory process, without unduly harming military autonomy and professionalism. Likewise, legislated limitations on the size of the standing forces during peacetime can have positive benefits for civil-military relations. On the negative side, certain institutional arrangements have the potential to hurt civilian control, as Goldwater-Nichols did by unifying the military and creating a powerful voice in the chairman of the JCS. However, the emphasis on institutions can take us only so far.[66] In this case, the moral obligation on the part of both the military and civilians to respect each other's proper roles, as well as the virtue to act according to this duty, is critical.[67] Thus, even a powerful chairman of the JCS in charge of a large unified military can be self-limiting and thus "cause" healthy civilian control.

Notes

1. Harold D. Lasswell, *The Analysis of Political Behavior: An Empirical Approach* (London: Kegan Paul, Trench, Trubner& Co., 1948), 26. Lasswell earlier refers to the military as "specialists on violence" and discusses the management of violence in Harold. D. Lasswell, "The Garrison State," *American Journal of Sociology* 46, no. 4 (January 1941): 455–468.

2. The most notable among these are Richard Kohn's article "Out of Control" and the numerous responses to it. See Richard H. Kohn, "Out of Control: The Crisis in Civil-Military Relations," *National Interest* 35 (Spring 1994): 3–17; and Colin Powell, John Lehman, William Odom, Samuel Huntington, and Richard Kohn, "An Exchange on Civil-Military Relations," *National Interest* 36 (Summer 1994): 23–31. Similar discussions are found in Don M. Snider and Miranda A. Carlton-Carew, eds., *U.S. Civil-Military Relations: In Crisis or Transition* (Washington, D.C.: The Center for Strategic and

International Studies, 1995); Charles J. Dunlap, Jr., "Welcome to the Junta: The Erosion of Civilian Control of the U.S. Military," *Wake Forest Law Review* 29, no. 2 (Summer 1994): 341–92; Charles J. Dunlap, Jr., "The Origins of the Military Coup of 2012," *Parameters* 22, no. 4 (Winter 1992/1993): 2–22; James Kitfield, "Standing Apart," *National Journal* 30, no. 24 (June 13, 1998): 1350–58; Eliot A. Cohen, "Civil-Military Relations: Are U.S. Forces Overstretched?" *Orbis* 41, no. 2 (Spring 1997): 177–86; Thomas E. Ricks, *Making the Corps* (New York: Scribner, 1997); A. J. Bacevich, "Civilian Control: A Useful Fiction?" *Joint Forces Quarterly*, no. 6 (Autumn/Winter 1994–95): 76–79; Mackubin Thomas Owens; "Civilian Control: A National Crisis?" *Joint Forces Quarterly*, no. 6 (Autumn/Winter 1994–95): 80–83; and articles by a number of scholars in a symposium on civil-military relations in the Spring 1998 edition of *Armed Forces and Society*. For more recent discussions during the Bush presidency, see Richard H. Kohn, "The Erosion of Civilian Control of the Military in the United States Today," *Naval War College Review* 55, no. 3 (Summer 2002): 9–59; Mackubin Thomas Owens, "Rumsfeld, the Generals, and the State of U.S. Civil-Military Relations," *Naval War College Review* 59, no. 4 (August 2006): 68–80; Damon Coletta, "Courage in the Service of Virtue: The Case of General Shinseki's Testimony before the Iraq War," *Armed Forces and Society* 34, no. 1 (October 2007): 109–21; Michael C. Desch, "Bush and the Generals," *Foreign Affairs* 86, no. 3 (May/June 2007): 97–108; and Richard B. Myers and Richard Kohn, Mackubin Thomas Owens, Lawrence J. Korb, and Michael C. Desch, "Responses: Salute and Disobey? The Civil-Military Balance, Before Iraq and After," *Foreign Affairs* 86, no. 5 (September/October 2007): 147–56.

3. Don M. Snider and Miranda A. Carlton-Carew, "The Current State of U.S. Civil-Military Relations: An Introduction," in *U.S. Civil-Military Relations: In Crisis or Transition*, ed. Don M. Snider and Miranda A. Carlton-Carew (Washington, D.C.: Center for Strategic and International Studies, 1995), 16. Likewise, Michael Desch argued that "there is a remarkably broad range of ideas on what constitutes 'good' or 'bad' civil-military relations." Michael C. Desch, *Civilian Control of the Military: The Changing Security Environment* (Baltimore, MD: Johns Hopkins University Press, 1999), 3. And following Snider and Carlton-Carew, the term "effective civilian control" is used as a synonym for healthy or good civil-military relations. See pg. 15.

4. This discussion follows similar categorizations offered by Snider and Carlton-Carew, "Introduction," 15–16; and Desch, *Civilian Control of the Military*, 3–5. It is not intended to be exhaustive but representative of the major approaches.

5. Samuel P. Huntington, *The Soldier and the State: The Theory and Politics of Civil-Military Relations* (Cambridge, MA: Harvard University Press, 1957), 84–85.

6. Desch, *Civilian Control of the Military*, 4–5.

7. Kenneth W. Kemp and Charles Hudlin, "Civil Supremacy over the Military: Its Nature and Limits," *Armed Forces and Society* 19, no. 1 (Fall 1992): 7–26.

8. Richard H. Kohn, "The Erosion of Civilian Control," 16; and Richard H. Kohn, "How Democracies Control the Military," *Journal of Democracy* 8, no. 4 (1997): 143.

9. Peter D. Feaver, *Armed Servants: Agency, Oversight, and Civil-Military Relations* (Cambridge, MA: Harvard University Press, 2003), 298–302; see 4–6, 65–68.

10. Feaver, *Armed Servants*, 68. On different types of military advice, see Richard K. Betts, *Soldiers, Statesmen, and Cold War Crises*, Morningside Edition (New York: Columbia University Press, 1991), 11–12.

11. Feaver, *Armed Servants*, 301.

12. Allan R. Millett, *The American Political System and Civilian Control of the Military: A Historical Perspective* (Columbus: Mershon Center, Ohio State University, 1979), quoted in Dunlap, "Welcome to the Junta," 344.

13. Dunlap, "Welcome to the Junta," 344.

14. See Dunlap, "Welcome to the Junta," 344.
15. Desch, *Civilian Control of the Military*, 4; Snider and Carlton-Carew also point this one out.
16. See the gap literature discussed in Peter D. Feaver, and Richard H. Kohn, eds., *Soldiers and Civilians: The Civil-Military Gap and American National Security* (Cambridge: MIT Press, 2001). An example of this argument can be found in Richard Danzig, *The Big Three: Our Greatest Security Risks and How to Address Them* (Washington, D.C.: NDU Press, 1999), 53–55. He notes there that "while maintaining a professional and merit-based military, responsible decision makers also need to address the need to bring the DoD and American society closer together," and that "more attention needs to be paid to opportunities to expose members of the military and civilian populations to one another."
17. Rebecca L. Schiff, "Civil-Military Relations Reconsidered: A Theory of Concordance," *Armed Forces and Society* 22, no. 1 (Fall 1995): 7.
18. Snider and Carlton-Carew, 15; and see Desch, *Civilian Control of the Military*.
19. See Eliot A. Cohen, *Supreme Command: Soldiers, Statesmen, and Leadership in Wartime* (New York: Free Press, 2002).
20. Indeed, as Patricia Shields points out, "All theories of democratic civil-military relations have a normative component." Patricia M. Shields, "Civil-Military Relations: Changing Frontiers," *Public Administration Review* 66, no. 6 (November/December 2006): 926. On the "civil-military problematique," see Peter D. Feaver, "The Civil-Military Problematique: Huntington, Janowitz, and the Question of Civilian Control," *Armed Forces and Society* 23, no. 2 (Winter 1996): 150–158.
21. It is worth noting at the outset that the ability of any system of civilian control to actually provide for healthy civil-military relations may be hindered or aided by structural factors at the systemic level. As Desch shows in his realist-inspired work, the external threat environment can impact the quality of civil-military relations. See Desch, *Civilian Control of the Military*.
22. Huntington, *Soldier and the State*, 83.
23. Ibid., 84.
24. Cohen, *Supreme Command*, 4.
25. Huntington, *Soldier and the State*, 83 and 85.
26. Including those who rely on norms of subordination to achieve civilian control in a fashion analogous to the inculcation of professionalism. See David Hendrickson, *Reforming Defense: The State of Civil-Military Relations* (Baltimore: Johns Hopkins University Press, 1988); and Kemp and Hudlin, "Civil Supremacy."
27. See Huntington, *Soldier and the State*, 84; Feaver, *Armed Servants*, 7; and Cohen, *Supreme Command*, 229.
28. Desch's reply in Myers et al., "Responses," 156.
29. Desch, "Bush and the Generals," 108.
30. Huntington's main flaw, however, is that he thought that objective civilian control could be fulfilled only if American society changed. In particular, he thought that America would have to become more conservative and less individualistic: more like West Point and less like Highland Falls. Otherwise, America would not allow the military to be autonomous or professional enough to achieve objective control. See Huntington, *Soldier and the State*, 464–466; as well as Feaver, *Armed Servants*, 19–20. Most importantly, this is flawed because an America that became more like West Point in order to achieve civilian control would have lost the game at the outset. It would have lost its soul to save it. This could hardly be a good solution to the problem of civilian control. Fortunately, a conservative society is not a necessary condition for

the enactment of objective control. Liberals can also see the wisdom of such a solution and restrain themselves from undue interference in military matters. Of course, this may be more difficult for liberals, as certain recent encroachments have shown. However, that does not mean it is impossible.

31. Huntington, *Soldier and the State*, 83.
32. Morris Janowitz, *The Professional Soldier: A Social and Political Portrait* (1960; reprint New York: Free Press, 1971); 420–40. For a nice discussion of Janowitz's argument, see Arthur D. Larson, "Military Professionalism and Civilian Control: A Comparative Analysis of Two Interpretations" *Journal of Political and Military Sociology* 2 (Spring 1974): 57–72.
33. Huntington, *Soldier and the State*, 351. And see 350–4.
34. Schiff, "Civil-Military Relations," 12. It is hard to believe that these things will prevent intervention, given that what will necessitate such cooperation will look a lot like intervention unless the standard for civilian control is the absence of a military coup. For criticism of Schiff's position, see Richard S. Wells, "The Theory of Concordance in Civil-Military Relations: A Commentary," *Armed Forces and Society* 23, no. 2 (Winter 1996): 269–75.
35. Feaver coins this term. See Peter D. Feaver, *Guarding the Guardians: Civilian Control of Nuclear Weapons in the United States* (Ithaca, NY: Cornell University Press, 1992).
36. See Desch, "Bush and the Generals."
37. See Peter D. Feaver, "Civil-Military Relations," *Annual Review of Political Science* 2 (1999): 225. Subjective control theorists also commonly utilize this mechanism for civilian control. See Huntington, *Soldier and the State*, 82; and Feaver, *Armed Servants*, 81.
38. Three important caveats about Feaver's work should be noted. First, Feaver's work is largely a positivist attempt to explain and predict patterns of civil-military relations. However, it has strong but implicit normative/prescriptive content, and thus it should be considered a normative theory as well. Second, his work is complicated and not easily captured by the categorical framework utilized here. Indeed, it crosses the boundaries here, often purposely, since he is trying to subsume older theories under his agency theory. For example, while institutions are critical for Feaver, he also relies on the military accepting a certain moral commitment to civilian rule for things like punishment to work. See Feaver, *Armed Servants*, 90. Thus, he shares a critical feature of objective control. Moreover, in common with the subjective control theorists, Feaver's monitoring mechanisms include using accession policies for "selecting and promoting personnel who will share civilian preferences" (ibid., 79; and see 59). Third, and more damaging to any prescriptions based on agency theory, Feaver tends to rely quite a bit on a strong president (to put bite into the threat of punishment) and professional norms to make his agency theory work. However, if these variables are doing a lot of the driving, it might be argued that these are the keys to civilian control, not institutions per se.
39. Feaver, *Armed Servants*, ch. 3.
40. Ibid., 57.
41. Cohen, *Supreme Command*, 208–9.
42. Ibid., 13.
43. Ibid., 6.
44. On the advantages of civilians in determining security and risk levels, see Ibid., Hendrickson, *Reforming Defense*, 25, and Desch, "Bush and the Generals."
45. This follows from Dunlap, "Welcome to the Junta;" and Dunlap, "Origins."
46. Albright highlights the importance of this even within Huntington's schema. See David E. Albright, "A Comparative Conceptualization of Civil-Military Relations,"

World Politics 32, no. 4 (July 1980): 555. On Finer and others who share this view, see S. E. Finer, *The Man on Horseback: Military Intervention into Politics* (New York: Praeger, 1962); Kemp and Hudlin, "Civil Supremacy"; and Hendrickson, *Reforming Defense.*
47. Kemp and Hudlin, "Civil Supremacy," 22.
48. See Jayamaha Buddhika, Wesley D. Smith, Jeremy Roebuck, Omar Mora, Edward Sandmeier, Yance T. Gray, and Jeremy A. Murphy, "The War as We Saw It," *New York Times*, August 19, 2007, 11 (WK); and for a recent example of an appeal for redress occasioned by the war in Iraq, see http://www.appealforredress.org/.
49. Although, as Desch reminded me, the military must still be taught to understand that war is continuation of politics à la Clausewitz (private conversation). It does not rule out the necessity of liberally educating military leaders so that they can handle the complexities of the modern battlefield, particularly when dealing with complex situations that they will confront in counterinsurgency warfare. Unfortunately, folks like Sam Sarkesian and Robert Connor think the military should engage in "enlightened advocacy." The last thing we need is another savvy political interest group that can manipulate civilians, especially given its ease due to the divided control between the executive branch and Congress. See Sam C. Sarkesian and Robert E. Connor, Jr., *The U.S. Military Profession into the Twenty-First Century: War, Peace, and Politics*, 2nd ed. (London: Routledge, 2006), 71–2.
50. Hendrickson, *Reforming Defense*, 28. Damon Coletta also calls for political restraint, courage, and personal virtue on the part of military leaders, with particular reference to General Eric Shinseki's famous testimony before Congress before the Iraq War. Without arguing one way or the other about Coletta's particular judgment on Shinseki, his overarching call for restraint on the part of military leaders is well-taken. See Coletta, "Courage," 110.
51. Quoted in Owens, "Rumsfield," 74.
52. For a different view on resignation, see Feaver, *Armed Servants*, 301. For a similar view, see Desch, "Bush and the Generals," 108. My difference with Desch on this is that he would allow it if their advice is being ignored. I think this might set the bar too low, though in practice, few would resign simply for being ignored.
53. See Huntington, *Soldier and the State*, ch. 4.
54. On the effects of internal orientation, see Stanislav Andreski, "On the Peaceful Disposition of Military Dictatorships," *Journal of Strategic Studies* 3, no. 3 (December 1980): 3–10; Dunlap, "Welcome to the Junta;" Dunlap, "The Origins"; and Desch, *Civilian Control of the Military.*
55. Hendrickson, *Reforming Defense*, 25.
56. Desch, "Bush and the Generals," 108.
57. Contra the subjective control and assertive control advocates.
58. Desch's reply in Myers et al., "Responses," 156.
59. See Dunlap, "Welcome to the Junta;" and Dunlap, "The Origins"; and Desch, *Civilian Control of the Military.*
60. He notes that if that was not the case, it was still wrong because he was "injecting himself improperly into a political campaign." Korb's response in Myers et al, "Responses," 152.
61. Fred Kaplan, "Pete the Parrot Departs," *Slate*, October 5, 2007, http://www.slate.com/id/2175310/.
62. Quoted in Desch, "Bush and the Generals," 97.
63. See ibid., 107–108.
64. Snider and Carlton-Carew, "Introduction"1; Coletta, "Courage," 119; and Suzanne Nielsen, "The Army Officer as Servant," *Military Review* 3, no. 1 (January–February 2003): 17.

65. See Finer, *Man on Horseback*; and A. R. Luckham, "A Comparative Typology of Civil-Military Relations," *Government and Opposition* 6, no. 1 (Winter 1971).
66. I think this is generally true about politics. Without certain virtues in the principles and agents, institutional arrangement can have only limited effect. This is an old argument in political science, perhaps nowhere more interesting than in the famous Mill-Macaulay debate. See Jack Lively and John Rees, *Utilitarian Logic and Politics: James Mill's Essay on Government, Macaulay's Critique, and the Ensuing Debate* (Oxford: Clarendon, 1978).
67. Here, I follow in the footsteps of Finer, Hendrickson, and Kemp and Hudlin—not to mention Huntington.

16

Understanding Civil-Military Relations during the Clinton-Bush Era

Mackubin Owens

During the 1990s, a number of events led observers to conclude that all was not well with civil-military relations in America. These events generated an often acrimonious public debate in which a number of highly respected individuals concluded that American civil-military relations had become unhealthy at best and that they were "in crisis" at worst. In the words of the distinguished military historian Richard Kohn, the state of civil-military relations during this period was "extraordinarily poor, in many respects as low as in any period of American peacetime history."[1]

Some observers claimed that the civil-military tensions of the 1990s were a temporary phenomenon, attributable to the perceived antimilitary character of the Clinton administration. But civil-military tensions did not disappear with the election and reelection of George W. Bush. If anything, civil-military relations have become more strained as a result of clashes between the uniformed services and Bush's first secretary of defense, Donald Rumsfeld, over efforts to "transform" the U.S. military from a Cold War force to one better able to respond to likely future contingencies and the planning and conduct of U.S. military operations in Afghanistan and Iraq.

Civil-Military Relations from Clinton to Bush

The serious systemic problems affecting American civil-military relations that scholars and public policy experts identified during the decade of the 1990s included:

- the U.S. military had become more alienated from its civilian leadership than at any other time in American history;

- there was a growing gap between the U.S. military as an institution and civilian society at large;
- the U.S. military had become politicized and partisan;
- the U.S. military had become resistant to civilian oversight, as illustrated by the efforts to dictate when and under what circumstances it would be used to implement U.S. policy;
- officers had come to believe that they had the right to confront and resist civilian policymakers, to *insist* that civilian authorities heed their recommendations; and
- the U.S. military was becoming too influential in inappropriate areas of American society.[2]

The likely and very dangerous outcome of such trends, went the argument, was a large, semiautonomous military so different and estranged from society that it might become unaccountable to those whom it serves. Those who advanced this view worried about the expansion of the military's influence and were concerned about the possibility of a military that was contemptuous of American society and unresponsive to civilian authorities.

Most writers who took this line acknowledged that the crisis was not acute—it did not, for instance, involve tanks rumbling through the streets or soldiers surrounding the parliament building or the presidential palace. Instead, they said, it was subtle and subversive—like a lymphoma or a termite infestation—destroying silently from within and appearing as mutual mistrust and misunderstanding, institutional failure, and strategic incapacitation.[3] If the problem had not yet reached the danger point, they contended, that time was not too far off if something was not done soon.

Not all scholars agreed with this assessment. Some argued that American civil-military relations were not in crisis but in transition as a result of the Cold War's end and changes in American society.[4]

Nonetheless, of the three criteria for judging the state of civil-military relations in the United States during the past decade and a half, only military effectiveness would seem to rate high marks, although the time necessary to adjust to the insurgency in Iraq might be seen as detracting from the excellence of the uniformed military. Comity or harmony between civilians and the uniformed military has ranged from average to poor, and the attitude of up-and-coming officers concerning the role of military advice raises serious questions regarding the future of constitutional balance.

Comity or Harmony between Civilians and the Uniformed Military

Nothing was more illustrative of the lack of comity in civil-military relations during this period than the unprecedented instances of downright hostility on the part of the uniformed military toward President Bill Clinton, whose antimilitary stance as a young man during the Vietnam War years did not endear him to soldiers.[5]

Many of the most highly publicized disputes between the uniformed military and the Clinton administration reflected cultural tensions between the military as an institution and liberal civilian society, mostly having to do with women in combat and open homosexuality in the military. The catalog included the very public exchange on the issue of military service by open homosexuals between newly elected President Clinton on the one hand and the uniformed military and Congress on the other, "Tailhook," the Kelly Flinn affair, and the sexual harassment scandal at Aberdeen, Maryland.[6]

Civil-military disharmony did not disappear with the election of George W. Bush. Issues having to do with the "transformation" of the U.S. military and the conduct of the Iraq war have created serious tensions between the uniformed military and the Bush administration, making it clear that civil-military relations continue to be contentious, characterized by mutual suspicion and misunderstanding.

To begin with, the instances of military officers undercutting Secretary of Defense Donald Rumsfeld and his policies in pursuit of their own goals—what Peter Feaver has called "shirking" (e.g., anti-Rumsfeld leaks to the press, "foot-dragging," and "slow-rolling")—that had similarly plagued the Clinton administration, continued apace.[7] In addition, public criticism by military officers of civilian leaders continued as well.

For instance in April 2006, a number of retired army and Marine Corps generals publicly called for the resignation of Secretary of Defense Rumsfeld. Much of the language they used was intemperate, indeed contemptuous. One described the actions of the Bush administration as ranging from "true dereliction, negligence, and irresponsibility" to "lying, incompetence, and corruption." Another called Rumsfeld "incompetent strategically, operationally, and tactically." The seemingly orchestrated character of these attacks suggested that civil-military disharmony had reached a new and dangerous level.[8]

Although the critics in this case were retired general officers, observers of what the press called the "revolt of the generals" believed that these retired flag officers were speaking on behalf not only of themselves, but of many active duty officers as well. As Richard Kohn has observed, retired general and flag officers are analogous to the cardinals of the Roman Catholic Church. While there are no legal restrictions that prevent retired members of the military—even recently retired members—from criticizing public policy or the individuals responsible for it, there are some important reasons to suggest that the public denunciation of civilian authority by soldiers, retired or not, undermines healthy civil-military relations. Kathleen Mahoney-Norris in the next chapter fully explores these issues.

Constitutional Balance

The cornerstone of U.S. civil-military relations is civilian control of the military, a principle that goes back to the American Revolution and the precedent established by George Washington, who willingly subordinated himself and his army to civilian authority. "Washington's willing subordination, of himself and the army he commanded, to civilian authority established the essential tenet of that service's professional ethos. His extraordinary understanding of the fundamental importance of civil preeminence allowed a professional military force to begin to flourish in a democratic society. All of our military services are heir to that legacy."[9]

During the Clinton administration, critics charged that the subordination of the military establishment to civilian control was under assault. During the 1992 presidential campaign, General Colin Powell, then chairman of the Joint Chiefs of Staff (JCS), published an op-ed piece in the *New York Times* warning about the dangers of intervening in Bosnia. Not long afterward, he followed up with an article in *Foreign Affairs*. Both were criticized as illegitimate attempts by a senior military officer to preempt the foreign policy agenda of an incoming president. As such, they constituted a serious encroachment by the military on civilian "turf." Critics argued that it was unprecedented for the highest ranking officer on active duty to go public with his disagreements with the president over foreign policy and the role of the military.

A second example of constitutional overreach was the military's purported resistance to involvement in constabulary missions. Critics contended that such instances were further examples of an illegitimate expansion of the military's influence into inappropriate areas. They argued that the uniformed defense establishment had succeeded in making military, not political, considerations paramount in the political-military decision-making process—dictating to civilians not only how its operations would be conducted, but also the circumstances under which the military instrument would be used.

This purported role reflected the post-Vietnam view dominant within the military that only professional military officers could be trusted to establish principles guiding the use of military force. Taking its bearings from the so-called Weinberger doctrine, a set of rules for the use of force that had been drafted in the 1980s, the U.S. military did everything it could to avoid what came to be known—incorrectly—as "nontraditional missions": constabulary operations required for "imperial policing," for example, peacekeeping and humanitarian missions.

The clearest example of a service's resistance to a mission occurred when the army, arguing that its proper focus was on preparing to fight conventional wars, insisted that the plans for U.S. interventions in Bosnia, Kosovo, and elsewhere reflected the military's preference for "overwhelming force." As one contemporary source reported, the military greatly influenced the Dayton Agreement establishing an implementation force (IFOR) to enforce peace in Bosnia-Herzegovina. Many interpreted such hostility as just one more indication that the military had become too partisan (Republican) and too politicized.[10]

Closely related to the influence of the uniformed military on the political decision to employ the military instrument was the issue of resources for defense and readiness. Here the target was not only the president but also Congress. By 1998, this issue had become so acrimonious that "the Joint Chiefs and U.S. senators engaged in public accusations of dishonest testimony and lack of support."[11]

More troubling for constitutional balance in the long run is a survey of officer and civilian attitudes and opinions undertaken by the Triangle Institute for

Security Studies (TISS) in 1998–99, which discovered that "many officers believe that they have the duty to force their own views on civilian decision makers when the United States is contemplating committing American forces abroad."

When "asked whether military leaders should be neutral, advise, advocate, or insist on having their way in the decision process" to use military force, 50 percent or more of the up-and-coming active duty officers answered "insist" on the following issues: "setting rules of engagement, ensuring that clear political and military goals exist, developing an 'exit strategy,'" and "deciding what kinds of military units will be used to accomplish all tasks." In the context of the questionnaire, "insist" definitely implied that officers should try to compel acceptance of the military's recommendations.[12]

Ironically, some journalists who would normally reject the idea that military officers should "insist" that elected officials or their constitutional appointees adopt the former's position seem to be all for it when it comes to the Bush administration and Donald Rumsfeld. For instance in a March 2005 column for the *Washington Post*[13] handicapping the field to succeed Air Force General Richard B. Myers as chairman of the Joint Chiefs of Staff (CJCS), David Ignatius raised a central question of U.S. civil-military relations: To what extent should the uniformed military "push back" against the policies of a president and his secretary of defense if the soldiers believe the policies are wrong?

Ignatius wrote that "when you ask military officers who should get the job, the first thing many say is that the military needs someone who can stand up to . . . Rumsfeld. The tension between Rumsfeld and the uniformed military," he continued, "has been an open secret in Washington these past four years. It was compounded by the Iraq war, but it began almost from the moment Rumsfeld took over at the Pentagon. The grumbling about his leadership partly reflected the military's resistance to change and its reluctance to challenge a brilliant but headstrong civilian leader. But in Iraq, Rumsfeld has pushed the services—especially the Army—near the breaking point."

"The military is right," concluded Ignatius. "The next chairman of the JCS must be someone who can push back." In support of his argument, Ignatius invoked the very important book by H. R. McMaster, *Dereliction of Duty: Lyndon Johnson, Robert McNamara, the Joint Chiefs of Staff, and the Lies That Led to Vietnam*, the subject of which is how the JCS failed to challenge Secretary of Defense Robert McNamara adequately during the Vietnam War.[14] Many serving officers believe the book effectively makes the case that the JCS should have more openly voiced their opposition to the Johnson administration's strategy of gradualism, and then resigned rather than carry out the policy.

Agency Theory: Understanding the Civil-Military Relations during the Clinton-Bush Era

The most persuasive theoretical explanation for the pattern of civil-military relations during the Clinton-Bush era is provided by Peter Feaver in his remarkable book *Armed Servants*. Feaver's explanation of the extent to which civilians exercise control over the uniformed military is based on "agency theory," which was originally developed by economists to analyze the relations between a principal who delegates authority and an agent to whom that authority is delegated. In political science, the most fruitful applications of the principal-agent framework have been in the areas of executive and legislative interaction with the bureaucracy. The problem that agency theory seeks to analyze is this: given different incentives, how does a principle ensure that the agent is doing what the principal wants him to do? Is the agent "working" or "shirking"?

The major question for the principal is the extent to which he will monitor the agent. Will monitoring be intrusive or nonintrusive? This decision is affected by the cost of monitoring. The higher the cost of monitoring, the less intrusive the monitoring is likely to be.

The agent's incentives for working or shirking are affected by the likelihood that his shirking will be detected by the principal and that he will then be punished for it. The less intrusive the principal's monitoring, the less likely the agent's shirking will be detected.

In applying agency theory to civil-military relations, Feaver acknowledges the unsuitability of the term "shirking" when describing the action of the military agent when it pursues its own preference rather than those of the civilian principal. But he contends that the alternatives are even less suitable.

Feaver argues that shirking by the military takes many forms. The most obvious form of military shirking is disobedience, but it also includes foot-dragging and leaks to the press that are designed to undercut policy or individual policymakers.

Feaver posits four general patterns of civil-military relations: (1) civilians monitor intrusively; the military works; (2) civilians monitor intrusively; the military shirks; (3) civilians monitor unintrusively; the military works; and (4) civilians monitor unintrusively; the military shirks.

Feaver contends that the civil-military relations pattern that prevailed during the Cold War was pattern 1: civilians monitored intrusively; the military worked. Agency theory predicts that this outcome will occur when there is a wide gap between the preferences of the civilians and the military, when the costs of intrusive monitoring are relatively low, and when the military thinks the likelihood of punishment for shirking is fairly high.

Feaver argues persuasively that the evidence from this period supports these hypotheses. Of critical importance was the firing of a popular military hero (Douglas MacArthur) by an unpopular president (Harry Truman). This dramatic action shaped the expectations of the military concerning the likelihood of punishment for shirking during the Cold War period.

Feaver explains the post–Cold War "crisis" in civil-military relations in a way that integrates a number of features that arose in the 1990s—the end of the Cold War, a growing gap between civilian and military elites, the personal history of President Clinton, the creation of a powerful CJCS by the Goldwater-Nichols Defense Act of 1986, and the occupation of this office by a popular, politically savvy general—Colin Powell.

Feaver argues that civil-military relations pattern 2 prevailed during the 1990s: civilians monitored intrusively; the military shirked. The cost of intrusive monitoring went down. The preferences of civilian and military elites diverged in many important ways, increasing incentives for the military to pursue its own preferences.

Finally, the expectation of punishment for shirking decreased as a result of the election of Bill Clinton, whose equivocal relationship with the military made punishment unlikely. Combined with a powerful and popular military leader and an absence of consensus regarding security affairs across the executive and legislative branches, the civilian principals were in a relatively weakened position vis-à-vis the military agents.

Although Feaver did not examine civil-military relations during the Bush administration, it seems fair to conclude that agency theory explains much of the tension between civilian principals and the uniformed military during that period as well. The fact is that Secretary of Defense Rumsfeld believed that civilian control had eroded during the Clinton years, and he sought to reestablish it. It is not surprising that the uniformed military resisted this attempt.

Contemporary Civil-Military Relations and the American Tradition of Civilian Control

The very public attacks on civilian authorities by officers during both the Clinton and Bush administrations fly in the face of the American tradition of civilian control of the military. Should active duty and retired officers of the army and navy in 1941 have publicly debated the Lend-Lease program or the occupation of Iceland? Should Douglas MacArthur have resigned over the Europe-first strategy? Should generals in 1861 have discussed in public their opinions of Lincoln's plan to reprovision Fort Sumter, aired their views regarding the right of the South to secede from the Union, or argued the pros and cons of issuing the Emancipation Proclamation?

The view of the soldier, no matter how experienced in military affairs he or she may be, is still restricted to the conduct of operations and military strategy, and even here, as Cohen shows, the civilian leadership still reserves the right to make operational decisions. Civilian control of the military means at a minimum that it is the role of the statesman to take the broader view, deciding when political considerations take precedence over even the most pressing military matters. The soldier is a fighter and an adviser, not a policymaker. And in the American system, only the people at large—not the military—are permitted to punish an administration for even "grievous errors" in the conduct of war.

In addition, it is clear in retrospect that the uniformed military does not necessarily get things right that the civilian leadership gets wrong. A case in point is Secretary of Defense Rumsfeld and the conduct of the Iraq War.

The Uniformed Military's Case against Rumsfeld

The central charges in the case against Secretary Rumsfeld include willfully ignoring military advice and initiating the war with a force that was too small; failing to adapt to the new circumstances once things began to go wrong; failing to foresee the insurgency that now rages in that country; and ignoring the need to prepare for postconflict stability operations.[15]

This criticism of Rumsfeld by uniformed officers is predicated on two assumptions. The first is that soldiers have the right to a voice in making policy regarding the use of the military instrument, that indeed they have the right to *insist* that their views be adopted. The second is that the judgment of soldiers is inherently superior to that of civilians when it comes to military affairs. In times of war, civilians should defer to military expertise. Both of these assumptions are questionable at best, and they are at odds with the principles and practices of American civil-military relations.

First, in the American system, the uniformed military does not possess a veto over policy. Indeed, civilians even have the authority to make decisions in what would seem to be the realm of purely military affairs. As Eliot Cohen has shown, in practice, American civil-military relations do not actually conform to what some have dubbed the "normal theory of civil military relations," which holds that civilians determine the goals of war and leave the strategy and execution of the war to the uniformed military.[16] As Cohen illustrates in *Supreme Command*, successful wartime presidents, such as Abraham Lincoln and Franklin Roosevelt, "interfered" extensively with military operations—often driving their generals to distraction.[17]

It is also the case that the invocation of *Dereliction of Duty* in support of the position that the uniformed military is entitled to "insist" that its advice be followed is based on a misreading of the book. As Richard Kohn—who was McMaster's academic adviser for the dissertation that became *Dereliction of Duty*—has observed, McMaster

> neither says nor implies that the chiefs should have obstructed U.S. policy in Vietnam in any other way than by presenting their views frankly and forcefully to their civilian superiors, and speaking honestly to Congress when asked for their views. It neither states nor suggests that the chiefs should have opposed President Lyndon Johnson's orders and policies by leaks, public statements, or by resignation, unless an officer personally and professionally could not stand, morally and ethically, to carry out the chosen policy.[18]

This serious misreading of *Dereliction of Duty* has dangerously reinforced the increasingly widespread belief among officers that they should be advocates of particular policies rather than simply serving in their traditional advisory role.

Second, when it comes to military affairs, soldiers are not necessarily more prescient than civilian policymakers. This is confirmed by the historical record. Abraham Lincoln constantly prodded George McClellan to take the offensive in Virginia in 1862. McClellan just as constantly whined about insufficient forces. Despite the image of civil-military comity during World War II, there were many differences between Franklin Roosevelt and his military advisers. George Marshall, the greatest soldier-statesman since Washington, opposed arms shipments to Great Britain in 1940 and argued for a cross-Channel invasion before the United States was ready. History has vindicated Lincoln and Roosevelt.

Many are inclined to blame the U.S. defeat in Vietnam on the civilians. But the U.S. operational approach in Vietnam was the creature of the uniformed military. The conventional wisdom today is that the operational strategy of General William Westmoreland, emphasizing attrition of the Peoples' Army of Vietnam (PAVN) forces in a "war of the big battalions"—sweeps through remote jungle areas in an effort to fix and destroy the enemy with superior fire power—was counterproductive. By the time Westmoreland's successor could adopt a more fruitful approach, it was too late.[19]

During planning for Operation Desert Storm in late 1990 and early 1991, General Norman Schwarzkopf, commander of U.S. Central Command (CENTCOM), presented a plan calling for a frontal assault against Iraqi positions in southern Kuwait followed by a drive toward Kuwait City. The problem was that this plan was unlikely to achieve the foremost military objective of the ground war: the destruction of the three divisions of Saddam Hussein's Republican Guard. The civilian leadership rejected the early war plan presented by CENTCOM and ordered a return to the drawing board. The revised plan was far more imaginative and effective.[20]

While the military must make its point strongly in the councils of government, it must also be recognized that the military will not always be correct when it comes to policy recommendations. As CJCS in 1990, Colin Powell preferred sanctions against Iraq to the use of force. As noted above, Marshall opposed arms shipments to Great Britain in 1940. History has vindicated the position of the civilians in these cases.

In the case of Rumsfeld, it seems clear that although he made some critical mistakes, no one did better than he when it came to predicting what would transpire. Did Rumsfeld foresee the insurgency and the shift from conventional to guerilla war in Iraq? No, but neither did his critics in the uniformed services.[21]

Indeed, Tom Ricks reported in the December 25, 2004, *Washington Post* that Major Isaiah Wilson III, who served as an official historian of the campaign and later as a war planner in Iraq, placed the blame squarely on the army.[22] Ricks wrote,

> Many in the Army have blamed Defense Secretary Donald H. Rumsfeld and other top Pentagon civilians for the unexpectedly difficult occupation of Iraq, but Wilson reserves his toughest criticism for Army commanders who, he concludes, failed to grasp the strategic situation in Iraq and did not plan properly for victory. He concludes that those who planned the war suffered from "stunted learning and a reluctance to adapt."

Rumsfeld's Pentagon is often charged with shortchanging the troops in Iraq by failing to provide them with the necessary equipment—for example, armored "humvees." But a review of army budget submissions makes it clear that its priority, as is usually the case with the uniformed services, was to acquire "big ticket" items. It was only after the insurgency and the improvised explosive device (IED) threat became apparent that the army began to push for supplemental spending to "up-armor" the utility vehicles.

And while it is true that Rumsfeld downplayed the need to prepare for post-conflict stability operations, it is also the case that in doing so he was merely ratifying the preferences of the uniformed military. When it comes to postconflict stability operations, the real villain is the Weinberger-Powell Doctrine, a set of principles long internalized by the U.S. military that emphasizes the requirement for an "exit strategy." But if generals are thinking about an exit strategy, they are not thinking about "war termination"—how to convert military success into political success. This cultural aversion to conducting stability operations is reflected by the fact that operational planning for Operation Iraqi Freedom took eighteen months, while planning for postwar stabilization began halfheartedly only a couple of months before the invasion.[23]

In retrospect, it is easy to criticize Rumsfeld for pushing the CENTCOM commander, General Tommy Franks, to develop a plan based on a smaller force than the one called for in earlier plans, as well as for his interference with the Time-Phased Force Flow and Deployment (TPFFD) that lays out the schedule of forces deploying to a theater of war. But hindsight is always 20-20, permitting us to judge another's actions on the basis of what we know now, not what we knew then. Thus the consequences of the chosen path—to attack earlier with a smaller force—are visible to us in retrospect, while the very real risks associated with an alternative option—for example, taking the time to build up a larger force at the cost of losing the opportunity to achieve surprise—remain provisional.

The debate over the size of the invasion force must also be understood in the context of Rumsfeld's perception of civil-military relations during the Clinton administration. As suggested above, Rumsfeld believed that civilian control of the military had eroded during the Clinton years. In keeping with the civil-military relations pattern posited by Feaver (civilians monitored; the military shirked), the services simply dragged their feet when they didn't want to do something.

It seems clear that Rumsfeld was thinking of the Balkans case of the 1990s—in which the army simply overstated the force requirements—when the army chief of staff expressed his opinion that the invasion of Iraq would require a larger force than had been apportioned for the mission. To Rumsfeld, the situation appeared to be that the army always replied, "The answer is 350,000 soldiers. What's the question?"

Accordingly, Rumsfeld was inclined to interpret the army's call for a larger force to invade Iraq as just one more example of what he perceived as foot-dragging. In retrospect, Rumsfeld's decision not to deploy the 1st Cavalry Division was a mistake, but again he had come to believe that the TPFFD, like the "two major theater war" (2MTW) planning metric, had become little more than a bureaucratic tool that the services used to protect their shares of the defense budget.

It is clear that Rumsfeld is guilty of errors of judgment regarding both transformation and the conduct of the Iraq war. With regard to the former, his "business" approach to transformation is potentially risky. Rumsfeld's approach stresses an economic concept of *efficiency* at the expense of military and political *effectiveness*. But war is far more than a mere targeting drill. As the Iraq war has demonstrated, the destruction of the "target set" and the resulting military success does not translate automatically into the achievement of the political goals for which the war was fought in the first place.[24] But the U.S. military does need to transform and, as suggested above, the actual *practice* of transformation in the Rumsfeld Pentagon has been flexible and adaptive, not doctrinaire.

With regard to the Iraq war, Rumsfeld's original position regarding the Iraq war was much more optimistic than the facts on the ground have warranted. But he has eventually acknowledged changes in the character of the war and adapted to them. In addition, Rumsfeld's critics have been no more prescient than he. We should not be surprised. Again, as Carl von Clausewitz reminds us, war takes place in the realm of chance and uncertainty.

Conclusion

The past two decades have revealed profound fissures in the framework of U.S. civil-military relations. These fissures are the result of changes that have occurred since the end of the Cold War. These changes include the shift to an all-volunteer force that many believe to be alienated from American society at large and the replacement of the "Soldier's Code" or "Marshall Ideal"—the belief that officers should remain apolitical—with the admonition to "find its voice" and address the public directly on policy matters.

> Prominent scholars and former officers urge today's leaders to speak out in the public square on policy debates. Instead of being a passive and neutral cog in the political system, "adhering to a notion of the military profession as a silent order of monks isolated from the political realm," the U.S. military was urged to be politically engaged.[25]

Not surprisingly, a consequence of these changes has been the increasing politicization of the officer corps.

Social changes have also affected the military as an institution and civil-military relations.[26] These changes were particularly evident during the 1990s: the emergence of "cultural relativism" and the imposition of nonmilitary social, ethical, and political criteria on the uniformed seriously challenged traditional military culture.

These fissures have been exacerbated by the protracted war in Iraq. Unfortunately, the peculiar dynamics of political resistance to the Bush presidency, particularly the Iraq war, have distorted the debate that must occur if these fissures are to be repaired. The dominant narrative places the blame for Iraq on the Bush administration. According to this narrative, the great failure of the Bush administration was its refusal to heed the military voice. An interesting result of the distortion of the debate has been the spectacle of political liberals in the United States—who would not have been caught dead saying a good word about the military in the past—now embracing the purported military perspective in attacking the policies of the Bush administration.[27]

But as argued above, this narrative has things wrong. Under the American system of civilian control, the uniformed military advises the civilian authorities but has no right to insist that its views be adopted. Of course, uniformed officers have an obligation to stand up to civilian leaders if they think a policy is flawed.

They must convey their concerns to civilian policymakers forcefully and truthfully. If they believe the door is closed to them at the Pentagon or the White House, they also have access to Congress. But the American tradition of civil-military relations requires that they not engage in public debate over matters of foreign policy, including the decision to go to war. Moreover, once a policy decision is made, soldiers are obligated to carry it out to the best of their ability, whether their advice is heeded or not.

In addition, the historical record illustrates that the military does not necessarily get the things right that the civilians get wrong. Finally, the "bright line" that purportedly delineates the strictly military realm from the policy realm of the civilians is not as clear as some would have it.[28] As Elliott Cohen argues in *Supreme Command*, civilians and soldiers engage in an "uneasy dialogue" based on different experiences and perspectives.

Cohen's cases illustrate that the great democratic statesmen of the past did not accept an artificial dividing line that separates the two spheres. They went far beyond merely defining policy. They aggressively inserted themselves into the planning and supervision of the war, constantly "querying, prodding, suggesting, arbitrating," and occasionally overruling their military advisors. They went far beyond merely offering guidance or goals. They selected commanders, fired others, meddled when necessary, and drove the refinement of strategies and plans until they were satisfied.[29]

Of course such involvement engenders resistance. This explains, in light of Feaver's agency theory, why civil-military relations during the Bush years in particular were so characterized by a lack of comity and harmony.

Notes

1. Richard H. Kohn, "The Erosion of Civilian Control of the Military in the United States Today," *Naval War College Review* 50, no. 3 (Summer 2002): 10.
2. Cf. Kohn, "Erosion of Civilian Control" and Richard H. Kohn, "Out of Control: The Crisis in Civil-Military Relations," *National Interest*, no. 35 (Spring 1994); Russell Weigley, "The American Military and the Principle of Civilian Control from McClelland to Powell," special issue, *Journal of Military History*, October 1993; Edward Luttwak, "Washington's Biggest Scandal," *Commentary* 97, no. 5 (May 1994); Charles Dunlap, "The Origins of the Coup of 2012," *Parameters*, 22 (Winter 1992–93); Charles Dunlap, "Welcome to the Junta: The Erosion of Civilian Control of the Military," *Wake Forest Law Review*, 29, no. 3 (Summer 1994); Gregory Foster, "Confronting the Crisis in Civil-Military Relations," *Washington Quarterly* 20, no. 4 (Autumn 1997); Andrew Bacevich and Richard H. Kohn, "Grand Army of the Republicans," *New Republic*, December 8, 1997, 22–25; and Ole Holsti, "Of Chasms and Convergences: Attitudes and Beliefs of Civilians and Military Elites at the Start of a New Millennium," in *Soldiers and Civilians: The Civil-Military Gap and American National Security*, ed. Peter Feaver and Richard Kohn (Cambridge, MA: MIT Press, 2001).
3. Foster, "Confronting the Crisis," 15.
4. See, for instance, Douglas Johnson and Steven Metz, "American Civil-Military Relations: A Review of the Recent Literature," in *US Civil Military Relations: In Crisis or Transition?* ed. Don M. Snider and Miranda A. Carlton-Carew

(Washington, D.C: Center for Strategic and International Studies, 1995), 201, and Michael Desch, *Civilian Control of the Military: The Changing Security Environment* (Baltimore: Johns Hopkins University Press, 1999), 141.

5. For examples of the hostility of the uniformed military toward President Clinton, see John Lancaster, "Accused of Ridiculing Clinton, General Faces Air Force Probe," *Washington Post*, June 8, 1993, 21; "A Military Breach?" *Seattle Post-Intelligencer*, June 11, 1993, 10; David H. Hackworth, "Rancor in the Ranks: The Troops vs. the President," *Newsweek*, June 28, 1993; Rowan Scarborough, "Marine Officer Probed for Blasting Clinton," *Washington Times*, November 11, 1998, 1, and "Major Gets Punished for Criticizing President," *Washington Times*, December 7, 1998; C. J. Chivers, "Troops Obey Clinton Despite Disdain," *USA Today*, November 18, 1998; and Jane Perlez, "For 8 Years, a Strained Relationship with the Military," *New York Times*, December 28, 2000, A13.

6. Cragg Hines, "Clinton's Vow to Lift Gay Ban Is Reaffirmed," *Houston Chronicle*, November 12, 1992, A1; Barton Gellman, "Clinton Says He'll 'Consult' on Allowing Gays in Military," *Washington Post*, November 13, 1992, A1; U.S. Department of Defense, Office of the Inspector General, *The Tailhook Report: The Official Inquiry into the Events of Tailhook '91* (New York: St. Martin's, 1993); William McMichael, *The Mother of All Hooks* (New Brunswick, NJ: Transaction, 1997); Elaine Sciolino, "B-52 Pilot Requests Discharge That is Honorable," *New York Times*, May 18, 1997, A1; Bradley Graham, "Army Leaders Feared Aberdeen Coverup Allegations," *Washington Post*, November 11, 1996, A1.

7. Peter Feaver, *Armed Servants: Agency, Oversight, and Civil-Military Relations* (Cambridge, MA: Harvard University Press, 2005).

8. Greg Newbold, "Why Iraq Was a Mistake," *Time*, April 17, 2006, 42–43; David S. Cloud and Eric Schmitt, "More Retired Generals Call for Rumsfeld Resignation," *New York Times*, April 14, 2006, A1.

9. William Calhoun, "Washington at Newburgh," http://www.claremont.org/publications/pubid.416/pub_detail.asp.

10. According to Clinton administration officials, the agreement "was carefully crafted to reflect demands from the military. . . . Rather than be ignored . . . the military, as a price for its support, has basically gotten anything it wanted. Warren Strobel, "This Time Clinton Is Set to Heed Advice from Military," *Washington Times*, December 1, 1995, 1. But military resistance to Clinton's foreign policy predated Bosnia. See, for example, Richard A. Serrano and Art Pine, "Many in Military Angry Over Clinton's Policies," *Los Angeles Times*, October 19, 1993, 1.

11. Kohn, "Erosion of Civilian Control," 21n 5. Cf. Eric Schmitt, "Joint Chiefs Accuse Congress of Weakening U.S. Defense," *New York Times*, September 30, 1998, 1; and Elaine Grossman, "Congressional Aide Finds Spending on 'Core Readiness' in Decline," *Inside the Pentagon*, June 28, 2001, 1.

12. Ole Holsti, "Of Chasms and Convergences: Attitudes and Beliefs of Civilians and Military Elites at the Start of a New Millennium," in *Soldiers and Civilians*, ed. Peter Feaver and Richard Kohn, pp. 84, 489, and tables 1.27, 1.28.

13. David Ignatius, "Rumsfeld and the Generals," *Washington Post*, March 30, 2005, A15. http://www.washingtonpost.com/wp-dyn/articles/A11309-2005Mar29.html.

14. H. R. McMaster, *Dereliction of Duty: Lyndon Johnson, Robert McNamara, the Joint Chiefs of Staff, and the Lies That Led to Vietnam* (New York: HarperCollins, 1997).

15. See, for example, Michael C. Desch, "Bush and the Generals," *Foreign Affairs*, 86, no. 3 (May/June 2007). For a contrary view, see Mackubin Thomas Owens, "The Military's Place," *Foreign Affairs*, 86, no. 5 (September/October 2007), and "Rumsfeld, the

Generals, and the State of U.S. Civil-Military Relations," *Naval War College Review* 59, no. 4 (Autumn 2006): 68–81.

16. The origin of this understanding of civil-military relations can be traced to Samuel Huntington, *The Soldier and the State: The Theory and Politics of Civil-Military Relations* (Cambridge, MA: Belknap Press, Harvard University, 1957).

17. Eliot Cohen, *Supreme Command: Soldiers, Statesmen, and Leadership in Wartime* (New York: Free Press, 2002).

18. Kohn, Erosion of Civilian Control, 16.

19. Lewis Sorley, *A Better War: The Unexamined Victories and Final Tragedy of America's Last Years in Vietnam* (New York: HBJ/Harvest Books, 2000).

20. See Michael Gordon and Bernard Trainor, *The Generals' War: The Inside Story of the Conflict in the Gulf* (Boston: Little, Brown, 1995).

21. On the general topic of the uniformed military's failure to adapt to conditions in Iraq, see Frank Hoffman, "Dereliction of Duty Redux?: Post-Iraq Civil-Military Relations," *Orbis*, 52, no. 2 (Spring, 2008). For a forceful indictment of the failure of senior army leadership to prepare for the insurgency in Iraq, see Paul Yingling, "A Failure of Generalship," *Armed Forces Journal* (May 2007).

22. Thomas E. Ricks, "Army Historian Cites Lack of Postwar Plan: Major Calls Effort in Iraq 'Mediocre,'" *Washington Post*, December 25, 2004, A01, http://www.washingtonpost.com/wp-dyn/articles/A24891-2004Dec24.html.

23. On Rumsfeld and the plans for the Iraq War, see Michael Gordon and Bernard Trainor, *Cobra II: The Inside Story of the Invasion and Occupation of Iraq* (New York: Pantheon, 2006).

24. Frederick W. Kagan, *Finding the Target: The Transformation of American Military Policy* (New York: Encounter Books, 2006).

25. Hoffman, "Dereliction of Duty Redux?" Cf. Sam C. Sarkesian and Robert E. Connor, Jr., *The U.S. Military Profession into the Twenty-First Century: War, Peace and Politics* (London: Frank Cass, 1999), 167.

26. Charles C. Moskos, John Allen Williams, and David R. Segal, eds., *The Postmodern Military: Armed Forces after the Cold War* (New York: Oxford University Press, 2000), and John Allen Williams, "The Military and Society: Beyond the Postmodern Era," *Orbis* 52, no. 2 (Spring 2008).

27. Ignatius, "Rumsfeld and the Generals" (see note 17). The most absurd example of Bush's opponents' use of the military against him is Martin Lewis's call for former CJCS General Peter Pace to use the Uniform Code of Military Justice to "relieve" the president of his role as commander in chief. Martin Lewis, "General Pace, You Can Save the US—By Arresting Bush for 'Conduct Unbecoming,'" *Huffington Post*, August 25, 2007, http://www.huffingtonpost.com/martin-lewis/general-pace-you-can-sa_b_61785.html. This is just the most extreme example of disdain for President Bush trumping the Constitution. It is, of course, essentially a call for a military coup.

28. Desch, "Bush and the Generals" (see also note 19).

29. Cohen, *Supreme Command.*

17

The Retired Officer and the State

Kathleen A. Mahoney-Norris

Secretary of Defense Donald Rumsfeld's resignation in December 2006 elevated the issue of civilian control of the military into public view and partisan debate. According to the *New York Times*, Mr. Rumsfeld's resignation may have been delayed due to the administration's concern about undue influence from the U.S. military. Specifically, the influence allegedly came from *retired* officers. The *New York Times* noted that retired generals who had called for Rumsfeld's dismissal "had in effect ensured Mr. Rumsfeld's job security, because the White House was unwilling to take any action that could be interpreted as the civilian leadership buckling under pressure from the military establishment."[1] Assuming the *Time's* analysis is correct, it highlights how the public statements and actions of retired senior military officers may have important—and potentially detrimental—effects on national security policy. More disturbing is the possibility that this represents only part of a larger trend toward questionable and counterproductive involvement by retired officers in policy matters, and even in partisan politics.

The criticisms of U.S. government policy in Iraq by recently retired general officers represent one aspect of this problem; it is a problem that is compounded by the trend of retired officers serving as "expert" media commentators on military operations. A second issue involves presidential candidates who have tried to garner the endorsements of retired senior military leaders in order to burnish their national security credentials.

Retired officers have long enjoyed varying levels of influence within the U.S. government—especially within the Department of Defense (DoD)—and within other sectors of society such as the defense industry. This chapter contends, however, that retired senior officers may now exercise undue influence on U.S. policy in three ways: (1) politicians seek out retired officers to support and legitimize partisan positions or particular candidates; (2) policymakers use retired military officers to support and legitimize policies related to national security and military matters; and (3) the general public—which commonly has very limited knowledge of the military—does not discriminate between the statements and actions of retired officers and those of active duty officers.[2] These factors are compounded because retired senior officers often maintain a network of influential friendships with active duty members of the profession, and thus may serve as a proxies in representing military views to the public. Additionally, within the military itself, active duty members generally continue to regard retired senior officers as part of the military profession, and thus may give their opinions undue weight.[3]

In this chapter I examine the troubling implications of *retired senior officers*[4] becoming publicly involved in both national security issues and related political debates. (I do not specifically address the defense industry sector, which has already garnered a substantial literature.[5]) While there are established legal limits on the free speech and political activities of active duty military personnel, no such limits are placed on retired military members. Should there be—or should senior retired military officers restrict their own actions as part of a professional military ethic or in deference to professional norms?

There are strongly held viewpoints on this question. As Frederick Kagan has argued, "retired generals are citizens in good standing with all the rights of their fellow citizens—rights that they have laid their lives on the lines to protect."[6] On the other hand, Richard Kohn contends that "those in the know understand that four-stars never really 'retire,' but, like princes of the church, embody the core culture and collectively represent the military community as authoritatively as the active-duty leadership."[7]

In examining this issue, I first outline the parameters of the current problem. I then consider the concept of military professionalism, raising questions relative to this concept as originally posited by Samuel Huntington and Morris Janowitz some fifty years ago.[8] I address the professional attributes of expertise, corporateness, and responsibility, demonstrating that retired senior officers generally possess these essential attributes—or are at least *perceived* to retain these attributes. Based on this analysis, I propose that senior officers should consider adopting self-limitations on their actions, once retired, as part of the professional responsibility they still owe to the state and to society. This chapter concludes by recommending some professional norms for senior military officers as they retire and become nominally private citizens.

The Parameters of the Problem

Tensions over civil-military relations are not new, nor is it the case that retired military officers have never been involved in public policy debates or partisan politics. Rather, this research argues that, based on the present confluence of the three factors noted above, it is appropriate—indeed, necessary—to examine the specific role of *retired* senior military officers. This is because of the apparently increasing politicization of the military and the significance of national security and defense issues, coupled with the ignorance of policymakers and the public about the U.S. military and defense matters.

A perceived "civil-military gap" between the Clinton administration and the military led recently to the "Project on the Gap between the Military and Civilian Society," sponsored by the Triangle Institute for Security Studies (TISS).[9] Based on extensive data and studies produced for that project, Peter Feaver and Richard

Kohn concluded that there was cause for concern, particularly if the trends noted continued. For example, based on survey data finding that military officers were becoming more openly partisan, they argued that

> the development of any partisan identity, or behaving like "just another interest group," is dangerous . . . If it were viewed as just another interest group, the military would lose the respect and support of the American people, money from Congress, and recruits from American society. Uniformed advice would be less trusted by the civilian leadership. Military professionalism would weaken. Officers who maintain (as many do) that they separate their personal views and voting behavior from their duties may underestimate the subtle and potentially corrosive effects of partisanship on their behavior, leadership, morale, and attitude towards the president.[10]

In fact, Kohn and other analysts of civil-military relations have gone so far as to charge that "Republicans have increasingly regarded the 1.4 million members of the all-volunteer military and their families as a political interest group—a part of the Republican coalition."[11] For example, during the 2000 and 2004 elections, officials of the Republican Party made much of their concern about military absentee votes being counted properly, with the clear implication that those votes would all favor Republican candidates. Republican Party officials and lawmakers even pursued a series of steps to ensure that these military votes would arrive in a timely enough manner to be counted. The implications of this are explored by Donald Inbody in chapter 12 of this volume.

Retired senior officers are adding to this concern by becoming much more overtly involved in political campaigns. Of course, in the United States it is not unusual for retired military officers to run for public office (generals Andrew Jackson, Ulysses S. Grant, and Dwight D. Eisenhower represent successful presidential candidates from different eras) or for individual retired officers periodically to endorse political candidates. In the 1992 presidential campaign, General P. X. Kelley, former Marine Corps commandant, campaigned for then-president George H. W. Bush (Republican), while Admiral William Crowe, former chairman of the Joint Chiefs of Staff (CJCS), endorsed candidate Bill Clinton (Democrat). The problem is that this trend has expanded dramatically as groups of retired officers have endorsed presidential candidates in an increasingly polarized context. For instance, some eighty-five senior retired military officers endorsed George W. Bush when he ran for president in 2000.[12] Military historian Andrew Bacevich expressed concern over the many three- and four-star officers not only endorsing candidates but appearing at national party conventions and on television, "apparently oblivious to the fact that such activities subverted the identity of the soldier as apolitical servant of the state."[13] Furthermore, Bacevich argued that a particularly significant and negative partisan turning point occurred with the candidacy of General Wesley Clark in the 2004 presidential contest. According to Bacevich, General Clark

> embraced naked political partisanship. Clark aggressively touted his credentials as a lifelong military professional—not simply as a veteran—to advance his political ambitions. The unspoken but self-evident basis of his run for the presidency was

that four-star rank constituted all the qualifications necessary for political responsibilities at the highest level. He ran for office *as* a general. In doing so Clark trampled all over the principle, reconstituted by soldiers in the aftermath of Vietnam, that the justification for a distinctive profession of arms derives in part from the fact that it inhabits a space apart from and above politics.[14]

In addition to this trend of partisanship, efforts to directly affect national policy need to be considered. Military historians such as Dennis Showalter trace increased public involvement by military officers to more retired officers serving as commentators on television and writing autobiographies or books related to national security. In addition, as he points out, this generation of senior leaders is not only the best educated in history, but also contains "intellectuals who are less willing than an earlier generation to keep quiet about policy disagreements."[15] This reluctance to keep quiet was clearly influenced by the debacle of the Vietnam War—almost universally viewed by the officer corps as an example of why the military must be more involved in policymaking involving war—and why civilians must also respect the operational autonomy of the military.

Of course, it would be inaccurate to claim that retired officers prior to the twenty-first century had never expressed their concern over national security policies. Well-known figures such as generals Douglas MacArthur, Maxwell Taylor, and Curtis LeMay all commented forcefully on key issues once they had retired (and in some cases, while still on active duty).[16] In addition, retired officers have periodically been employed by the executive or legislative branches to validate preferred national security or defense policy positions. For example, Huntington noted with disapproval how a congressional subcommittee (the Jenner subcommittee) in the 1950s deliberately used the testimony of retired Korean War commanders in order to criticize the Truman administration's conduct of the Korean War. Huntington concluded that "military professionalism and objective civilian control become impossible if the administration punishes officers for presenting their professional opinions to Congress, [or] if congressmen insist upon using the soldiers to embarrass the administration."[17]

The relevance of Huntington's concerns were underscored in the fall of 2007 when General David Petraeus, the American military commander in Iraq, testified before Congress about the Bush administration's strategy in Iraq. The Bush administration's attempt to portray General Petraeus as an "unbiased professional" was attacked by some elected officials who questioned the general's independence from the administration's position.[18] Questions about the general's bias arose in the wake of an earlier op-ed piece that he had written in September 2004 on the status of Iraqi security forces; an op-ed that former defense official Lawrence Korb labeled "patently false and misleading." But Korb's concern went far deeper: "If Petraeus wrote and published the article on his own initiative, he was injecting himself improperly into a political campaign. If he was encouraged (or even authorized) to do so by his civilian superiors, they were abusing military professionalism for partisan political purposes."[19]

While General Petraeus was an active duty officer at the time, the negative reactions by policymakers underscore the pitfalls of retired senior officers adding to the perceived politicizing of national security issues. As one active duty four-star officer commented with regard to retired officers criticizing the administration's policy on Iraq, "They are entitled to their views, but I believe them to be wrong. And it is unfortunate they have allowed themselves to become in some respects, politicized."[20] The comment on politicization resonates within the military, reinforcing the traditional feeling that "the military must remain above politics if it is to retain its position of prestige within the larger society . . . [This] proceeds from the assumption that politics—the life blood of a liberal democracy—is something bad, or at least beneath the dignity of a professional soldier, and is to be eschewed."[21]

Some retired general officers have also publicly indicated their discomfort with the policy of speaking out. One of the most common reasons given was voiced by recently retired air force chief of staff General John Jumper, who was concerned that "public criticism hurts the morale of the troops in the field."[22] Four recently retired general officers echoed Jumper's concerns when they editorialized in the *Wall Street Journal* that while their fellow retired officers were entitled to freedom of speech, they believed that it was inappropriate for any senior military officer to publicly criticize Secretary Rumsfeld or other members of the civilian U.S. leadership, because

calling for the secretary's resignation during wartime may undercut the U.S. mission and incites individual challenge to the good order and discipline of our military culture. At best, such comments may send a confusing message to our troops deployed on dangerous missions in Afghanistan and Iraq. At worst, they can also inspire and motivate the evil forces we seek to defeat.[23]

Yet not everyone sees the involvement of retired officers in policy debates to be objectionable—in fact, quite the contrary. Frederick Kagan argues that "there is great danger in making vital decisions about an ongoing armed struggle without hearing the views of all available experts"; so limiting debate "runs the serious risk of depriving the American people and their leaders of the critical advice and information they need to make sound decisions."[24] Kagan's viewpoint is endorsed by numerous retired general officers, including, understandably, those who publicly spoke out to urge Secretary Rumsfeld to resign or who criticized the conduct of operations in Iraq.

In view of the often tense civil-military relations under Secretary Rumsfeld, it is not altogether surprising that a number of retired general officers would speak out publicly about their disagreement with U.S. security policy on Iraq, blaming Secretary Rumsfeld and the Pentagon's civilian leadership personally for many of the problems. Many of these officers were particularly concerned, too, that the military would be blamed for the lack of success in Iraq. They did not want a repeat of what was felt to be the betrayal of the Vietnam War. It is instructive to note, though, that the Bush administration fired back at these dissenters with public statements of support from both active duty and *retired* general officers.[25] According to one report, administration officials "were far more comfortable seeing retired generals fight it out on the airwaves than having to debate uniformed war critics themselves from the civilian confines of the White House."[26] Regardless of their status, though, military historians have commented that "it is highly unusual for active or *retired* officers to openly question their leaders"[27] and that "the level of wartime criticism is notable."[28]

These public attempts by retired senior officers to influence national security debates, allied with the trend of growing political partisanship, clearly have negative implications for civil-military relations. First, if the military (including retired officers) is perceived as an interest group with a partisan agenda, policymakers may be more likely to doubt the objectivity of the military advice they receive. As it is, assessing the validity of military advice may be particularly problematic for today's policymakers and elected officials who have less direct experience or knowledge of the military and defense issues in the wake of the end of the Vietnam War, the end of the draft, and changing societal norms. As TISS survey data indicate, "not only are there fewer people with military experience in the political elite, but veterans are now under-represented rather than over-represented [relative to their comparable cohort in the population as a whole] in the national political leadership."[29] Bianco and Markham trace this underrepresentation in Congress specifically to the end of conscription, with "the resulting asymmetric decline in the probability of military service for high-education, high socio-economic status individuals who typically run for Congress."[30]

This trend is occurring at the same time as military officers are not only better educated, but generally more inclined to advocate rather than advise on military matters. The TISS surveys found that 50–60 percent of up-and-coming officers "now believe that it is their role to insist rather than merely advise or advocate in private, on key decisions, particularly those involving the use of force."[31] Surely this tendency among active duty military officers would only be reinforced when retired senior officers join openly in national security debates to challenge civilian policymakers. This would be especially true if dissenting retired officers asserted that they were speaking for their active duty colleagues.[32]

Besides the negative impact within the U.S. military of retired officers speaking out, there is the potential for causing confusion and mistrust among the public at large. That is because the U.S. public is even less informed about military and defense issues than civilian policymakers are. Thus, Kagan's comment that no one is obliged to take what retired generals say "seriously" misses the point that the public is ill-prepared to make judgments on that score, and may place undue trust in any military member, whether on active duty or retired.[33]

In this regard, the fact that a September 2007 poll of U.S. citizens revealed that they would trust military commanders to bring the Iraq War to an end by extremely large margins—rather than the Bush administration or Congress—is illustrative of public opinion about the military.[34] This finding substantiates recent studies and polls that have generally found the public to have very high confidence in the military.[35] Many would argue that in a democracy such extreme trust in an unelected institution is not a healthy sign and that it reflects poorly on societal knowledge about what constitutes appropriate civil-military relations. It also leaves the public vulnerable to continuing exploitation of military issues for partisan political purposes.

It would clearly be detrimental to civil-military relations for the military to be perceived as partisan or as just another interest group, instead of as a neutral instrument of the country and its people.[36] Again, the expanding involvement of retired senior officers in public debate adds to the problem as the line is further blurred—whether deliberately or not—between the military and society; between a professional officer and a citizen. The average citizen does not make a distinction between retired senior officers and those still serving, especially if they are recently retired. The print media compound this problem for the average citizen by usually mentioning only in passing that the "general" or "admiral" they are quoting is actually retired.

It is important to note that many senior officers, whether retired or not, recognize these concerns. In this regard, retired air force general Charles Boyd's remarks to a group of lieutenant colonels and colonels about the propriety of retired officers calling for Secretary Rumsfeld's resignation are worth quoting:

> It's very difficult for a general to take off his uniform—even if he wants to. He has professional knowledge, he has experience relating to an arcane subject, little known or understood by the average civilian . . . and so when he speaks he has a special kind of credibility . . . Yet when he does, if he does so in criticism of a political policy, or of a particular politician, he—himself—immediately becomes politicized. His nobility of purpose is lost in the ensuing, inevitable, counter attack. His retired status becomes obscured—he is a military man involved in a political debate. While the public knows there is a legal distinction between the active duty and retired officer's right to speak publicly, when the retired officer does so in what becomes useful to one side in partisan debate, the substance of his argument takes on political taint—and to a degree, the military's purity as a whole is diminished.[37]

Assuming there is merit in the argument made to this point—that healthy civil-military relations in the United States require that retired senior officers consider their actions carefully—the next logical step might be to propose norms of conduct, or guidelines, for retired officers to consider. This first requires an examination of the three components of military professionalism: expertise, corporateness, and responsibility.

Expertise

First, it would be disingenuous to claim that military expertise disappears with the removal of the uniform. Recall Huntington's characterization of the military profession's expertise as resting on "the management of violence" in order to fulfill the function of "successful armed combat."[38] Yet as Huntington admits, there are "limited opportunities of the officer to acquire practical experience at the most important elements of his vocation."[39] Thus, the fact that the retired officer is no longer actively directing the operations of forces in combat does not disqualify the officer from being considered a professional. Comparatively few officers have the opportunity to manage violence during their career, as such opportunity is dependent upon the international context (sustained military operations in Afghanistan and Iraq have recently provided more officers with that opportunity). Rather, as retired officers maintain their professional development by continuing to educate themselves in military skills and related arts, and by consulting or working on defense issues, they may very well maintain their professional expertise.

The truth of these observations is borne out by the fact that after they retire, senior officers are sought out specifically for their military expertise by a large variety of organizations. Whether it is as commentators on military operations and defense matters for the media, as educators or policy experts for universities and think tanks, or as managers and leaders within the defense industry sector,[40] retired officers are regarded as experts. Most telling of all is that these officers have consistently been appointed on the basis of their professional expertise to serve on either presidential or congressional commissions dealing with critical national security and defense issues. For example, under the George W. Bush administration, both the executive and legislative branches have appointed retired senior officers to serve on commissions and panels[41] dealing with terrorism and the Iraq War.[42]

Corporateness

"Corporateness" (Huntington) or "system of internal administration" (Janowitz) is another requirement that pertains to the military as a profession. In this sense, the military is recognized as a distinct institution with its own values, standards, and rules, requiring and fostering a special degree of trust and bonds among its members. On many levels, retired military officers still have an explicit relationship with their client—the state—and with the military community. As Swain points out, "it is a false proposition that upon retirement officers revert to full civilian status in so far as the obligations they undertook at their commissioning."[43] This is because, according to congressional Title 10 legislation dealing with the armed forces, "retired officers remain members of the armed forces by law and regulation."[44] It is also noteworthy that within the military itself, retired officers are still considered members of the profession in the sense that they may be censured (or even court-martialed) for past actions. For instance, retired Lt. General Philip R. Kensigner Jr. was recently censured by Army Secretary Pete Geren for errors and deceptions related to the friendly-fire death of Corporal Pat Tillman in Afghanistan.[45] And, under certain national security conditions, "it is DoD policy that military retirees be ordered to active duty as needed to perform such duties as the Secretary concerned considers necessary in the interests of national defense"—presuming they are medically fit and meet certain age restrictions.[46]

Additionally, all retired military members receive a pension from the government, free or heavily subsidized medical care, and a retiree identification card that entitles them to many of the same services that they enjoyed while on active duty. They may wear their uniforms at ceremonies or official functions, "a privilege granted in recognition of faithful service to the country."[47] All of this substantiates the perception that retired officers are still considered to be a part of the military profession and community.

Furthermore, as Huntington remarks, "the corporate structure of the officer corps includes not just the official bureaucracy but also societies, associations, schools, journals, customs, and traditions."[48] Thus, in the case of the retiree, official linkages with the bureaucracy are further reinforced by continuing networks of friendship with members still in the profession; networks that are quite strong at the general officer level. Within the wider active military community, retired members continue to be afforded the respect customarily given to all general officers. Janowitz highlights the fact that retired officers' roles in professional associations "are very important in strengthening the social solidarity of the regular officer both during active duty and *after retirement*."[49] Thus, it would be entirely too simplistic to accept the claim that an officer ceases to be a military professional once retired, particularly if he or she remains actively engaged within the military community.

Responsibility

In Huntington's construct, the third component of military professionalism consists of responsibility, which for the military means a duty to "the military security of . . . [its] client, society."[50] Huntington views the officer as motivated by "a technical love for his craft and the sense of social obligation to utilize this craft for the benefit of society."[51] In fulfilling this responsibility, the officer references "an explicit code expressed in law and comparable to the canons of professional ethics of the physician and lawyer."[52] For Janowitz, too, a professional group's system of self-administration "implies the growth of a body of ethics and standards of performance."[53] Clearly, military officers have a unique professional responsibility to protect the state, which may include the ultimate sacrifice of one's life. In the United States, military officers are specifically bound by the oath they swear to uphold the Constitution of the United States and by the Uniform Code of Military Justice (UCMJ), which places stricter standards upon military members than civilian laws allow.

It is this component of responsibility that provides the strongest justification—normatively and pragmatically—for advocating professional norms, or guidelines, for retired senior officers. For, as Allan Millett points out, "without constant self-policing and task success, a profession can narrow its own freedom and destroy public trust as rapidly as it gained its relative autonomy."[54] Certainly one could disagree with the contention that retired officers effectively remain members of the military profession, and thus make a reasoned argument that they should not be bound by the ethics of the profession. However, as pointed out above, in a democracy it is the *perceptions* of policymakers and the public that matter. Any perception that the military cannot be trusted as a neutral—and ethical—public servant because of active or retired officers' actions can only be deleterious for a democracy.

Millett's admonition therefore applies equally to both active and retired military members: "The contingent nature of professional autonomy requires that a profession be sensitive to its public image, particularly to reassure its clients that it knows what it is doing even if they do not."[55] In fact, this point goes to the heart of recent public controversies surrounding disagreement between active and retired senior leaders over operations in Iraq and other national security issues: Does the military leadership know what it is doing? The concern, as outlined above, is whether this level of public disagreement might not erode the confidence of policymakers and the public in the U.S. military as a whole. Clearly, it is not in society's interest for professional military judgment to be seen as suspect because of acrimonious public debates within the profession, or as compromised because it is politicized.

Professional Norms for Retired Senior Officers

The concept of ethics is naturally embedded in the whole notion of professionalism. As part of his well-known consideration of the topic, Huntington argued that the more the officer corps demonstrated adherence to an ideal model, a "professional military ethic," the more professional they were.[56] While Huntington has much more to say about this topic and the associated "military mind," what is most pertinent here is his argument that "politics is beyond the scope of military competence, and the participation of military officers in politics undermines their professionalism, curtailing their professional competence, dividing the profession against itself, and substituting extraneous values for professional values. The military officer must remain neutral politically."[57] Obviously, Huntington is talking about active duty officers, and he is attempting to establish the necessity for "objective control" of the military (versus "subjective control"), but his points also bear directly on the implications of retired senior officers inserting themselves into partisan political debate on national security and related policy issues.

McKinlay clearly agrees with Huntington when he notes that "professionalization inhibits any personal political action as this is quite clearly contrary to the development of social responsibility."[58] He makes a convincing argument for the importance of informal controls, because they "relate to the internalization and socialization of non-political values by the military. The acquisition of such a set of values may be precipitated on account of the development of a specific normative code of conduct ... [which] would lead the military to eschew spontaneously certain forms of action."[59] His account of professionalization is particularly useful for thinking about the situation of retired senior officers, who are not legally subject to restrictions upon their activities. They must be convinced of the necessity to adhere to certain norms, whether based primarily on (1) concerns about the integrity of the military profession, (2) healthy civil-military relations in a democracy, or (3) effective national security policymaking.

Civil-military relations scholar Marybeth Peterson Ulrich has advocated that one way to achieve those norms would be for the profession itself to take the lead in internally educating— and fostering—appropriate standards of behavior.[60] She suggests that as it is active duty leadership that has the core responsibility to the state, they should set the norms for retired officers.

Self-regulation has the merit of including retirees as part of the military profession—thus matching perceptions about their status—and entails both rights and obligations. This does not mean that retired officers would be expected to restrict their activities as if they were active duty officers. Retired officers should consider the impact that their actions might have on active duty members, policymakers, and the public.

While guidelines and norms might seem clear in the abstract, applying them to particular situations is always difficult. It might be helpful, thus, to envision a continuum of activities where the closer a retired senior officer comes to discussing ongoing operations or sensitive national security issues, the more the retiree should remain silent. This would apply even in the area of retired officers who are hired to serve as media commentators based on their expertise. As well-known retired general and media commentator Perry Smith has written, "I have thought for more than 12 years that the role of the military analyst was to analyze, to explain and educate, and not to criticize . . . [T]here are lots of people in the media who serve the role of critic. They don't need the help of retired colonels and generals to do that."[61] Of course, this is a fine line to walk, especially in the midst of ongoing operations. An example of how fine this line might be is represented by the dilemma of retired military officers who have publicly criticized the use of torture in "the global war on terrorism" as being corrosive to professional military ethics, whether endorsed by civilian authorities or not.[62]

This same idea of a continuum could be applied in endorsing candidates for office or in speaking out on partisan political issues based specifically on national security or military expertise, as opposed to more general public policy issues. For example, a retired officer stating that he or she is endorsing a candidate based on the retiree's judgment and expertise in national security would be suspect. It would be particularly suspect if the endorsement were offered collectively by a group of retired general officers. In that regard, the trend toward group endorsements is particularly troubling, as it may look to the public (and to active duty members) as if the military as an institution is endorsing a candidate or a position.

A matrix that considers a number of options might also be useful for applying norms. For instance, in advising active duty army leaders about how they should respond to potentially questionable national security policymaking, Wong and Lovelace offer a model for consideration. The model "illustrates some of the options available to senior military leaders when confronted with policy formulation that, in their professional opinion, they believe is flawed."[63] Those options might include retiring, resigning, acquiescing, or reaching a compromise with civilian policymakers. Yet, according to Wong and Lovelace, the higher the stakes for national security and the greater the resistance to military advice, the greater the "responsibility to the nation and the profession to do what is right."[64] In their opinion, doing what is right when national security is at risk does not include the option of retirement, as "retiring removes the officer from a position of influence during a critical time to the nation."[65] Of course they are correct to note that an officer who has resigned or retired does not have the same legal authority as an active duty officer, although this chapter has demonstrated that senior retirees do indeed possess influence. The more important point is that how this influence is employed must be carefully weighed in terms of national security and perceptions of the military profession in the eyes of civilian policymakers and the public.

In the end, there are no easy answers. But this chapter has argued that as the retired senior officer is still generally perceived to belong to the military profession—both within the military and by the public—the retiree must carefully consider his or her actions with respect to national security and partisan politics. In fact, the retired senior officer still owes a duty to the military profession, to the state, and to society. It would be advisable for senior active duty leadership to explicitly recognize this duty and to assist senior retirees by establishing, promoting, and providing education on norms of professional conduct for retired senior officers through the methods discussed above. For as Wong and Lovelace perceptively suggest, "the crux of the issue lies in the *culture* that surrounds all the ranks in the military—not just the generals."[66] Thus, only with a concerted, combined approach can the U.S. military play its part in ensuring healthy, nonpartisan civil-military relations within the United States, along with optimal national security policymaking.

Notes

1. Jim Rutenberg, "Removal of Rumsfeld Dates Back to Summer," *New York Times*, November 10, 2006, A.22.
2. This point was made explicitly by an active duty four-star officer in an Army War College survey: "The public doesn't distinguish between active duty general [officers] and retired general [officers]. As a result, the entire military is politicized." Cited in Marybeth Peterson Ulrich, "Infusing Normative Civil-Military Relations Principles in the Officer Corps" (Newport, RI: United States Naval War College, National Security Decision Making Department, 2005), p. 15.
3. As one active duty general officer noted, "My concern is the effect of a retired general officer's commitment to a political party immediately after retirement on junior officers. Rather than the junior officer taking time to be fully informed on the current issues, there may be a tendency to blindly follow a senior that they admire for his/her service accomplishments." Cited in Ibid.
4. Retired "senior" military officers are considered to be those who have achieved general officer (U.S. Army, Air Force, and Marines) or flag (U.S. Navy) rank. According to then-secretary of defense Donald Rumsfeld, there were "6,000 or 7,000 retired generals and admirals" in April 2006. Cited in David S. Cloud, "Here's Donny! In His Defense, a Show Is Born," *New York Times*, April 19, 2006. While there are clearly some influential colonels and naval captains, this work primarily considers those officers who have attained stars. Certainly the public, along with the military itself, accords an almost automatic respect to any individual with the appellation "general" or "admiral."
5. In addition, legal restrictions and public policy with regard to the defense sector already exist, which is not the case in the national security and political spheres.
6. Frederick W. Kagan, "Let the Generals Speak," *Weekly Standard* 11, no. 32 (May 8, 2006): 15–17.
7. Richard H. Kohn, "General Elections: The Brass Shouldn't Do Endorsements," *Washington Post*, September 19, 2000, A23.
8. Samuel P. Huntington, *The Soldier and the State: The Theory and Politics of Civil-Military Relations* (Cambridge, MA: The Belknap Press of Harvard University Press, 1957); and Morris Janowitz, *The Professional Solider: A Social and Political Portrait* (Glencoe, IL: Free Press, 1960).

9. Peter D. Feaver, Richard H. Kohn, and Lindsay P. Cohn, "Introduction: The Gap between Military and Civilian in the United States in Perspective," in *Soldiers and Civilians: The Civil-Military Gap and American National Security*, ed. Peter D. Feaver and Richard H. Kohn (Cambridge, MA: The Belfer Center for Science and International Affairs at the John F. Kennedy School of Government, Harvard University), 2001, pp. 1–11.

10. Peter Feaver and Richard H. Kohn, "Conclusion: The Gap and What It Means for American National Security," in Feaver and Kohn, *Soldiers and Civilians*, pp. 459–473, p. 466. Also see Ole R. Holsti, "A Widening Gap between the U.S. Military and Civilian Society?—Some Evidence, 1976–96," *International Security* 23, no. 3 (Winter 1998/99): 5–42. Holsti's extensive survey data on the political and ideological identifications of U.S. civilian and military leaders from 1976 to 1996 found that the proportion of Republican military officers grew from fewer than one-third in 1976 to two-thirds of survey respondents by 1996.

11. Andrew J. Bacevich and Richard H. Kohn, "Grand Army of the Republicans," *New Republic* 217, no. 23 (December 8, 1997): 22–25.

12. Kohn, "General Elections."

13. Andrew J. Bacevich, *The New American Militarism: How Americans Are Seduced by War* (New York: Oxford University Press, 2005), p. 62.

14. Ibid., emphasis in original.

15. Scott Shane, "Civilians Reign over U.S. Military by Tradition and Design," *New York Times*, April 16, 2006, 1–18.

16. MacArthur's disagreement with Truman administration policy in the Korean War, whether in uniform or out, represents a classic case study of civil-military relations. See other policy criticisms in Maxwell D. Taylor, General, U.S. Army (Retired), *The Uncertain Trumpet* (New York: Harper & Brothers), 1960. Also see the deliberately titled *America Is in Danger*, by General Curtis E. LeMay with Major General Dale O. Smith (New York: Funk & Wagnalls, 1968).

17. Huntington, *Soldier and the State*, p. 418.

18. Steven Lee Myers and Megan Thee, "Americans Feel Military Is Best at Ending the War," *New York Times*, September 10, 2007.

19. Lawrence J. Korb, "Political Generals," *Foreign Affairs* 86, no. 5 (September-October 2007): 152–153.

20. David S. Cloud and Eric Schmitt, "More Retired Generals Call for Rumsfeld's Resignation," *New York Times*, April 14, 2006.

21. Leonard Wong and Douglas Lovelace, "Knowing When to Salute," Strategic Studies Institute Op-Ed (Carlisle, PA: Strategic Studies Institute, June 2007), p. 5, available at http://www.strategicstudiesinstitute.army.mil/newsletter/op-ed.cfm.

22. John Yellig, "Retired Officer Decries Criticism of Rumsfeld," *Charlottesville (VA) Daily Progress*, May 2, 2006.

23. John Crosby et al., "In Defense of Donald Rumsfeld," *Wall Street Journal*, April 17, 2006, A16.

24. Kagan, "Let the Generals Speak."

25. Cloud, "Here's Donny!" On the other hand, the retired generals who have spoken out have been careful to point out that their criticism was not coordinated. Cited in Michael R. Gordon, "As Policy Decisions Loom, a Code of Silence Is Broken," *New York Times*, April 16, 2006, 1.18.

26. Mark Manzetti and Jim Rutenberg, "Pentagon Memo Aims to Counter Rumsfeld Critics," *New York Times*, April 16, 2006.

27. Mark Sappenfield, "At Pentagon, a Delicate Civil-Military Balance," *Christian Science Monitor*, April 20, 2006 (emphasis added), http://www.csmonitor.com/2006/0420/po2s02-usmi.html.

28. Charles Babington, "Senate Panel Considers Hearing on Rumsfeld," *Washington Post*, April 26, 2006, A04.

29. Feaver and Kohn, "Conclusion," p. 464.

30. William T. Bianco and Jamie Markham, "Vanishing Veterans: The Decline of Military Experience in the U.S. Congress," in Feaver and Kohn, *Soldiers and Civilians*, pp. 275–287, 286.

31. Ibid., p. 465. For Feaver and Kohn, this has occurred at least in part in the wake of events such as the Vietnam War, "which the military blames on civilian micro-management, failed strategies, and acquiescent military leaders" (p. 465).

32. See, for example, recently retired United States Marine Corps Lt. General Gregory Newbold's comments that he only went public with his criticisms with "'the encouragement of some still in positions of military leadership' and in order to 'offer a challenge to those still in uniform.'" Cited in Thom Shanker, "Third Retired General Wants Rumsfeld Out," *New York Times*, April 10, 2006, A6.

33. Kagan, "Let the Generals Speak."

34. In September 2007 a *New York Times*/CBS News Poll found that only 5 percent would trust the Bush administration to resolve the war, 21 percent would most trust Congress, and 68 percent would most trust the military commanders. Cited in Myers and Thee, "Americans Feel Military Is Best."

35. See the findings and analysis in Paul Gronke and Peter D. Feaver, "Uncertain Confidence: Civilian and Military Attitudes about Civil-Military Relations," in Feaver and Kohn, *Soldiers and Civilians*, pp. 128–161.

36. Kohn, "General Elections."

37. Charles G. Boyd, General, USAF (Ret.), "Remarks by General Charles G. Bloyd, USAF (Ret.)," Air University Graduation, May 25, 2006, Reprinted in *The Wright Stuff* 2, no. 1 (January 4, 2007), Air University, Maxwell Air Force Base, AL, http://www.maxwell.af.mil/au/aunews/archive/july/generalJuly06/BoydSpeaks.html, (acessed July 1, 2007).

38. Huntington, *Soldier and the State*, p. 11.

39. Ibid., p. 13.

40. As early as 1960, Morris Janowitz pointed to the fact that "the post-retirement employment of generals and admirals became conspicuous with the growth in the size of the officer corps. In the years immediately after World War II, some four to five hundred high-ranking officers became available for civilian employment" (Janowitz, *Professional Solider*, p. 373). Echoing President Dwight Eisenhower's concern about a growing "military-industrial complex," Janowitz further highlighted that "within the defense contract industries . . . the presence of retired military officers is widespread and indicates a new type of interlocking directorate between industry and the military establishment. All the major aircraft and missile companies employ retired admirals and generals in key management posts" (p. 376).

41. The administration has also relied upon the formal Defense Science Board, a standing committee of retired military officers and former government officials, to investigate key military issues. Also of note, the DoD leadership has continued to informally consult about policy in the Iraq War with a group of retired generals and civilian analysts, as recounted in Manzetti and Rutenberg, "Pentagon Memo."

42. For example, in 2007, the U.S. Congress created a twenty-member commission (the Independent Commission on the Security Forces of Iraq), composed of retired senior military officers, to assess the status of Iraqi security forces and report back to

Congress. Karen DeYoung, "Iraqi Army Unable to Take Over Within a Year, Report Says," *Washington Post*, September 6, 2007.

43. Richard Swain, "Reflection on an Ethic of Officership," *Parameters* 37, no. 1 (Spring 2007): 4–22, 19.

44. Ibid.

45. Neil A. Lewis, "Retired General Is Censured for Role in Tillman Case," *New York Times*, August 1, 2007. Other retired and active-duty general officers were admonished, too.

46. Department of Defense Directive Number 1352.1, "Management and Mobilization of Regular and Reserve Retired Military Members," July 16, 2005, p. 2.

47. "Retiree Uniform Regulations," http://www.military.com/benefits/retiree/retiree-uniform-regulations (accessed August 5, 2007).

48. Huntington, *Soldier and the State*, p. 16.

49. Janowitz, *Professional Soldier*, p. 382, emphasis added.

50. Huntington, *Soldier and the State*, p. 15.

51. Ibid.

52. Huntington, *Soldier and the State*, p. 16.

53. Janowitz, *Professional Soldier*, p. 6.

54. Allan R. Millett, "Military Professionalism and Officership in America," A Mershon Center Briefing Paper (Columbus, OH: The Mershon Center of the Ohio State University, 1977), p. 3. Certainly, the U.S. military understands the absolute necessity for maintaining public confidence in the military as an institution; a painful and well-remembered legacy in the aftermath of the Vietnam War. See Thom Shanker, "At the Pentagon, Concern about Blame for the Situation in Iraq," *New York Times*, November 10, 2006, A22.

55. Millett, "Military Professionalism," p. 4.

56. "The professional ethic is broader than professional ethics in the narrow sense of the code governing the behavior of the professional man toward nonprofessionals. It includes any preferences and expectations that may be inferred from the continuing performance of the military occupational role." Huntington, *Soldier and the State*, p. 61.

57. Ibid., p. 71. Other scholars point out that historically, politicization has usually been associated with military ineffectiveness: . . . "Only by eventually divorcing itself from politics was the U.S. officer corps able to embark upon a protracted but ultimately successful process of professionalization." Bacevich and Kohn, "Grand Army of the Republicans," 25.

58. R. D. McKinlay, "Professionalization, Politicization and Civil-Military Relations," in *The Perceived Role of the Military*, ed. M. R. Van Gils (Rotterdam, The Netherlands: Rotterdam University Press, 1971—Contributions to Military Sociology Vol. 1) pp. 245–265, 254. This is because, as McKinlay lays out earlier in his model of professionalization, the fifth dimension requires that the expertise developed "be applied and harnessed to socially responsible uses . . . thus, the orientation of the application of this knowledge must be to community rather than personal, group or organizational interests" (p. 251).

59. Ibid., p. 251.

60. Ulrich, "Infusing Normative Civil–Military Relations," p. 16.

61. Smith, Perry, "Armchair Generals," *Wall Street Journal*, April 17, 2003, A.12. Smith was careful to point out, though, that there would be an exception to criticize "if the war plan was terribly flawed or if our political and military leaders were being dishonest."

62. David R. Irvine, "The Demise of Military Accountability," *Salt Lake Tribune*, January 29, 2006. Irvine, himself a retired army general officer, recounted the outrage expressed by some forty retired generals and admirals meeting specifically to support congressional legislation forbidding torture.
63. Wong and Lovelace, "Knowing When to Salute," p. 4.
64. Ibid., p. 5.
65. Ibid. As they emphasize, resigning equates to "forfeiting . . . membership in the profession" and is not considered to be a viable option." In fact, "resigning is such a drastic option that it has been over 40 years since a general officer resigned from the Army (and he later requested reinstatement)" (p. 4).
66. Ibid., p. 6, emphasis added.

18

Women, Women, Everywhere . . .

Judith Hicks Stiehm

Introduction

Women have never been exempt from war. Their roles have included providing justification for war, as well as serving as victim, support, and warrior. In general, women have been more active when conflict has occurred in their homeland, whether in a defensive war, a war for independence, or a civil war. Also, their numbers have tended to be larger in irregular or insurgent forces than in forces in which the enlisted are trained and commanded by a well-established government. In recent years, however, even in the latter, women have become more numerous and their assignments more varied. Two factors contributing to this have been stronger norms against sex discrimination and the end of conscription. This essay discusses the American experience to illuminate reasons given for limiting women's military service; the changes in women's military participation since World War II, especially since 1972; and the experience of women now serving in uniform.

Reasons Given for Resisting Women's Military Service

American culture, at least now, includes a strong norm (and a significant amount of law) against discrimination based on race, ethnicity, religion, sex, and sometimes sexual orientation. This has not always been the case. For instance, women have had the vote for less than one hundred years, and the Equal Rights Amendment has still not been ratified. Opposition to women's military service has also been a strong norm, and while that resistance has been eroding, opposition to women's service in combat—especially ground combat—remains strong. Nevertheless, women are slowly being integrated into the U.S military.

In 1976 Congress directed that the U.S. military academies be opened to women. The services opposed the legislation, arguing that they trained combat leaders and because military women could not serve in combat, they should not attend the academies. This was argued even though a significant number of academy graduates went into noncombat specialties, including intelligence, logistics, and administration. In a series of in-depth interviews with officer faculty and staff at the U.S. Air Force Academy, I found deep resistance to the presence of women. Even though only a small percent of air force personnel have a combat mission, the reasons offered tended to focus on combat.[1]

The principal theme was that women should not be subjected to war's suffering. Because most of America's wars have been fought "over there," Americans may be susceptible to the idea that noncombatants need not suffer in war. Of course, they do. A small dose of reality quickly changed the position of most officers to one of "Our" women should not suffer. In particular they were concerned that women who served in combat might become prisoners of war (POWs) and that abusive treatment of American women prisoners would affect the judgment of the women's peers and commanders, and that it could also affect public opinion. This was largely due to the ethic of chivalry, which calls for men to protect women.

Officers gave additional reasons for not wanting women to fight by their side. One was based on the perception that women are small and weak and cannot do their share. (The average difference in size between women and men in the United States is only five inches and twenty-five pounds.) Physical standards could, of course, be set for all recruits or for all military specialties. Further, technology has greatly reduced the importance of having a capacity for chin-ups. Gone are the days when men marched into battle; today they fly in via helicopter, drop in via aircraft, or drive in via wheeled or tracked vehicles. However, there was, and continues to be, a strong sentiment that the mere presence of women reduces an all-important military element—cohesiveness.[2]

Other arguments have included the possibility that an enemy facing a mixed-sex unit might fight harder, might outdo itself, in order to avoid the humiliation of being defeated by women. In short, chances for an enemy surrender, a highly desirable goal, would be reduced. An alternative view was that an enemy that saw women in U.S. ranks would interpret that as weakness or desperation. Less often set forth were arguments about society's need for nurturers, and, after a war, society's need to have numerous women available to replenish the population. (Even if large numbers of men were lost, the remaining few could father many children if there were enough women available.)

Bias against women in the military continues even though most American men do not serve in the military, and of those who do, only limited numbers ever see combat. Rigorous training is required to prepare men to kill. Part of that training often implicitly or explicitly involves mythologies that connect masculinity to military service, that aver that the warrior should and *can* protect, and that those in uniform are all at risk and prepared to sacrifice. Even if their military occupations are in support, those in uniform are considered ready for a call to combat. They can be substituted for the fallen.[3]

The point is that for many men (and women), it has been important to reserve the role of warrior—the military combatant who exercises society's force—to men. Since government is the institution with a monopoly on the legitimate use of force, there has long been a link between full citizenship and military service. Still, as women have begun to play more active roles in government, their roles in the military have also expanded. Indeed, it is possible that before long the military may even call a woman commander in chief.

Changes in Women's Military Service

In a graveyard in Carlisle, Pennsylvania, there is a monument to Molly Pitcher, who "manned" a cannon in the War for Independence. Nurses found their way to the battlefield during the Civil War. In 1901, the army created a Nurse Corps, and the navy followed suit in 1908. During World War I a small number of women were inducted into the navy. It was not until World War II, however, when the society was mobilized, food was rationed, and tin cans were collected that women joined/were admitted into the military in significant numbers. Rosie the Riveter was emblematic of the women who stepped into men's civilian jobs, but other women put on uniforms to "release a man for war." Hundreds of thousands joined the Women's Army Corps (WACS), the Women's Reserve of the U.S. Naval Reserve (WAVES), the Women in the Air Force (WAFS), and the marines, too. Of the women in uniform, almost seventy thousand were nurses. In fact, almost a quarter of all American nurses volunteered for service. Military women served in the United States and abroad, on ships and on planes.

Women were demobilized after WW I, and after WW II it was decided that a small number could have regular active duty status. However, Congress decreed that none would rise higher than the rank of lieutenant colonel—except on a temporary basis when they were assigned to lead a corps—and that the total number of women would not exceed 2 percent of active duty personnel. In fact, even during the Korean War, women volunteers did not compose even 1 percent of personnel. In 1967, the era of Vietnam, the cap on women and on their promotions was removed, and they began to move into jobs other than clerical and medical. By 1970, two women, both nurses (nurses have regularly served as women's military vanguard), had become generals, and marine and army women were serving in Vietnam.

Major change began in 1972. That year the Equal Rights Amendment passed both houses of Congress with the requisite two-thirds vote. In debate it was specifically decided *not* to protect women from the draft. However, it was also decided to end the draft. The military scrambled. It would need recruits, and plans were made to increase the number of women. They did. In 1972 one out of every thirty recruits was a woman; by 1976 one in thirteen was.[4]

One of the most dramatic changes occurred in 1975 when the Department of Defense (DoD) decreed that discharge for pregnancy would be voluntary. Maternity uniforms were created, and it became possible for women to have a full military career without sacrificing motherhood.

By 1976, women were accepted into the Reserve Officers' Training Corps (ROTC), as well as by the academies. Air force women joined army and navy women in pilot training, and the WAC, the last of the women's corps, was abolished. Other changes included carrots for women who were willing to enter "nontraditional" fields—that is, not medical or clerical—but not so "nontraditional" as to include combat. This meant that the ratio of enlisted women to officer women became more like that of enlisted men to officer men—that is, around 85 percent to 15 percent.[5] Basic training (except for the Marine Corps) was sex integrated, women received defensive weapons training, and their uniforms grew pants. Some even became drill instructors for male recruits.

However, women were still restricted by law from flying in combat planes or serving on combat ships, and they were restricted from ground combat by policy. At first the air force argued that since pilots had to be interchangeable, women could not fly at all. That policy soon came to an end. Similarly, the navy first sought to keep navy women off all ships. The judiciary overruled the navy, and women began sea rotations like their male counterparts. During the Reagan years, there was a "pause" in changes for women, but they were needed, and there was no rollback. In 1980, however, Congress mandated a single personnel and promotion system for women and men in all of the services. This put women into direct competition with their male peers.

During the Clinton administration in 1993, against air force advice, the restriction on women as pilots of combat aircraft was removed. So, too, was the restriction on women's presence on combat ships (with the navy's support). This meant that virtually all air force slots were opened to women, as were more than 90 percent of all navy slots.[6] Over two-thirds of army positions were opened, as were more than 60 percent of marine positions.

Women's deployment with their units has led to women's near participation in combat on the ground. One hundred seventy army women participated in the 1983 invasion of Grenada, and two women (among 800) commanded companies in the 1989 invasion of Panama. Forty-one thousand women (7 percent of all personnel in theater) served in the Persian Gulf War. Fifteen women were killed there, and two became POWs. One POW was Rhonda Cornum, a physician. The account of her cool and professional conduct probably influenced Congress in its decision to lift the legislative restrictions on women's combat service.

Women in Today's Military

Today, the U.S. military is regularly engaged in limited ground combat in Afghanistan and Iraq against terrorists, insurgents, and criminals. It is not possible to geographically isolate that combat, and military women who seem to be "everywhere" cannot be kept safe. The prohibition against the assignment of women to ground units below brigade level continues to exist. Nevertheless, women, who make up 9 to 10 percent of U.S. troops in Iraq, are regularly exposed to hostile fire and bombings. Still, fewer than a hundred have been killed, and only a handful of them have become POWs. Women serve as guards on convoys and as sentries at checkpoints. Some have gone on raids—because women were needed to guard, search, or interrogate Iraqi women. Thus far there has been little debate about women's role in Iraq. Almost certainly this is because every woman is a volunteer. One must assume that there would be many and grave objections raised if a draft were reinstated in which women and men were drafted and assigned to combat units in the same way. Because they are needed, some women have been attached—although not "assigned"—to direct support units. They do not participate in infantry, artillery, or cavalry units, but they command army military police companies, fly air force and navy attack aircraft, and provide intelligence for the Marine Corps.

The Women's Research and Education Institute has been monitoring the status of women in the armed forces since 1989. Their 2005 report, *Women in the Military: Where They Stand*, tells us where they stood at the end of 2004.[7]

Women make up 15 percent of officer and 15 percent of enlisted active duty personnel. These numbers hold true for the army and navy, while for the marines the number is only 6 percent, and for the air force, 20 percent. Interestingly, the coast guard, a military service but under the Department of Homeland Security during peacetime, has no restrictions at all on women's service, but it is only a little over 10 percent women. Across the military, restrictions on the service of women cannot account for such low numbers. Data suggest that women do have less of a propensity to join the military than men do, but the military may also not be as eager or as skilled in recruiting them.

There has been some concern about how representative the military is of the U.S. citizenry. As an institution, the military has rightly taken some pride in its 1948 directive to racially integrate, and in its ability to offer an opportunity for low-income minorities to join the middle class. Women minorities have benefited as well as men; however, results have not been uniform across the services, ranks, and racial groups.

Eighty percent of women officers in the coast guard are white; in the navy, 74 percent; in the air force, 73 percent; in the marines, 66 percent; and in the army, only 60 percent. The differences are even more dramatic among enlisted women: 75 percent of enlisted women in the coast guard are white; in the air force, 59 percent; in the marines, 51 percent; in the navy, 48 percent; and in the army, only 38 percent. Black women make up 42 percent of the army's enlisted women; for the navy, 31 percent; for the air force, 26 percent; for the marines, 18 percent; and for the coast guard, only 10 percent. If one assumes that roughly 10 percent of the population is black, black women are greatly overrepresented among enlisted women, most notably in the army. Hispanic women make up 10 percent of enlisted and 5 percent of officers, with a preponderance in the marines. Less than 1 percent of women officers and about 2 percent of enlisted women are American Indian. There is some tendency for them to cluster in the navy and marines. Asian/Pacific Islander women represent 6 percent of women officers and 5 percent of enlisted women. Few join the coast guard, but they are about equally represented in the other services.

A limited number of enlisted women serve in the senior enlisted ranks. In 2004, their numbers ranged from 5 percent of the total for the marines to 12 percent for the air force. The percent of women holding the O-6 rank of colonel or (navy) captain fell in the same range. There were thirty-nine women generals or admirals in September 2004, representing 0.4 percent of those at flag rank. Each service has, at some time, had at least one woman with the rank of three stars.

As more military women follow the career track of successful men, these numbers may increase. Many senior women entered when their choices were more constricted than at present. Still, women and men do concentrate in different military occupations. Over 40 percent of men officers serve in tactical operations, whereas only 11 percent of women do so. In contrast, 38 percent of women are in health care, as opposed to 13 percent of men. Administrative assignments claim 12 percent of women and 6 percent of men. Differences are smaller for the categories of intelligence, engineering and maintenance, scientific and professional, supply and logistics, and student/trainee. These fields claim about 40 percent of both men and women, but in the past were considered "nontraditional" for women.

A higher percentage of enlisted women serve in health care specialties (16 percent versus 5 percent of men), as they do in support and administration (33 percent to 13 percent). A higher percentage of men (19 percent versus 5 percent for women) serve in gun crew and seamanship capacities, and 23 percent of men versus 9 percent of women serve in power/mechanical equipment repair. The differences in electronic equipment repair; communications and intelligence; technical specialty; crafts; service and supply; and student/trainee are smaller. It must be remembered, however, that even if there is a higher percentage of women than men (33 percent versus 13 percent) serving in a specialty like administration, because women compose a much smaller percentage of the total, *most administrators are still men.*

Women now compose over 17 percent of Reserve and National Guard officers and enlisted. They make up over 20 percent of the army, navy, and air force reserves, but are smaller components of the army and air national guard. The Reserve and the National Guard had but limited use during the Cold War. However, with the end of conscription and the extended hostilities in Iraq, many members have been called to service there. Many probably didn't anticipate such service when they first chose to join the Reserves or the Guard.

Among American veterans, 7 percent are women, up from 4 percent in 1986. Close to half are under the age of forty-five, while only 18 percent are over sixty-five.

The military has not been immune to incidents of sexual assault and harassment. One might expect that a hierarchal structure that can issue and enforce orders could set an example for society by erasing such behavior. However, the military is also a male-dominated institution where "masculinity" is valued, sexual prowess is admired, women are vastly outnumbered, and complaining to superiors is not esteemed. While officers may have fewer difficulties than enlisted personnel, and the newest recruits may be the most vulnerable, survey results show that the military has not been able to excise sexual assault and harassment.

Much of military policy has mirrored civilian policy. Thus, in 1980 the DoD adopted the Equal Employment Opportunity Commission (EEOC) guidelines on sexual harassment and established an overall definition of harassment. A series of DoD surveys on sexual harassment suggest that the problem has not been resolved, but it was the 1991 Tailhook scandal involving naval aviators that brought outrageous behavior by active duty officers to public notice. While most officers were "unable" to identify particular offenders, the secretary of the navy, who had been present at the Las Vegas convention, did resign. So did the woman navy officer who lodged a complaint. The incident bruised the navy and everyone involved. Since that time, the navy has required all personnel to undergo annual training to prevent sexual harassment.

In 1997, the public was dismayed by charges (and later convictions) of rape, sexual assault, and sexual harassment leveled against army drill sergeants at the army's Aberdeen Proving Grounds in Maryland. At the same time, the army's top enlisted man, its sergeant major, was charged with sexual harassment. In a court-martial he was acquitted of harassment, but convicted of obstruction of justice. A further example of misbehavior at the top involved the senior woman in the army, Lt. General Claudia Kennedy, who brought charges against a major general who had been nominated for the position of deputy inspector general of the army, a position in which he would be in charge of issues related to sexual harassment. Her charges were upheld; he did not receive the appointment.

The air force made headlines over a series of sexually related incidents at the Air Force Academy in 2003. And Congress held hearings related to charges made by servicewomen concerning their treatment in Iraq in 2004.

A series of task forces and committees have issued reports over the years. The latest response from DoD came in 2005. It provided for increased support for victims, including provisions for confidentiality and new training standards.

The American public holds the military in high esteem, and thus may be especially critical of the fact that it has not set an example for civilians in regard to the treatment of uniformed women.[8] The military stands for equality of treatment and teamwork. Women have found that it doesn't always work that way. Formal and legal approaches have not solved the problem. What is difficult to assess is what is occurring or could occur informally and beneath public notice. Is part of the problem the fact that women are complaining more? Have some service members learned how to handle things informally? If so, how? Are men becoming more conscious of boundaries that women expect to be able to enforce? It should be remembered that different American cultures permit different language, jokes, and even touching. When individuals from different groups meet in the military, some may have to learn to ignore behavior they find offensive; others may have to learn new self-restraint. The military expects to be able to demand uniform behavior. Women rightly expect respect and to be able to control their own sexuality.

Tomorrow

It took decades for nurses to become firmly established as regular military officers. While they were once the vanguard, they are now so thoroughly incorporated that sometimes when women in the military are being studied, nurses are set aside as "not an issue," as not needing consideration. This is probably because they so dominate a necessary profession in the American society at large that they also dominate that profession within the military as well. Women set the standards in the nurse corps. As the head of one nurse corps told me, "We will never let a man become head of the corps."

There is a question to be answered as to whether women will ever be well incorporated as long as they remain a small minority, not just in the military, but in the different specialties as well. What if women were to concentrate themselves, or were concentrated, in a field like intelligence? Or in electronic repair? Would they then gain the same acceptance as the nurses have? Civilian training for intelligence is not dominated by women. Could they, or could the military, intentionally create a women-dominated specialty within the military that is not dominated by women in civilian life? Indeed, if one really wanted to better utilize women in the military, would there be an advantage in simply giving them one of the services—for example, the air force?

The military can use many more women than now serve, although its overall level of 15 percent is higher than that of all but a few other nations' militaries. Still, the smaller number of women means they are more highly selected. Military women are generally of higher quality than are the men—that is, they have more degrees, higher test scores, and fewer waivers. Could and should the military raise its overall quality by increasing the percent of women to, say, 25 percent? What strategies would be needed to do so?

The military probably has the best large-scale child-care programs in existence. With more women in the military and working the full range of shifts, this became a necessary support. Additionally, the navy plans to experiment with a two-year break in active service to allow members a better opportunity to parent their newborns and reduce the numbers of women who end their military careers because of family considerations.

The military has also developed a wide range of other programs to support the family. These should not be perceived merely as women's programs, even though the Defense Advisory Committee on Women in the Services (DACOWITS) has been tasked to study these programs and give advice about them. In large part, the programs are designed to assist retention—not just retention of officers, but retention of the far more numerous senior enlisted.

It is predicted that tomorrow's military will be engaged in more missions—for example, peace stabilization—that require working directly with ordinary citizens of foreign countries. The purpose is often referred to as "winning hearts and minds." Officer-to-sheik relations are important, but so are relations with ordinary Iraqis. With limited numbers of women in the military, the military is missing an opportunity to connect with 50 percent of the population in countries like Iraq and Afghanistan. The American press recently reported efforts by the U.S. military to recruit local women in Iraq to persuade their husbands to cease resistance. Soldiers have also gone into schools to ask children about suspicious activity they may have seen. Such efforts may be limited (and also controversial), and whether they have born fruit is not known, but it may be that women would be more effective at such tasks than men are. For instance, we know that in domestic disturbances, police officers have found that women officers are more successful than men in creating calm. It seems certain that women's skills and others' perceptions of women are valuable in many situations where U.S. troops need to work with civilian populations. Hence, there may be a need for more women or, perhaps, for different assignments for them.

Classical peacekeeping operations are numerous and have proven important in ending conflict. Such operations occur where both (all) sides have agreed to end hostilities and invite the presence of peacekeepers; and where peacekeepers are neutral, limited to observing and reporting, and exercise force only in self defense. By definition, peacekeepers are military troops. While many nations are eager to have their militaries participate in such missions, there has been some opposition in this country to using U.S. troops for these missions. There is a fear that they will lose their fighting edge or, at the least, that such missions will require not just training but retraining.[9] Again, this may be another area in which more women, who regularly serve as military police, will be needed.

But the $64 question is what will happen if the draft is reinstated. Tolerance of the expanded role of women surely has been based on the fact that all are volunteers. Pictures of a woman deploying to Iraq in battle fatigues and kissing the baby she is leaving behind have not created a stir. There would be a stir if that mother did not want to go to Iraq and did not even want to be in the military!

Notes

1. This discussion is drawn from the postscript in Judith Hicks Stiehm, *Bring Me Men and Women: Mandated Change at the U.S. Air Force Academy* (Berkeley: University of California Press, 1981), pp. 288–301.
2. A second, continuing concern is the "readiness" of women personnel for deployment. In such discussions, the percent of men who are not "ready" is often overlooked.
3. See Judith Hicks Stiehm, "Myths Necessary to the Pursuit of War," in *Arms and the Enlisted Woman* (Philadelphia, PA: Temple University Press, 1989).
4. Also, in 1972, the Supreme Court gave women service members the same benefits for their dependents that men received. The case was *Frontiero v. Richardson*.
5. Women who entered the military and were given "nontraditional" jobs were doubly nontraditional. Once in service, they encountered, as their peers, subordinates, and commanders, men who were likely to hold the most traditional views about sex roles. Some women sought acceptance by "acting like a soldier." The Catch-22 was that in doing so, they tended to fulfill the stereotype of the butch lesbian, and lesbians were (and are) subject to discharge. In fact, under the current "don't ask, don't tell" policy, lesbians make up a third of those discharged, although only 15 percent of the military are women.
6. Women are not allowed to serve on submarines, because the cramped quarters make privacy virtually impossible.
7. Lory Manning, *Women in the Military: Where They Stand*, 5th ed., report of Women's Research and Education Institute (Arlington, 2005).
8. Congressional anger about the treatment of military women probably reflects public opinion. Legislators' response has generally been to tell the military to shape up. However, there are individuals, again including women, who believe that the problem is putting women where they do not belong. In particular, there is some sentiment in favor of sex-segregating basic training.
9. In *Men, Militarism and UN Peacekeeping* (Boulder, CO: Lynne Rienner, 2004), Sandra Whitworth discusses the many downsides to giving highly militarized troops a mission that requires different skills and practices.

19

Contracting for Services in U.S. Military Operations

Deborah D. Avant

When the United States deploys its forces around the world, an increasingly important part of its operations falls to personnel outside the uniformed U.S. military per se. Increasingly, the U.S. military has been using what some call contractors, others call private military and security companies, and still others call mercenaries. In this chapter, I will briefly describe the private security industry and the larger global market for force of which it is a part; then I will discuss some of the benefits and risks the United States faces with its increasing use of private forces.

To get an idea of the private security industry's role in U.S. military operations, consider the recent experience in Iraq. When the United States defeated the Iraqi army in 2003, between one in ten and one in six people deployed by the United States to the theater were civilian employees of private security companies (PSCs) who were performing the work that used to be done by uniformed personnel. As lawlessness followed the fall of Saddam Hussein and U.S. forces were stretched thin, an "army" of private security forces surged into the country—to train the Iraqi police force, the Iraqi army, a private Iraqi force to guard government facilities and oil fields, and simply to protect expatriates working in the country. In May 2004, Secretary of Defense Donald Rumsfeld estimated that in excess of twenty thousand private security personnel were in the country (making private soldiers the second largest component of the "coalition of the willing"). In fact—if one combines the set of support and training personnel with the estimated set of private and site security personnel, the numbers are much higher than that. As many as fifty-eight thousand private security personnel may have been working in the country at that time. The Pentagon's first census of the number of contractors in Iraq, released in December 2006, counted one hundred thousand contractors, including Iraqis contracted for services.

These people are citizens of countries as varied as Fiji, Israel, Iraq, Nepal, El Salvador, the Philippines, South Africa, the United Kingdom (UK), and the

United States. They are employed by more than fifty different PSCs. In addition to the one hundred thousand people working for the United States, others work for the British government, the Iraqi government, and for private firms and international nongovernmental organizations (NGOs). The experience in Iraq is not unique—it is only the latest manifestation of a trend toward the privatization of security that mushroomed during the 1990s.

Private security companies have become more and more involved in the *delivery* of security services. A few examples illustrate this trend. When the 1995 Dayton Accords required that the Bosnian military be rebuilt, MPRI, an American firm, was hired to advise and train the Bosnian military. Since 1994, every international civilian police officer the United States has sent abroad has been a Dyncorp employee. Every multilateral peace operation conducted by the United Nations (UN) in the 1990s was accomplished with the presence of PSCs.

The private sector is also increasingly involved in *financing* security services. Both NGOs and transnational corporations finance security in unstable parts of the world. This includes global corporations (e.g., BP, Exxon, and DeBeers), as well as international NGOs (e.g., CARE and the World Wildlife Fund), and many others have contracted with PSCs for site security and security planning all over the globe.

The industry that has grown to meet this demand consists of companies that provide a wide range of military and policing services. On the military side, they provide such services as operational support, advice and training, and logistical support. On the policing side, they provide site security, crime prevention, and intelligence. The range of services provided by an individual company varies considerably—with some providing close to the full range of services and others specializing in one or more segments of the market.

All PSCs, however, operate as service sector companies frequently do. They are contract organizations with a relatively small set of full-time employees and a capacity to bring in large numbers of specialists for a given contract. These contract employees may have little loyalty to the company that hired them; in fact, they are often on the rosters of many different companies. Once in a theater—like Iraq—they may switch employers frequently as contracts (some as short as six weeks) come and go.

This use of PSCs by the United States provides a variety of benefits. First, let me outline the benefits:

1. *Surge and flexibility*
   As seen in Iraq, PSCs can provide "surge" capacity to quickly field additional forces. Without the political and bureaucratic lead time required for mobilizing military forces, PSCs can move forces in to accomplish a wide variety of tasks. As quickly as these forces can appear, they can disappear. Once dangers pass or local forces are trained and deployed, contracts can lapse, and these personnel can be quickly demobilized.
2. *Specialized skills*
   PSCs can also more easily field the kinds of forces that are most needed. They recruit from databases of mostly retired military and police personnel. This makes it easier for them to hire people with particular types of experience.

For instance, a PSC can specifically recruit retired military police (MPs), civil affairs officers, and members of special forces. They can also recruit personnel with specific skills (e.g., language or area expertise) or talents (e.g., establishing order after civil war). It is much more difficult for national military organizations to find people with such skills and experience and to deploy them to a particular arena.

3. *Ability to recruit internationally*

   As mentioned earlier, PSCs have been able to recruit people from a wide range of countries. As one U.S. army staff sergeant put it in 2004, "We're trying to get more international participation here and the contractors can hire internationally."

4. *Finally, political cost*

   It is (at least perceived to be) *politically* less costly to field PSCs. Private contractors are perceived to be working for profit, and by choice; therefore, sending them abroad is not held to the same standard as sending national troops who are deployed by their own government. Thus, in the wake of the end of the Cold War, when U.S. forces were downsized to satisfy political demands, outsourcing tasks (e.g., logistics through the Logistics Civilian Augmentation Program [LOGCAP]) was seen as a way of doing more with fewer troops. Similarly, for those who believe that a long-term commitment is crucial to successful nation building in Iraq and who worry that the United States cannot sustain such a long-term commitment, the use of PSCs provides a way to substitute for troops and enhance staying power.

The use of PSCs also entails a number of costs and risks. Some of these are practical and short-term, whereas others are more political and of longer term:

1. *First, cost*

   PSCs may be more expensive than military forces—particularly under circumstances in which the United States wants to provide the same level and quality of service as the military does or when there are high levels of danger. The latter issue arose in Iraq. Surge capacity comes at a high price. Recruiters must deal with supply and demand. The huge demand for security precipitated by the Iraqi situation created a sellers' market. People working for PSCs in Columbia, for instance, reported offers to move to Iraq at three times their current salary. Even in less volatile situations, the privatization (or, more accurately, competition) for security services sometimes saves money because it inspires new ideas about how to deliver a service that requires fewer people or fewer or different materials. The more the United States wants PSCs to do exactly what the military does, the more it limits this flexibility. Without flexibility, the use of PSCs can actually increase costs. For instance, in its initial outsourcing of the Reserve Officers' Training Corps (ROTC) training, the army required certain levels of fitness, training, and experience that produced trainers almost indistinguishable from active duty equivalents—but at an additional cost. This is an area for more study. But one should not assume that privatizing saves money.

2. *Reliability*

   If the government does try to minimize costs, it may forgo quality by hiring a company that will deploy fewer personnel or personnel with fewer skills or professionalism, both of which could exacerbate worries that there is nothing to compel contractors to remain on the battlefield once bullets begin to fly. In Iraq, there were periodic reports that supply was inadequate, both during the conflict and particularly as the insurgency accelerated in the spring and summer of 2003, because civilian contractors failed to show up. According to Lt. General Charles S. Mahan Jr., the army's senior logistics officer, "We thought we could depend on industry to perform these kinds of functions . . . [but it got] harder and harder to get [them] to go in harms way."[1]

3. *Integration*

   Two kinds of issues are associated with integration: the integration of contracted personnel with regular personnel and the degree to which parsing tasks to be contracted impedes integration. The integration of contracted personnel has been a constant worry in Iraq. It has impeded information sharing and has muddied the definition of roles. Contracted tasks are also harder to change in the field. There is little or no flexibility to deviate from the contract. As the insurgency heated up in Iraq and as requirements changed, one of the major results was that contracting officers—those who could actually change contracts—were in high demand and low supply.

   Just as important, however, has been the fact that contracting itself requires the divvying up of tasks that are subsidiary to the overarching goal. Even if the task is clear, once it is assigned to a contractor, successful execution of the task may thwart integration with the larger goal. An example of this is the way in which personal security details have impeded the counterinsurgency effort. PSCs are given the job of keeping important individuals safe. Their strategy for doing this, however—driving at very high speeds, not stopping at intersections, and so forth—has kept officials safe, but sometimes at the cost of alienating the very public the United States and the fledgling Iraqi government are trying to win over. This issue was made dramatically apparent when employees of Blackwater opened fire at a Baghdad intersection in September 2007.

4. *Legal Ambiguity*

   The laws of war have been designed for traditional militaries. The legal status of personnel deployed by PSCs is often unclear, as are the mechanisms by which their rights and responsibilities are meted out. This poses problems for both private security personnel and those they operate around. Unless they are commissioned by a government, they are not *combatants*. To the degree that they are seen to be working toward the achievement of military objectives, however, neither are they *noncombatants*. This poses serious risks for individuals who might not be accorded prisoner of war (POW) status if captured by the enemy, and they may face criminal prosecution for acts they commit in the line of duty.

This legal limbo also introduces more risks *from* security personnel. Private security personnel are not generally governed by military justice systems (though the circumstances under which they may be prosecuted within the US military justices system was recently expanded by Congress). When PSC personnel break laws, it is often unclear how to hold them accountable. Sometimes this is because the law they are subject to is unclear, while at other times it is because either there is no practical legal forum in which to prosecute them or there are serious practical hurdles to their prosecution. For whatever reason, few private security personnel have even been indicted for alleged criminal behavior in Iraq. Though these are the most serious legal issues, others abound—for example, fraud against companies found not fulfilling their contract or wrongful death claims against companies that lose personnel in the execution of their contracts.

The two final risks are of longer term and more political:

5. *Political change*
The political process works differently when the United States hires contractors. It is less transparent; it advantages the executive branch over the legislature; it enhances the influence of private interests in the policymaking process; and sometimes it also advantages the foreign government or private corporation that is paying for the service.
6. *Change in the military profession*
The blurring of lines between what soldiers do and what private security personnel do may also inhibit military innovation. Making costly changes may be less attractive than outsourcing. It may also erode the professional ethos of the military. Opportunities in the private sector have already had an impact on retention rates, and some worry that as the military must compete with the private sector, it will lose unique and important professional qualities that are crucial to successful security operations in a democratic setting.

In considering the best way forward vis-à-vis America's use of contractors in military operations, there are a variety of viewpoints, but they all boil down to three broad alternatives. One option is to scale back the use of PSCs, define core military functions, and move PSCs away from these core functions (reducing concerns about reliability and integration). This option would still require that the United States deal with the practical concerns surrounding cost and think creatively about practical ways to hold PSC personnel legally responsible for their actions. This option would do the most to assuage long-term political concerns, but this would also require a strategy to substitute for the level of private force the United States currently uses—either by reducing U.S. commitments, adding to and changing the structure of the U.S. military, or finding other partners.

A second option is to simply accept the reality that PSCs will play a significant (and perhaps even larger) role and allow the market to take its course. Even advocates of free markets agree, however, that the effective functioning of markets requires some legal structure. Interestingly, many PSCs have argued as much—requesting some regulatory framework to enhance the legitimacy of reputable firms, minimize risk, and reduce the operational inefficiencies associated with a market of multiple standards.

The third option is to find new tools that reward proper behavior by PSCs and new instruments for prosecuting wrongdoings. The creation of professional, ethical, and/or legal standards may be one way to move this scenario forward. For instance, one could imagine a system to license private security professionals—whereby professional standards could be issued, individuals could lose their license for violations, and PSCs could demonstrate their commitment to proper behavior by hiring only licensed personnel. This might ease some concerns with reliability. There are a variety of efforts—in the United States as well as in the UK and Europe—to begin thinking about standards. Though they are in their infancy, these efforts hold some promise. This path requires paying much more attention to the legal instruments already available, as well as to new ones, to address criminal actions. This option, however does not address the deeper, more long-term ways in which contracting for force reallocates authority over force in a fairly undemocratic way. If market options are destined to play a larger role in American military force, all Americans should be thinking hard about how not only contractors but also government officials can be held to account for the private use and abuse of force.

Note

1. Anthony Bianco and Stephanie Anderson Forest, with Stan Crock in Washington and Thomas F. Armistead in Iraq, "Outsourcing War," *Business Week*, September 15, 2003.

20

Odd Couples: The DoD and NGOs[1]

Linton Wells II and Charles Hauss

This chapter was written in late 2007; it could not have been written twenty years earlier. We would almost certainly never have met. Working together would have been out of the question.

Vietnam was still a raw political wound for both the military and the peace-building communities. The Cold War did not yet show signs that it would soon end, which meant that the peace movement saw little room in which to cooperate with a military that was part and parcel of the arms buildup under presidents Jimmy Carter and Ronald Reagan.

But, the global political tectonic plates have shifted dramatically twice since then, and they have reshaped our lives as both scholars and practitioners. This career naval officer and career pacifist find themselves on the same political side more often than not.

We, individually, had little to do with making this change happen. Still, we find ourselves working together in response to these dramatic shifts at home and abroad.

As Thomas Friedman reminds us, the Berlin Wall fell on 11/9, and the terrorist attacks on the World Trade Center and the Pentagon occurred on 9/11. The calendar numbers may have been a coincidence, but the political similarities are not.

The collapse of communism in Eurasia made it possible for the United States and other Western powers to intervene to try to end conflicts in such different places as Bosnia and Somalia. Whereas we were divided over military involvement in Grenada and Nicaragua, we agreed on the need for the military and nongovernmental organizations (NGOs) to be engaged in post–Cold War hot spots. Indeed, on the thirtieth anniversary of filing his conscientious objector application, Hauss found himself writing an op-ed article supporting American military operations in Kosovo.

Then 9/11 came. Wells was on an airplane that morning. Hauss was involved in a false anthrax scare a few days later. In the days and weeks that followed, both our political responsibilities had changed.

Most people in the NGO community tried to come up with nonviolent strategies to respond to the terrorist attacks. Not everyone endorsed the war in Afghanistan,[2] but a surprising number of NGO activists did, *faute de mieux*.

Pentagon officials were not surprised by how easy it was to topple the Taliban or, for that matter, Saddam Hussein's regime two years later. What was surprising was the tenaciousness of the resistance against the United States and its allies that has led to thousands of American deaths and countless more casualties among Afghans and Iraqis. Serving officers and Defense Department (DoD) officials soon realized that there was more to realizing political goals than military conquest.

As a result, people like the two of us began attending conferences and other events together. Once we learned to speak each other's language (Pentagonese is a foreign language to NGOs, and vice versa), we found plenty of areas of common ground, which we explore below.

At first the invasion of Iraq threw a monkey wrench into our cooperation. Unlike the case with Afghanistan, almost no one in the NGO community supported the invasion. DoD professionals had no choice but to support their commander in chief. Yet, as the situation in Iraq deteriorated after the fall of the Baathist regime, officers who had served in Iraq or Afghanistan began to realize that their skill set did not involve postwar reconstruction, let alone conflict prevention.

Our goal for this chapter is to outline the work our communities have been doing together in the last few years on three levels. First is how our thinking has begun to converge and to show us areas where we can work together. Second, we will provide a few examples of that newfound cooperation. Finally, we will close with some problems we can already see and others we anticipate.

We have personally been involved in much of what we are discussing. However, we are delighted to note that there are so many initiatives involving NGOs, the DoD, and the United States and foreign governments that we can no longer keep up with them all. Recently, we have each taken new jobs so that we can concentrate full time on these budding relationships.

That said, this is also new turf intellectually as well as politically, which, of course, is the premise of this book that is trying to bring military and political studies together.

Convergence: The Military

The shift in U.S. military thinking may seem surprising to some readers, given the widespread criticism of Bush administration policies in academic and journalistic circles. But important changes have been endorsed at the highest level at DoD and have the support of both civilian policymakers and serving officers. The changes also antedate 9/11. That something was afoot with the military became clear late in the 1990s when then-marine commandant General Charles Krulak argued that the United States had to expect to deploy troops who would be doing three things—fighting, peacekeeping, and offering humanitarian relief—often in the same place and at the same time.

Since 2001, the military and policymakers in the security community have realized that not only were they going to be involved in operations other than traditional war, but also that they did not know very much about how to do so.[3] A key initiative came with the Defense Science Board's (DSB) "summer study" in 2004. The board used what is now a fairly standard typology of the stages of a conflict.[4] Phase 0 for conflict prevention, phases 1–3 for precombat and combat operations, phase 4 for postconflict stabilization, and phase 5 for reconstruction (or reconciliation in NGO-speak).

The DSB report also made the argument that we have to assume that these operations will take up to ten years each and that we should expect to be involved in a few of them at all times, though few would be as intense as Iraq or Afghanistan.

What was new was the board's emphasis on phases 4 and 5. Their work culminated in the publication of Directive 3000.05 in late 2005. In simplest terms, the directive stated that military support to stability, security, transition, and reconstruction operations was to be as important as warfighting itself.[5]

Even more intriguing was the similarity between the DSB report and one of the most influential books on conflict resolution, Michael Lund's *Preventing Violent Conflict*.[6] Most people who teach courses in international conflict resolution use Lund's curve that all but mirrors the DSB's formulation. From private communications with the authors of both reports, we know that the DSB was not aware of Lund's work and that as far as Hauss knows, no one in the NGO world has read the DSB report other than people he sent it to.

At about the same time, President Bush extended the logic of 3000.05 to the civilian side of the government in NSPD 44 (National Security Presidential Directive).[7] Most notably, it charged S/CRS (State/Coordinator for Reconstruction and Stabilization) as the lead civilian office for this work. Although S/CRS is housed at the Department of State, it was established to bring together participants from all the relevant civilian departments and agencies, as well as from the military.

This line of thinking was reinforced by the 2006 Quadrennial Defense Review (QDR). It makes almost no mention of a military role in conflict prevention and resolution, but its emphasis on "long wars" implies that the military is going to be doing a lot more than just fighting battles. That said, the QDR was inspired in large part by the realization that "phase 0" operations would have to be a major part of its work with potential allies and adversaries in conflict-prone zones. Reveron's chapter in this book captures the full scope of phase 0 operations.

Even more than any doctrinal statement or interagency collaboration, the DoD has been driven by concerns that it had not expected before 9/11. From a military perspective, the new challenges are daunting in large part because they are so outside the parameters of what the military did before the end of the Cold War. Nevertheless, a desire for change is percolating up from the ranks of serving officers. In part, it reflects their desire to simply do their jobs well, as reflected in the popularity of a website, companycommander.com, that a group of captains created to share with each other their frustrations with their own commanders. Very few serving officers have gone public with their concerns, although many do so privately. One rare exception is the summer 2007 article by Lt. Colonel Paul Yingling, who has served in both Bosnia and Iraq and has taught political science at West Point.[8]

Officers, including General David Petraeus, who have seen the importance of all the phases of war, have concentrated their efforts on what one marine colonel called "making momma happy" as part of postwar reconstruction. Australian colonel David Kilkullen, arguably the world's leading counterinsurgency expert, has argued that victory in a place like Iraq cannot be won by military means alone. Kilkullen serves as one of the core group of advisors working with General Petraeus.[9]

General Petraeus may be best known for championing what the Bush administration calls "the surge," or the sharp increase in the number of troops assigned to Iraq to try to quell the insurgency. Far less publicized, though, is his extensive background as a peacekeeper in Haiti, Bosnia, and Kuwait. Further, he was one of the few commanders who were successful in forging stability and starting reconstruction when he commanded the 101st Airborne's occupation of Mosul and Nineveh. In large part this was because "he made momma happy."

The U.S. military has had little choice but to pay more attention to postcombat reconstruction, stabilization, and reconciliation. This is also true of most North Atlantic Treaty Organization (NATO) countries that have an office akin to S/CRS. Indeed, many have gone further than the United States in developing such capacities inside the military. One example is the Canadian military, which has long required that all cadets at the Royal Military College take a year-long course on peacekeeping. The lead instructor for the course, David Last, is a recently retired colonel (and Ph.D. in political science) who was one of the first officers to work seriously with NGOs, dating back to his service in Bosnia. As early as 1992, Last made contact with the Canadian peace movement on the (mistaken) assumption that it could help him design a peace garden in Cyprus, where he was then serving as a peacekeeper.

To reinforce the importance of phase 4 operations, many DoD officials have clearly been arrested by a statistic in Thomas Barnett's *The Pentagon's New Map*.[10] Fully half of the conflicts that come to an end through some sort of cease-fire or treaty break out in violence again within five years. Thus, there is a growing sense of urgency about phase 0 operations. Put as simply as possible, preventing violence from breaking out at all is preferable to intervening to end it and having to pick up the pieces afterward. It may well be that the quagmire in Iraq and Afghanistan will spur efforts in this direction. As planners anticipate where and how the military might be called on to intervene in the future, their attention may often be drawn to the prevention of conflicts. Thus, in a recent paper based on a fact-finding mission to countries from Darfur to Niger, Colonel Cindy Jebb of West Point and three of her fellow colonels wrote about the need to protect human security in all its aspects if the kind of fighting we currently see in Darfur is to be prevented from spreading westward.

Although we have no hard evidence for this assertion, it seems to us that the values and the culture of the military have changed more than they have in such agencies as the State Department and the U.S. Agency for International Development (USAID). The sweeping changes advocated by the likes of Barnett, Jebb, or Kilkullen are a contrast to the limited reforms proposed by Dennis Ross, arguably the most innovative diplomat of our time.[11]

Just as important were other events that started as natural rather than human disasters. The most important was the tsunami that devastated much of Asia in the days after Christmas 2004. The navy deployed the carrier *Abraham Lincoln* and the hospital ship, *Mercy*, to Indonesia. Two things became clear very quickly. First, the military can work with NGOs when they share a common purpose. After all, who is in favor of a tsunami? Second, the U.S. military has capacities that no other organization in the world can match. The *Lincoln* was able to generate as much as 100,000 gallons of drinkable water a day. Its crew of 5,000–6,000 approaches the number of Foreign Service Officers at the State Department.

The corporate sector is also now involved. Microsoft, for instance, has an office of humanitarian relief, which is run by a veteran aid worker from the World Health Organization (WHO). In August 2006, a group of military and civilian relief workers who had worked together since the 1990s organized the Strong Angel III demonstration in which they examined responses to a complex humanitarian emergency—in this case, a simultaneous terrorist attack and outbreak of pandemic flu in San Diego. One of the organizers of Strong Angel has retired from the navy and took the lead of InSTEDD (Innovative Support to Emergencies, Diseases and Disasters), an independent entity started with funding from Google.

During the week in which we finished this chapter, the National Defense University hosted a demonstration project for the STAR-TIDES nonprofit research project[12] that is investigating ways to support stressed populations with (1) information sharing, (2) low-cost logistics and (3) social networks. The focus is on approaches that are easy to use in disaster zones, postwar stabilization, and economic development, including but not limited to

1. shelters, including the "hexayurts," demonstrated in 2006 at Strong Angel 3; the "ShelterBox," begun by a Rotary Club in the United Kingdom (UK); "Uni-Fold" prefabricated accordion shelters; and more;
2. simple water-purification systems;
3. cooking systems, such as high-efficiency wood gas stoves and solar cookers;
4. solar panels charging AA batteries for distribution to the settlement members (other renewables may be included—e.g., wind and micro-hydro);
5. lighting, heating, and cooling approaches;
6. sanitation infrastructures concepts;
7. information and communications technologies (ICT), including collaboration tools and identity/privilege management approaches suitable for austere environments.

STAR-TIDES development continues and subsequently has supported decision makers addressing real-world contingencies such as the Southern California fires and Bangladesh floods.

In sum, leadership at DoD increasingly has come to recognize that without the ability to engage effectively with civil-military mission partners (including NGOs, aid organizations, and commercial firms) outside the boundaries of the DoD enterprise, they *cannot* achieve the social, political, and economic goals for which military forces are increasingly committed. Such engagement is not a nice-to-have adjunct to the kinetic phases of war, but needs to be a core part of national and military strategy.

This requires the ability to share unclassified information across the boundaries of military networks. This means that we all need to communicate using similar information and communications technologies (ICT), whatever our home organizations. But ICT alone will not be enough. What policies should govern how much information we share with each other, especially when some of it may be based on classified sources? Moreover, underlying networks should be independent of local unreliable power, and should be supported by lift to put them in place quickly.

These capabilities are needed now, from Iraq to Haiti to the southern Philippines, and they will be needed in the future for other stabilization and reconstruction, humanitarian assistance, and disaster relief missions. They can also be used to build the capacity of nations to prevent conflicts. Many of these issues can become opportunities as the structure of the new Africa Command (AFRICOM) is put in place, since an assumption is that civilians in government and in NGOs will have to be part of its work if it is going to succeed.

Critics have properly pointed out shortcomings in the new statements from the Bush administration. Directive 3000.05 calls for a massive shift in DoD priorities, something that cannot happen quickly or easily in such a large and hierarchical organization.[13] Similarly, S/CRS remains seriously underfunded and understaffed, and it is by no means clear how much career diplomats are willing to work with NGOs, let alone with DoD.

Our point is not to make a case about Iraq, but simply to note that many of the men and women who have served in this century's wars see the need for change.

We see similar changes in the civilian side of government. Hauss recently interviewed a senior state department officer who joined the department because he believed that Secretary Condoleezza Rice was serious in her commitment to "transformative diplomacy."

Convergence: The NGOs

Change in the NGO community is far less uniform and often far less enthusiastic. This should hardly be surprising, if for no other reason than that NGOs tend to be anything but hierarchically organized, and many intentionally try to avoid anything that smacks of military-like discipline.

The NGOs have also been less consistent because they are far more varied than the military. There are dozens of types of NGOs, including those that focus on human rights, humanitarian relief, development, conflict resolution, the environment, and more. They also vary tremendously in size. Some have no more than a handful of employees; others, such as World Vision, have annual budgets well in excess of $1 billion. Some operate only in one or two locations; others have a presence just about everywhere. Some raise their money privately, while others hold large government contracts.

We will limit our attention to two kinds of NGOs: U.S.-based humanitarian and conflict resolution NGOs that have significant operations in other countries. We do so because their reaction to cooperation with the military has been rather different and tells us a lot about the challenges both sets of "odd couples" face.

Humanitarian groups tend to work "on the ground" even when a conflict is at its height. Organizations like Doctors Without Borders have built their reputations for their courageous work under the most dangerous of circumstances. Many are reluctant to work closely with the military. Doing so can put them in danger. What's more, many of the senior leaders of their umbrella association, Interaction, think that working directly with the military compromises their neutrality. This has been a particularly difficult issue in Iraq and Afghanistan, where many NGOs have decided to leave or not to start projects.

What's more, there is a deep wariness toward the military among most NGOs. At the conferences and workshops we attend, you have no trouble figuring out who the soldiers and who the NGO representatives are, even before the former put on their dress uniforms for the formal photograph.

But the chasm between the two worlds is shrinking. Humanitarian NGOs have typically been "on the ground" before the military arrives and will still be there when the troops leave. Just as the military understands it needs the expertise of the NGOs, the NGOs are coming to appreciate the resources that the military can bring to a humanitarian effort.[14]

Still, the wariness continues. The humanitarian and development NGOs typically believe that they have to maintain strict neutrality toward all government actors. However, the development of protocols for military/NGO interactions in combat zones has gone a long way toward improving these relationships. Perhaps even more important than the protocols themselves is the fact that it was largely brokered by a retired air force officer who is now on the staff of the United States Institute for Peace (USIP). Indeed, it is a sign of how much the military and NGOs are willing to work together that USIP has stepped in to help the two communities work with each other.[15] Similar discussions are taking place between conflict resolution NGOs and the military and civilian contractors through the International Peace Operations Association.

Many humanitarian NGOs are still reluctant to be too close to the military in the field. Washington is a different story. There is little or no danger for either side to meet regularly there. As a result, Interaction recently created a staff position to build relationships with the military. Many of its larger member organizations have security officers who try to do the same.

The conflict resolution NGOs are different. They are also smaller. More than 150 groups belong to Interaction, and the Alliance for Peacebuilding has about fifty. Search for Common Ground is one of the Alliance's largest members, but with a budget of about $20 million, it is dwarfed by many of Interaction's members of Interaction.

That said, conflict resolution groups have been more open to working with the military than their humanitarian counterparts because they see neutrality in different terms. Their operating assumption is that NGOs have to work actively with all the parties to a dispute if any progress is going to be made in settling it. And, in most of the conflict-wracked regions of the world, the military is one of those parties.

September 11 was a shock for NGOs, especially for those based in Washington and New York. The adjustment was difficult. A number of leaders in the field were talking privately and sometimes writing openly about what should be done. Some, but by no means all of them, came to the conclusion that they could *not* come up with a nonviolent response to 9/11. Even the people who opposed the war in Afghanistan understood the need to hold al Qaeda responsible for what it had done.

A number of NGOs, or at least individuals in NGOs, saw the need to work with the military. The predecessor of the Alliance for Peacebuilding helped the United States Military Academy develop a course, Winning the Peace, that is taken by cadets majoring in the social sciences. Others were invited to places like the Peace Keeping and Stabilization Operations Institute at the Army War College. Some worked directly with the Joint Forces Command. Two or three people even got security clearances.

Like the humanitarian groups, some conflict resolution NGOs worried that they would be tainted by close cooperation with the military or that they might have their integrity compromised. But, DoD officials made it clear that they did not need or want NGO help in phases 1–3. They also understood from the beginning that it would be easier for the NGOs and DoD to work together in Washington than in the field, where having e-mails from .mil addresses on one's laptop could be tantamount to a death sentence if it were stolen.

Iraq slowed things down. Almost no one in the NGO world supported the war. Few of the conflict resolution NGOs were willing to work in Iraq; none would take money from the U.S. government. But as the conflict dragged on and on, the NGOs had to admit that, like the government, they lacked good ideas for stabilizing the situation in a way that would allow Iraqis to rebuild their society and American troops to leave.

Like Interaction, the Alliance for Peacebuilding has created a position to coordinate its work with all U.S. agencies, not just the military. Representatives from the military, S/CRS, and USAID attended its annual retreat in 2007.[16]

Eastern Mennonite University (a member of the Alliance) has been running a project it calls "3D Security" for development and diplomacy as well as defense.[17] So far, the organization has opened an office on Capitol Hill so it can engage in lobbying.

Finally, there is a growing convergence among humanitarian and conflict resolution NGOs themselves. Many of the humanitarian and development organizations have realized that they cannot build a country's infrastructure if the hospitals or schools or roads they help build are destroyed in future combat. Therefore, some of the largest of them, including World Vision, MercyCorps, and the Catholic Relief Services, have created conflict resolution practices. Meanwhile, conflict resolution groups have realized that they have to do more than just help forge agreements that bring fighting to an end. Creating what Kenneth Boulding called stable or lasting peace more than twenty years ago requires meeting the kinds of human needs that Colonel Jebb and her colleagues wrote about. That is the only way to address the issues that gave rise to conflict in the first place.

What Has Been Done

We think we have been able to accomplish a lot. Clearly we have come a long way in five years; however, as the military might say, the deliverables have been limited.

Our greatest and longest-lasting accomplishments have come in humanitarian relief, which is the "low hanging fruit" of our endeavors. After all, no one is in favor of a tsunami or a devastating hurricane. Building on the experience that culminated in the Strong Angel and related exercises, we have seen a team of dedicated military officials and NGO professionals who have been working together for at least a decade. The same individuals keep reappearing in disaster zones ranging from the invasion of Iraq to the tsunami to the earthquake in Pakistan. The tsunami, in particular, showed the NGOs what DoD—and only DoD—can do, given its vast resources. And, because this was the first time that massive numbers of troops and NGOs hit the ground running at the same time, they had to cooperate and, despite a few glitches, found it fairly easy to do so. It was not as easy in Iraq and Afghanistan, where the Office of the Secretary of Defense (OSD) forced civil affairs and other officers to break most lines of communications with NGOs, at least in country. The weaknesses were most obvious in the aftermath of Hurricane Katrina, when it was almost two weeks before the military joined the relief effort in any significant way. While the NGOs probably learned more than the military from these efforts, the military had a steep learning curve as well. It began to realize just how counterproductive many information-sharing restrictions can be—for example, those that prohibit NGO representatives from seeing maps based on unclassified imagery. More intriguingly, a lot of military personnel were on the ground in Banda Aceh after the tsunami and saw how local and international NGOs were able to work with the Indonesian authorities and rebels to end a revolution that had wracked the region for more than a generation.

A second area of some—and great potential—success is in education and training. Many rising officers who have come back from Afghanistan and Iraq understand that the young men and women under their command need to understand far more than they do about other cultures and about techniques for conflict resolution. Therefore, both the Marines and the Joint Forces Command are negotiating with a small NGO for online and other forms of electronically distributed conflict resolution training. As yet, the flag officers who need to approve such projects have not bought into them.

That said, the NGO community is actively involved in expanding education and training at the military academies, the command and staff colleges, and the war colleges, epitomized by the Winning the Peace course at West Point. As noted earlier, it was jointly developed by the NGO community, the permanent military faculty at the academy, and two faculty members on short-term tours who have rotated out to the Joint Forces Command and Tikrit, Iraq, respectively.

The Academy's catalog describes the course as follows:

> This course helps prepare future lieutenants for what else they need to know while deployed besides military tactics and strategy. Bringing together subject matter experts from BS&L, DFL, DMI, English, G&EnE, History, Law, SOSH, U.S. governmental agencies, IGOs, and NGOs, we cover topics as varied as counterinsurgency, cultural awareness, players on the ground, governance and economics, and legal, moral, and ethical considerations leaders will face while deployed. We also spend a night and several days in a multiethnic U.S. city interacting with Egyptian Copts, Muslims, Hindus, and various Christian denominations to more fully

understand how groups with different beliefs can live and work together. This course aims to help create "soldier statesmen" at the Company Grade level for the U.S. Army, and is open to any interested junior or senior.

Since the catalog went to press, the academy has also gotten a major grant from the John D. and Catherine T. McArthur Foundation to fund internships for cadets interested in working with NGOs in the developing world.

The other academies have not gone as far, but the Air Force Academy drew on a colonel already on the faculty who holds a Ph.D. in conflict resolution to help ease on-campus tensions surrounding the role of evangelical Christians.

With the support of Congressman Sam Farr (a former Peace Corps volunteer), the Naval Postgraduate School now has a degree-granting program in postconflict studies. The Peace Keeping and Stabilization Operations Institute at the Army War College has a veteran NGO leader on its staff. More generally, the faculties at the war colleges have diversified their permanent and visiting faculty to reflect the various demands of the post–9/11 world.

Again, the learning process goes both ways. The military students get a crash course about the world of NGOs, and the NGO representatives learn just how smart and thoughtful academy cadets and war college students are.

There is also a move afoot to bring the NGO community more squarely into the policymaking process. This is occurring through what is called the interagency process. It is a concerted effort not only to foster cooperation within the government, but also increasingly to include NGO representatives in broad policy discussions. This, of course, extends far beyond the military. However, given the relative size of the personnel and budget of DoD compared to that of all the other civilian agencies combined, the military is at the heart of these efforts.

Finally, although it may not be concrete, the most important development of the deliverables is that we are talking to each other. One event at a conference we attended suggests how important "mere" talking can be. The Highlands Forum organized a session on NGO/DoD cooperation that was held at a small hotel near Gettysburg, Pennsylvania. We were taken around the battlefield by James McPherson, the leading historian of the war and the battle. McPherson then came back to the hotel for dinner and led a group of senior DoD and NGO leaders in a discussion of the parallels between what was unfolding in Iraq and what happened in the American South after the Civil War. By the time the evening was over, we realized that we are all in the same boat, a boat we can keep afloat only by working together.

As we argue in the next section, we live in very different cultures. Especially for people of our generation, there is a significant amount of ignorance and mistrust between the military and the NGOs, though we are delighted that this is less of a problem among people a generation younger than we are.

It has, quite frankly, taken us a long time to develop the levels of trust that cooperation on controversial subjects requires. Certainly, the two of us have reached that point, not just with each other, but also with dozens of other people on either side of what seems to be a disappearing divide.

Problems on the Horizon

Do not think that all of this is occurring quickly or easily. It is not.

To begin with, as noted above, we live and work in very different worlds. One of the things we learned after 9/11 was just how little conflict resolution professionals and academics knew about national security. The military's lack of knowledge about NGOs was only slightly less.

One trivial but symbolically important story tells it all. Wells asked one of his then-deputies, Spanky Kirsch, to work with Hauss and others on NGO and OSD cooperation. The two of them agreed to meet for lunch at Kramerbooks and Afterwards, which Washington insiders know is not a place conservative Republicans tend to frequent. Kirsch had a meeting at a think tank five or six blocks away on K Street. Instead of walking for five minutes on Connecticut Avenue, he got on the Metro and managed to get lost. The lunch took place and Kirsch decided that he could enjoy the world of the tree-huggers. Then, Wells and Kirsch invited Hauss to a meeting at the Pentagon. Hauss asked Kirsch (who had to escort him) how many people worked in the building. Twenty-three thousand. How many other conscientious objectors were in the building? None. Hauss simultaneously realized that the last time he had been in the building, the French were still fighting in Vietnam.

Kirsch fell in love with Kramerbooks. Hauss showed off his stack of yellow Pentagon visitors' badges and introduced Kirsch as his younger, Catholic, and conservative brother, as he does whenever they go to meetings together.

Getting to this point has taken time and hard work, and there aren't a lot of people in the NGO world who are comfortable working with the Pentagon. In the conflict resolution world, that number may not top thirty. It is higher among humanitarian and development NGOs, but not by much.

Funding is always an issue. Most foundations that have traditionally funded NGOs are not likely to do so for DoD-related work. But there is also reluctance on the part of many in the NGO community to take funding from DoD, which is the source of many potential grants and consulting contracts.

In addition, much of what we could do together requires security clearances. That is true, for instance, for attending most predeployment training exercises. However, as far as we know, only two conflict resolution NGO professionals have one. Hauss does not, because he doesn't want to even be accused of working with classified material.

Finally, we do disagree. We do not view Iraq the same way. We are closer on Afghanistan, but differences still exist and probably will on most issues our country faces in the years to come.

Bowling Together

The bottom line for this chapter is that we encourage our colleagues in the worlds of the NGOs and DoD to keep searching for ways to work together that reflect one of the most important new concepts introduced into political science in our professional lifetimes.

In *Bowling Alone*, Robert Putnam addresses civic engagement and social capital in the United States.[18] In a portion of the book that has not gotten enough attention, Putnam stresses the need for "bridging" social capital in which we literally build bridges across ideological or cultural divides. We don't have to agree, but we do have to talk. We have to build trust. We have to at least come close to laughing when we disagree.

That is what we do.

Notes

1. The positions presented in this article do not represent either those of the Defense Department or those of the Alliance for Peacebuilding. We would like to thank Dick O'Neill, Spanky Kirsch, Eric Rasmussen, Dave Warner, Gretchen Sandles, Tina Schweiss, Cindy Jebb, John Agoglia, and Chic Dambach for helping us clarify our views.
2. Matthew Hersey and Charles Hauss, *Terrorism and Conflict Resolution*, in *Terrorism: Concepts, Causes and Conflict Resolution*, ed. Dennis Sandole and R. Scott Moore (Fort Belvoir/Arlington, VA: Defense Threat Reduction Agency and the Institute for Conflict Analysis and Resolution, 2002), 130–142.
3. Some would argue that DoD has had experience with these sorts of operations in the Balkans, in Kurdistan, and in other operations going back as far as the Philippine American war. If so, there are many lessons that need to be relearned.
4. http://www.acq.osd.mil/dsb/reports/2004-12-DSB_SS_Report_Final.pdf.
5. http://www.dtic.mil/whs/directives/corres/html/300005.htm.
6. Washington: United States Institute of Peace, 1996.
7. http://www.fas.org/irp/offdocs/nspd/nspd-44.html.
8. Lt. Col. Paul Yingling, "A Failure in Generalship," *Armed Forces Journal*, May 2007, http://www.armedforcesjournal.com/2007/05/2635198.
9. George Packer, "Knowing the Enemy," *New Yorker*, December 16, 2006.
10. New York: Putnam, 2004.
11. Dennis Ross, *Statecraft* (New York: Farrar, Straus, and Giroux, 2007).
12. TIDES stands for Transportable Infrastructures for Development and Emergency Support. It is part of a broad research effort called STAR (Sustainable Technologies, Accelerated Research), hence the overall title STAR-TIDES. More information is at www.star-tides.net.
13. However, progress is being made. The uniformed leadership of the navy, Marine Corps and coast guard cosigned the "Maritime Strategy" in November 2007. One of its key points is that preventing war is as important as winning it. Similarly, the army revised its Operations Manual (FM 3-0) in February 2008 to incorporate many of the principles of 3000.05. So changes are underway, but an important question is whether the national security organizations can adapt fast enough to meet the challenges also underway in the rest of the world.
14. http://www.interaction.org.
15. http://www.usip.org/pubs/guidelines_pamphlet.pdf.
16. http://www.allianceforpeacebuilding.org.
17. http://www.3dsecurity.org.
18. Robert D. Putnam, *Bowling Alone* (New York: Simon and Schuster, 2000).

21

The Citizen-Soldier, Then and Now: The National Guard, Military Reserves, and ROTC

David L. Leal

When we assumed the Soldier, we did not lay aside the Citizen.

—*George Washington*

Introduction

This chapter discusses the theory and reality of the citizen-soldier, as both have proven important to the design and use of America's military forces. Concerns about the military in general and standing armies in particular were derived from, and caused by, the British. Such fears were particularly common in the founding era, and this cultural inheritance and the resulting constitutional design are essential to understanding the structure, size, and effectiveness of the American military.

Despite ten recent decades featuring two world wars, a Cold War, a "military-industrial complex," the events of 9/11, and two wars with Iraq, the U.S. armed forces would not be unrecognizable to the founding fathers. While they might be concerned about a large standing army, they would likely appreciate the essential role of "citizen-soldiers"—today, Reservists and the National Guard—in waging war. The American system of national and state militaries—built on a dual reserve and active duty system—is unique. While this is not always maximally effective in operational terms, it does maintain the world's most powerful military with little serious concern about its commitment to democracy, the Constitution, and civilian leadership.

This chapter, therefore, discusses three facets of the citizen-soldier: the National Guard, the national military Reserves, and the Reserve Officers Training

Corps (ROTC). In all three organizations, civilians engage in a part-time military role and thereby live in two worlds. In an era of substantial military engagement, there is growing concern about a gap between a military that is at war and a nation that is not. For many civilians, the citizen-soldier is the only connection they may have to the contemporary military. In the absence of a draft, the citizen-soldier serves as a rare bridge between the civilian and military worlds—and thereby makes real the global politics headlines that often seem disconnected from everyday American life.

The Citizen-Soldier Tradition

The story of the citizen-soldier begins in ancient Greece and Rome, and this model was on the minds of many during the Revolutionary War. According to Thomas Jefferson, it was necessary for "every citizen to be a soldier; this was the case with the Greeks and Romans and must be that of every free state."[1]

Discussed by thinkers ranging from Machiavelli to Adam Smith to Rousseau, the citizen-soldier can have different meanings and purposes. Cohen (1985, 122) noted that the citizen-soldier has been applied in America to such diverse entities as the colonial Minutemen and the contemporary All Volunteer Force (AVF)—but he asks what it means. In ancient Athens and Sparta—and a few contemporary nations like Switzerland—it meant that *all* male citizens, young and old, were also soldiers. Military obligation may not entirely capture the citizen-soldier ideal, however. For some, it indicates not only that citizens serve, but also that service imparts values that are useful for citizenship and that may in fact be necessary for citizenship. According to this view, military service "instilled in individuals the virtues necessary for self-governance aimed at the common good—selflessness, courage, camaraderie, patriotism, and civic virtue" (Snyder 1999, 8). Simply enrolling large numbers of civilians into the military is not enough; the citizen-soldier can be seen as a normative ideal that connects service with subsequent civic participation. In fact, there is abundant evidence that, at least in the United States, veterans participate in politics at higher rates than do nonveterans (Ellison 1992; Leal 1999; Leal and Teigen 2003). However, Snyder and Cohen observed that such a definition would exclude many from citizenship, including women (at some points in American history), those who do not meet physical or educational standards, and some immigrants.

Perhaps the citizen-soldier can be seen as a brake on tyranny; he or she is "not merely a soldier who can vote, but a sort of civilian-soldier" (Cohen 1985, 123). Yet Cohen notes that the twentieth century saw examples of nations with universal service but no freedom. He wrote that

> in liberal-democratic states, the true political argument for the use of citizen-soldiers is more subtle . . . To use a metaphor from business, in a cadre/conscript system the citizenry are day-laborers, not stockholders, persons whose services are needed and used, but who have no control over the enterprise of which they are part. According to this view the most proper as well as the most effective defense of nation rests with those with the largest stake in it.

There is nothing new about debates concerning the proper relations between armies and the societies they are tasked to protect. Many have concluded that the best guarantee of safety from armies is to make them resemble the general populace. Eighteenth-century British commentator William Blackstone (1979) wrote the following:

> To prevent the executive power from being able to oppress, says baron Montesquieu, it is requisite that the armies with which it is entrusted should consist of the people, and have the same spirit with the people . . . Nothing then, according to these principles, ought to be more guarded against in a free state, than making the military power, when such a one is necessary to be kept on foot, a body too distinct from the people.

Americans have long worried about the consequences of maintaining a large standing army. As Weigley (2001, 219) noted, "American colonists fully accepted the Whig antimilitary tradition and indeed integrated it into American political culture."

Despite such reservations, the colonies were not in a position to ignore military issues (Barber 1972, 299). Conflicts with Native Americans and fears of European incursions meant that some kind of military force was necessary. The colonists drew on their English heritage to create a militia system whereby all able-bodied, free white males were subject to brief calls for defensive purposes. By 1640, militias were in place in Connecticut, Maryland, Massachusetts, and Virginia; by 1671, the other six colonies had followed suit (Riker 1957, 11). Goldich (1985) noted that such militia were locally drawn, objected to extended service, and were reluctant to serve far from home. While individuals recognized the need to serve in certain locales, the system would essentially collapse in places where there was no direct threat.

Nevertheless, militias provided the backbone of the Minutemen and the Continental Army during the Revolutionary War. Cooper (1997) noted that at the start of the American Revolution, many citizens wanted to be soldiers, but this fad soon faded, and the Continental Army shrank. The colonies sought to avoid drafting men, preferring to recruit volunteers through land bounties and cash. The Continental Congress did set quotas by colony, and most colonies conscripted some men from their state militias into the Continental Army (Goldich 1985). However, "Response to this system was unenthusiastic and spotty, and it did not solve the never ending recruiting and strength problems of the Continental Army" (17).

Other problems with the militia system included the short terms of recruits and a shortage of federal money for pay and supplies. Some men simply refused to serve; others were ill-trained and ill-equipped; many left when their terms were up; and others served only reluctantly.

Nevertheless, the founding fathers worried that any army—even their own—was a potential source of tyranny. The army was almost entirely disbanded in 1784 after several troubling events, and at one point it was reduced to eighty men (Goldich 1985, 18). The American defense plan was to rely on a navy, a small army, and state militias.

The republic did strengthen the military powers of the federal government when it replaced the Articles of Confederation with the Constitution. The new Constitution explicitly gave the national government more military power and authority, although suspicions remained that the changes could lead to tyranny. This fear, as well as the typical state-national concerns that were prominent in the minds of the convention delegates, created a force with both state and national elements. Most prominently, the Constitution makes reference to both a national army and navy, as well as to state militias. Congress also received unlimited power to maintain an army, albeit with a two-year time limit for appropriations. According to Huntington (167), "Few provisions in the Constitution were agreed to with more reluctance." The constitutional militia clauses essentially put the militia under state control in peace and dual control in war. There were varied reactions. During the Virginia ratifying convention, Patrick Henry charged that

> your militia is given up to Congress, also, in another part of this plan: they will therefore act as they think proper: all power will be in their own possession . . . By this, sir, you see that their control over our last and best defense is unlimited. If they neglect or refuse to discipline or arm our militia, they will be useless: the states can do neither—this power being exclusively given to Congress. The power of appointing officers over men not disciplined or armed is ridiculous; so that this pretended little remains of power left to the states may, at the pleasure of Congress, be rendered nugatory.[2]

Arguing in favor of the militia clause in Federalist No. 29, Alexander Hamilton wrote the following:

> Where in the name of common sense are our fears to end if we may not trust our sons, our brothers, our neighbours, our fellow-citizens? What shadow of danger can there be from men who are daily mingling with the rest of their countrymen; and who participate with them in the same feelings, sentiments, habits and interests?[3]

The reliance on a militia system continued into the mid-twentieth century. American armies and navies were kept small and underfunded except in times of war—"to arm hastily in time of war, and to disarm with even greater haste in time of peace" (Barber 1972, 301). Goldich (1985, 18) noted that since the system had worked—in the sense that defeat was avoided in the Revolutionary War and the War of 1812, not to mention in other frontier conflicts—the new nation saw no reason to change.

More generally, Huntington noted that Americans traditionally saw large military forces as a threat to liberty, a threat to democracy, a threat to economic prosperity, and a threat to peace. One reaction is the policy of transmutation, whereby the distinctly military nature of the armed forces is reduced. This is found in the historic reliance on the militia, as well as in the quote by Josephus Daniels in 1915: "You cannot have an institution in America that is not Americanized" (157).

The Evolution of the National Guard

The development of the National Guard from state and local militias is chronicled by Cooper (1997) and Fogelson (1989), from which this section is largely drawn except where noted. The Militia Act of 1792 confirmed the place of the militia and implemented the Constitutional militia provisions. It required compulsory enrollment by all free, white, able-bodied males between the ages of eighteen and forty-five. Members of the militia were required to use their own weapons and equipment, and they could not be called to service by the president for more than three months per year (Goldich 1985, 16). Despite this legislation, the state militias were largely ignored by Congress, which provided little guidance or financing.

This system largely collapsed by the 1830s. Men were uninterested in serving, and the states were unwilling to compel participation. The existing militias were composed of a wide variety of volunteer units that spontaneously emerged from the 1830s to the Civil War. The reliance on such units was a concession to reality, not a deliberate policy change (Cooper 1997, 15).

These militia units were essentially private associations with much in common with fraternal organizations. They were largely cohesive along ethnic, occupational, and class lines, and they elected their own officers, designed their own uniforms, raised private funds, wrote their own rules, and experienced little state regulation (Fogelson 1989, 5). The units "attracted both native Americans, seeking to preserve the cohesion of their communities, and newcomers, trying to create cohesive communities of their own" (Fogelson 1989, 7). However, armed ethnic units were sometimes viewed with alarm by native-born whites, and some state governments disbanded or confiscated weapons from ethnic or Roman Catholic units (Snyder 1999).[4]

A key problem was that volunteer units were poorly trained and the officers poorly qualified. Huntington (1957) noted that when the militia was called out—as during the War of 1812 and the Spanish-American War—the result was sometimes chaotic and featured national-state bickering. In addition, the use of amateur soldiers could prove problematic. Mahon (1983) noted the cruelty of some militia toward Native Americans and Mexicans during frontier wars and the Mexican-American War. Regular soldiers sometimes had to come to the rescue of civilians to prevent volunteer atrocities.

During the Civil War, states made some effort to reinvigorate their militias, but most soldiers and sailors were recruited as volunteers or conscripts through centralized, national efforts. By 1873, fifteen of thirty-seven states reported no militia forces, although a few provided significant financial support. Some states called these forces the National Guard; other states used a variety of names, including the Indiana Legion and the Massachusetts Volunteer Militia.

The volunteer militias occasionally served a police purpose, especially during strikes (Fogelson 1989, 7–8). A number of events, in particular the 1877 railroad strike, created a fear of impending class warfare. Local police forces were not very developed, were easily overwhelmed during a strike or civil disorder, and were sometimes sympathetic to the strikers. While the regular army was a potential alternative, its use was opposed by southerners with memories of Reconstruction and by others who saw the potential of tyranny in an army operating domestically. Given the nature of these units, many performed poorly. This led to reforms, including increased state funding, the construction of large and expensive armories, and an emphasis on tactical knowledge and drill. Most states changed their military codes to divide the militia into (1) active and organized units known as the National Guard and (2) all other able-bodied men into an inactive category (Skowronek 1982, 104). While militia effectiveness grew, many Guardsmen wanted to focus on military training, as the role of labor policeman was not seen as interesting, glamorous, or appropriate.

A variety of forces opposed National Guard reforms. Some in the regular army wanted to replace the National Guard with a national reserve. Some state politicians and party machines opposed greater federal involvement, as they feared losing the patronage of appointing guard officers (Skowronek 1982, 96). A key event was the Spanish-American War in 1898, when "in the eyes of the Army, and many historians, the Guard failed miserably" (Cooper 1997, 97). The mobilization was chaotic, disease swept army camps, some guardsmen refused to serve, and some states told guardsmen that they were not obliged to serve. As Cooper (1997, 106) observed, there was a belief that "the individual's right to refuse to volunteer was implicit in the ethos of the nineteenth-century republican citizen soldier. By its very definition, volunteering was an act of conscience and patriotism, not an obligation."

The National Guard as we know it today was created by the federal Dick Act (or Militia Act) of 1903. This was a significant triumph for the Guard and the National Guard Association. According to Riker (1957, 61), "Considering that the chief officials of the Regular Army had during four generations distrusted the militia and had built up a military theory that had no role for it, the Dick Act represents also a great triumph of state bureaucracies over the national one."

The act abolished the nonvolunteer militia codified by tradition and the Militia Act of 1792. The old unorganized militia was now called the "reserve militia," while the National Guard became the "organized militia." The latter would receive federal support, and the law gave the president authority to call them to federal service for nine months to stop an invasion, suppress insurrection, or enforce federal law. Amendments in 1908 eliminated the time limit and specified that service could be outside the United States.

In 1916 Congress passed the National Defense Act, which created the Reserve Officers Training Corps (ROTC), reorganized the army, created an Organized Reserve Corps, and significantly changed the Guard. It allowed the president to decide the organization, branch, and tasks of Guard units; set uniform enlistment standards; required officers to pass federal tests; lengthened annual drill time; and required Guardsmen to take dual state and national oaths. The president was also allowed to draft Guardsmen into federal service with congressional authorization, and he could use a national draft during wartime to add to the ranks of the army. In exchange, federal appropriations for the Guard increased by nine times, and states were responsible only for administrative and armory costs.

According to Skowronek (1982, 232), "The most controversial section of the act [Section 1] ensured the National Guard its position as the first-line offensive reserve to be called directly after the expansion of the regular army." However, this would prove to have little meaning in twentieth-century warfare. As Fogelson (1989) noted, "World War I permanently altered the state soldiery's place in manpower policy" (171). The federal army reorganized and renamed Guard units, and while the Guard contributed 12 percent of soldiers to the war effort, this was overwhelmed by those recruited as federal volunteers and draftees. This was accentuated by similar dynamics in World War II.

The Rise of the Reserves

The creation of the army reserve is well documented in Crossland and Currie (1984), from which this section is largely drawn except where noted. This organization grew out of the debates surrounding the militia and the National Guard. In 1915, Secretary of War Lindley Garrison proposed a "Continental Army" plan, which would essentially replace the state Guard with a national Reserve. This idea was opposed by the Guard, many members of Congress, and ultimately President Woodrow Wilson (Fogelson 1989). Thus, instead of replacing the National Guard with a national Reserve, the United States simply added it.

The U.S. Army Reserve began in 1908 with the creation of a Medical Reserve Corps. Congress then created a Regular Army Reserve in 1912, which was accomplished by creating a seven-year enlistment term with about half of this time to be served in a reserve capacity.

Other branches of the armed forces also established federal and state reserve units, although this chapter concentrates on Army Reserve units because the preponderance of military personnel are in the army. There are seven reserve components, six within the Department of Defense (DoD) (Moxon 1985). In addition to the Army Reserve and the Army National Guard, these consist of the Navy Reserve (formerly the Naval Reserve; established in 1915), the Marine Corps Reserve (established in 1916), the Air Force Reserve (established in 1948), and the Air National Guard (established in 1947). The seventh is the Coast Guard Reserve (established in 1941), which was previously located in the U.S. Department of Transportation but is now within the U.S. Department of Homeland Security.

The National Defense Act of 1916 established the "Regular Army, the Volunteer Army, the Officers' Reserve Corps, the Enlisted Reserve Corps, the National Guard while in the service of the United States, and such other land forces as are now or may hereafter be authorized by law" (Crossland and Currie 1984, 28). In 1918, all distinctions between the multiple subdivisions were dropped; all Reserve, Guard, and active duty commissions were simply in the U.S. Army. The National Defense Act of 1920 redefined the army and its subunits as consisting of the Regular Army, the Organized Reserves, and the National Guard. According to Goldich (1985, 23), "When superficialities are stripped away, it can be seen that this system, firmly established by 1920, has survived to the present day."

Between the world wars, the active duty military was small. In September 1939, there were about 187,000 regulars in the army, about 200,000 National Guardsmen, and about 120,000 members of the Organized Reserve Corps (Binkin and Kaufmann 1989, 38). However, many officers on the Reserve list received little training and little pay, and the "Organized Reserve units themselves remained only skeletons, having few enlisted personnel and minimal equipment" (Crossland and Currie 1984, 53). Nevertheless, the existence of many Reserve officers trained during the interwar period was a useful resource. Over 140,000 Reserve officers were serving in active duty capacities by the end of 1942, and almost 200,000 by early 1945. From September 1, 1943, to May 31, 1944, 52.4 percent of officers killed in action were Reserve officers. In total, one-quarter of army officers were Reserve officers.

After the passage of the National Defense Act of 1947, a committee studied the Reserve and Guard components. President Harry Truman favored unification, but the idea was dropped. That year also saw the admission of women to the Reserves through membership in the nursing and medical corps, and in 1950 this was expanded to women without prior military service. The Armed Forces Reserve Act of 1952 eliminated the Officers' Reserve Corps and the Enlisted Reserve Corps. The Organized Reserve Corps became simply the Reserve.

In contrast to World War II and the Korean War, the Vietnam War saw relatively little use of the reserves. In fact, according to Binkin and Kaufmann (1989, 20–21), the Reserves "became a haven for draft-averse 'volunteers' seeking to avoid service in Vietnam. Reserve units were stripped of essential equipment and reserve training came to a virtual standstill. By the end of the 1960s, according to the official historical account, the Army Reserve was in 'disrepair and disarray,' and its 'ability to go to war was near zero.'"

The end of the draft and the beginning of the AVF led to a shortfall of personnel in the reserves, although Binkin and Kaufmann (1989, 22) argue that this was ultimately "most responsible for breathing life back into the reserves in the early 1970s." In the short term, it was problematic because the Total Force policy (discussed below) required the reserves to assume a more significant role. Yet the reserves were no longer drawing men who did not want to serve in Vietnam, and it was neither a full-time job nor a particularly prestigious activity. This created recruiting problems, but benefits were increased, recruiting efforts were intensified, and as occurred in the active duty military during this time, the number of female enlistees increased.

The 1970s saw the adoption of the "Total Force," which meant that military operations in the future would rely on a mix of active and reserve forces, depending on the task at hand. It was officially adopted in 1973, and according to an August 23, 1973, memo from Secretary of Defense James R. Schlesinger, "Total Force is no longer a 'concept.' It is now the Total Force Policy which integrates the Active, Guard and Reserve forces into a homogenous whole" (Duncan 1997, 141).

According to Brown (1993, 53), "We have found in the total force a superb combination of federal or state governance; national or local representation; and professional or citizen-soldier competence, uniquely suited to America—a state, a nation, and a democracy—all of which reflect the diversity of a continent."

More important, the reorganization meant that the nation would have difficulty engaging in extended operations without using all three components. No longer could the United States wage a conflict almost exclusively with active duty forces, as illustrated by the current war in Iraq (Binkin and Kaufmann 1989, 34).

Guard and Reserve: Contemporary Organization and Deployments

For the Reserve and Guard, there are several organizational categories that involve time commitment, likelihood of recall to active duty, and pay. The first is the Ready Reserve, which is divided into the Select Reserve and the Individual Ready Reserve. The Select Reserve is what most people see as the Reserves. The approximate time requirement is one weekend a month and two weeks per year (in addition to any mobilizations), and Reservists receive pay for each day of training. The Individual Ready Reserve (IRR) is a nontraining status with no real time commitment and no pay. However, members of the IRR can and have been called to active duty in recent years.

The Retired Reserve consists of all former active duty or Reserve officers and enlisted personnel who receive retirement pay or benefits, as well as individuals who are eligible for retirement pay after completing the requisite number of years of service but who have not yet reached the age of sixty. The Retired Reserve has three categories, but all members are subject to recall to active duty.

The Standby Reserve contains active duty and reserve personnel who are designated as key civilian employees or are experiencing a temporary disability or hardship. They do not train and are not assigned to units. Relatively few individuals are in this category.

There are several basic paths to joining the Reserves or the National Guard. The first derives from service in the active duty military. The typical new soldier, sailor, airman, or marine signs an eight-year contract. The time is usually divided between active duty and reserve status. For instance, one might serve four years of active duty, followed by four years in a reserve status. The various branches offer different combinations.

A person may also join the Reserves or National Guard directly. Without prior service, an individual will experience Army Basic Training and Advanced Individual Training, which will determine their Military Occupational Specialty (MOS), which is called Air Force Specialty Code for those in the Air National Guard. The recruit is then placed on reserve status, which will consist mostly of Select Reserve status with sometimes two years of IRR (the Guard equivalent is called Inactive National Guard) service at the end.

The composition of the Reserves and the Guard varies significantly in terms of prior experience. The vast majority of air and navy reservists come from active duty status (Duncan 1997, 307); the proportion with prior service is much lower for the Army Reserve and the Army National Guard.[5]

While Reservists and Guardsmen have often been called "weekend warriors," this description—and the implication they were somehow "playing soldier"—is now a thing of the past (Jopar 2003). In fact, the "one weekend a month, two weeks a year" slogan is rarely heard today in light of the greater use of reserve forces in the wars in Iraq and Afghanistan.

Duncan (1997, xi) noted that during the first Gulf War, almost 246,000 Reservists and Guardsmen were ordered to active duty. Many others volunteered for humanitarian work in Operation Restore Hope in Somalia, and others volunteered for Operation Just Cause in Panama, for Operation Provide Comfort in Iraq, and for operations against drug trafficking. However, for those Reservists and Guardsmen, the first Gulf War was a one-time event, which separates it from the multideployment experience of many military personnel in this decade.

According to a Congressional Research Service report, the total number of personnel deployed to Iraq and Afghanistan from September 2001 to November 30, 2006, included over four hundred thousand in the National Guard and Reserve: 230,778 from the Guard and 181,437 from the Reserve. By comparison, just over a million (1,044,939) active duty personnel had served in these nations. This means that about 28 percent of deployed military personnel were from reserve components.[6]

A number of issues have arisen from such heavy deployments. These include the length of each deployment, the number of deployments, the amount of time between deployments, health issues, and the transition back to civilian life. A survey conducted by *Stars and Stripes* in 2003 revealed several common difficulties experienced by reservists, including differential treatment vis-à-vis active duty units, assignment to tasks they were not trained to perform, and low morale due to repeated activations (Jopar 2003). Whether such problems are widespread and whether they will translate into recruiting and retention shortfalls are unclear. Some governors are also worried that heavy National Guard deployments to Iraq deprive their states of sufficient personnel to cope with natural disasters.

In addition, the National Guard and Reserve began the war with shortages of personnel and equipment. In addition, "cross-leveling"—the practice of deploying units borrowing people and equipment from units remaining at home—is "causing chaos," according to Lt. General Jack C. Stultz, head of the Army Reserve (Tyson 2006). Local units are sometimes taken apart and the components reassembled into multistate forces, which "goes against the culture of the Reserve and particularly that of the Guard, which prides itself on building hometown teams that fight together" (Tyson 2006).

Employment issues are also a source of concern. Federal law—the Uniformed Services Employment and Reemployment Rights Act (USERRA)—guarantees reemployment for activated Reservists and prohibits discrimination against employees who serve in the Reserves. State laws cover similar issues for members of the National Guard.[7] Nevertheless, not all employers are aware of their obligations, and reservists must sue if their rights are violated.

Casualties are unfortunately inevitable with deployments. According to the Saban Center for Middle East Policy at the Brookings Institution, the total number of U.S. military fatalities from March 19, 2003, to September 1, 2007, was 3,011. The National Guard accounted for 436 and the Reserves for 287—a total of 723, or 24 percent.[8]

ROTC[9]

Another place where the civilian and military worlds interact is on the college campus. At many universities, the sight of a student in a military uniform is common. On other campuses, the military is a distant institution with few visible affiliations. Why are some students in uniform, what are they doing, what are the costs and benefits to the individual, and what are the implications for the nation? This section will discuss these questions, as well as provide a brief history of the ROTC.

ROTC: A Short History

Given long-standing American suspicions of standing armies, how did a program begin that trained military officers on college campuses? Michael Neiberg (2000) has written the most comprehensive history of ROTC, from which the following account is largely drawn. He explains that although ROTC officially started just before the U.S. entry into World War I, its roots are intertwined with those of the modern American university. While the Morrill Act of 1862 is best known for the creation of the land grant university system, it also required these institutions to offer military training. The act was unclear as to what this meant in practice, but by 1900, forty-two colleges and universities offered training programs of varied quality with War Department support.

As noted above, the National Defense Act of 1916 created ROTC, which incorporated the various existing collegiate programs. ROTC was designed to provide officers for the Reserve and National Guard, but it did not provide scholarships. It was divided into a two-year program for freshmen and sophomores, which was mandatory at many schools, followed by a two-year "Advanced Course" leading to a Reserve or Guard appointment. The 1916 act also attempted to establish a standard educational and training curriculum.

Despite relatively unenthusiastic military support, ROTC had produced 40 percent of Reserve officers by 1940. While ROTC was suspended during World War II in favor of shorter officer training programs, the availability of ROTC-trained officers was credited with playing an important role in the mobilization of the military after Pearl Harbor. ROTC was reinstated in 1946, and the 1948 Gray Commission recommended keeping it for three reasons: it was cheap, it was in the best citizen-soldier tradition, and the military needed college-educated officers who could understand new technologies.

As the military expanded during the Cold War, ROTC transitioned from preparing Reserve and Guard officers to commissioning active duty officers. In the 1960s, colleges and universities that required ROTC began to abolish this requirement, and enrollments fell. In 1964, the ROTC Revitalization Act for the first time funded a large number of scholarships (5,500); it allowed cross-enrollment by students at nearby universities, created a two-year program option, and dropped the number of "contact" hours with cadets. Enrollment increased, but some students used ROTC to postpone being drafted, and numbers substantially dropped after 1969 when the draft lottery made it clear who was likely to be called.

While a variety of alternatives to ROTC were debated during the late 1960s and early 1970s, the DoD ultimately decided to keep ROTC as the primary means of commissioning young officers. The arguments in its favor included relatively low costs; the importance of a balanced officer corps; the need for capable, flexible, and independent officers; the value of an "intellectually capable" military leadership; and the contribution of ROTC to closing civil-military gaps (Coumbe 1999).

With the implementation of the AVF in 1973, the challenge for the military was to attract students to ROTC without the motivation of the draft. Many units were initially placed on probation for having low numbers of cadets, but numbers were increased through (1) a recruiting campaign that focused on scholarships and opportunity, (2) the unrestricted admission of women, beginning with the air force in 1970, (3) a focus on increased diversity recruitment, and (4) loosened hair, uniform, and drill regulations.

Numbers

Any discussion of the officer corps will probably call to mind a picture of the military service academies at West Point, Annapolis, and Colorado Springs. However, ROTC programs produce almost twice the number of officers as do these academies.

There are 273 campuses that sponsor Army ROTC units, 71 that sponsor Navy/Marine Corps (NROTC) units, and 144 that sponsor Air Force (AFROTC) units.[10] For most service branches, the plurality of officers is commissioned through these ROTC programs. For example, in fiscal year (FY) 2004, the U.S. Military Academy at West Point commissioned 976 men and women as active duty second lieutenants. By comparison, Army ROTC programs nationwide contributed over 3,300 active duty second lieutenants—2,285 were on scholarship and 1,077 were nonscholarship participants. In addition, another 858 active duty officers were produced by Officer Candidate/ Training Schools (OCS/OTS), 724 by Direct Appointment, and 383 by other means. Thus, of the total 6,303 new U.S. Army active duty commissions, over half came from Army ROTC. For the entire DoD, of the 19,084 active duty officers commissioned in 2004, 6,866 were from army, navy, and air force ROTC units, and 3,413 were from the service academies.[11] In addition, for the 2003–2004 academic year, Army ROTC produced an additional 554 Reserve officers and 614 National Guard officers. ROTC is also an important source of racial, ethnic, and gender diversity in the military (see Leal 2007 for additional discussion of this and other ROTC topics).

The Civil-Military Gap and ROTC

The most significant recent scholarship on the civil-military gap is Feaver and Kohn's volume (2001), which outlines the problems, investigates the realities, and discusses consequences and strategies for the future. What solutions did they propose? They suggested (1) increasing the military presence in civilian society,

(2) increasing civilian understanding of the military, and (3) improving instruction on civil-military relations in professional military education. One step forward is ROTC, which "provides a singular opportunity to increase contacts between the military and future civilian leaders" (470). However, they pointed out that opponents of ROTC include not only some academics but also "bean-counters and 'culture-warriors' in the Pentagon and Congress" (470). In addition, a recent article in the Wall Street Journal (Jaffe 2007) discussed the closure of many northeastern and urban ROTC units, and Desch (2001, 322) suggested that ROTC units should be better distributed across the nation and include "elite" universities.

One reason for this geographic change is cost; there may be pressure to support "efficient" programs at southern and western state universities that produce many officers rather than smaller units on elite and urban campuses that produce relatively few second lieutenants and ensigns. This trend might be accentuated in these times of tight resources as well as declining reenlistment rates of West Point graduates (Bender 2007). While the 2006 U.S. Supreme Court ruling in Rumsfeld v. FAIR could lead to the return of ROTC units at some Ivy League (or other) campuses, it remains to be seen whether DoD will seek to reestablish programs that might generate relatively few—albeit well-educated—new officers.

Why is a regionally concentrated ROTC a problem? As the Wall Street Journal article pointed out, urban closures negatively affect diversity. Second, an officer corps drawn disproportionately from particular regions enhances the civil-military gap. Some Americans may begin to see the military as led by unusual "others," not by people like themselves. Third, military effectiveness is enhanced by well-educated officers, and many of the top-rated American universities are in the Northeast and urban areas. As Cohen noted (2005), "it is education that provides the intellectual depth and breadth that allows soldiers to understand and succeed in America's wars." Relatedly, in surveying centuries of military history, Kennedy and Neilson (2002, xi) concluded that "war fighting is the greatest challenge to a student's capacity for dealing with the unknown, and those trained, as opposed to educated, have seldom managed to muster the wherewithal to cope with that environment."

Conclusions

The Continental Congress thought that standing armies were "inconsistent with the principles of republican governments, dangerous to the liberties of a free people, and generally converted into destructive engines for establishing despotism" (Fogelson 1989, 3). Nevertheless, the United States developed a large, professional, and permanent military force in the twentieth century, and there is little alternative today.

The contemporary U.S. system is a hybrid one, reflecting both cultural concerns about the military inherited from England and issues of federalism that were central in the founding era. The military relies on volunteers for both the active duty and reserve components, the latter being divided between the national

Reserves and the state National Guards. In addition, many future military officers are trained on civilian college campuses. The U.S. military therefore includes many citizen-soldier components, which results in a force that generally reflects the American (male) population.

Nevertheless, there are difficulties with the current system. According to Kennedy (2005), "the tradition of the citizen-soldier has served the indispensable purposes of sustaining civic engagement, protecting individual liberty—and guaranteeing political accountability." Nevertheless, he worries that so few serve in a contemporary military that is "extraordinarily lean and lethal, even while it is increasingly separated from the civil society on whose behalf it fights." Another problem is that while the war in Iraq is fought mostly by volunteer active duty and reserve military personnel, large numbers of contractors now fill many military roles (see Deborah Avant's chapter in this volume).

The distance between civilian society and the military concerns some. Career soldiers have often felt distrusted by civilians; they also have seen themselves as the carriers of certain values missing in civilian society. Nevertheless, "The culture gap has never been so wide, however, as to prevent soldiers from remembering that they are Americans first, and respecting the Constitution of the United States accordingly" (Weigley 2001, 216). While military and civilian values and practices cannot be identical, it is by no means clear that serious problems are on the horizon. How the military will interpret the Iraq war—particularly in terms of individual, partisan, and institutional blame and credit—will be worth watching because it may determine future civil-military fissures.

Finally, what might the future bring for the citizen-soldier? We might begin by recognizing that much is changing with the Guard and the Reserve. According to the National Governors Association, "Since September 11, 2001, our national leaders have had a paradigm shift in their thinking on national defense. The National Guard of the United States is no longer considered a strategic reserve. It is now recognized as a ready and relevant operational reserve from which units are regularly rotated into and out of combat operations."[12] When U.S. citizen-soldiers are used so often and for so long, America's contemporary militia moves even further away from its colonial origins.

To continue the status quo will involve greater demands on those willing to serve and will require acceptance of high operational tempo and frequent absences from family, jobs, and friends. As Tyson (2006) noted, "ordering more citizen-soldiers out of their communities and into war zones imposes a special burden, as reservists are older and more likely to have families and civilian jobs, and must also shoulder the task of responding to homeland disasters and other emergencies." Will this lead to a self-selection process that will move reservists further away from the average American? Will this new role attract a different type of citizen-soldier—perhaps one with more focus on the soldier? This may be foreshadowed by the increasing military use of the term "Warrior-Citizen."

The alternatives to the current system are few and largely impractical. While the active duty forces could expand and the Guard/Reserve forces could be deemphasized, the latter are likely permanent features of the U.S. military. Goldich (1985) noted that the Guard/Reserve system was not ideally suited to a potential war in Europe with the Soviet Union, which would have required the fast mobilization of a large number of well-trained units. If this fact was not enough to change military practices and overcome centuries of embedded cultural and political values, it is unclear what could.

Some argue that a draft would distribute the sacrifice of service across the nation more equally, and thereby restrain politicians from sending the armed forces into combat. A draft is not supported by a high-technology military that prefers volunteers to reluctant and randomly selected conscripts—and few in the general public or Congress favor it.

One way to revitalize the citizen-soldier is to expand the Reserve, the Guard, and ROTC. Given the growing cost of higher education, students might be receptive to a new scholarship program that brings associate degree holders, or those who complete two or three years of college credits, into an advanced enlisted rank. In addition, a more expansive or more targeted use of the IRR could make available to the military a number of people who possess skills or abilities of occasional but not regular utility (see Treverton et al. 2003). On the other hand, while such ideas might bring the civilian and military worlds into greater contact, they can go only so far in addressing the larger issues noted above.

To conclude, Senator Chuck Hagel (R-NE) expressed some of the difficulties with the current state of the military while not claiming there were easy answers (Henderson 2007):

> I don't think you want a free society where you've got a very clear difference between the people and the paid professional military . . . It disconnects the people from the kind of commitment and sacrifice that goes into this . . . You then raise another generation of Americans thinking they have no obligations, thinking they have no responsibilities, thinking that they're born into this world as an American so we'll pay these kids over there to go join the armed forces. That's the real danger here. Service. Citizenship. What is the responsibility of a citizen?

Notes

1. Quoted in Eliot A. Cohen, *Citizens and Soldiers: The Dilemmas of Military Service* (Ithaca, NY: Cornell University Press, 1985).
2. http://press-pubs.uchicago.edu/founders/documents/a1_8_16s10.html.
3. http://press-pubs.uchicago.edu/founders/documents/a1_8_15s9.html.
4. See also Johnson (1992) for a history of African Americans in militias and the National Guard.
5. For the number of personnel in each reserve category, see U.S. Census Bureau (2007).
6. http://www.almc.army.mil/library/Newsltrspr07.htm.
7. http://esgr.org/default.asp.
8. Military Casualty Information, Statistical Information and Analysis Division, Department of Defense, (http://siadapp.dior.whs.mil/personnel/CASUALTY/oif-deaths-total.pdf).
9. This section is from an earlier essay on the ROTC published in *PS: Political Science & Politics* Leal (2007).
10. Although unit numbers vary according to how they are counted.

11. http://www.dod.mil/prhome/poprep2004/download/download.html.
12. Policy Position HHS-03: Army and Air National Guard. http://www.nga.org.

References

Axe, David. 2007. *Army 101: Inside ROTC in a Time of War*. Columbia: University of South Carolina Press.

Barber, James Alden, Jr. 1972. "The Military Services and American Society: Relationships and Attitudes." In *The Military and American Society*, ed. Stephen E. Ambrose and James Alden Barber, Jr. New York: Free Press.

Bender, Bryan. 2007. "West Point Grads Exit Service at High Rate: War's Redeployments Thought a Major Factor." *Boston Globe*, April 11. Available at: www.boston.com/news/nation/articles/2007/04/11/west_point_grads_exit_service_at_high_rate/. Accessed April 19, 2007.

Binkin, Martin, and William W. Kaufmann. 1989. *U.S. Army Guard & Reserve: Rhetoric, Realities, Risks*. Washington, DC: Brookings Institution.

Blackstone, William. 1979. *Commentaries on the Laws of England: A Facsimile of the First Edition of 1765–1769*. Chicago: University of Chicago Press.

Brown, Frederic J. 1993. *The U.S. Army in Transition II*. Washington, DC: Brassey's.

Cohen, Eliot A. 2005. "Neither Fools Nor Cowards." *Wall Street Journal*, May 13.

Cohen, Eliot A. 1985. *Citizens and Soldiers: The Dilemmas of Military Service*. Ithaca: Cornell University Press.

Cooper, Jerry. 1997. *The Rise of the National Guard: The Evolution of the American Militia, 1865–1920*. Lincoln: University of Nebraska Press.

Coumbe, Arthur. 1999. "Why ROTC? The Debate over Collegiate Military Training, 1969–1973." *Air & Space Power Journal*. Available at: www.airpower.maxwell.af.mil/airchronicles/cc/coumbe.html. Accessed April 19, 2007.

Crossland, Richard B., and James T. Currie. 1984. *Twice the Citizen: A History of the United States Army Reserve, 1908–1983*. Washington, DC: Office of the Chief, Army Reserve.

Desch, Michael. 2001. "Explaining the Gap: Vietnam, the Republicanization of the South, and the End of the Mass Army." In *Soldiers and Civilians: The Civil-Military Gap and American National Security*, edited by Peter Feaver and Richard Kohn. Cambridge: MIT Press.

Duncan, Stephen M. 1997. *Citizen Warriors: America's National Guard and Reserve Forces & the Politics of National Security*. Novato, CA: Presidio Press.

Ellison, Christopher G. 1992. "Military Background, Racial Orientations, and Political Participation among Black Adult Males." *Social Science Quarterly*, v73: 361–378.

Feaver, Peter, and Richard Kohn. 2001. "Conclusion: The Gap and What It Means for American National Security." In *Soldiers and Civilians: The Civil-Military Gap and American National Security*, ed. Peter Feaver and Richard Kohn. Cambridge: MIT Press.

Feaver, Peter, Richard Kohn, and Lindsay Cohn. 2001. "The Gap Between Military and Civilian in the United States in Perspective." In *Soldiers and Civilians: The Civil-Military Gap and American National Security*, ed. Peter Feaver and Richard Kohn. Cambridge: MIT Press.

Fogelson, Robert M. 1989. *America's Armories: Architecture, Society, and Public Order*. Cambridge: Harvard University Press.

Goldich, Robert L. 1985. "Historical Continuity in the US Military Reserve System." In Bennie J. Wilson III (ed.), *The Guard and Reserve in the Total Force: The First Decade 1973–1983*. Washington, DC: National Defense University.

Henderson, Kristin. 2007. "Their War." *Washington Post.* July 22, W10.

Huntington, Samuel. 1957. *The Soldier and the State: The Theory and Politics of Civil-Military Relations.* Cambridge: Harvard University Press.

Jaffe, Greg. 2007. "A Retreat From Big Cities Hurts ROTC Recruiting." *Wall Street Journal,* February 27.

Johnson, Charles, Jr. 1992. *African American Soldiers in the National Guard: Recruitment and Deployment During Peacetime and War.* Westport, CT: Greenwood.

Jopar, David. October 18, 2003. "It's a Whole New World for Guardsmen and Reservists, No Longer 'Weekend Warriors.'" *Stars and Stripes.*

Kennedy, David M. July 25, 2006. "The Best Army We Can Buy." *New York Times* (op-ed).

Kennedy, Gregory C., and Keith Neilson, eds. 2002. *Military Education: Past, Present, and Future.* Westport, CT: Greenwood.

Leal, David L. 2007. "Students in Uniform: ROTC, the Citizen-Soldiers, and the Civil-Military Gap." *PS: Political Science & Politics,* v40: 479–83.

_____. 1999. "It's Not Just a Job: Military Service and Latino Political Participation." *Political Behavior,* v21: 153–174.

Leal, David L., and Jeremy Teigen. 2003. "Veteran Status and Political Participation." Paper presented at the 2003 International Biennial Conference of the Inter-University Seminar on Armed Forces and Society. Chicago, IL, October 24–26.

Mahon, John K. 1983. *History of the Militia and the National Guard.* New York: Macmillan.

Moxon, Arthur L. 1985. "US Reserve Forces: The Achilles' Heel of the All-Volunteer Force?" In Bennie J. Wilson III (ed.), *The Guard and Reserve in the Total Force: The First Decade 1973–1983.* Washington, DC: National Defense University.

Neiberg, Michael S. 2000. *Making Citizen-Soldiers: ROTC and the Ideology of American Military Service.* Cambridge: Harvard University Press.

Philbin, Edward J., and James L. Gould. 1985. "The Guard and Reserve: In Pursuit of Full Integration." In Bennie J. Wilson III (ed.), *The Guard and Reserve in the Total Force: The First Decade 1973–1983.* Washington, DC: National Defense University.

Riker, William H. 1957. *Soldiers of the States: The Role of the National Guard in American Democracy.* Washington, DC: Public Affairs Press.

Skowronek, Stephen. 1982. *Building a New American State: The Expansion of National Administrative Capacities 1877–1920.* Cambridge: Cambridge University Press.

Snyder, R. Claire. 1999. *Citizen-Soldiers and Manly Warriors: Military Service and Gender in the Civil Republican Tradition.* Lanham: Rowman & Littlefield.

Treverton, Gregory F., David Oaks, Lynn Scott, and Justin L. Adams. 2003. "Attracting 'Cutting-Edge' Skills Through Reserve Component Participation." Santa Monica: RAND.

Tyson, Ann Scott. November 5, 2006. "Possible Iraq Deployments Would Stretch Reserve Force." *Washington Post,* A1.

U.S. Census Bureau. 2007. *Statistical Abstract of the United States.* Washington: U.S. Census Bureau.

Weigley, Russell F. 2001. "The American Civil-Military Cultural Gap: A Historical Perspective, Colonial Times to the Present." In *Soldiers and Civilians: The Civil-Military Gap and American National Security,* ed. by Peter Feaver and Richard Kohn. Cambridge: MIT Press.

Conclusion

Judith Hicks Stiehm and Derek S. Reveron

For most of its history, the United States has had a tradition of maintaining only a small standing military, the primary mission of which was to fight wars. In the twenty-first century, this and other traditions may be eroding. The military finds itself increasingly tasked with non-warfighting missions, evidenced by Hurricane Katrina relief operations in the United States, reconstruction operations around the world, and medical-care delivery in the developing world. As notions of traditional security have given way to concerns with human security, the range of military operations has expanded. No longer is the military solely charged with fighting and winning the country's wars.

At the same time that military roles have changed, civil-military relations also appear to be changing. Prior to the Vietnam era, the military was largely removed from politics, but there are indications that the military is becoming partisan and that politicians are finding it equally advantageous to associate themselves with the military. The Iraq War gave rise to the "revolt of the generals," spawned angry captains, and gave rise to veteran groups against the war. Thus, one goal of this volume has been to invite citizens to consider whether to reemphasize tradition, or whether norms about the military should evolve—and, if so, in which direction. While the military is government's essential vehicle for maintaining territorial integrity and security, its use since 1989 has impacted diplomatic and economic relationships. The military is increasingly charged not only with setting the conditions for stability but with a follow-on development mission because the requirements for that mission are too large for other federal departments or international organizations.

While we have not tackled issues related to the economy, we have tried to take the reader "inside defense" to examine the new ways in which diplomacy and the military are interacting. The first section focused on the international arena, where we may be learning the limits of the effective use of force, as well as the complexity of the relationship between diplomacy and the military and the imbalance between the two. The second section examined the formal relationship between the military and the branches of the federal government. In each instance, the military receives direction from a constitutional authority. However, the military is assigned the crucial responsibility of educating the civilian authorities that legitimate it, equip it, and assign it to its missions.

The military has a necessary role in the policymaking process, yet that process is inevitably political. This makes it difficult for the military to separate its role as expert from its role as advocate. And when experts believe they are not listened to, they may find themselves lapsing into advocacy and, thus, into the political realm. While there are no well-founded fears that advocacy will lead to a military coup in the United States, it does create a tension between those who formulate policy and those who implement it. This dynamic demands greater involvement of the public in the issues raised in the third section of this book. What is the proper balance among those in voluntary, contracted, and conscripted military service? What limits should be placed on those who serve? Should limits be placed on veterans after service? How can military personnel and civilian society best interact?

Perhaps the military's growing experience with nongovernmental organizations (NGOs) can provide guidance for determining how those with different visions and practices—but with a common purpose—can cooperate. When Stiehm was doing fieldwork in Bosnia, she was able to conduct a series of interviews with young soldiers and young NGO staffers. She found that the two held strong negative stereotypes of each other.[1] Soldiers saw NGO workers as "disaster junkies" who were naïve, unpunctual, undisciplined, self-righteous, antimilitary, and unpatriotic. Soldiers, in turn, were seen as "boys with toys" who were immature, rigid, authoritarian, conformist, arrogant, impatient, insensitive, and homophobic. What was far more important, both groups began to realize, was what they shared. Members of both groups were young, adventurous, committed to service, prepared for hardship, practical, responsive to the "power of the moment," and dedicated to making a difference.

While their approaches were different, both groups were equally dedicated to problem resolution. And both groups recognized that they needed each other to bring security and normalcy to Bosnia. The lessons learned there and those emerging from Iraq can help to improve the way the military interacts with NGOs, with other federal departments, and with society at large. By going "inside defense," we hope this volume informs thinking through the lessons of Iraq and how those lessons will impact the military of the future and the government that employs it.

Fundamentally, citizens have ultimate responsibility for understanding these lessons and how the government acts on their behalf in domestic and international politics. This responsibility includes understanding, respecting, and cooperating with the military. Too often civilian society appears to be willfully ignorant about the military and too easily swayed by policy entrepreneurs promoting its virtues or denigrating its faults. Hopefully, this volume has provided a foundation for understanding the military and has suggested questions that society must address.

Notes

1. I have posted "The Challenge of Civil-Military Cooperation in Peacekeeping" on my website: www.judithstiehm.com.

About the Authors

Deborah D. Avant is professor of Political Science and Director of International Studies and the Center for Research on International and Global Studies at the University of California, Irvine. She is the author of *Political Institutions and Military Change: Lessons from Peripheral Wars* and *The Market for Force: The Consequences of Privatizing Security*, as well as numerous articles in journals such as *International Organization, International Studies Quarterly, Armed Forces & Society*, and the *Review of International Studies and Foreign Policy*. Her doctoral work was done at the University of California, San Diego.

Stephen Biddle is a senior fellow at the Council on Foreign Relations. From 2001 to 2006 he was professor of security studies at the Strategic Studies Institute at the U.S. Army War College. He has been on the faculty of political science at the University of North Carolina, Chapel Hill, and has held research positions at the Institute for Defense Analyses, Harvard's Belfer Center for Science and International Affairs, and the Kennedy School of Government's Office of National Security Programs. His book *Military Power: Explaining Victory and Defeat in Modern Battle* won the Council on Foreign Relations' Arthur Ross Award Silver Medal for 2005. His articles have appeared in *Foreign Affairs; International Security; Survival;* the *Journal of Politics;* the *Journal of Conflict Resolution;* and *Security Studies*. He holds AB, MPP, and Ph.D. degrees from Harvard University.

Russell A. Burgos is a lecturer in the Department of Political Science at the University of California, Los Angeles. He is also the Middle East program director for the military-security Track II diplomacy program at the Institute on Global Conflict and Cooperation at the University of California, San Diego. He has published or has forthcoming articles in *Security Studies; Perspectives on Politics; PS: Political Science & Politics;* and the *International Studies Review;* and is at work on a contracted manuscript titled *From the Potomac to the Tigris: The United States and Iraq from the Great War to the Long War*. A veteran of Operation Iraqi Freedom, Dr. Burgos has taught at the University of California, Los Angeles; Claremont McKenna College; and Pepperdine University. He received MA and Ph.D. degrees from UCLA, an MA from The George Washington University, and a BA from Loyola University–Chicago.

Brendan J. Doherty is an assistant professor of political science at the United States Naval Academy, where he teaches courses on the presidency and American politics. He earned his Ph.D. from the University of California, Berkeley, and his B.A. from Dartmouth College. In 2006–2007, he served as a congressional fellow of the American Political Science Association. His dissertation, "The Politics of the Permanent Campaign: Presidents, Fundraising, and the Electoral College," was an empirical examination of the evolving nature of the permanent campaign for the presidency over the past quarter century. His published work includes studies of presidential travel, Senate leadership, speech restrictions in judicial campaigns, the Marshall court and federalism, the political participation of dual citizens, and the targeting of Spanish-speaking voters in presidential elections.

John Garofano is a professor of strategy and policy at the U.S. Naval War College. From 2000 to 2003 he was senior fellow in the International Security Program at the Kennedy School of Government while working on a book on civil-military relations and U.S. decisions on the use of force. He has published on military intervention, the Vietnam War, civil-military relations, and Asian security in such journals as *International Security; Asian Survey; Contemporary Southeast Asia;* and the *Naval War College Review.* Dr. Garofano has taught at the U.S. Army War College, the University of Southern California, and the Five Colleges. He received a Ph.D. from Cornell University, an MA from the School of Advanced International Studies at The Johns Hopkins University, and a B.A. from Bates College.

Kenneth E. Harbaugh is a JD candidate at Yale University Law School and a former U.S. Navy pilot. From 2002 to 2005, he served as an assistant professor at The Citadel, where he taught naval history. While on active duty, he commanded an EP-3 combat reconnaissance crew, and flew missions in support of Operation Southern Watch and Operation Enduring Freedom. He recently returned from Afghanistan, where he worked as an independent consultant for the International Center for Transitional Justice. He earned his BS (summa cum laude) from Duke University.

Charles Hauss teaches political science half-time at George Mason University and is head of government liaison with the Alliance for Peacebuilding. He is the author of ten books, including two on conflict resolution and a forthcoming volume on rethinking national security.

Captain Donald S. Inbody is a retired Navy Captain and a doctoral candidate in government at the University of Texas at Austin. He holds master's degrees from the Naval War College, the Naval Postgraduate School, and Wichita State University. He has commanded a ship and a Naval Reserve Officer Training unit, served with the 103rd and 104th Congresses as a budget liaison officer with the Secretary of the Navy, and directed one of the Department of Defense command and control analytic think tanks.

His dissertation research examines party identification, voting patterns, and political attitudes of the post–Cold War American military.

David L. Leal is an associate professor in the Department of Government at the University of Texas at Austin and a faculty associate of the UT Center for Mexican-American Studies. His interests include Latino politics, public policy, the military and society, and religion and politics. He has published over two dozen articles in journals such as the *Journal of Politics; Armed Forces & Society;* the *British Journal of Political Science; Political Research Quarterly; American Politics Research; Political Behavior; Social Science Quarterly;* and *Educational Policy.* His other publications include the book *Electing America's Governors* (Palgrave Macmillan, 2006), the coedited volume *Latino Politics: Identity, Mobilization, and Representation,* and a number of book chapters. He is currently a member of the editorial boards of *American Politics Research* and *Social Science Quarterly.* He received his Ph.D. in political science from Harvard University in 1998.

Kathleen A. Mahoney-Norris is associate professor of national security studies and director of the Strategy and War Studies Division at the USAF Air Command and Staff College. She is a political scientist with a focus on the Latin American region, civil-military relations, democratization and human rights, and international organizations. She earned a Ph.D. in international studies from the University of Denver's Graduate School of International Studies and an MS from the National War College. She has edited *Democratization and Human Rights,* along with other publications. Colonel Mahoney-Norris recently retired from the USAF Reserve with over twenty-six years of active duty and reserve service as an intelligence officer and political-military affairs officer. She also taught at the USAF's Air War College and at the University of Colorado.

Michael F. Morris is a colonel in the U.S. Air Force. In addition to serving as a flight, squadron, and deputy group commander, he has served on a number of headquarters staffs, including the air staff in the Pentagon. Colonel Morris also served as a legislative fellow in the Senate Appropriations Committee (Defense Subcommittee) of the U.S. Senate, as a member of the air force's legislative liaison staff, and in the Operations Group for the Chief of Staff, United States Air Force. He also taught security and strategy at the U.S. Naval War College in Newport, Rhode Island. Colonel Morris has been published in *Flashpoints in the War on Terrorism.* He holds a bachelor's degree in business administration from East Texas State University, a master's degree in business administration from the University of Montana, and a master's degree in national security and strategic studies from the U.S. Naval War College, graduating with distinction.

Mackubin Owens is associate dean of academics for electives and directed research and professor of national security affairs at the U.S. Naval War College. He specializes in the planning of U.S. strategy and forces, especially naval and power projection forces; the political economy of national security; national security organization; strategic geography; and American civil-military relations. From 1990 to 1997, Dr. Owens was editor in chief of the quarterly defense journal *Strategic Review* and adjunct professor of international relations at Boston University. His articles on national security issues have appeared in such publications as *International Security; Orbis; Armed Forces Journal; Comparative Strategy;* the *Wall Street Journal;* the *New York Times;* the *Los Angeles Times;* the *Jerusalem Post,* and many others. He is coeditor of the textbook *Strategy and Force Planning.* He is currently working on a book for the University Press of Kentucky, tentatively titled *Sword of Republican Empire: A History of US Civil-Military Relations.* Dr. Owens earned his Ph.D. in politics from the University of Dallas, his MA in economics from Oklahoma University, and his BA from the University of California, Santa Barbara.

James P. Pfiffner is university professor in the School of Public Policy at George Mason University. His major areas of expertise are the presidency, American national government, and public management. He has written or edited ten books on the presidency and American national government, including *The Strategic Presidency: Hitting the Ground Running* (2nd edition, 1996), *The Modern Presidency* (4th edition, 2004), and *The Character Factor: How We Judge Our Presidents* (2004). His professional experience includes service in the director's office of the U.S. Office of Personnel Management (1980–81), and he has been a member of the faculty at the University of California, Riverside, and California State University, Fullerton.

Derek S. Reveron is an associate professor of national security affairs at the Naval War College in Newport, Rhode Island. He received a diploma from the Naval War College, an MA in political science and a Ph.D. in public policy analysis from the University of Illinois at Chicago. He specializes in U.S. foreign policy, civil-military relations, and intelligence. He is the author of *Promoting Democracy in the Post-Soviet Region* (2002), the editor of *America's Viceroys: the Military and U.S. Foreign Policy* (2004), and the coeditor of *Flashpoints in the War on Terrorism* (2006). His numerous book chapters and articles have appeared in *Orbis; Defense and Security Analysis;* the *International Journal of Intelligence and Counterintelligence; Low Intensity Conflict & Law Enforcement;* and the *National Review Online.* Additionally, he sits on the editorial boards of the *Defense Intelligence Journal* and the *Naval War College Review.* Before joining the Naval War College faculty, Dr. Reveron taught political science at the Joint Military Intelligence College, the National Defense University, and the U.S. Naval Academy.

William Ruger is an assistant professor in the Department of Political Science at Texas State University–San Marcos. He is also a research fellow in foreign policy studies at the Cato Institute and the book review editor for *Armed Forces and Society.* Before joining Texas State, he was a fellow at Liberty Fund and also taught international relations at Wesleyan University and Brigham Young University. He holds a Ph.D. in politics from Brandeis University and an AB from the College of William and Mary.

Stephen M. Saideman is Canada Research Chair in International Security and Ethnic Conflict and associate professor of political science at McGill University. He received his Ph.D. in political science from the University of California, San Diego, in 1993. In addition to his books, *The Ties That Divide: Ethnic Politics, Foreign Policy and International Conflict, For Kin or Country: Xenophobia, Nationalism and War (with R. William Ayres),* and *Intra-State Conflict, Governments and Security: Dilemmas of Deterrence and Assurance* (edited with Marie-Joëlle Zahar), he has published articles in *International Organization, Comparative Political Studies,* the *Journal of Peace Research,* and *Security Studies,* among several other journals. He spent a year on the U.S. Joint Staff working in the Strategic Planning and Policy Directorate on Balkans issues as part of a Council on Foreign Relations international affairs fellowship. As a result of this experience, his work is increasingly focused on civil-military relations in the United States, Canada and multilateral interventions.

Judith Hicks Stiehm is professor of political science at Florida International University where she served as provost and academic vice president for four years. She has taught at San Francisco State University, the University of Wisconsin, the University of California, Los Angeles, and the University of Southern California. She has been a visiting professor at the U.S. Army Peacekeeping Institute and at the Strategic Studies Institute at Carlisle Barracks. Her books include *Nonviolent Power: Active and Passive Resistance* (1972); *Bring Me Men and Women: Mandated Change at the U.S. Air Force Academy* (1981); *Arms and the Enlisted Woman* (1989); *It's Our Military Too!: Women and the U.S. Military* (1996); *The U. S. Army War College: Military Education in a Democracy* (2002); and *Champions for Peace: Women Winners of the Nobel Prize for Peace* (2006).

Jeremy M. Teigen is an assistant professor of political science at Ramapo College specializing in American government and elections. He attended graduate school at the University of Texas at Austin, receiving a Ph.D. in government in 2005. He has published articles in *Political Research Quarterly, Armed Forces & Society,* and *Social Science Quarterly.*

Linton Wells II is the transformation chair and a distinguished research professor at the National Defense University. He moved to NDU in June 2007 after sixteen years in the Office of the Secretary of Defense, during which time, among other things, he helped build bridges with the NGO community. He attended graduate school at The Johns Hopkins University, receiving an MS in engineering in mathematical sciences and a Ph.D. in international relations. He is also a 1983 graduate of the Japanese National Institute for Defense Studies in Tokyo, the first U.S. naval officer to attend there. In twenty-six years of naval service, Dr. Wells served in a variety of surface ships, including command of a destroyer squadron and guided missile destroyer. In addition, he acquired a wide range of experience in operations analysis; Pacific, Indian Ocean, and Middle East affairs; C3I; and special access program oversight.

Isaiah Wilson III is an academy professor with the Department of Social Sciences at the U.S. Military Academy at West Point and director of American politics and public policy. He is an army aviator, military historian, and strategist, and he is a graduate of the U.S. Army's School of Advanced Military Studies. He holds a BS in international relations from the U.S. Military Academy, master's degrees in public policy and government from Cornell University and the U.S. Army's Command and General Staff College and School of Advanced Military Studies; and a Ph.D. from Cornell University. LTC Wilson is a life member of, and recent International Affairs Fellow (IAF) with, the Council on Foreign Relations. He is the author of the recently released book, *Thinking Beyond War: Civil-Military Relations and Why America Fails to Win the Peace* (Palgrave Macmillan) and currently serves on the faculty of the National War College (Washington, D.C.) as the 2007–08 West Point Fellow. Wilson also founded and directs Project: ThinkBeyondWar, a multiyear, interdisciplinary, and multi-agency collaborative research initiative dedicated to the reformation of the 'American way of war and peace' commensurate with the post-9/11 security environment.

Daniel Wirls is professor of politics at the University of California, Santa Cruz. He is author of *Buildup: The Politics of Defense in the Reagan Era* (Cornell University Press, 1992) and coauthor of *Invention of the United States Senate* (Johns Hopkins University Press, 2004), as well as of articles and chapters on Congress, American political development, and the politics of public policy.

Stephen D. Wrage earned his BA in classics at Amherst College. On graduating he went to Athens for two years where he taught in a Greek school and served as assistant to its president. Returning to the United States, he taught at St. Albans School in Washington, D.C., worked at the Brookings Institution for Dr. Helmut Sonnefeldt, and attended the Johns Hopkins School of Advanced International Studies. He served as assistant dean of the School of Foreign Service at Georgetown University and wrote his dissertation—a study of human rights in American foreign policy—at Johns Hopkins under the direction of Dr. Robert Osgood. He has published scholarly articles and books on a variety of topics in ethics and American foreign policy and is the author of a number of widely used case studies of actual ethical quandaries experienced by officers in the American military. In 1995 he spent a Fulbright year in Singapore and has written about that severely controlled society for the *Washington Post*, the *Los Angeles Times*, the *Asian Wall Street Journal*, and the *Atlantic Monthly*. In 2004 he published *Immaculate Warfare*, a study of the ethical, practical, and command issues raised by precision-guided munitions.

Index

CPSIA information can be obtained
at www.ICGtesting.com
Printed in the USA
FFOW02n2104090118
44459510-44252FF